T0140009

Communications in Computer and Information Science   **2017**

Rationale

The CCIS series is devoted to the publication of proceedings of computer science conferences. Its aim is to efficiently disseminate original research results in informatics in printed and electronic form. While the focus is on publication of peer-reviewed full papers presenting mature work, inclusion of reviewed short papers reporting on work in progress is welcome, too. Besides globally relevant meetings with internationally representative program committees guaranteeing a strict peer-reviewing and paper selection process, conferences run by societies or of high regional or national relevance are also considered for publication.

Topics

The topical scope of CCIS spans the entire spectrum of informatics ranging from foundational topics in the theory of computing to information and communications science and technology and a broad variety of interdisciplinary application fields.

Information for Volume Editors and Authors

Publication in CCIS is free of charge. No royalties are paid, however, we offer registered conference participants temporary free access to the online version of the conference proceedings on SpringerLink (http://link.springer.com) by means of an http referrer from the conference website and/or a number of complimentary printed copies, as specified in the official acceptance email of the event.

CCIS proceedings can be published in time for distribution at conferences or as post-proceedings, and delivered in the form of printed books and/or electronically as USBs and/or e-content licenses for accessing proceedings at SpringerLink. Furthermore, CCIS proceedings are included in the CCIS electronic book series hosted in the SpringerLink digital library at http://link.springer.com/bookseries/7899. Conferences publishing in CCIS are allowed to use Online Conference Service (OCS) for managing the whole proceedings lifecycle (from submission and reviewing to preparing for publication) free of charge.

Publication process

The language of publication is exclusively English. Authors publishing in CCIS have to sign the Springer CCIS copyright transfer form, however, they are free to use their material published in CCIS for substantially changed, more elaborate subsequent publications elsewhere. For the preparation of the camera-ready papers/files, authors have to strictly adhere to the Springer CCIS Authors' Instructions and are strongly encouraged to use the CCIS LaTeX style files or templates.

Abstracting/Indexing

CCIS is abstracted/indexed in DBLP, Google Scholar, EI-Compendex, Mathematical Reviews, SCImago, Scopus. CCIS volumes are also submitted for the inclusion in ISI Proceedings.

How to start

To start the evaluation of your proposal for inclusion in the CCIS series, please send an e-mail to ccis@springer.com.

Ying Tan · Yuhui Shi
Editors

Data Mining and Big Data

8th International Conference, DMBD 2023
Sanya, China, December 9–12, 2023
Proceedings, Part I

 Springer

Editors
Ying Tan (iD)
Peking University
Beijing, China

Yuhui Shi
Southern University of Science and Techn
Shenzhen, China

ISSN 1865-0929   ISSN 1865-0937 (electronic)
Communications in Computer and Information Science
ISBN 978-981-97-0836-9   ISBN 978-981-97-0837-6 (eBook)
https://doi.org/10.1007/978-981-97-0837-6

Preface

The Eighth International Conference on Data Mining and Big Data (DMBD 2023) was held on December 9–12, 2023 in Sanya, China. DMBD 2023 served as an international forum for researchers to exchange the latest advances in theories, models, and applications of data mining and big data as well as artificial intelligence techniques. DMBD 2023 was the eighth event after the successful first event (DMBD 2016) at Bali Island of Indonesia, second event (DMBD 2017) at Fukuoka City of Japan, third event (DMBD 2018) at Shanghai of China, fourth event (DMBD 2019) at Chiang Mai of Thailand, fifth event (DMBD 2020) at Belgrade of Serbia, sixth event (DMBD 2021) at Guangzhou of China and seventh event (DMBD 2022) at Beijing of China virtually.

These two volumes (CCIS vol. 2017 and vol. 2018) contain papers presented at DMBD 2023. The contents of those papers cover some major topics of data mining and big data. The conference received 79 submissions, at least three reviewers per submission in a double-blind review. The committee accepted 38 regular papers to be included in the conference program with an acceptance rate of 48.1%. The proceedings contain revised versions of the accepted papers. While revisions are expected to take the referee's comments into account, this was not enforced and the authors bear full responsibility for the content of their papers.

DMBD 2023 was organized by the International Association of Swarm and Evolutionary Intelligence (IASEI), and co-organized by Peking University and Southern University of Science and Technology, Computational Intelligence Laboratory of Peking University (CIL@PKU), Advanced Institute of Big Data, Beijing, Key Lab of Information System Requirement, Science and Technology on Information Systems Engineering Laboratory, and technically co-sponsored by City Brain Technical Committee, Chinese Institute of Command and Control (CICC), International Neural Network Society, and also supported by Nanjing Kangbo Intelligent Health Academy, Springer-Nature, and Beijing Xinghui High-Tech Co. The conference would not have been such a success without the support of these organizations, and we sincerely thank them for their continued assistance and support.

We would also like to thank the authors who submitted their papers to DMBD 2023, and the conference attendees for their interest and support. We thank the Organizing Committee for their time and effort dedicated to arranging the conference. This allowed us to focus on the paper selection and deal with the scientific program. We thank the Program Committee members and the external reviewers for their hard work in reviewing the submissions; the conference would not have been possible without their expert reviews. Furthermore, this work is partially supported by the National Natural Science Foundation of China (Grant No. 62250037, 62276008, and 62076010), and also partially supported by the National Key R&D Program of China (Grant No. 2022YFF0800601).

Finally, we thank the EasyChair system and its operators for making the entire process of managing the conference convenient.

December 2023

Ying Tan
Yuhui Shi

Organization

General Chair

Ying Tan   Peking University, China

Programme Committee Chairs

Yuhui Shi   Southern University of Science and Technology, China

Wenbin Zhang   Michigan Technological University, USA

Advisory Committee Chairs

Xingui He   Peking University, China

Gary G. Yen   Oklahoma State University, USA

Technical Committee Co-chairs

Benjamin W. Wah   Chinese University of Hong Kong, China

Guoying Wang   Chongqing University of Posts and Telecommunications, China

Enhong Chen   University of Science and Technology of China, China

Fernando Buarque   Universidade of Pernambuco, Brazil

Haibo He   University of Rhode Island Kingston, USA

Jihong Zhu   Tsinghua University, China

Jin Li   Guangzhou University, China

Kay Chen Tan   Hong Kong Polytechnic University, China

Nikola Kasabov   Auckland University of Technology, New Zealand

Qirong Tang   Tongji University, China

Yew-Soon Ong   Nanyang Technological University, Singapore

Yi Zhang   Sichuan University, China

Invited Speakers Session Co-chairs

Andres Iglesias   University of Cantabria, Spain
Shaoqiu Zheng   28th Research Institute of China Electronics
                                Technology Group Corporation, China

Special Session Co-chairs

Ben Niu   Shenzhen University, China
Kun Liu   Advanced Institute of Big Data, China

Publications Co-chairs

Radu-Emil Precup   Politehnica University of Timisoara, Romania
Weiwei Hu   Tencent Corporation, China

Publicity Co-chairs

Eugene Semenkin   Siberian Aerospace University, Russia
Junqi Zhang   Tongji University, China

Finance and Registration Chairs

Andreas Janecek   University of Vienna, Austria
Suicheng Gu   Google Corporation, USA

Conference Secretariat

Wenbo Yan   Peking University, China

Program Committee

Muhammad Abulaish   South Asian University, India
Abdelmalek Amine   Tahar Moulay University of Saida, Algeria
Sabri Arik   Istanbul University, Turkey
Nebojsa Bacanin   Singidunum University, Serbia
Carmelo J. A. Bastos Filho   University of Pernambuco, Brazil

Chenyang Bu	Hefei University of Technology, China
Bin Cao	Tsinghua University, China
Junfeng Chen	Hohai University, China
Walter Chen	National Taipei University of Technology, Taiwan, China
Shi Cheng	Shaanxi Normal University, China
Prithviraj Dasgupta	U. S. Naval Research Laboratory, USA
Khaldoon Dhou	Texas A&M University Central Texas, USA
Hongyuan Gao	Harbin Engineering University, China
Weifeng Gao	Xidian University, China
Ke Gu	Changsha University of Science and Technology, China
Roshni Iyer	UCLA, USA
Ziyu Jia	Beijing Jiaotong University, China
Mingyan Jiang	Shandong University, China
Colin Johnson	University of Nottingham, UK
Liangjun Ke	Xi'an Jiaotong University, China
Lov Kumar	National Institute of Technology, Kurukshetra, India
Germano Lambert-Torres	PS Solutions, Brazil
Tai Le Quy	Leibniz University Hannover, Germany
Ju Liu	Shandong University, China
Jun Liu	Carnegie Mellon University, USA
Kun Liu	Advanced Institute of Big Data, China
Qunfeng Liu	Dongguan University of Technology, China
Yi Liu	Advanced Institute of Big Data, China
Hui Lu	Beihang University, China
Wenjian Luo	Harbin Institute of Technology (Shenzhen), China
Haoyang Ma	National University of Defense Technology, China
Jinwen Ma	Peking University, China
Chengying Mao	Jiangxi University of Finance and Economics, China
Mengjun Ming	National University of Defense Technology, China
Seyedfakhredin Musavishavazi	BAuA, Federal Institute for Occupational Safety and Health, Germany
Sreeja N. K.	PSG College of Technology, USA
Qingjian Ni	Southeast University, China
Neelamadhab Padhy	GIET University, India
Mario Pavone	University of Catania, Spain
Yan Pei	University of Aizu, Japan
Xin Peng	Hainan University, China

Additional Reviewers

Cai, Long
Dhou, Khaldoon
Hu, Zhongyuan
Jin, Feihu
Lei, Jiaqi
Lian, Xiaoyu

Weinan, Tong
Wenbo, Yan
Zhang, Yixia
Zhang, Yixuan
Zhang, Zhenman

Contents – Part I

Contents – Part II

Machine Learning for Medical Applications

Data Mining Methods

Data Analytics Methods in Human Resource Demand Forecasting

Wei Wang[1], Jin Zhu[2], and Pingxin Wang[3](✉) ⓘ

[1] Logistics Group, Jiangsu University of Science and Technology, Zhenjiang 212100, China
[2] School of Economics and Management, Jiangsu University of Science and Technology, Zhenjiang 212003, China
[3] School of Science, Jiangsu University of Science and Technology, Zhenjiang 212003, China
wangpingxin@just.edu.cn

Abstract. Human resources are the first resource for enterprise development, and a reasonable human resource structure will increase the effectiveness of an enterprise's human resource input and output. Based on a deep understanding of forecasting mining technology, this paper discusses the multiple linear regression method and BP neural network algorithm for human resource demand forecasting. Through modeling, statistical index analysis and significance test, the data mining algorithms are analyzed and compared. The regression equation is obtained, and the demand forecast is made on the number of the enterprise personnel, and the feasibility of the multiple regression model is verified. At the same time, the BP neural network algorithm is described in detail, and an example is given to compare the forecasting results of multiple linear regression method and BP neural network algorithm.

Keywords: Data Analytics · Multiple Llinear Regression · BP Neural Network · Human Resource Demand Forecasting

1 Introduction

Currently, the world is developing rapidly, and companies must analyze their employee numbers and structure in order to adapt to increasingly complex external environmental changes. Human resource demand forecasting models can help companies predict the total amount of human resources needed and achieve rational allocation. Compared to traditional personnel management, modern human resource management focuses more on using scientific and technological means for scientific management [1].

Forecasting refers to the scientific judgment of the future development trends and patterns of the predicted object through correct methods and approaches, using effective historical and current information of the predicted object itself. However, due to the uncertainty of information, it inevitably leads to difficulties and problems in forecasting. The demand for human resources in enterprises includes both overall demand and individual demand, as well as demands in terms of quantity, quality, and structure. Human resource demand forecasting refers to the pre-analysis and forecasting of the quantity of human resource demand, age structure, professional structure, educational level structure, professional technical position structure, and skill structure during a certain period in the future [2, 3].

Human resource demand forecasting is an important aspect of human resource planning. It requires a comprehensive consideration of various internal or external factors and an accurate understanding of the relationship between enterprise development and human resource demand. The methods for human resource demand forecasting can generally be divided into two categories: qualitative forecasting methods represented by status quo planning method, experience forecasting method, Delphi method, descriptive method; quantitative forecasting methods represented by trend forecasting method, labor productivity analysis method, linear regression method, time series method. The former is influenced by subjective experience of forecasters with generally low accuracy in forecasting continuity and weak ability to handle complex environments. The latter has a wide range of applications with high accuracy in forecasting but requires higher sample data.

Based on the characteristics of enterprise human resource demand, this paper constructs a predictive model based on data mining technology. By analyzing historical personnel numbers over the years for forecasting purposes, we provides reasonable suggestions for future workforce construction for enterprises.

2   Related work

2.1 Human Resource Demand Forecasting methods

The existed human resource demand predication methods can usually be divided into qualitative method and quantitative method, of which qualitative research and application earlier. Qualitative forecasting means that managers and experts with rich experience and comprehensive analytical capabilities rely on familiar business knowledge, using personal experience and analytical judgment based on the historical data and current situation of the enterprise, to some extent, the development of human resources in the future of the enterprise to make a certain degree of forecasting, and then through a certain form of synthesis of the views of various experts, as the main basis for predicting the future situation of human resources.

With the development of data technology, there are more and more quantitative researches on human resource forecasting, which use historical data or various factors to forecast the demand of human resource. According to the relatively complete historical human resource statistics, the enterprise managers use certain mathematical methods to process and sort them scientifically and reveal the laws between the relevant factors and variables, so as to predict the future development of human resources changes. Its main features are the use of statistical data and mathematical models to predict, pay attention to the development of human resources in the quantitative analysis, less subject to subjective factors.

The ultimate goal of demand forecasting is to find the trend of data. There are some similar ideas and steps between qualitative and quantitative methods, but there are also big differences in processing methods. Because of the different application scope and technical characteristics of each method, the choice of different methods will have a direct impact on the forecasting results and quality. In the process of human resource demand forecasting, the qualitative forecasting method is often influenced by the emotion or experience ability of experts, therefore, the quantitative method can be used to analyze the human resource data of enterprises accurately and form a reasonable forecasting result.

2.2 Multiple Regression Analysis

The method of regression analysis is to look for the relevant factors that can affect the level of human resource demand exactly, if there is some certain relationship between these factors and the level of human resource demand, at this time, we can use the method of mathematical statistics to express the relationship quantitatively, so as to simulate the demand for personnel regression equation, and then forecast. The key to this approach is to identify variables that are highly relevant to personnel requirements. Xie [4] studied the variable analysis model based on employee satisfaction, and He [5] made regression analysis on the human resource level factors in the western region, and studied the comprehensive evaluation system of human resource level Zheng [6] used regression method to forecast the human resource demand of Inner Mongolia Electric Power Group.

The establishment of the regression analysis model is realized by determining the causality between the dependent variable and the independent variable, then we evaluate whether the regression model has a good fitting degree by statistical index and test. If the fitting degree is good, the independent variable reaches the basic condition of forecasting. To some extent, the regression analysis method solves the problem of demand forecasting, but the Regression analysis is more demanding on the quantity and quality of the selected. samples, if we do not have a certain amount of data in line with the statistical law, it is not suitable to use multiple linear regression method for demand forecasting. Based on the statistical laws of independent and dependent variables, this chapter carries out multivariate Regression analysis to ensure the accuracy of human resource demand forecasting.

2.3 Data Mining methods

Data mining refers to the non-trivial process of revealing hidden, previously unknown and potentially valuable information from a large amount of data in a data set. The forecasting based on data mining is a decision support process, which is mainly based on artificial intelligence, machine learning, pattern recognition, statistics, database, visualization technology, etc., to analyze enterprise data in a high degree of automation, make inductive reasoning, and excavate potential patterns from it to help decision makers adjust market strategies, reduce risks, and make correct decisions. The following methods are frequently used data mining methods.

Association rules are a kind of knowledge and rules that can be found in the database to reflect the relationship between things. On the premise that there is indeed a certain regular relationship between things, the value of one or more things can be predicted through one or more things [7].

Decision trees are a method of classifying data based on its attributes. Decision tree method has the advantages of comprehensibility and intuitiveness. Compared with neural networks, the decision-making process that leads to the result can be explained clearly. However, processing complex data is the short board of decision tree processing, and the number of processing branches is very large, so it is difficult to manage. At the same time, there are also problems such as data missing value processing [8]. Common algorithms include ID3, C4.5, CART, and CHAID.

Based on the Bayesian theorem of posterior probability, Bayesian network is a method based on statistical processing of data [9]. Uncertain events are connected through a network to predict outcomes related to other events, with network variables either visible or hidden in the training sample. Bayesian network has the functions of classification, clustering, forecasting and causality analysis, and its advantages are easy to understand and good forecasting effect, but bad forecasting effect for low probability events.

Rough set theory [10] is often used to deal with uncertainty or ambiguity. It can not only show the internal structural relations of noisy data or inaccurate data, but also be used for correlation analysis and feature reduction. Rough set is a mathematical model of vague concepts. Since there is no requirement on the initial value of data or additional information, it is widely used in uncertain and incomplete information classification and information acquisition. The emergence of rough set theory and technology has a great role in promoting the efficiency of data mining and knowledge discovery.

5 Statistical analysis

Statistical analysis is mainly based on the principles of statistics and probability theory, and is a more accurate data mining technology. It is a model-based method, including regression analysis, factor analysis and discriminant analysis, which is easy to understand and accurate to describe results.

6 Neural networks

Neural networks [1] are one of the most commonly used data mining techniques, first proposed by psychologists and neurobiologists, aiming to develop and test computational simulations of nerves. It is very similar to the process of repeated learning in the human brain. Firstly, it learns and trains based on samples, and then distinguishes different features and patterns between various samples. The sample set should be as representative as possible, and in order to accurately fit various sample data, the system should train and learn hundreds or even thousands of times to finally identify potential patterns. When it encounters new sample data, the system will automatically predict and classify based on the training results [11, 12]. Neural networks perform well in predicting complex problems, possessing high tolerance for noisy data and the ability to classify untrained data.

The ultimate goal of data mining is to discover valuable knowledge information. The above methods have similar ideas and steps, but there are also significant differences in processing methods. Table 1 provides a comparison of the characteristics of the main data mining techniques mentioned above.

Due to the different application fields and technical characteristics of various methods, choosing different methods will have a direct impact on the results and quality

Table 1. Comparison of Main Technical Methods of Data Mining

Methods	Characteristic
Association rules analysis	Classification, clustering
Decision trees	Inductive classification
Bayesian network	Clustering and forecasting,
Rough set	Uncertainty classification
Statistical analysis	Clustering
Neural network	Classification, clustering

of mining. This paper intends to use multiple regression analysis and neural network algorithms for data mining and forecasting.

3 Data Analytics Methods in Human Resource Demand Forecasting

3.1 Multiple Regression Analysis Method

The standard equation for multiple regression is shown in Equation 1,

$$\hat{y} = b_0 + b_1 x_1 + b_2 x_2 + \cdots + b_p x_p + \varepsilon, \tag{1}$$

where $\hat{y}$ is predication value of dependent variable, b_0 is regression constant, p is the number of independent variables. $b_i (i = 1, 2, \cdots, p)$ are the regression coefficients, $x_i (i = 1, 2, \cdots, p)$ are the independent variables and ε is random error.

The human resource model measures n sets of independent observations $y_k, x_{k1}, x_{k2}, \cdots, x_{kp} (k = 1, 2, \cdots, n)$ and uses the unbiased estimation of regression analysis to obtain the correct regression coefficients and constants, and ultimately obtain the fitted regression equation.

In a multiple regression model, the proportion of the variation of the independent variable affected by the variation of the dependent variable is determined by using a determination coefficient R^2, which is the ratio of the sum of squares of the regression to the sum of squares of the population. Its calculation is shown in Equation 2. The closer it is to 1, the better the fit of the model, and the closer it is to 0, the worse the fit of the model.

$$R^2 = \frac{\sum\limits_{i=1}^{n} \left(\hat{y}_i - \bar{y}_i \right)^2}{\sum\limits_{i=1}^{n} \left(y_i - \bar{y}_i \right)^2}, 0 \leq R \leq 1 \tag{2}$$

In a multiple regression model, as the number of samples increases, the determination coefficient will also increase, which easily leads to the illusion that the more independent variables, the better the fitting effect. In order to reduce the impact of the number of independent variables and sample size on the regression analysis results, a correction coefficient is introduced as shown in Equation 3. The correction coefficient divides the sum of squares of residuals and the sum of squares of total deviations by their respective degrees of freedom to eliminate the influence of the number of variables on the goodness of fit, which can accurately reflect the goodness of fit.

$$\text{Adjusted}R^2 = 1 - \frac{\sum\limits_{i=1}^{n}(y_i - \hat{y}_i)^2 \Big/ n - p - 1}{\sum\limits_{i=1}^{n}(\hat{y}_i - \bar{y}_i)^2 \Big/ n - 1} \tag{3}$$

The linear relationship test is divided into F-test and t-test, which are used to test the significance test of the overall linearity of the equation and the significance test of variables, respectively. By specifying a significance level α, a rejection domain H0 with all b values of 0 is determined for testing and judgment. The significance of the entire regression relationship is verified through the F-test, but due to the significant linear relationship between the respective variables and the target variable after their interaction, it does not mean that each independent variable has a significant linear relationship with the target variable. Therefore, the t-test is also needed to verify the significance of each parameter variable in the regression process with respect to the dependent variable. Therefore, it is necessary to use a combination of F-test and t-test of linear hypothesis to detect the linear relationship between variables.

3.2 BP Neural Network Algorithm

In a neural network, the output of one neuron can be the input of another neuron. Figure 1 is a simple schematic diagram of the neural network structure, where each circle represents a neuron. The entire neural network is a three-layer structure consisting of input layer, hidden layer, and output layer [13–15].

BP (Back Propagation) neural network was proposed by Rumelhart, McCelland, and others. Rumelhart systematically explained the application of error backpropagation algorithm in neural networks for the first time. With the migration of the times, the theory of BP neural network has been continuously improved and updated, and has now become one of the most widely used neural network models.

The BP neural network is divided into two parts: one is the forward propagation of information; Part of it is the back propagation of errors [15]. The topology structure is generally a three-layer structure, consisting of three parts: input layer, several intermediate hidden layers, and output layer. Each layer of neurons only accepts the input of the previous layer of neurons, and there is no connection between neurons in the same layer. The signal propagates through the input layer and hidden layer before being transmitted to the output layer. If there is an error between the calculated output and the actual output, it enters the error back propagation stage, and the weights of each layer of neurons are adjusted, continue forward propagation until an output value that meets the error standard or reaches the specified number of propagation times is obtained.

BP neural network algorithm has three main steps.

Input layer   Hidden layer   Output layer

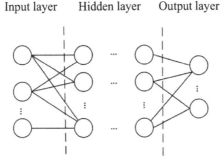

Fig. 1. Schematic diagram of neural network

(1) Data preprocessing

Before conducting neural network training, it is necessary to preprocess the data. Mainly by reducing the randomness of the data to ensure the learning speed and forecasting accuracy of the neural network.

Data preprocessing is an important part of training neural networks, and the performance of neural networks is to some extent affected by the quality of data processing results. The most common method of data processing is to normalize the original data, which means that the input data is completely limited to a certain interval through certain transformations, making the numerical values of the data become a relative value relationship. The normalization of data can be achieved by using a linear function transformation method, which subtracts the minimum sample value from the indicator sample value and then divides it by the maximum difference of the indicator sample, namely,

$$y_i = \frac{x_i - \min x_i}{\max x_i - \min x_i}(i = 1, 2, \cdots, n). \tag{4}$$

(2) Determination of BP Neural Network Structure

1. Design the number of layers in the network. According to the definition and characteristics of neural networks, three-layer neural networks are the most superior. If the network design structure is reasonable and the weight values of neural nodes are appropriate, it can approximate any continuous function [16].
2. Design of input layer nodes. The number of input layer nodes refers to the number of input features, which have a significant impact on the forecasting results [17].
3. Design of hidden layer nodes. The number of nodes in the hidden layer is related to the accuracy and learning efficiency of the entire BP network, so it is necessary to determine the number of nodes based on the actual operation results, with the minimum total sample error [18].
4. Output layer node design. The design of the number of output layer nodes is determined based on actual needs, and the number of output nodes is set to several.

(3) Simulate training and predict

Firstly, establish input layer data samples, normalize the samples, construct a BP neural network, train the samples, and complete the training when the total error of the network meets the accuracy requirements.

4 Experimental Analysis

4.1 Result Analysis of Multiple Linear Regression Forecasting for Human Resources

The key point of regression analysis forecasting methods is to identify various factors that affect the total demand for human resources. The factors that are highly related to the number of personnel required by enterprises are mainly reflected in two aspects: firstly, the determined influencing factors have a certain relationship with the basic characteristics of the enterprise and industry; Secondly, the identified influencing factors should be linearly correlated to a certain extent with the final predicted goal of the required number of employees. Based on the above two considerations and combined with enterprise development experience, scatter plots were selected from multiple human resource indicators that affect the company's development, such as business volume, production level, human resource turnover ratio, production volume, wage growth rate, R&D investment rate, and employee satisfaction. Finally, independent variables such as turnover, wage growth rate, and R&D investment rate were determined for multiple regression analysis. After conducting SPSS data statistical analysis, the results Tables 2and 3 were obtained.

Table 2. Determination coefficient

Model	R	R^2	Adjusted R^2
Multiple Regression Analysis	0.995	0.989	0.984

Table 3. Analysis of variance

Model	Sum of squares	Degree of freedom	Mean square	F	Significance
Regression	234483.706	3	78161.235	186.217	0.000
Residual	2518.394	6	419.732	–	–
Total	237002.100	9	–	–	–

Table 2 is the determination coefficient table. It can be seen from Table 2 that the determination coefficient R=0.995, R^2=0.984, Adjusted $R^2 = 0.984$ which indicates a good fit of the model. Table 3 is an analysis of variance table, which displays the results of regression fitting analysis of variance. Significance represents the probability that the F-value in the F-test is greater than the critical value specified by F. The results show that when the regression equation contains three different independent variables in the

Table 4. Analysis of regression coefficient

Model	Non-standardized coefficient		t	Significance
	B	error		
Constant	3406.021	32.717	104.104	0.000
Turnover	6.075	0.376	−16.155	0.000
Wage growth rate	1.794	1.856	0.967	0.371
R&D investment rate	−74.783	27.453	−2.724	0.034

text, its significance probability value is less than 0.001, rejecting the assumption that the regression coefficients are all 0, and the equation fitting effect is good.

Table 4 shows the regression process statistics and t-test result coefficient analysis. From the statistical quantities in the table, it can be concluded that the multiple linear regression analysis model is:

$$\hat{y} = 3406.021 - 6.075x_1 + 1.794x_2 - 74.783x_3 \qquad (5)$$

Based on the obtained regression Equation (5), we can obtain the forecasting results and error analysis of multiple linear regression analysis as shown in Table 5.

Table 5. Multiple linear regression forecasting results and errors

Years	Electricity sales(100 millilon Kw·h)	Salary growth rate (%)	R&D funding investment enrollment rate (%)	Number of personnel	Forecasting results	Error
1	49.1	10	1	3035	3050	−0.52%
2	53.5	6	1.41	3001	2986	0.82%
3	58	11.2	0.8	3012	3013	−0.06%
4	63	0.2	1.56	2900	2906	−0.24%
5	71.8	0.3	1.13	2873	2885	−0.45%
6	81.6	8	1.4	2825	2819	0.18%
7	91.5	7.9	1.2	2800	2774	0.94%
8	100.9	11	1.82	2655	2676	−0.82%
9	110.7	10	1.7	2640	2624	0.48%
10	118	10.6	1.35	2598	2607	−0.36%
11	123.97	10	1.5		2558	
12	130	10.5	1.55		2519	
13	134.5	11	1.6		2489	

From the forecasting results and error analysis, it can be seen that the predicted value of human resource demand based on multiple regression is basically consistent with the actual situation of the enterprise. This can provide certain guidance for the company in predicting human resource demand to a certain extent, and also verify the effectiveness and feasibility of the multiple linear regression human resource demand forecasting model established in this article.

4.2 Result Analysis of BP Neural Network Forecasting for Human Resources

As a new technology in the field of artificial intelligence, BP neural network has a solid theoretical foundation, rigorous derivation process, and clear algorithm flow. Due to its powerful functionality, the BP algorithm has become the most widely used artificial neural network.

In order to show the forecasting effect of BP neural network forecasting for human re-sources, this paper uses the data set in subsection 4.1 and compares the results with multiple linear regression forecasting. According to the steps of BP neural network algorithm, we firstly establish input layer data samples, normalize the samples and construct a BP neural network. By using the neural network, the samples were trained and the process was stop until the total error of the network meets the accuracy requirements. Based on the above steps, the forecasting results and error analysis of BP neural network are shown in Table 6.

Table 6. BP neural network forecasting results and errors

Years	Electricity sales (100 millilon Kw·h)	Salary growth rate (%)	R&D funding investment enrollment rate (%)	Number of personnel	Forecasting results	Error
1	49.1	10	1	3035	3035	0.00%
2	53.5	6	1.41	3001	2998	0.10%
3	58	11.2	0.8	3012	3012	0.00%
4	63	0.2	1.56	2900	2898	0.07%
5	71.8	0.3	1.13	2873	2870	0.10%
6	81.6	8	1.4	2825	2831	−0.21%
7	91.5	7.9	1.2	2800	2801	−0.04%
8	100.9	11	1.82	2655	2655	0.00%
9	110.7	10	1.7	2640	2637	0.11%
10	118	10.6	1.35	2598	2599	−0.04%
11	123.97	10	1.5		2599	
12	130	10.5	1.55		2593	
13	134.5	11	1.6		2591	

Comparing Table 5 and Table 6, it is not difficult to find that the BP neural network has better forecasting performance compared to multiple linear regression, with relatively small errors. This is because neural networks can continuously accept new sample information and adjust the attributes of the model itself, with generalization ability and dynamic characteristics, ensuring its strong adaptability. Therefore, the BP algorithm has be-come the most widely used artificial neural network, but it also has some following disadvantages.

(1) The error convergence speed is slow.

After the training of neural networks reaches a certain level, standard BP neural net-work algorithms often have the disadvantage of slow learning speed. Increasing the number of training times does not significantly reduce the error, and sometimes there may even be oscillations. The error increases instead of decreasing, seriously affecting the convergence speed of the network [19, 20]. This situation is particularly serious for complex problems.

(2) BP neural network is easy to fall into local minima

During the learning process of BP neural networks, the reduction of error values may sometimes be in a stagnant state, but after a certain degree of training, it can continue to significantly decrease, which is trapped in a local minimum. The neural network may mistakenly think that it has found the optimal value and stop training.

Conclusions

With the continuous development and progress of society, more and more enterprises human resources data appeared. How to extract information from these human resource data has become an urgent need in the development and construction of enterprises, and data analytics technology brings new opportunities for the forecasting of human resource demand.

This paper studies multiple linear regression method and BP neural network algorithm in human resource demand forecasting, respectively. Firstly, we discuss the method of multiple regression analysis, modeling multiple linear regression analysis, conducting fit tests using statistical indicator determination coefficient R2 and correction determination coefficient R2, conducting overall significance tests and independent variable significance tests using F-test and t-test, and obtaining regression equations based on actual data. Finally, the number of personnel in the enterprise was verified and predicted based on the obtained regression equations, verified the feasibility of the regression analysis model. At the same time, the BP neural network algorithm is described in detail, and an example is given to com-pare the forecasting results of multiple linear regression method and BP neural network algorithm. By comparing the above two methods, we find that the BP neural network has better forecasting performances than multiple linear regression. Also we point out the disadvantages of BP neural network algorithm.

Acknowledgments. This work was supported in part by National Natural Science Foundation of China (Nos. 62076111 and 61773012), Natural Science Foundation of the Jiangsu Higher Education Institutions of China (No. 15KJB110004), and Postgraduate Research & Practice Innovation Program of Jiangsu Province.

Disclosure of Interests.. The authors declare no conflict of interest.

References

1. Lu, X.: A human resource demand forecasting method based on improved BP algorithm. Comput. Intell. Neurosci. ID 3534840 (2022)
2. Wang, Z.: A genetic algorithm-based grey method for forecasting food demand after snow disasters: an empirical study. Nat. Hazards **68**(2), 675–686 (2013)
3. Haque, M.M., Rahman A., Hagare, D., Kibria, G.: Probabilistic water demand forecasting using projected climatic data for bluemountains water supply system in Australia. Water Res. Manage. **28**(7), 1959–1971 (2014)
4. Xie, B.: Regression analysis of the impact of human resource management on enterprise performance. Stat. Decis. **13**, 83–85 (2013)
5. He, E.: Analysis on factors influencing regional differences in the level of human resources in western China. Zhejiang University (2011)
6. Zheng, H.: Research on performance evaluation and prediction of human resource demand of Inner Mongolia electrical corporation. Tianjin University (2013)
7. Leu, J., Lo, C., Liu, C.: Development and test of fixed average k-means base decision trees grouping method by improving decision tree clustering method. J. Appl. Sci. **9**(3), 528–534 (2009)
8. Idoudi, R., Ettabaa, K.S., Solaiman, B., et al.: Ontology knowledge mining based association rules ranking. Procedia Comput. Sci. **96**, 345–354 (2016)
9. Borsuk, M.E., Stow, C.A., Reckhow, H.A.: A Bayesian network of eutrophication models for synthesis, prediction, and uncertainty analysis. Ecol. Model. **173**(2–3), 219–239 (2004)
10. Pawlak, Z.: Some issues on rough sets. In: Peters, J.F., Skowron, A., Grzymała-Busse, J.W., Kostek, B., Świniarski, R.W., Szczuka, M.S. (eds.) Transactions on Rough Sets I. LNCS, vol. 3100, pp. 1–58. Springer, Heidelberg (2004). https://doi.org/10.1007/978-3-540-27794-1_1
11. Lin, L.: Electronic human resource management and organizational innovation: the roles of information technology and virtual organizational structure. Int. J. Hum. Resour. Manage. **22**(02), 235–257 (2011)
12. Guo, J., Wang, H., Gao, Y., Zhiwen, Z.: A new data mining method of iterative dimensionality reduction derived from Partial Least-Squares Regression. In: The 3rd International Conference on Intelligent Information Technology Application (IITA 09), IEEE CPS Press, pp. 471–474 (2009)
13. Ganapathy, J., García Márquez, F.P.: Data mining and information technology in transportation - a review: In: Proceedings of the Fifteenth International Conference on Management Science and Engineering Management, vol. 79, pp. 849–855 (2021)
14. Witold, P.: The benefits and drawbacks of data mining technologies. WIREs: Data Min. Knowl. Disc. **10**(1), e1344 (2020)
15. Pagaiya, N., Phanthunane, P., Bamrung, A., et al.: Forecasting imbalances of human resources for health in the Tailand health service system: application of a health demand method. Hum. Resour. Health **17**(1), 4 (2019)
16. Meehan, R., Ahmed, S.: Forecasting human resources requirements: a demand model. Hum. Resour. Planning **13**(4), 297–307 (1990)
17. Kenney, R.: Questions for Delphi. Antioch Rev. **77**(1), 90–91 (2019)
18. Niederberger, M., Koberich, S.: Coming to consensus: the Delphi technique. Eur. J. Cardiovasc. Nurs. **20**(7), 692–695 (2021)

19. Michel, J., Daniel, R., Michel, J., et al.: Human resource flexibility and the relation-ship between work-family enrichment and job satisfaction: regression analysis. Horizonte Empresarial **12**(1), 53–62 (2013)
20. Bleischwitz, R., Nechifor, V., Winning, M., et al.: Extrapolation or saturation-r. Glob. Environ. Change **48**, 86–96 (2018)

A Localization Correction Algorithm of Location-Based Services Based on Point Clustering

Jianqiao Sheng[1]($\boxtimes$), Liang Zhang[1], Yicao Zhang[1], Jingxuan Xu[1], and Jiaqi Wu[2]

[1] Information and Communication Branch, State Grid Anhui Electric Power Co., Ltd., Hefei, China
cambridgeace@sina.com.cn

[2] State Grid Anhui Electric Power Co., Ltd., Huainan Power Supply Company, Huainan, China

Abstract. Cell phone location-based services (LBS) is the basis of many smartphone applications, and location accuracy is the most core parameter of location-based services. Currently, LBS can be realized in two ways: GPS positioning and network base station positioning. Among them, the accuracy of network base station positioning is relatively low, and the phenomenon of positioning point drift will occur. Most of the positioning point drift occurs in the stationary state of the positioning object by the network positioning of the random positioning deviation, to the application of LBS-based services have brought about an impact. To address this problem, this paper first uses k-means algorithm to cluster the positioning data points, the positioning points are divided into different sets, to distinguish which are the positioning data when the positioning object is moving, which are the points generated by the drift deviation when it is stationary, and then use the expectation to obtain relatively accurate positioning information, to achieve a certain degree of correction of the positioning drift deviation. In this paper, based on android platform, we call the basic Gaode positioning API to obtain the positioning service, and store the positioning data in the cell phone database through greenDao component as the collected positioning points, in addition to the data sharing function and so on. This paper further implements the k-means algorithm for the collected positioning data, verifies the above ideas, and achieves certain results.

Keywords: Cell phone location services · k-means algorithm; android · Gaode location APIs

1 Introduction

Mobile location-based services are location-based services that rely on the networks of mobile telecommunication operators to obtain precise location information about the user, including latitude and longitude coordinates. This service not only provides the user's current geographic location, but also predicts the user's likely future location based on the user.s movement trajectory. Whether it is for city navigation, outdoor adventure, or finding rescue in an emergency, mobile location services play an important role [1].

The use of cell phones to determine the orientation refers to the combination of wireless networks and cell phones, cell phone holders can be detailed coordinates (longitude and latitude, including three-dimensional data), or some of the base users to provide value-added services through the information, voice, SMS. Now, the use of cell phones to determine the location of the technology, it can be broadly divided into: base station positioning, WiFi positioning, GPS positioning. GPS positioning is a high-precision positioning technology, can reach 10 m or even smaller accuracy, but the premise is that the cell phone hardware needs to support the Global Positioning System. Nowadays, most users' cell phones are equipped with this function. Another positioning technology is base station positioning based on cell phone signals, which has an accuracy of about one hundred meters, and it is a technology that relies on cellular mobile communications. Finally, WIFI positioning is an emerging positioning technology that has been adopted by many large software companies. It calculates location through WiFi hotspots and also provides fairly accurate results for indoor positioning of multiple users. This technique is accomplished by detecting WiFi router address location software (ID) and then utilizing its collaborative WiFi location database and map data to accomplish the positioning.

However, under the conditions of the mobile environment, with the configuration of the hardware equipment of the cell phone and the needs of the holder, the problem of random drift of positioning will occur. In order to address this problem, this paper firstly utilizes the k-means algorithm to cluster the positioning data points, and divides the positioning points into different sets, in order to differentiate which are the data positioned when the positioning object is moving, and which are the points generated by the drift deviation when it is stationary, and then utilizes the expectation solving to obtain the relatively accurate positioning information, and realizes a certain degree of correcting the deviation of the positioning drift. This paper is based on android platform, call the basic gaode positioning API to obtain positioning service, the positioning data will be stored in the cell phone database through greenDao component, as the collected positioning points, in addition to the data sharing function and so on. This paper further implemented k-means algorithm for the collected positioning data to verify the above ideas and achieved certain results.

2   Cell Phone Location and Location Service Bias

2.1   Cell Phone Positioning

So far, the cell phone positioning technology, which is widely used by everyone, mainly contains three kinds: base station positioning, WiFi positioning, and GPS positioning.

GPS positioning: has a relatively high degree of precision, but it needs to have a global positioning system cell phone hardware under the conditions of being able to support it, the current ordinary users of cell phones, now contain this template. For containing 24 satellites, it is distributed in the distance of 6 km from the ground, if you want to orbit the earth, it takes 12 h to surround, so that people on the ground, will be in any point in time can observe more than 4 satellites. For the integrated GPS, it requires the possession of a cell phone with a smart system attached to it, and its built-in GPS board, which only contains the function of receiving, but does not have the function of transmitting. 24 GPS satellites are constantly sending information to the earth containing important parameters such as time, such as satellites pointing to the earth, and the cell phone receives this information, and it will use the signals from multiple satellites, and at the same time it will be based on the order and time difference sent by the satellites, and the time difference will be based on the order and time difference sent by the satellites. The order and time difference sent by the satellites, using these two variables and based on the three satellites their respective 3D coordinates (X,Y,Z), to calculate the location of the phone. Considering the clocks between the phones and the time difference between them and the satellites, a fourth satellite needs to be introduced, but in fact four unknowns are needed, which include X,Y,Z and the clock difference, which can form four equations to be solved in order to obtain specific information about the location of the phone such as latitude, longitude and elevation.Base Station Positioning: Based on cellular phone signals, the accuracy range of about one hundred meters is positioned through the base station, with certain accuracy requirements, and is a technology based on cellular mobile communications [2].

WIFI positioning: This is a newborn positioning method. It is also accurate in calculating the orientation and multi-user indoor positioning accuracy through WiFi hotspot. It is to detect the WiFi router address positioning software (ID), and then in its cooperation with the WiFi location database and map data to complete the positioning. Using WiFi positioning, the phone must support and enable WiFi. Its accuracy depends on the density of the WiFi location database WiFi router details, the accuracy of about 200 m.

2.2 Location Service Bias

As an important indicator to measure the performance of the cell phone's GPS, it contains many kinds of factors, such as the positioning precision and positioning accuracy of the cell phone positioning service, the location information of the cell phone positioning service will be accompanied by a variety of changes in time, resulting in a variety of deviations from the phenomenon occurs. This paper introduces a brief table of GPS error, as shown in Table 1:

Table 1. GPS positioning error

Factors	range of inaccuracy
Satellite clock error	0–1.5 m
Satellite orbit error	1–5 m
Errors introduced by the ionosphere	0–30 m
Errors introduced by the atmosphere	0–30 m
Noise from the receiver itself	0–10 m
Multiple Reflections	0–1 m
Total Positioning Error Total Positioning Error	About 28 m

Typically, the actual satellite navigation information, which already includes atmospheric correction parameters, has the potential to reduce the error to a range of 0.5 to 0.7, and within about the last two years, the GPS error, which may have been reduced to a range of 10 m or even less [3].

There are several reasons for the bias in positioning services:

1) Pure base station localization. Base station signal strength, density, etc.;
2) Positioning is definitely not allowed.
3) Base station positioning + GPS.

There are GPS devices, assuming they have been turned on, because GPS signals work poorly indoors, and will be strong and weak at times if possible (to accomplish GPS, it must be at least three satellites). Under the combined effect of base station positioning + GPS, all time positioning will be biased, so there will be a positioning offset every minute. LBS positioning is to locate to the location of the base station, not the location of your device, so the LBS positioning has little to do with the location of your device, but rather depends on the device SIM card access to which base station, where your location is, and access to the base station is affected by the The access to the base station is affected by the density of the base station, the number of users of the base station, but not close to which base station access to which base station, which is automatic, uncontrollable and unknown, so there is a problem of positioning drift.

Based on this principle can know the global positioning system, GPS tracking device does not send out signals, only receive satellite positioning to send data to solve the problem after the operation. But if in the urban high-rise area, it often faces some of the searchable satellite number is small, the actual use of the process, in general, three satellites can realize the initial positioning. From this, horizontal coordinates, vertical coordinates and height can be determined. Satellite tracking satellite signals are blocked, the GPS tracking device in weak signal conditions, the direct capture may be just one star or two stars. If the GPS tracking orientation is slightly adjusted, you can usually get three stars or four stars, then the received signal is often part of the reflected signal emitted by the satellite. Therefore, people who have used GPS probably have this experience: when the cell phone terminal containing GPS is at a standstill, the coordinate information obtained by the cell phone positioning service includes longitude and latitude, and it will appear to float around a point, and sometimes deviate from certain positions, and even show signs of speed. The industry refers to this phenomenon as "drift" [4].

Two states of GPS drift: static position drift, velocity (position) drift.

Static velocity drift can be resolved with zero velocity at rest. Positioning position offset phenomenon is more commonly occurring, this is due to a question of the degree of precision, now many civilian ships, if it is under 10 m, then it is good condition is 5 m. For the need for a higher degree of fineness of the measurement of the situation, if you want to achieve a more ideal accuracy, then you need to use differential technology to compensate, but this product is very expensive, and the market is not very popularize this product, not very suitable for the public [5].

3   Core Technology

3.1   Clustering Algorithm

General clustering algorithms. It is categorized into five main types, which mainly include segmentation methods, hierarchical methods, density based methods, grid based methods and model based methods.

Method of division: First k divisions are created, k being the number of divisions to be created; then, accuracy is increased by using a cyclic localization technique, which, in order to help improve the quality of the divisions, usually consists of dividing an object from one set to another [6].

Hierarchical approach: For an experimentally obtained data or a given data, a hierarchy is created to decompose these data into a collection of data. It can be divided into two operations, mainly from top to bottom (decomposition) and from bottom to top (merging).

Density-based approach: Clustering of objects is accomplished based on density division. It is the clustering method used to grow by the density around the object you are detecting.

Grid-based approach: First, in the condition containing the entire object, the space in which it is located is divided into a finite number of modules, which are able to form a lattice-like structure; the lattice structure is then utilized to complete the clustering.

Model-based approach: The pattern or style of each clustering is first envisioned and then modeled so that the corresponding model can be found, along with the data to which it applies. For ease of use, this paper uses one of the simplest and most effective clustering algorithms, the k-means algorithm. k-means algorithm, as a kind of clustering algorithm that is now gaining popularity among people. It is the clustering function that is accomplished by taking the average of the sample data derived or calculated for each cluster as the point representing the entire cluster [7].

Algorithm Steps:

1) Find a centroid in all the data clusters and let it be the initial clustering center for each aggregate group to get the initial clustering center;
2) Divide the data samples a bit, according to a minimum distance formula that can be computed, into the aggregation group closest to it;
3) Calculate the mean of an aggregate group and use it as a new clustering center;
4) Continue running steps 2 and 3, and if the center of this cluster remains the same, run step 5;
5) Finish and the result gives K clusters.

3.2   Implementation of Localization in ANDROID Systems

Android SDK is a simple set of positioning LBS positioning service interface, you can use this API to get the positioning results (including global positioning, page positioning assistance H5), reverse geocoding (textual description of the address), as well as geofencing function. As of now, there are two main types of maps related to positioning in China; a Gaode map and a Baidu map. Google has made the maps developed by Gaode make our country a map produced by Apple as their data provider. Whether it is the ability to locate or the accuracy of the data, the experience on the Gaode map will not disappoint the user, and the function is more powerful and user-friendly; Baidu map application program interface through the application program interface to support the Android device application program interface to build a powerful interactive application, but also to achieve the positioning, local search, direction and other data services [8, 9].

3.2.1 GPS-Based Positioning

The goal achieved by Android system is achieved through the smartphone realization process, including the use of the phone in the function of the Global Positioning System (GPS), and the use of the operator's network base stations and Wi-Fi networks to achieve the goal. The positioning process is shown in Fig. 1.

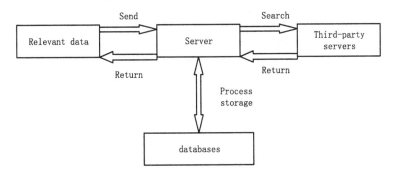

Fig. 1. Positioning process data flow diagram

In Android, for the developer's consideration, Google supplies a complete API interface that is used to allow it to implement the location determination aspect of the Global Positioning System. In the interface supplied by the developer, it is possible to obtain the current location of the device based on a specific wrapper class, but it is also necessary to periodically change the current location information requested by the hardware device [10].

3.2.2 Network Base Station Based Localization

When the cell phone is in the power-on state, it automatically registers information with the base station in the GSM cellular network in which the signal is the strongest according to each base station's own ID, so we can obtain information about the user's geographic location through the base station's ID by utilizing the correspondence between the base station's ID and geographic location provided by a third party. The user's cell phone broadcasts a signal, which is then picked up by base stations near different locations. Since the distance of the user from the location base station is different, the time at which the base station receives the signal sent by the user will be slightly different. Further by analyzing the time difference between the time when the signal is received by different base stations, the location of the user can be calculated [11].

In addition, a large number of applications in the 5G era require accurate positioning, such as industrial AGV, asset tracking, etc., especially indoor accurate positioning, but satellite positioning can not be used indoors, and LTE and WiFi positioning technology is not accurate. For this reason, 5G has added a positioning function in the R16 version, which utilizes the MIMO multibeam feature to define indoor positioning techniques such as cellular cell-based signal round-trip time (RTT), signal time difference of arrival (TDOA), angle-of-arrival measurements (AoA), angle-of-departure measurements (AoD), and so on [12, 13].

3.3 Expectation Model for Location Data

The data for localization in this paper contains two parameters: longitude and latitude. The indoor collected localization data will appear floating deviation, what I want to do is, the collected localization data with deviation to find out the corresponding expectation respectively. In this paper, it is through the expectation model to realize the correction of bias in probability statistics, the definition of mathematical expectation is as follows:

Let the law of distribution of a discrete random variable X be:

$$P\{X = x_k\} = p_k, k = 1, 2, 3...... \tag{1}$$

If the series $\sum_{k=1}^{\infty} x_k p_k$ converges absolutely, the sum of the series $\sum_{k=1}^{\infty} x_k p_k$ is said to be the mathematical expectation of the random variable X, denoted E(X). i.e..

$$E(X) = \sum_{k=1}^{\infty} x_k p_k \tag{2}$$

Through the above explanation, in the outdoor situation, generally through the GPS positioning, its accuracy can reach a few meters; in the indoor will be through the 3G or wifi signal positioning, their accuracy can only reach the range of 50–100 m, so if you are stationary, the positioning data will appear positioning "drift" phenomenon! Therefore, it is necessary to approximate a more accurate data by correcting the deviation. The basic idea is as follows:

(1) Firstly, the k-means algorithm distinguishes the points that are far away from each other and finds out which points are stationary drifting;
(2) The stationary drifting points are used to obtain more accurate information by solving the expectation.

4   Positioning Data Acquisition Program Design and Implementation

4.1   Positional Data Structure

The localization data in this paper includes localization longitude and localization latitude. The specific data structure is shown in Table 2:

Table 2. Data structures for positioning

Variable Name	Variable Meaning
private Double lat;	latitude
private Double lng;	longitude
private Double accuracy;	accuracy
private String proder;	localization source
private String province;	User's province
private String city;	User's city
private String desc;	User's location
private String phoneId;	phone number
private DaoSession daoSession;	Activation data
private LocationDao myDao;	Storage of documents

4.2   Positioning Process

Specifically, first set up the positioning service class and the positioning parameter class to get the positioning client information and initialize it. Set the positioning interval to 2 min. Then set the specific positioning service parameters, including setting the positioning mode to high-precision mode, requesting the method of obtaining the address, and setting the positioning listener. Use the data storage ORM framework greenDAO provided by the Android platform to store the data. GreenDAO is a lightweight and fast ORM solution for mapping objects to SQLite database. Pass the positioning service information through the Intent mechanism to start and stop the positioning service. Rewrite the update location service method. Set the positioning client information, start the local positioning service as well as the positioning listener service, run the notification in the service foreground, and create a new thread: check whether the positioning service is started regularly, and restart the positioning service if it is not started. Check if the location user is available, if so start the location. The method called to start the positioning service returns a value indicating not to kill this service. Destroys location service information such as location threads and determines if there are still running processes. Creates a database access session and inserts it into the database. Open the positioning listener service to get information about the current positioning service program and create a json file to store the data in the database as a way to complete data collection (Fig. 2).

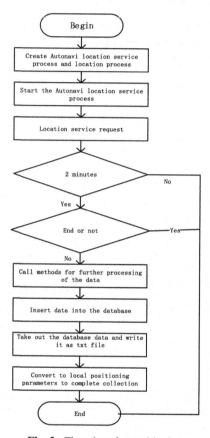

Fig. 2. Flowchart for positioning

5 Experimental Analysis

First of all, let's analyze each function of the main function interface as follows: Click the "START LOCATION" button to start tracking your location information to get the location data. Click the "SAVE DATA TO FILE" button to store the location data in the user-specified location and convert it to a txt file, as shown in Fig. 3.

Fig. 3. Initiating localization versus data localization

Click the "VIEW LOCATION" button to get an overview of the map information. Click the "STOP LOCATION" button to stop the location service and display the prompt as shown in Fig. 4.

Fig. 4. Viewing the map and stopping the positioning

After clustering using the k-means algorithm, the test data samples were divided into 20 classes for analysis and the running results are shown in Fig. 5:

```
print:cluster[0][0]= (32. 09303927951389, 118. 80970757378472)
print:cluster[0][1]= (32. 0926318359375, 118. 80826199001736)
print:cluster[0][2]= (32. 09159, 118. 80826199001736)
print:cluster[0][3]= (32. 09159, 118. 809318)
print:cluster[0][4]= (32. 09159, 118. 809318)
print:cluster[0][5]= (32. 09159, 118. 809318)
print:cluster[0][6]= (32. 09159, 118. 809318)
print:cluster[0][7]= (32. 09257378472222, 118. 80820692274305)
=======================================
print:cluster[1][0]= (32. 177683919270834, 118. 7199205186632)
=======================================
print:cluster[2][0]= (32. 077023, 118. 81006)
print:cluster[2][1]= (32. 0758997938836804, 118. 81007111545138)
print:cluster[2][2]= (32. 07592881944444, 118. 8104066297743)
print:cluster[2][3]= (32. 07601345486111, 118. 81044976128472)
print:cluster[2][4]= (32. 076815321180554, 118. 8100721571806)
print:cluster[2][5]= (32. 077023, 118. 81006)
=======================================
print:cluster[3][0]= (32. 205126, 118. 724041)
print:cluster[3][1]= (32. 205126, 118. 724041)
print:cluster[3][2]= (32. 205126, 118. 724041)
print:cluster[3][3]= (32. 205126, 118. 724041)
print:cluster[3][4]= (32. 205126, 118. 724041)
print:cluster[3][5]= (32. 205126, 118. 724041)
print:cluster[3][6]= (32. 205126, 118. 724041)
print:cluster[3][7]= (32. 205126, 118. 724041)
print:cluster[3][8]= (32. 20519070095486, 118. 72461263020833)
print:cluster[3][9]= (32. 205250651041666, 118. 72629150390625)
=======================================
print:cluster[4][0]= (32. 110277, 118. 777926)
print:cluster[4][1]= (32. 110277, 118. 777926)
=======================================
```

Fig. 5. Clustering results of k-means algorithm

The points obtained after clustering by the k-means algorithm are depicted in a scatter plot under the coordinate system as shown in Fig. 6, and the processed points are then plotted on a scatter plot, as shown in Fig. 7:

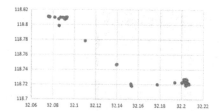

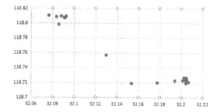

Fig. 6. Coordinates of points after clustering   **Fig. 7.** Plot of processed coordinates

6 Summarize

Location-based information service (LBS) has been quite popular in today's society, which can integrate the virtual network life with the real geographic location information. In the technical application based on location service, the foundation is the positioning technology, which obtains the user's precise positioning information through the cell phone device and uploads the positioning information to the server side. According to the user's different function choices, the server side processes the positioning data accordingly and adopts the corresponding recommendation algorithms to return the results of the processing of the data to the user. In this paper, through the introduction of the location service, to realize the positioning service, especially the cell phone in the stationary state, the positioning of the random drift problem, for this problem, this paper adopts the clustering method, to achieve the distinction between the stationary and running state positioning data, and then for the stationary state of the drift of the positioning data and the real positioning of the position of the deviation expectancy of the positioning of the cell phone under the stationary state of the corrective bias.

References

1. Wang Yan, W., Hao, M.T.: Research on forum information recognition technology based on K-center point clustering algorithm. Comput. Eng. Des. **21**(01), 45–56 (2009)
2. Chengmin, W., Tiyan, Z., Chuyun, S.: Optimization model and simplified gradient algorithm for K-center point clustering method. Control. Eng. **54**(S2), 57–60 (2009)
3. Jigui, S., Jie, L., Lianyu, Z.: Research on clustering algorithm. J. Softw. **24**(01), 34–37 (2008)
4. Liu, J.L.: Application of k-center point clustering algorithm to hierarchical data. Comput. Eng. Des. **40**(24), 30–31 (2008)
5. Shuhui, Z.: Analysis and implementation of K-center point algorithm - PAM. Fujian Comput. **12**(06), 34–39 (2008)
6. Yunping, S., Daxin, X.: Analysis and application of K-means based clustering algorithm. J. Xi'an Univ. Technol. **30**(01), 47–50 (2006)
7. Xiaomin, Y., Yunhao, C.: Spatial clustering analysis under constraints - an improved K-center point clustering algorithm. Surv. Mapp. Inf. Eng. **23**(03), 40–43 (2006)
8. Chen, S.: On the implementation and analysis of commonly used clustering algorithms. J. Fujian Radio Telev. Univ. **56**(06), 80–83 (2006)
9. Zhou, H., Yuan, Q., Cheng, Z., Shi, B.: PHC: a fast partition and hierarchy-based clustering algorithm. J. Comput. Sci. Technol. **34**(3), 45–50 (2003)
10. Huang, Z.: Extensions to the k-means algorithm for clustering large data Setswith categorical values. Data Min. Knowl. Disc. **12**(3), 34–40 (1998)
11. Kim, J.W., Kim, J.Y., Kim, C.S.: Semantic LBS: ontological approach for enhancing interoperability in location based services. In: Meersman, R., Tari, Z., Herrero, P. (eds.) On the Move to Meaningful Internet Systems 2006: OTM 2006 Workshops. OTM 2006. LNCS, vol. 4277, pp. 792–801. Springer, Heidelberg (2006). https://doi.org/10.1007/11915034_103
12. An, J., Cheng, C.Q., Song, S.: Geohash-based regional query for facet data. Geogr. Geog. Inf. Sci. **29**(5), 31–35 (2013)
13. Kaufman, L., Rousseeuw, P.J.: Finding Groups in Data: An Introduction to Cluster Analysis. Wiley, New York, pp. 100–240 (1990)

Comparison of Prediction Methods on Large-Scale and Long-Term Online Live Streaming Data

Huan Chen⬤, Shuhui Guo⬤, Siyu Lai⬤, and Xin Lu(✉)⬤

College of Systems Engineering, National University of Defense Technology, Changsha 410073, China
xin.lu.lab@outlook.com

Abstract. Effective prediction of online live streaming traffic plays a crucial role not only in optimizing network resource allocation for enhancing viewer experience but also in assessing factors impacting audience retention and the overall sustainability of streaming platforms. This study conducts a comprehensive evaluation of machine learning methods for online live streaming traffic prediction using extensive hourly traffic data. The dataset comprises 1,385,444,808 live streaming entries and encompasses 30,690,841 unique streamers from the Douyu platform, spanning December 2020 to April 2023. Various experimental settings are employed to compare the performance of these methods. Our findings reveal that among ten methodologies considered, the Bidirectional Long Short-Term Memory, Extra Tree (ET), and Random Forest models demonstrate consistent and robust performance. Particularly, the ET model exhibits outstanding accuracy and precision in predicting daily viewer counts when incorporating pertinent features. In the domain of large-scale and long-term live streaming data prediction, machine learning approaches surpass traditional time series forecasting methods. Moreover, our analysis underscores the significance of incorporating streamer count in enhancing the accuracy of network traffic prediction. Interestingly, while hourly features show limited impact, in certain scenarios, their inclusion may even diminish the predictive efficacy of the models.

Keywords: Online live streaming · Machine learning · Time series prediction · Extra Tree · Bi-LSTM

1 Introduction

Online live streaming, among the myriad Internet applications, has experienced rapid evolution propelled by its strong interactivity and the liberation from temporal and spatial constraints [1]. Since 2016, the surge in online live streaming has led to the emergence of numerous platforms, including Twitch, Douyu TV, TikTok, and others, captivating millions of users globally. The content spectrum of online live streaming has expanded from entertainment-focused gaming to diverse applications encompassing education, culture, sports, tourism, and beyond [2]. The onset of the COVID-19 pandemic further accelerated the momentum of online live streaming [3], facilitating the emergence of novel streaming methods such as "remote learning" [4], "e-commerce live streaming" [5], and "social live streaming" [6]. This evolution triggered a fervor for live streaming, exemplified by the staggering statistics: by December 2022, China recorded a soaring 751 million live streaming users, marking an increase of 47.28 million from December 2021, constituting a significant 70.3% of the total Internet user base [7].

The increasing coverage and popularity has brought numerous challenges to online live streaming platforms [8]. For example, game live streaming emphasizes on clarity and smoothness, while business live streaming requires stability. Faced with the differences in technology requirements, as well as the surge in traffic, platform operators need to use various technologies to maintain the stability and fluency of the platform. Another challenge is the high volume and frequency of "Danmu" (a subtitle system in online video platforms that allows users to overlay moving comments onto a playing video that are synchronized to the video timeline [9]), which puts great pressure on the system and imposes excessive technical requirements on the platform. Network traffic prediction can help platform operators optimize network management, and provide users with a smooth and stable live streaming experience. Furthermore, it can also evaluate the impact of factors such as viewers' behaviors, content preferences, and platform performance on the number of viewers, helping to understand the dynamic relationship between streamers and viewers, and further revealing factors that contribute to audience retention and overall platform sustainability.

In recent years, some scholars have been devoted to the research of live streaming prediction. In the related research on predicting the popularity of live streaming rooms, Kaytoue et al. [10] observed a strong correlation between the initial popularity of live streams and their future popularity. Based on this finding, they developed a linear regression model that utilizes the historical viewer count to predict the future viewer count. Furthermore, Jia et al. [11] demonstrated a strong correlation between the popularity of a live streaming room and the frequency at which the streamer conducts live streams. Arnett et al. [12] found through analysing live streaming data from Twitter, YouTube, and Instagram that the timing of account creation by streamers does not directly affect their popularity (measured by the number of viewers and fans). How, having a social media account is crucial for the growth of popularity. Netzorg et al. [13] propose a temporal analysis method that utilizes all relevant information available at time t to predict the eventual absolute popularity (measured by the number of fans) at time $t + \delta$. The predictive results indicate that the behaviors of streamers play a significant role in predicting their popularity.

In other related research on live streaming prediction, Nascimento et al. [14] created a linear regression model to predict the amount of chat based on the number of viewers logged into a channel. In an effort to infer the future income of streamers with users' attributes as features, Tu et al. [15] identified GBDT as one of the most effective/accurate decision tree algorithms compared to Cart, AdaBoost, and RF. They also find that streamers' income is most affected by the number of fans, and that streamers with more fans tend to receive more virtual gifts. Chen et al. [16] collected over 9.5 million Danmu data from 500 live streaming rooms on Douyu platform and proposed a novel model that integrates multiple types of semantic information from Danmu, including sentiment, topics, as well as information on the viewers, and used these information to predict the value of virtual gifts sent by the viewers. The results showed that the gifting behaviours of viewers can be well predicted with features extracted from the Danmu data.

We can see that the majority of online live streaming studies focused on statistical analysis of live streaming data, while only a few attempted to study on traffic prediction. What's more, most of these prediction studies were limited with small sample size, short observation periods, and low generalizability of prediction results, etc. The accuracy and effectiveness of predictions still need to be further verified and improved in practical applications. To overcome these limitations, this study aims to conduct a thorough comparative analysis of various methods and models employed for traffic prediction based on large-scale, long-term live streaming data. Additionally, we will integrate different features to enhance the accuracy and interpretability of predictions. We utilize large-scale and long-term online live streaming data to employ different methods for prediction. Then, through analyzing factors which affect the traffic of live streaming platforms, we extract different features for prediction and evaluate their contribution in improving prediction accuracy with various algorithms.

2　Dataset and Methods

2.1　Live Streaming Data

Douyu, founded in 2016, is the leading online live streaming platform in China. As a typical live streaming platform, it has a large number of active users and provides rich live streaming services. According to Douyu's 2022 annual financial report [17], in the fourth quarter, the Monthly Active Users (MAU) on its mobile platform reached 57.4 million, while the number of paying users remained stable at 5.6 million.

In this study, continuous live streaming data from Douyu, including room ID, room name, live streaming category ID, streamer ID, nickname of streamer, start time of streaming, time of data retrieval, number of live viewers, and number of fans, were obtained with a deliberately developed crawler system by scraping all streaming rooms using Douyu's open data interface (API). The original dataset used in this study covers a time span of 839 days, from December 25, 2020, to April 12, 2023, with a time interval of 10 min. The dataset consists of 1,385,444,808 tuples, involving 30,690,841 unique streamers. As the focus of this study is primarily on the number of streamers and the number of viewers on the platform, the dataset is aggregated into daily and hourly basis, respectively. A summary of the original dataset is provided in Table 1.

Table 1. Overview of the original dataset.

Category	Description
Period of analysis	2020.12.25–2023.04.12
Duration	839 days
Time interval	10 min
Tuples	1,385,444,808
Number of unique streamers	30,690,841
Data attribute fields	room_id, room_name, cate_id, owerner_id, nick_name, show_time, now_time, online, fans

2.2 Prediction Methods

To assess the efficacy of live streaming prediction methodologies, we conduct a systematic comparison of prediction performance between two categories of methods: traditional time series prediction techniques and machine learning algorithms. Specifically, we evaluate ARIMA, SARIMA, BP, RNN, LSTM, GRU, Bi-LSTM, Random Forest, XGBoost, and Extra Tree models.

ARIMA. As the most widely used traditional time series prediction method [18]. $ARIMA(p, d, q)$ integrates the main features of autoregression (AR), differencing (I), and moving average (MA) models to address issues such as non-stationarity of time series, correlation between observations, and residual errors [19]. Equation (1) demonstrates the $ARIMA(p, d, q)$ model using the lag polynomial L [20, 21].

$$\left(1 - \sum_{i=1}^{p} \varphi_i L^i\right)(1 - L)^d = \left(1 - \sum_{j=1}^{q} \theta_j L^i\right)\varepsilon_t. \tag{1}$$

In the equation, L^i denotes the lag operator, φ_i represents the autoregressive model parameter, θ_j represents the moving average parameter, and ε_t is the error term.

SARIMA. SARIMA extends ARIMA by including the seasonal terms (P, D, Q) to capture repetitive patterns within the data's seasonal cycles. Assuming that y_t is a non-stationary time series, w_t represents a Gaussian white noise process, $E_p(B^m)$ represents a seasonal moving average polynomial, $\Theta_Q(B^m)$ demonstrates a seasonal moving average polynomial, and B is a backshift operator. Equation (2) presents the SARIMA model [22].

$$E_p(B^m)\phi_p(B)(1 - B^m)^D(1 - B)^d y_t = \Theta_Q(B^m)\theta_q(B)w_t. \tag{2}$$

Backpropagation (BP). BP is a key algorithm in neural networks that enables the optimization of the network's parameters, specifically the connection weights between neurons. It works by propagating the error from the network's output back to its inputs, allowing the weights to be adjusted in a way that reduces the error [23]. This iterative process gradually brings the network's output closer to the desired target output, and achieves better prediction performance.

Recurrent Neural Network (RNN). RNN is a robust ANN that can store and utilize information from previous time steps as input for the current time step, and use existing time series data to predict future data over a specific length of time [22]. This architecture enables RNN to effectively handle sequential data with temporal dependencies and remember important features of the input sequential data, making it widely used for time series prediction tasks. The single RNN cell is represented mathematically by Eq. (3) [22].

$$h_t = \tanh(W[h_{t-1}, x_t] + b). \tag{3}$$

where b represents the bias matrix, W denotes the weight matrix, and h_t and h_{t-1} are the hidden states at the current and previous time steps, respectively.

Long Short Term Memory (LSTM) [24]. LSTM differs from the basic structure of traditional RNNs, it introduces a long-term memory cell state and utilizes "gates" (forget gate, input gate, output gate [20]) to regulate the state and output at different time steps. By employing this approach, LSTM addresses issues such as gradient vanishing, gradient exploding and insufficient long-term memory capacity commonly encountered in RNNs [25], demonstrating significant effectiveness in handling sequential problems. The LSTM unit structure is shown in Fig. 1.

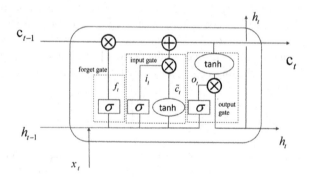

Fig. 1. The LSTM unit structure.

Gated Recurrent Unit (GRU). GRU is another variation of the RNN model. Similar to LSTM, GRU introduces a long-term memory cell state and utilizes "gates" (the reset gate and update gate) to control information and regulate the states and outputs at different time steps [26, 27]. Compared to LSTM, the GRU model has fewer parameters and is computationally more efficient but may exhibit slightly weaker modeling capabilities in certain tasks.

Bidirectional Long Short Term Memory (Bi-LSTM). Bi-LSTM is a variant of the LSTM model, proposed by Graves et al. [28] in 2005. The hidden layer of Bi-LSTM consists of both forward LSTM cell states and backward LSTM cell states [29]. One LSTM cell state considers the forward input and past information, while the other considers the backward input and future information. This structure enables simultaneous consideration of past and future information, resulting in improved predictive performance [30]. The Bi-LSTM network structure is shown in Fig. 2.

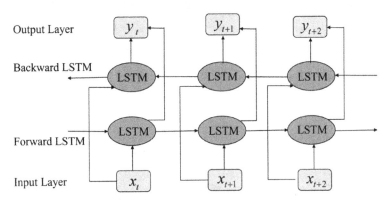

Fig. 2. The Bi-LSTM network structure.

Random Forest (RF). The core idea of Random Forest is to make predictions and classifications by constructing a set of decision trees [31]. Each decision tree is built independently, based on different random samples and feature subsets [32]. And final prediction result of the random forest is determined by voting or averaging the predictions from each decision tree [33].

Extreme Gradient Boosting (XGBoost) [34]. XGBoost is an ensemble learning algorithm based on gradient boosting algorithm and decision tree [34, 35]. It iteratively trains multiple weak learners (typically decision trees) and combines them to create a strong classifier for predicting and classifying complex data. In each iteration, XGBoost fits the residuals of the previous model to gradually improve the prediction performance. Additionally, XGBoost employs innovative techniques such as regularization [36], automatic handling of missing values, and parallel computing to enhance both the accuracy and efficiency of the model.

Extra Tree (ET). ET builds an ensemble of unpruned decision or regression trees according to the classical top-down procedure [37–40]. Its two main differences with other tree-based ensemble methods are that it splits nodes by choosing cut-points fully at random and that it uses the whole learning sample (rather than a bootstrap replica) to grow the trees [41]. Each individual tree within ET is trained on the original dataset, and during the construction process, ET randomly selects a feature value to split the tree. By combining the predictions from multiple trees, typically through voting or averaging, ET can make accurate predictions and handle complex datasets with high dimensional feature spaces. A schematic diagram of an extra tree algorithm is shown in Fig. 3.

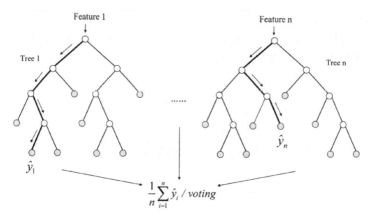

Fig. 3. Extra Tree Algorithm

2.3 Experimental Design

We evaluate the importance of different variables and incorporate different features into the models for prediction and fitting online streaming data. Therefore, the experimental has two parts: the first part does not involve feature inputs, while the second part includes the addition of features for prediction.

We select data from December 25, 2020, 00:00 to April 12, 2023, 24:00 using a sliding window approach to construct training and validation datasets for prediction. The prediction target is the viewer count for each hour of the next day, totaling 24 h. Specifically, the sliding window size is 168, including past 168 time steps, with a pre-diction time window size of 24.

The univariate live streaming data is used as both input and output in the first part, while multivariate data (including streamer count, hours of the day, and the combination of both) is used as input with univariate output in the second part. Evaluation metrics such as MAPE, MAE, MSE, and RMSE are calculated to assess the prediction performance.

3 Results

3.1 Data Overview and Temporal Analysis

Basic Statistics. In this section, we investigate the distribution of viewer count for all live rooms on the platform at a specific moment. For example, on April 12, 2023, at 21:00 (as shown in Fig. 4 (a)), the number of viewers in different live rooms follow a power-law distribution with an exponential cutoff [29]. In other words, the distribution of viewer count in the top-ranked (less than 1%) live rooms follows a power-law distribution, represented by the Zipf distribution (as shown in Eq. (4)). However, beyond that, the distribution of viewer count follows an exponential distribution, represented by Eq. (5). The specific forms of the distributions and the values of their parameters can be found in Table 2.

$$y = cx^{\beta}. \tag{4}$$

$$y = ax^{\left(-\frac{x}{t}\right)} + y_0. \tag{5}$$

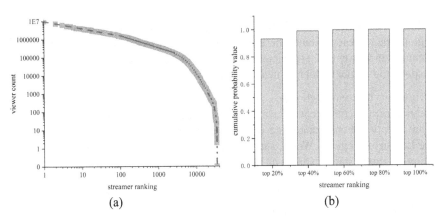

(a)   (b)

Fig. 4. (a) displays the distribution of viewer count in the live rooms on the platform at 21:00 on April 12, 2023. The horizontal axis represents the ranking of the streamers, and the vertical axis represents viewer count. (b) depicts a cumulative probability bar chart of the viewer count in the top 20% to 100% rankings of streamers.

Table 2. Fitting results of distributions of viewer count.

	range of x	range of parameters	R^2
Zipf Distribution	[1, 100]	$c = 9.83 \times 10^6$ $\beta = -0.40$	0.99684
	[100, 2700]	$c = 3.41 \times 10^7$ $\beta = -0.66$	0.99799
Exponential Distribution	[2700, 20000]	$a = 4.33 \times 10^5$ $t = 2794$ $y_0 = 1118$	0.99982
	[20000, 35000]	$a = 1.53 \times 10^4$ $t = 7961$ $y_0 = -196$	0.98439

The analysis of the viewer count variations reveals a strong heterogeneity across live rooms, with a few highly popular top-ranked live rooms attracting the majority of the viewer, while the tail-end live rooms have very few viewers. Furthermore, a cumulative probability bar chart of the viewer count was plotted (as shown in Fig. 4 (b)), confirming that the viewer distribution on the platform follows the Pareto Principle, also known as the 80/20 rule. This highly heterogeneous distribution pattern has resulted in a few streamers becoming internet celebrities, as they possess greater attractiveness and influence over the viewers compared to ordinary streamers. This further validates the rationale behind the increased live streaming load caused by internet celebrities' live shows or official live events.

Major Events. To gauge the influence of significant events on streaming metrics, we analyze a segmented subset of streaming data spanning from September 22, 2022, to January 22, 2023, with a specific focus on major esports tournaments within this timeframe. The graphical representation of these pivotal events, showcased in Fig. 5, illustrates the fluctuations in viewer count (depicted by the blue line) juxtaposed with the timelines of the esports tournaments (highlighted in colored regions).

Observing the trends delineated by the blue line, it becomes evident that esports tournaments generally coincide with an uptick in viewer count. However, notable exceptions warrant attention. For instance, the yellow and purple regions in the visual correspond to the League of Legends World Championships. Notably, the yellow segment, encapsulating the group stage, exhibits an upward trajectory in traffic. Conversely, the purple segment, encapsulating the quarter-finals, semi-finals, and finals, displays a downward trend. This divergence could be attributed to the limited advancement of Chinese teams beyond the quarter-finals during the 2022 League of Legends World Championships.

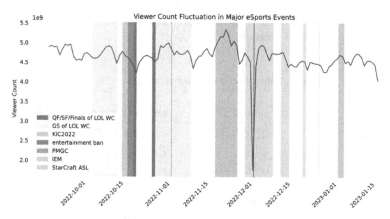

Fig. 5. Changes in the number of viewers associated with major esports events.

Furthermore, the red segment represents an aberrant dip in traffic on December 6, 2022, attributable to a nationwide entertainment suspension in remembrance of former president Jiang Zemin. This suspension led to the cessation of public entertainment activities across the country, profoundly affecting streaming traffic on that day.

General Viewer Characteristics. Line graphs illustrating the trends in the number of streamers and viewers over time are generated from the online live streaming data, as shown in Fig. 6. Studies have shown that the domestic live streaming platform load showed a significant intra-day effect, showing inverted N-type [12]. Our data also exhibits this pattern. As seen in Fig. 6 (a), the load variation on the live streaming platform follows a clear pattern within a day: viewer count in the live rooms decreases starting from midnight and gradually rises after reaching a minimum value at around 6–8 am (typically 7 am). Thereafter, it reaches the peak of the day between 9–11 pm, followed by a decline. Moreover, it appears that the fluctuations in both the number of viewers and the number of streamers are synchronized.

Figure 6 (b) represents the average traffic variation trend from Monday to Sunday. It demonstrates that the number of streamers and viewers remain relatively stable throughout the week, ranging from approximately 72,000 to 74,000 streamers and 404 million to 425 million viewers. Additionally, the changes in the average number of streamers and viewers are not perfectly synchronized but exhibit a similar trend. Specifically, the quantities gradually increase from Monday to Saturday, reaching a peak on Saturday, and then decrease (although there may be slight fluctuations on certain days).

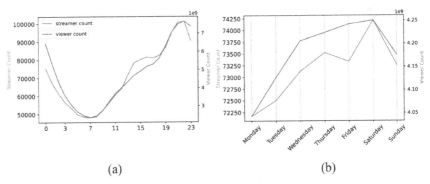

(a)   (b)

Fig. 6. Daily traffic data and weekly traffic Data. In (a), the traffic changes within a day are plotted in hours, while in (b), the average traffic changes from Monday to Sunday are plotted.

Stationarity Test and Data Autocorrelation Analysis. In this case, We employ the Augmented Dickey-Fuller (ADF) test to assess the stationarity of the data. According to the ADF test, the test statistic is calculated as -6.35, and the p-value is $2.685557e{-}08$, indicating that the series is stationary. This implies that the fluctuations in the time series data are predictable in the long run and not influenced by long-term trends. Furthermore, autocorrelation analysis conducted on the series of viewer count revealed two significant peaks at lag 24 and lag 168, as shown in Fig. 7. This indicates that the live streaming traffic data exhibits a cyclic pattern of autocorrelation with a period of one day (24 h) and one week (7 days, 168 h), which aligns with typical characteristics of network traffic data. This finding suggests that time can be considered as an important feature in designing prediction algorithms for live streaming traffic data. By incorporating features such as hours of the day and days of the week, we can capture the cyclic patterns and enhance the accuracy of predictions.

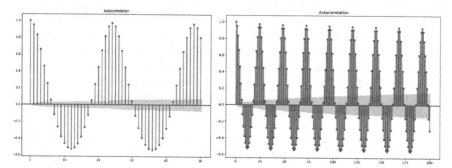

Fig. 7. Autocorrelation test result plot for different lag periods. The autocorrelation plot illustrates the strength of the correlation between lag periods and observed values. The horizontal axis represents the lag periods, with the left plot showing a lag of 50 and the right plot showing a lag of 200. The vertical axis represents the autocorrelation coefficient.

3.2 Univariate Prediction

This section showcases the prediction performance and comparative analysis of ten different models used in this study for forecasting the viewer_count for the next 24 h in a univariate forecasting task. The specific results are presented in Table 3 and Fig. 8, which display error levels, comparisons between models, and the fit be-tween predicted and actual values in the validation set.

The accuracy of final predictions depends on the selection of model parameters. We employed grid search to find optimal hyperparameters and further improved performance through fine-tuning. For instance, the Bi-LSTM model was tested with various hidden layer sizes, learning rates, and iterations, determining the best parameter combination. The final model parameters are as follows:

① ARIMA: the order values for p, d, and q are set as 6, 0, and 5 respectively.
② SARIMA: the order is set as (2,0,2), and the seasonal order is set as (2,0,2,12).
③ BP: the input layer size is 168, the output layer size is 24, the hidden layer size is 150, the learning rate is 0.001, and it iterates for 150 rounds.
④ RNN: the first layer size of 256, with a tanh activation function and a hidden state sequence at each time step; the second layer size is 100, with a tanh activation function and does not return a sequence. The final layer is a fully connected layer with 24 neurons. The loss function used is mean squared error, the optimizer is Adam with a learning rate of 0.001, and the training batch size is 64.
⑤ LSTM: only one hidden layer with 20 neurons and uses the ReLU activation function.
⑥ GRU: a hidden layer size of 256, an output layer size of 24, a batch size of 32, and a learning rate of 0.0003.
⑦ Bi-LSTM: the input layer, hidden layer, and output layer have 168, 128, and 24 neurons respectively. The training iterations, batch size, activation function, loss function, and optimization function are 150, 128, LeakyReLU, MAE, and Nadam. The learning rate is dynamically adjusted based on epochs (reduced to 1/10 every 50 epochs).
⑧ RF: 100 regression trees.

⑨ XGBoost: 1000 estimators, each with a maximum depth of 3 and a learning rate of 0.01. Additionally, training will stop early if there is no improvement in the validation set error for 50 consecutive rounds.

⑩ ET: 100 regression trees with a random state of 0.

Among the evaluated models, the Bi-LSTM model demonstrates the most outstanding performance. Specifically, the Bi-LSTM model achieves the lowest MAPE value of 0.00994, as well as the smallest MAE, MSE, and RMSE values. Compared to the worst-performing AMIRA model, the Bi-LSTM model has an MAPE value that is only 4.75% of its MAPE value, resulting in a 95.25% improvement in accuracy. Compared to the relatively better-performing RF model, the Bi-LSTM model shows a 2.55% improvement in accuracy.

These results indicate that the Bi-LSTM model exhibits minimal errors and high accuracy in predicting online live streaming traffic. In contrast, other neural network models such as RNN, LSTM, and GRU, as well as the traditional time series model SARIMA, perform relatively poorer. This suggests that the Bi-LSTM model, based on the bidirectional long short-term memory network, possesses an advantage in network traffic forecasting tasks. However, it is worth noting that apart from the Bi-LSTM model, several other models also display commendable performance. For instance, the Random Forest (RF), XGBoost, and Extra Tree (ET) models yield relatively good results across multiple evaluation metrics.

Table 3. Comparison of evaluation metric values for each model (without features).

Model	MAPE	MAE	MSE	RMSE
AMIRA	0.2093	1.055×10^9	1.52×10^{18}	1.23×10^9
SARIMA	0.0144	7.35×10^7	9.45×10^{15}	9.72×10^7
BP	0.031	1.48×10^8	3.696×10^{16}	1.92×10^8
RNN	0.031	1.42×10^8	2.94×10^{16}	1.71×10^8
LSTM	0.0857	4.12×10^8	2.53×10^{17}	5.03×10^8
GRU	0.021	9.94×10^7	1.41×10^{16}	1.19×10^8
Bi-LSTM	**0.00994**	$\mathbf{5.11 \times 10^7}$	$\mathbf{5.409 \times 10^{15}}$	$\mathbf{7.35 \times 10^7}$
RF	0.0102	5.17×10^7	6.11×10^{15}	7.82×10^7
XGBoost	0.0175	8.56×10^7	1.01×10^{16}	1.01×10^8
ET	0.012	6.34×10^7	9.26×10^{15}	9.62×10^7

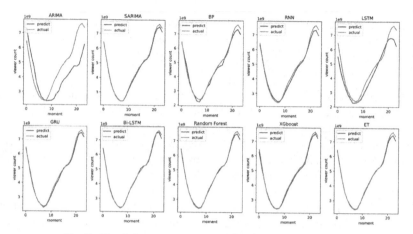

Fig. 8. The fitting performance of models (without features).

3.3 Feature Importance

In this partition, we incorporate additional features to predict viewer count. Specifically, we have chosen three features: streamer count, hours of the day, and the combination of both features. To emphasize the impact of features on the results, the model parameters in this section are set to be the same as those in the univariate prediction section. The selection of these features is based on their potential impact on the online live streaming platform's viewer count.

Figure 9 and Fig. 10 respectively illustrate the comparison of MAPE values under different conditions and the variation of four evaluation metrics. In Fig. 9, lighter colors indicate lower MAPE values and smaller model errors.

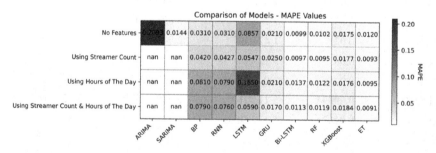

Fig. 9. The comparison of MAPE values with and without features.

Streamer Count. The error levels and comparison between different models after incorporating streamer count as an input feature for prediction are shown in Table 4. ARIMA and SARIMA models are excluded as they can only perform univariate forecasting. The results show that Bi-LSTM, RF and ET have similar performance. Among them, ET has the lowest MAPE value. However in terms of MAE, MSE, and RMSE, Bi-LSTM slightly outperforms ET and RF.

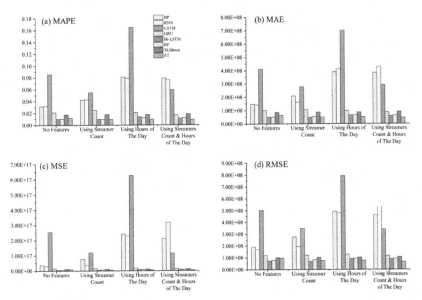

Fig. 10. The changes in evaluation metric values. The figure above illustrates the changes in four evaluation metrics - MAPE, MAE, MSE, and RMSE - under different scenarios: without features, with streamer count, with hours of the day, and with the combination of streamer count and hours of the day. These changes reflect the performance and variations of each model under different conditions.

Furthermore, BP, RNN, GRU, and XGBoost models perform between Bi-LSTM and LSTM models. While their MAPE values are slightly higher than the Bi-LSTM model, they remain relatively low. However, their MAE, MSE, and RMSE values are significantly higher than those of the Bi-LSTM model, indicating a larger gap between their predicted and observed values. The LSTM model performs the worst, with the highest MAPE value (0.0547), as well as highest MAE, MSE, and RMSE values, suggesting relatively large prediction errors.

Comparing these results with the previous univariate forecasting, after incorporating streamer count as a feature, the Bi-LSTM model's MAPE decreased from 0.00994 to 0.00967, indicating an improvement in prediction accuracy. Other metrics such as MAE, MSE, and RMSE also show improvements. LSTM, RF, and ET models are no exception to this. However, the BP model experiences a significant decline in performance after incorporating streamer count as a feature. Overall, there is an enhancement in overall prediction accuracy and a clear improvement in other metrics when considering the entire dataset. Nevertheless, incorporating this feature may not always lead to improvements and can potentially result in a decrease in prediction accuracy.

Hours of the Day. The error levels and comparison between different models after incorporating hours of the day for prediction are shown in Table 5. Incorporating hours of the day into the model results in varying levels of performance. In comparison to other models, Bi-LSTM, RF, and ET models exhibit better accuracy and lower percentage errors. Specifically, in this task, Bi-LSTM and RF models perform similarly. And ET

Table 4. Comparison of evaluation metric values for each model (with streamer count).

Model	MAPE	MAE	MSE	RMSE
BP	0.042	2.08×10^8	7.64×10^{16}	2.76×10^8
RNN	0.0427	1.62×10^8	3.73×10^{16}	1.93×10^8
LSTM	0.0547	2.76×10^8	1.19×10^{17}	3.46×10^8
GRU	0.025	1.06×10^8	1.47×10^{16}	1.21×10^8
Bi-LSTM	**0.00967**	$\mathbf{4.72 \times 10^7}$	$\mathbf{4.78 \times 10^{15}}$	$\mathbf{6.92 \times 10^7}$
RF	**0.00947**	$\mathbf{5.29 \times 10^7}$	$\mathbf{6.79 \times 10^{15}}$	$\mathbf{8.24 \times 10^7}$
XGBoost	0.0177	8.67×10^7	1.03×10^{16}	1.02×10^8
ET	**0.00927**	$\mathbf{4.93 \times 10^7}$	$\mathbf{5.70 \times 10^{15}}$	$\mathbf{7.55 \times 10^7}$

demonstrates the best performance, with an MAPE value of 0.00951, and the lowest values for MAE, MSE, and RMSE (4.93×10^7, 5.70×10^{15}, and 7.55×10^7, respectively). Compared to the worst-performing LSTM model, the ET model has an MAPE value that is only 5.76% of its MAPE value, resulting in a 94.24% improvement in accuracy. Compared to the relatively better-performing RF and Bi-LSTM model, the ET model shows a 22.05% and 30.58% improvement in accuracy, respectively. It is evident that when incorporating hours of the day as a feature, the ET model has the advantage.

Table 5. Comparison of evaluation metric values for each model (with hours of the day).

Model	MAPE	MAE	MSE	RMSE
BP	0.081	3.89×10^8	2.41×10^{17}	4.91×10^8
RNN	0.079	4.11×10^8	2.28×10^{17}	4.78×10^8
LSTM	0.165	7.18×10^8	6.27×10^{17}	7.92×10^8
GRU	0.021	9.76×10^7	1.63×10^{16}	1.28×10^8
Bi-LSTM	0.0137	6.48×10^7	8.35×10^{15}	9.14×10^7
RF	0.0122	6.48×10^7	8.80×10^{15}	9.38×10^7
XGBoost	0.0176	8.67×10^7	1.04×10^{16}	1.02×10^8
ET	**0.00951**	$\mathbf{5.10 \times 10^7}$	$\mathbf{5.82 \times 10^{15}}$	$\mathbf{7.63 \times 10^7}$

Considering the three tasks, the Bi-LSTM, RF, and ET models consistently display stable prediction performance, consistently ranking among the top three in terms of prediction accuracy. Specifically, before incorporating features, the Bi-LSTM model exhibits highest prediction accuracy, and the inclusion of the number of streamers as a feature further lowers its MAPE, indicating improved accuracy. However, the performance of the Bi-LSTM model does not significantly improve after incorporating hours of the day as a feature, whereas the ET model demonstrate superior performance and predictive accuracy. In contrast, the LSTM model consistently performs relatively poorly, with lower prediction accuracy before and after incorporating features, as evidenced by higher error metrics. Additionally, the BP and RNN models show relatively poor prediction performance. The GRU and XGBoost models demonstrate good prediction accuracy, ranking in the middle range. It can be observed that in this task, the ET model is more suitable for utilizing hours of the day for prediction.

Streamer Count and Hours of the Day. Table 6 displays the comparative error levels and results of different models upon integrating streamer count and hours of the day for prediction. Notably, upon inclusion of streamer count as a feature alongside hours of the day, all models showcased varying degrees of performance enhancement compared to solely incorporating hours of the day.

Several plausible explanations account for this observed phenomenon: First, the addition of streamer count furnishes the models with deeper insights into network live streaming load, establishing a correlation between streamer count and viewer count. This infusion of data grants the models enhanced understanding of data patterns and trends, consequently bolstering prediction accuracy. Second, the amalgamation of streamer count and hours of the day offers a more holistic and interconnected dataset. This amalgamated input empowers the models to decipher interactions among multiple features, facilitating a more comprehensive comprehension of the data and, consequently, more precise predictions.

Table 6. Comparison of evaluation metric values for each model (with streamer count and hours of the day).

Model	MAPE	MAE	MSE	RMSE
BP	0.079	3.84×10^8	2.11×10^{17}	4.59×10^8
RNN	0.076	4.29×10^8	3.18×10^{17}	5.64×10^8
LSTM	0.059	2.91×10^8	1.15×10^{17}	3.39×10^8
GRU	0.017	8.50×10^7	1.37×10^{16}	1.17×10^8
Bi-LSTM	0.0113	5.76×10^7	7.99×10^{15}	8.94×10^7
RF	0.0119	6.43×10^7	8.63×10^{15}	9.29×10^7
XGBoost	0.0184	9.00×10^7	1.12×10^{16}	1.06×10^8
ET	**0.00913**	**4.45×10^7**	**4.27×10^{15}**	**6.54×10^7**

Furthermore, in this task, the ET model continues to perform the best compared to the other models, with a MAPE value of 0.00913. It also achieves the lowest values in terms of MAE, MSE, and RMSE (4.45×10^7, 4.27×10^{15} and 6.54×10^7, respectively). The Bi-LSTM and RF models follow in performance, while the BP and RNN models exhibit relatively higher MAPE values, indicating larger errors in their predictions. Compared to the worst-performing BP model, the ET model has an MAPE value that is only 11.56%

of its MAPE value, resulting in a 88.44% improvement in accuracy. Compared to the relatively better-performing RF and Bi-LSTM model, the ET model shows a 23.28% and 19.20% improvement in accuracy, respectively.

When comparing these results with the previous three experiments, some trends and changes can be observed. Bi-LSTM, RF, and ET consistently demonstrate top performance among the models, with low MAPE, MAE, MSE, and RMSE values. And Bi-LSTM and ET outperform RF, indicating their stability and accuracy in dealing with large-scale and long-term online live streaming data prediction problems. The ET model, while slightly inferior to the Bi-LSTM model in the experiment without features (though still performing well), it consistently exhibits excellent or even the best performance in other experiments, making it the preferred model for predicting large-scale and long-term online live streaming load when features are incorporated.

Different models exhibit variations in handling different features. For instance, Bi-LSTM shows a stronger capability to leverage information from streamer count compared to hours of the day. Similarly, the ET model also demonstrates a similar pattern. However, the performance of the ET model is less influenced by the features and exhibits minimal fluctuations, demonstrating its relative stability.

4 Conclusions and Discussion

Our study centers on the analysis of extensive, prolonged online live streaming data. We conduct a thorough comparative assessment of diverse methods and models utilized for traffic prediction. Moreover, our approach involves the integration of various features aimed at augmenting prediction accuracy and refining the interpretability of prediction outcomes.

The findings highlight the performance stability of the Bi-LSTM, ET, and RF models in the realm of large-scale and long-term live streaming data prediction. Notably, the ET and Bi-LSTM models exhibit exceptional accuracy and precision, facilitating more precise forecasts of network traffic fluctuations while maintaining lower Mean Absolute Percentage Error (MAPE), Mean Absolute Error (MAE), Mean Squared Error (MSE), and Root Mean Squared Error (RMSE). Particularly, the ET model stands out as the most effective upon incorporating diverse features.

Our comparative analysis underscores the superiority of machine learning and deep learning models over traditional time series forecasting methods in predicting online live streaming traffic. The Bi-LSTM and ET models emerge as preferred choices, followed by RF, due to their superior performance.

In terms of feature integration, the inclusion of streamer count significantly enhances the performance of specific models. Conversely, the inclusion of hours of the day yields marginal improvements in predictive outcomes. Interestingly, experiments integrating both streamer count and hours of the day outperform experiments solely focused on hours of the day. However, some models exhibit slightly reduced performance in the combined approach compared to experiments solely reliant on streamer count. This reiterates the influential role of streamer count in improving prediction accuracy, while the impact of hours of the day remains minimal and, in some cases, may even diminish the predictive performance of the models.

Several potential avenues for optimization and future research merit consideration. First, while this study draws conclusions based on the provided dataset and specific problem parameters, selecting the optimal model should extend beyond individual model performance metrics. Factors like model complexity, training duration, interpretability, and scalability are crucial considerations that should influence the ultimate model selection. Expanding the scope of factors influencing viewer count for comprehensive analysis and prediction would be beneficial for future research. Incorporating additional variables that potentially impact live streaming traffic could offer a more holistic understanding of prediction dynamics. Furthermore, future investigations might delve into a more detailed examination of online live streaming traffic prediction. This could involve a targeted analysis, focusing on aspects intricately tied to live streaming operations. For instance, analyzing and predicting viewer counts for multiple or multiple-category live streaming rooms could provide valuable insights into granular operational aspects. Alternatively, exploring innovative ensemble models presents an opportunity to enhance operational efficiency. Novel approaches in ensemble modeling could specifically address concerns such as the training speed of the Bi-LSTM model, thus improving overall model efficiency.

References

1. Shu-Hui, G., Xin, L.: Live streaming: data mining and behavior analysis. Acta Phys. Sinica **69**(83) (2020)
2. Sharma, S., Gupta, V.: Role of twitter user profile features in retweet prediction for big data streams. Multimedia Tools Appl. **81**, 27309–27338 (2022)
3. Liu, X.: The market changes and causes of game live streaming industry from 2019 to 2020 by case study of HUYA. In: The 2022 International Conference on Economics, Smart Finance and Contemporary Trade (2022)
4. Heim, A.B., Patel, R.J.: Remote learning options. Science **377**(6601), 22–24 (2022)
5. Chen, H., Dou, Y., Xiao, Y.: Understanding the role of live streamers in live-streaming e-commerce. Electron. Commer. Res. Appl. **59**(C), 101266 (2023)
6. Qian, T.Y., Seifried, C.: Virtual interactions and sports viewing on social live streaming platforms: the role of co-creation experiences, platform involvement, and follow status. J. Bus. Res. **162**, 113884 (2023)
7. (CNNIC)ew, t.C.I.N.I.C.: The 51st edition of the "statistical report on internet development in china". Report 1009-3125 (2023)
8. Mengxuan, K., Junping, S., Pengfei, F.A.N.: Survey of network traffic forecast based on deep learning. Comput. Eng Appl. **57**(10), 1–9 (2021)
9. Yan, Z., Yang, Z., Griffiths, M.D.: "Danmu" preference, problematic online video watching, loneliness and personality: an eye-tracking study and survey study. BMC Psychiatry **23**(1), 523 (2023)
10. Kaytoue, M., Silva, A., Cerf, L., Meira Jr, W., Raïssi, C.: Watch me playing, i am a professional: a first study on video game live streaming. In: Proceedings of the 21st International Conference on World Wide Web, pp. 1181–1188 (2012)
11. Jia, A.L., Shen, S., Epema, D.H., Iosup, A.: When game becomes life: the creators and spectators of online game replays and live streaming. ACM Trans. Multimedia Comput. Commun. Appl. (TOMM) **12**(4), 1–24 (2016)
12. Arnett, L., Netzorg, R., Chaintreau, A., Wu, E.: Cross-platform interactions and popularity in the live-streaming community. In: The 2019 CHI Conference on Human Factors in Computing Systems, pp. 1–6 (2019)

13. Netzorg, R., Arnett, L., Chaintreau, A., Wu, E.: PopFactor: live-streamer behavior and popularity. In: International Conference on Web and Social Media (2021)
14. Nascimento, G., et al.: Modeling and analyzing the video game live-streaming community. In: 2014 9th Latin American Web Congress, pp. 1–9 (2014)
15. Tu, W., Yan, C., Yan, Y., Ding, X., Sun, L.: Who is earning? Understanding and modeling the virtual gifts behavior of users in live streaming economy (2018)
16. Chen, Z., Shen, J., Zhu, M., Hu, B., Liu, A.: Predicting virtual gifting behaviors in live streaming using Danmaku information. In: 2022 8th International Conference on Big Data Computing and Communications (BigCom), pp. 190–198 (2022)
17. Douyu reports fourth quarter 2022 unaudited financial results (2023/03/20 2023)
18. Zhang, Y., Meng, G.: Simulation of an adaptive model based on AIC and BIC ARIMA predictions. J. Phys: Conf. Ser. **2449**, 012027 (2023)
19. Siami-Namini, S., Tavakoli, N., Namin, A.S.: A comparison of ARIMA and LSTM in forecasting time series (2018)
20. Pierre, A.A., Akim, S.A., Semenyo, A.K., Babiga, B.: Peak electrical energy consumption prediction by ARIMA, LSTM, GRU, ARIMA-LSTM and ARIMA-GRU approaches. Energies **16**, 4739 (2023)
21. Guenoupkati, A., Salami, A.A., Kodjo, M.K., Napo, K.: Short-term electricity generation forecasting using machine learning algorithms: a case study of the Benin electricity community (C.E.B). In: TH Wildau Engineering and Natural Sciences Proceedings, vol.1 (2021)
22. ArunKumar, K., Kalaga, D.V., Kumar, C.M.S., Kawaji, M., Brenza, T.M.: Comparative analysis of gated recurrent units (GRU), long short-term memory (LSTM) cells, autoregressive integrated moving average (ARIMA), seasonal autoregressive integrated moving average (SARIMA) for forecasting covid-19 trends. Alexandria Eng. J. **61**(10), 7585–7603 (2022)
23. Sadeq, J.M., Qadir, B.A., Abbas, H.H.: Cars logo recognition by using of backpropagation neural networks. Measure. Sens. **26**, 100702 (2023)
24. Li, Y.F., Cao, H.: Prediction for tourism flow based on LSTM neural network. In: 6th International Conference on Identification, Information and Knowledge in the Internet of Things (IIKI). Procedia Computer Science, vol. 129, pp. 277–283 (2018)
25. Amalou, I., Mouhni, N., Abdali, A.: Multivariate time series prediction by RNN architectures for energy consumption forecasting. Energy Rep. **8**, 1084–1091 (2022)
26. Cho, K., Merrienboer, B.V., Bahdanau, D., Bengio, Y.: On the properties of neural machine translation: encoder-decoder approaches (2014)
27. Fu, R., Zhang, Z., Li, L.: Using LSTM and GRU neural network methods for traffic flow prediction (2016)
28. Graves, A., Schmidhuber, J.: Framewise phoneme classification with bidirectional LSTM and other neural network architectures. Neural Netw. **18**(5), 602–610 (2005)
29. Doulamis, A.D., et al.: A convolutional neural network face recognition method based on BILSTM and attention mechanism. Comput. Intell. Neurosci. **2023**, 2501022 (2023)
30. Li, Z.Y., Ge, H.X., Cheng, R.J.: Traffic flow prediction based on BILSTM model and data denoising scheme. Chin. Phys. B **31**(4), 214–223 (2022)
31. Alakus, C., Larocque, D., Labbe, A.: Covariance regression with random forests. BMC Bioinform. **24**(1), 258 (2023)
32. Lin, Y., Jeon, Y.: Random forests and adaptive nearest neighbors. J. Am. Stat. Assoc. **101**(474), 578–590 (2006)
33. Moon, J., Kim, Y., Son, M., Hwang, E.: Hybrid short-term load forecasting scheme using random forest and multilayer perceptron. Energies **11**(12), 3283 (2018)
34. Chen, T., Guestrin, C.: XGBoost: a scalable tree boosting system (2016)
35. Lei, T.M.T., Ng, S.C.W., Siu, S.W.I.: Application of ANN, XGBoost, and other ml methods to forecast air quality in Macau. Sustainability **15**(6), 5341 (2023)

36. Amjad, M., Ahmad, I., Ahmad, M., Wróblewski, P., Kamiński, P., Amjad, U.: Prediction of pile bearing capacity using XGBoost algorithm: modeling and performance evaluation. Appl. Sci. **12**(4), 2126 (2022)
37. Xia, B., Zhang, H., Li, Q., Li, T.: Pets: A stable and accurate pre dictor of protein-protein interacting sites based on extremely-randomized trees. IEEE Trans. NanoBioscience **14**(8), 882–893 (2015)
38. Zhou, Q., Ning, Y., Zhou, Q., Luo, L., Lei, J.: Structural damage detection method based on random forests and data fusion. Struct. Health Monit. **12**(1), 48–58 (2013)
39. Zhou, Q., Zhou, H., Ning, Y., Yang, F., Li, T.: Two approaches for novelty detection using random forest. Expert Syst. Appl. **42**(10), 4840–4850 (2015)
40. Xu, Y., Zhao, X., Chen, Y.: Research on a mixed gas classification algorithm based on extreme random tree. Appl. Sci.-Basel **9**(9), 1728 (2019)
41. Geurts, P., Ernst, D., Wehenkel, L.: Extremely randomized trees. Mach. Learn. **36**(1), 3–42 (2006)

Forecasting Chinese Overnight Stock Index Movement Using Large Language Models with Market Summary

Haiping Wang and Xin Zhou[✉]

Volatility Institute, New York University Shanghai, Shanghai, China
{hw2942,xinzhou}@nyu.edu

Abstract. Forecasting financial market movement constitutes a complex and pivotal research area within the realm of Financial Technology (Fintech). In this work, we investigate the ability of large language models to predict Chinese overnight stock index movement, utilizing market summary gleaned from news media sources. We fine-tune various pre-trained models to compare the performance with that of Generative Pre-training Transformer (GPT) models, specifically GPT-3.5 and GPT-4, as provided by OpenAI. The empirical findings underscore that the fine-tuned pre-trained models, characterized by fewer parameters and more straightforward architectures, surpass the esteemed GPT-3.5 and GPT-4 models in predictive metrics of accuracy and f1. All fine-tuned models are publicly available on the huggingface platform (https://huggingface. co/hw2942).

Keywords: Forecasting overnight stock index movement · Large language models · BERT · GPT

1 Introduction

Large language models (LLMs) ranging from Bidirectional Encoder Representations from Transformers (BERT) [7] to GPT [14] have gained public attention with reliable question answering feedback and interesting interactive experiences in chatbot interfaces. With the escalation of available training corpora, expansion of model parameters, and augmentation of computational resources, LLMs perform close or even better than human judgement in the areas, like sentiment analysis, language translation, text summarization and generation. To apply in finance, researchers pre-train LLMs with financial relevant corpora in different languages, such as corporate annual and quarterly filings, analyst reports, company announcements, earnings call transcripts, social media and financial news, to obtain FinBERT [6], BBT-Fin [12], BloombergGPT [16] and FinGPT [18]. Armed with these domain-specific pre-trained LLMs, a multitude of studies have effectively fine-tuned and optimized algorithms, culminating in compelling outcomes within various financial applications, including but not limited to quantitative trading, portfolio optimization, and financial sentiment analysis.

Y. Tan and Y. Shi (Eds.): DMBD 2023, CCIS 2017, pp. 48–62, 2024.
https://doi.org/10.1007/978-981-97-0837-6_4

Within the field of financial market, the prediction of stock market index assumes paramount importance due to its substantial influence on investors' trading strategy and regulatory decision-making process. However, the inherently dynamic and elusive nature of market poses a formidable challenge to accurately forecast market movement. Prior research efforts have predominantly focused on conventional statistical methodologies and machine learning models, leveraging historical transactional data and technical indicators. As LLMs emerge with enhanced performance, diverse textual sources comprising public news and social media have been harnessed to ascertain market trends. [11] examines the potential of ChatGPT and other LLMs in predicting stock market returns for the next trading day based on news headlines. Simultaneously, [17] conducts an extensive zero-shot analysis of ChatGPT's capabilities in multimodal stock movement prediction, resulting in underperformance when compared with traditional methods like linear regression using price features. As the duration of news impacting on market remains uncertain, it is untrustworthy to foresee daily market movements precisely. However, in the context of overnight stock index, where trading is dormant, overnight market news exhibits a correlation with the differential between morning opening prices and the preceding day's closing prices, thereby presenting an avenue for the prediction of overnight stock market index movement. [9] propose an LSTM Relational Graph Convolutional Network model to forecast overnight Tokyo Stock Price Index movement using overnight news. Recognizing the strong interactions around global stock markets, Ruize et al. [5] utilize the historical returns of international stock market index to predict the overnight return directions of nine target indices across Asia, Americas and Europe markets, achieving commendable evaluation metrics.

Previous studies have primarily placed emphasis on the forecast of daily market return, applying deep learning models based on historical prices and textual news data, with limited attention directed towards overnight stock index movement. This paper addresses this gap by conducting a comparative analysis of various LLMs with respect to overnight stock index forecasting. As shown in Fig. 1, our study consists of three procedures, that is data processing, fine-tuning and testing. Specifically, we exclusively collect overnight market summary from news media that isn't open-access and applied by preceding research. These summaries encapsulate succinct synopses of market events transpiring between the close of the former trading day and the commencement of the subsequent trading session, distinguishing them from isolated news articles or concise headlines employed in earlier studies. To facilitate our investigation, we implement prompts containing these market summaries with the GPT APIs, thereby obtaining predictions regarding the direction (up or down) of overnight stock index. Meanwhile, in order to establish a comparative benchmark with GPT, we engage in the fine-tuning of a diverse set of pre-trained LLMs. This ensemble encompasses models such as BERT, FinBERT, Robustly Optimized BERT Pretraining Approach (RoBERTa) [10], Linguistically-motivated bidirectional Encoder Representation from Transformer (LERT) [3], improved BERT with novel MLM as correction pre-training task (MacBERT) [2], Pre-training BERT with Permuted

Language Model (PERT) [4], Bidirectional and Auto-Regressive Transformer (BART) [8], Longformer [1], and BigBird [19]. Empirical findings substantiate that fine-tuned pre-trained models, featured by less parameters and simpler architectures, exhibit superior performance in comparison to the renowned GPT-3.5 and GPT-4 models, as evidenced by evaluation metrics of accuracy and f1 scores. Our research underscores that investors can avail themselves of a cost-effective and highly accurate means to validate overnight stock index movement, thereby aiding in risk management and the optimization of trading strategies.

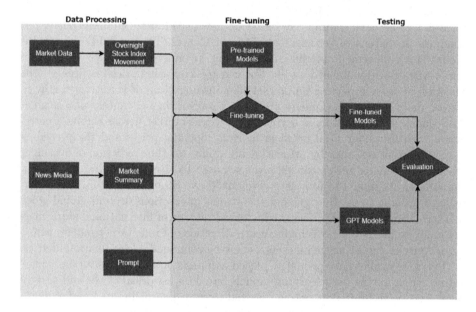

Fig. 1. A brief description of working flow

Our study contributes to the advancement of forecasting overnight stock market index on four key fronts. Firstly, our utilization of market summary sourced from news media represents a novel dataset, heretofore unexplored in prior research. This dataset reveals distinctive properties, characterized by its extensive text length and refined content, setting it apart from the limited scope of previous studies that focused solely on financial news or headlines. Secondly, we undertake the comprehensive collection and fine-tuning of Chinese LLMs to ascertain which model proves most adept in predicting overnight stock market index. Thirdly, our empirical findings present compelling evidence that LLMs with sizable parameter sets incurring high computational costs do not outperform fine-tuned pre-trained LLMs. Notably, our approach applies original pre-trained models through free open-access platform, subsequently fine-tuned via Google Colab at a relatively low computational cost. This renders our methodology accessible and cost-effective for a wide audience. Lastly, we have made all fine-tuned LLMs publicly available on the huggingface platform, with detailed information provided in the corresponding section for transparency and reproducibility. This ensures that our contributions are readily obtainable for further research and application within the academic community.

The subsequent sections of this paper are structured as follows. Section 2 provides a comprehensive description of the textual and numerical datasets used in our work, which consist of market summary and overnight stock index movement. In Sect. 3, we expound upon the LLMs engaged in our analysis, outlining their diverse structural configurations and detailing the fine-tuning methodology. The empirical results are presented and deliberated in Sect. 4. Finally, Sect. 5 summarizes our conclusions, highlighting the key insights garnered from our investigation and pointing out avenues for future research in this domain.

2 Data

2.1 Market Summary

In contrast to previous studies employing financial news or headlines, our approach involves the collection of market summary from news media using web crawler, characterized by their extensive textual content and distilled information. Specifically, we have selected wallstreetcn.com as our primary textual data source. This platform stands out as one of the most widely utilized applications among practitioners in the financial industry, enjoying a reputation as a preeminent financial information provider in China and consistently securing top rankings across various application markets. The market summary retrieved from wallstreetcn.com is extracted from morning reports, which are meticulously

Table 1. The market summary with original Chinese version and translated English version

Original Chinese version	Translated English version
美国CPI强化9月暂停加息预期，但旧金山联储主席点评称，美联储还有更多工作要做。三大美股指普集体转跌，虽未收跌，但标普纳指接近一个月低位。芯片股指三连跌。财报后迪士尼涨近5%。WeWork大反弹，涨超43%。	The strengthening of the U.S. CPI in September has temporarily suspended expectations of an interest rate hike, but the President of the San Francisco Fed commented that the Federal Reserve still has more work to do. The three major U.S. stock indices collectively turned lower, although they did not close lower, the S&P and Nasdaq were close to their one-month lows. Semiconductor stocks fell for the third consecutive session. Disney rose nearly 5% after the earnings report. WeWork had a major rebound, rising over 43%.
乐观财报季推动欧股走高，欧洲斯托克50指数涨超1%，LVMH率奢侈品股普涨。	Optimistic earnings season pushed European stocks higher, with the Euro Stoxx 50 index rising over 1%, and LVMH leading the luxury goods stocks in a general rise.
CPI公布后美债收益率加速下行，美联储官员讲话后拉升，十年和两年期美债收益率均回升超10个基点，30年期美债标售惨淡令美债进一步下跌。	After the CPI was announced, U.S. bond yields accelerated their decline, and after remarks from Federal Reserve officials, they rebounded. The yields on the ten-year and two-year U.S. bonds both rose by over 10 basis points, the sale of 30-year U.S. bonds was dismal, causing U.S. bonds to fall further.
美元指数刷新日低，此后转涨。日元兑欧元创2008年来新低，日元兑美元逼近去年日本干预汇市门槛。	The U.S. dollar index hit a new daily low and then turned higher. The yen hit a new low against the euro since 2008, and the yen against the dollar approached the threshold of Japan's intervention in the foreign exchange market last year.
美油跌落近九个月高位，一度跌超2%，欧洲天然气回落，跌近7%；黄金盘中转跌，连跌四日至两周低位。	U.S. oil fell from its highest level in nearly nine months, dropping over 2% at one point. European natural gas fell, dropping nearly 7%. Gold turned lower during the session, falling for the fourth consecutive day to a two-week low.
中国市场方面，美股时段，中概反弹，京东涨超2%，财报亮眼阿里涨近5%，离岸人民币收复7.21后回落超300点。沪指震荡反弹涨0.31%，券商股午后反弹，两市成交不足7000亿元。港股午后集体翻红，恒生科技收涨0.1%，券商再度走强，理想汽车涨2.4%。	In the Chinese market, during the U.S. stock market session, Chinese concept stocks rebounded, with JD.com rising over 2%. With impressive earnings, Alibaba rose nearly 5%, but offshore RMB fell over 300 points after recovering 7.21. The Shanghai Composite Index rebounded by 0.31% amid oscillations, with brokerage stocks rebounding in the afternoon. The trading volume in both markets was less than 700 billion yuan. Hong Kong stocks collectively turned higher in the afternoon, with the Hang Seng Tech Index closing up by 0.1%. Brokerage stocks strengthened again, and NIO rose by 2.4%.

curated by editors and include global political, macroeconomic, and market-related events occurring both the previous day and overnight. Market summary furnishes essential information to assist investors and the public in their decision-making approach. An illustrative example of market summary is presented in Table 1, excerpted from the wallstreetcn morning report dated August 11th, 2023[1].

As demonstrated in Table 1, the market summary provides comprehensive financial insights spanning international macroeconomic developments, foreign exchange rates, U.S. bond markets, and futures pertaining to commodities such as oil, gas, and gold. Additionally, it contains pertinent updates from mainstream stock markets in the United States, Europe, and China, all of which transpired prior to the opening of the Chinese stock market for the trading day. The dataset comprising market summaries involves a range of 96 to 745 tokens, spanning the period from 2019 to 2023, and contains data from 702 trading days. This dataset has been partitioned into 270 days for training, 32 days for validation, and 400 days for testing purpose.

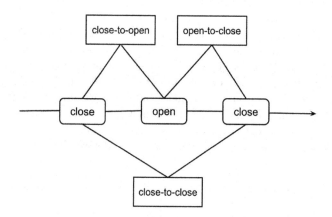

Fig. 2. Description of market movement

2.2   Overnight Stock Market Index Movement

In prior forecasting endeavors, three distinct methodologies have been applied for calculating market index movement: definitely, the close-to-close, close-to-open, and open-to-close approaches. As depicted in Fig. 2, the parameters derived from the close-to-close and open-to-close methods serve as indicators of daily movements, whereas the return yielded by the close-to-open method is designated as the overnight movement. It is noteworthy that during active trading hours, information disseminated by media outlets, corporations, and the public is absorbed

---

[1] https://wallstreetcn.com/articles/3695285?keyword=%E8%A7%81%E9%97%BB %E6%97%A9%E9%A4%90.

by the market in a nuanced and dynamic manner, rendering precise prediction of daily movement challenging. In stark contrast, owing to the absence of transactions during market closing hours, the market summary we compile, containing relevant financial information concerning non-trading periods, exhibits a pronounced correlation with overnight movement.

In this study, we focus on the overnight stock index movement specific to the Chinese market, namely the Shanghai Stock Exchange (SSE) Composite Index (000001.SH) and the SSE 50 Index (000016.SH). These indices are chosen to serve as the focal points of our investigation, representing key indicators of market performance within the SSE.

3   Models

3.1   BERT

BERT [7], developed by Google, is a pre-trained language model based on multi-layer bidirectional transformer encoder. There are two key stages in the proposed framework: pre-training and fine-tuning. During the pre-training phase, the BERT algorithm applies two unsupervised tasks, namely the masked language model (MLM) and next sentence prediction (NSP), drawing from the corpus comprised of BooksCorpus (800M words) and English Wikipedia (2500M words). In the MLM task, a specified percentage of input tokens is randomly masked, followed by the prediction of these masked tokens. To enhance the model's proficiency in discerning relationships between pairs of sentences, the NSP task involves binary classification aimed at predicting whether two segments are consecutive. In the subsequent fine-tuning step, leveraging the initialization with parameters from the pre-trained model, the BERT model undergoes optimization with labeled datasets tailored to designated downstream tasks. Notably, BERT has demonstrated its prowess by achieving state-of-the-art results across eleven distinct natural language processing (NLP) tasks, solidifying its status as one of the most extensively applied LLMs across a diverse array of applications.

3.2   FinBERT

Based on the foundational architecture of BERT, FinBERT [6] optimizes a pre-training process that entails the acquisition of both semantic and syntactic knowledge from an extensive corpus of unlabeled financial texts. The corpus consists of corporate annual and quarterly filing, financial analyst reports and earnings conference call transcripts, distinguishing it from the general knowledge applied in BERT. Since adapting to the financial domain, FinBERT has demonstrated superior performance to benchmark models in finance and accounting research. In terms of our study, we utilize the Chinese variant of FinBERT, specifically Mengzi-BERT-base-fin [21], which is pre-trained on Mengzi-BERT-base using 20G financial corpus composed of financial news, announcements, and financial research reports. This tailored pre-training approach imparts Mengzi-BERT-base-fin with a specialized proficiency for Chinese financial domain applications, aligning it closely with the objectives of our research.

3.3 RoBERTa

[10] conducted a comprehensive examination of hyperparameters selection and training data size during pre-training BERT. By implementing dynamic masking, omitting the NSP task, extending training sequences, and conducting longer-duration training with larger batch sizes, RoBERTa performs better than BERT across benchmarks like General Language Understanding Evaluation (GLUE), ReAding Comprehension from Examinations (RACE) and Stanford Question Answering Dataset (SQuAD). In an effort to augment the training data volume and subsequently improve end-task performance, the study incorporated five English-language corpora encompassing diverse sizes and domains, collectively amounting to 160GB of uncompressed text. This meticulous consideration of hyperparameters and training data characteristics underscores the nuanced approach undertaken to refine the efficiency of RoBERTa.

3.4 LERT

[3] proposed LERT, a pre-trained language model that is trained on MLM in addition to three distinct linguistic tasks, namely part-of-speech tagging, named entity recognition and dependency parsing. To better acquire linguistic knowledge, a linguistically-informed pre-training strategy is applied to each pre-training task, leading to the outcome of faster learning speed. With comprehensive and rigorous experiments on ten Chinese natural language understanding tasks, LERT brings substantial advancements over comparable baselines, illustrating the constructive impact of incorporating linguistic features in the pre-training procedure.

3.5 MacBERT

Different from BERT, MacBERT [2] introduces modifications to two key pre-training tasks, tailoring them for optimal application in Chinese language models. To alleviate the discrepancy between the pre-training and fine-tuning stages, researchers transform the original MLM as a text correction task, wherein the model is tasked with rectifying inaccuracies in text. Simultaneously, recognizing the limited effectiveness of NSP, sentence order prediction is implemented as an alternative pre-training task. Through training on an extended corpus of Chinese data sourced from Wikipedia dumps, encyclopedic content, news articles, and question-answering websites, MacBERT exhibits noteworthy improvements across a spectrum of ten distinct Chinese language tasks, which consist of machine reading comprehension, single sentence classification and sentence pair classification.

3.6 PERT

PERT [4] maintains an architecture akin to BERT, although notable distinctions arise in terms of input data and pre-training task. Introducing shuffled sentences as input data, PERT adopts the Permuted Language Model (PerLM) as its sole pre-training task. The primary objective of PerLM is to predict the positional arrangement of the original words within a scrambled sentence. Experimental outcomes demonstrate that PERT elicits enhancements in machine reading comprehension and named entity recognition tasks, albeit displaying comparatively suboptimal performance in text classification.

3.7   BART

Combining Bidirectional and Auto-Regressive Transformers, BART [8] is a denoising autoencoder for pre-training sequence-to-sequence models. There are two steps in pre-training stage, that is corrupting text with an arbitrary noising function and learning a model to reconstruct the original text. Significantly, various document-corruption strategies are explored with several previously proposed and novel transformations, which consist of token masking, token deletion, text infilling, sentence permutation and document rotation. After fine-tuning, BART performs comparably to RoBERTa on discriminative tasks, while achieving state-of-the-art results on several text generation tasks. In this work, we choose a Chinese variant of BART [15], pre-trained with 200GB cleaned text ranging from Chinese Wikipedia and a segment of WuDaoCorpus.

3.8   Longformer

Transformer-based models, exemplified by BERT, are inherently constrained by a maximum token limit of 512 for input sequences due to the self-attention operation, rendering them less suitable for processing lengthy text. To circumvent this limitation, Longformer employs an attention mechanism that combines a windowed local-context self-attention with a global attention mechanism motivated by the end task. This design allows Longformer to scale efficiently without truncating and chunking, bringing about a linear increase in memory usage as opposed to the quadratic increase observed in models with full self-attention. After pre-training and fine-tuning, Longformer consistently surpasses RoBERTa on a wide range of long document-level natural language tasks including text classification, question answering, and coreference resolution. Based on Longformer in [1], a Chinese variant of Longformer [20] which is pre-trained on WuDaoCorpus (180GB version) with rotary position embedding is applied in our experiment.

3.9   BigBird

Similar to Longformer, BigBird [19] addresses the challenge of handling long contexts in language tasks by implementing a sparse attention mechanism, leading to a linear reduction of dependency. Theoretical analysis affirms that BigBird serves as a universal approximator of sequence functions and attains Turing completeness, thus upholding the computational capabilities of models utilizing full attention. Empirical findings substantiate the effectiveness of BigBird, showcasing state-of-the-art performance across a range of NLP tasks, containing question answering and the classification of lengthy documents.

3.10   GPT

OpenAI introduced GPT-1 [14] based on the transformer architecture, which combines unsupervised generative pre-training with subsequent supervised discriminative fine-tuning. Unlike prior approaches that rely on supervised learning from extensive manually labeled data, GPT-1 deploys a language modeling objective on unlabeled data to initialize the parameters of the neural network model. With 117 million parameters and training on the BooksCorpus dataset, GPT-1 manifests the efficacy of this methodology across a diverse array of natural language understanding benchmarks.

Following the release of GPT-1 on June 11, 2018, OpenAI subsequently unveiled GPT-2 with 1.5 billion parameters on February 14, 2019, and GPT-3 with an unprecedented 175 billion parameters on May 28, 2020. Notably, a refined iteration known as GPT-3.5, which constitutes a subclass of GPT-3, was introduced on March 15, 2022, leveraging training data up until June 2021. Since its launch on November 30, 2022, ChatGPT, built upon the foundation of GPT-3.5, enables users to guide and customize conversations with regards to length, format, style, and language, swiftly becoming one of the most rapidly adopted consumer software applications in history by January 2023.

Presently, the most up-to-date iteration is GPT-4 [13], a large-scale, multi-modal model with the capacity to process both image and text inputs, while producing text outputs. OpenAI confirms that GPT-4 exhibits heightened reliability, creativity, and an enhanced ability to interpret nuanced instructions when compared to its predecessor, GPT-3.5.

3.11   Fine-tuning

In this work, we fine-tune the aforementioned pre-trained LLMs for comparison with GPT models. As the pre-trained LLMs are all available on the platform of huggingface, the fine-tuning process is executed using huggingface's Transformer module based on Python, resulting in fine-tuned LLMs open-accessed on this platform. The specific training hyperparameters are shown in Table 2, while details regarding the pre-trained LLMs and the lists of fine-tuned LLMs are presented in Table 3 and Table 4, respectively.

Table 2. The training hyperparameters of fine-tuning

parameter	value	parameter	value
optim	adamw_torch	evaluation_strategy	epoch
save_strategy	epoch	num_train_epochs	10
learning_rate	2.00E-05	push_to_hub	TRUE
load_best_model_at_end	TRUE	auto_find_batch_size	TRUE
save_total_limit	2	metric_for_best_model	accuracy/f1

Table 3. The detail of pre-trained LLMs

Model name	Pre-trained LLM	Details of the model
BERT	bert-base-chinese	12-layer, 768-hidden, 12-heads, 108M parameters
FinBERT	Langboat/mengzi-bert-base-fin	12-layer, 768-hidden, 12-heads, 102M parameters
RoBERTa	hfl/chinese-roberta-wwm-ext	12-layer, 768-hidden, 12-heads, 102M parameters
LERT	hfl/chinese-lert-base	12-layer, 768-hidden, 12-heads, 102M parameters
MacBERT	hfl/chinese-macbert-base	12-layer, 768-hidden, 12-heads, 102M parameters
PERT	hfl/chinese-pert-base	12-layer, 768-hidden, 12-heads, 110M parameters
BART	fnlp/bart-base-chinese	6 layers Encoder, 6 layers Decoder, 12 Heads and 768 Model dim
Longformer	IDEA-CCNL/Erlangshen-Longformer-110M	110M parameters
BigBird	Lowin/chinese-bigbird-wwm-base-4096	12-layer, 768-hidden, 12-heads, 105M parameters

Table 4. The lists of fine-tuned LLMs on the huggingface platform

Model name	Fine-tuned LLM of SSE Composite Index	Fine-tuned LLM of SSE50 Index
BERT	hw2942/bert-base-chinese-SSEC	hw2942/bert-base-chinese-SSE50
FinBERT	hw2942/mengzi-bert-base-fin-SSEC	hw2942/mengzi-bert-base-fin-SSE50
RoBERTa	hw2942/chinese-roberta-wwm-ext-SSEC	hw2942/chinese-roberta-wwm-ext-SSE50
LERT	hw2942/chinese-lert-base-SSEC	hw2942/chinese-lert-base-SSE50
MacBERT	hw2942/chinese-macbert-base-SSEC	hw2942/chinese-macbert-base-SSE50
PERT	hw2942/chinese-pert-base-SSEC	hw2942/chinese-pert-base-SSE50
BART	hw2942/bart-base-chinese-SSEC	hw2942/bart-base-chinese-SSE50
Longformer	hw2942/Longformer-110M-SSEC	hw2942/Longformer-110M-SSE50
BigBird	hw2942/chinese-bigbird-SSEC	hw2942/chinese-bigbird-SSE50

3.12 Prompt of GPT

In order to forecast overnight index movement, we exploit responses obtained from OpenAI's GPT-3.5 and GPT-4 APIs, utilizing carefully constructed prompts that furnish the necessary context and instructions. Prompts play a crucial role in enabling GPT models to adapt to particular contexts, thereby generating responses tailored to the users' requirements. In this work, we have devised prompts that seamlessly integrate background instructions with market summary from news media, with one example shown below:

As a financial market expert, based on the following information, assess whether the Shanghai Composite Index will open higher or lower. Ultimately, provide a judgment of whether it will rise or fall with detailed explanation. The content: Market summary

This carefully constructed prompt not only yields a judgment regarding overnight index movement, but also offers a comprehensive explanation rooted in the provided details. It is beneficial for investors and regulators to get an understanding of references for judging besides forecasting results, which is different from the output with only predicted labels for fine-tuned LLMs.

3.13   Evaluation Metrics

Since forecasting overnight index movement entails a binary classification of up and down, we use accuracy and f1 score as the evaluation metrics for both the fine-tuning training and testing experiments. These metrics are computed based on the underlying confusion matrix, as illustrated in Table 5. Within this framework, True Positive (TP) and True Negative (TN) signify instances where the actual and predicted labels align with the positive and negative categories, respectively. Conversely, False Positive (FP) and False Negative (FN) denote cases where the predicted labels deviate from the true labels. The accuracy and f1 are calculated by the following formulas:

$$accuracy = \frac{TP + TN}{TP + TN + FP + FN}$$

$$f1 = \frac{2 * TP}{2 * TP + FP + FN}$$

Table 5. Confusion Matrix

Actual/Predicted	Positive	Negative
Positive	True Positive (TP)	False Negative (FN)
Negative	False Positive (FP)	True Negative (TN)

4   Empirical Results

To ensure the robustness and reliability of our experimental results, we repeat the fine-tuning process of pre-trained LLMs ten times and select the best-performing model during testing for each LLM. The same procedure is applied to obtain responses via GPT-3.5 and GPT-4 APIs (0613-version) with ten iterations. As there are two settings for determining the best model during fine-tuning, we validate the performance of predicting overnight stock index movement with metrics containing accuracy and f1.

Beginning with the evaluation of the SSE Composite Index, Table 6 showcases the results with the parameter of metric for best model setting to accuracy. In this scenario, we observe that MacBERT achieves the highest testing accuracy of 0.72, while LERT demonstrates the best testing f1 of 0.686016. Notably, when compared to the naive method, MacBERT exhibits a substantial improvement of 25.76% in testing accuracy. Furthermore, all fine-tuned LLMs outperform the GPT models in relation to testing accuracy, which contrasts with prevailing perceptions.

When we shift the focus to f1 score as the metric for best model, Table 6 illustrates that RoBERTa reaches the highest testing f1 of 0.693548, while LERT

Table 6. The results of predicting overnight stock index movement

Model	SSE Composite Index		SSE 50 Index	
	Test Accuracy	Test f1	Test Accuracy	Test f1
metric_for_best_model: Accuracy				
Naive	0.5725		0.505	
BERT	0.6725	0.639566396	0.6075	0.604534
FinBERT	0.6575	0.601064	0.62	0.673428
RoBERTa	0.695	0.644068	0.65	0.681223
LERT	0.7025	0.686016	0.6325	0.672165
MacBERT	0.72	0.682051	0.685	0.697115
PERT	0.7025	0.655072	0.64	0.654244
BART	0.6925	0.681481481	0.6	0.607843
Longformer	0.6775	0.625	0.6125	0.595300261
BigBird	0.6875	0.666666667	0.615	0.619512
GPT-3.5	0.62	0.631068	0.6175	0.651481
GPT-4	0.6525	0.653367	0.62	0.646512
metric_for_best_model: f1				
Naive		0.598949212		0.662207
BERT	0.6475	0.648276	0.6325	0.664418
FinBERT	0.705	0.679347826	0.6625	0.691824
RoBERTa	0.715	0.693548	0.64	0.70082
LERT	0.7175	0.685237	0.685	0.690058
MacBERT	0.715	0.682927	0.675	0.70082
PERT	0.7075	0.664756	0.6575	0.682105
BART	0.6825	0.653950954	0.6325	0.650943396
Longformer	0.6525	0.643016	0.5925	0.634782609
BigBird	0.71	0.663212435	0.625	0.676724
GPT-3.5	0.62	0.631068	0.6175	0.651481
GPT-4	0.6525	0.653367	0.62	0.646512

attains the top testing accuracy of 0.7175. Based on the naive testing f1 score, RoBERTa showcases an improvement of 15.79%, underlining the compelling results secured in forecasting overnight index movement. Similarly, most LLMs outperform the GPT models, with the exception of BERT in terms of testing accuracy. GPT-4, on the other hand, lags behind the majority of fine-tuned LLMs, except for BERT and Longformer, with respect to testing f1 score. Given their intricate architectures, substantial training parameters, and associated high costs, it appears impractical to favor GPT models for our forecasting task. In contrast, fine-tuning pre-trained LLMs, which offer open access, emerges as a more viable option, given their satisfactory performance outcomes and cost-effectiveness.

To assess the robustness of our solution, we extend the experiment to predict the overnight SSE 50 Index movement. The results presented in Table 6 mirror those of the SSE Composite Index, further affirming that MacBERT obtains the highest accuracy of 0.685, marking a remarkable 35.64% improvement based on naive accuracy. Furthermore, when configuring the metric for best model as f1 score, the top performance in testing f1 score is achieved by RoBERTa and MacBERT, both scoring 0.70082, while LERT surpasses all other LLMs concerning testing accuracy with a score of 0.685.

Based on the aforementioned results, several key insights can be drawn regarding our task. Firstly, the market summary sourced from news media has proven to be a reliable and effective textual source for predicting overnight stock index movement, as evidenced by the convincing outcomes when compared to similar tasks in prior works [9]. Secondly, with regard to our financial forecasting task, fine-tuning pre-trained LLMs such as RoBERTa, LERT, and MacBERT emerges as a superior option, even though GPT models may accomplish commendable performance in general applications. Thirdly, our experiment underscores that LLMs characterized by intricate structures and substantial parameters do not invariably outperform models with simpler architectures and fewer parameters. This is exemplified by the relative underperformance of GPT-3.5 and GPT-4 in comparison with fine-tuned LLMs in our task. Thus, the choice of appropriate models should be contingent on the specific characteristics of the data and the nuances of the application scenarios at hand.

5   Conclusions

This paper has presented a novel study on forecasting overnight Chinese stock market index movement utilizing LLMs. Compared with text applied in prior works, such as financial news and titles, we collect market summary from news media featuring extensive and refined content. To assess the efficacy of various LLMs, we conduct fine-tuning on pre-trained LLMs accessible through the huggingface platform, which consist of BERT, FinBERT, RoBERTa, LERT, MacBERT, PERT, BART, Longformer and BigBird. Additionally, we employ the GPT-3.5 and GPT-4 APIs provided by OpenAI for comparative evaluation with fine-tuned LLMs. Our finding indicates that fine-tuned LLMs not only outperform baseline models but also surpass GPT models in predicting overnight index movement. Possessing fewer parameters and offering reduced computational cost, fine-tuned LLMs provide a practical tool for investors and regulators in the decision-making process.

In future work, our study can be enhanced along three dimensions. Firstly, the acquisition and evaluation of extra data resources from reputable news media with similar textual content will be undertaken to verify the performance. Secondly, leveraging the predictive results of overnight index movement, we intend to extend our investigation within the scope of financial applications, including portfolio optimization and risk management in practical trading scenarios.

Lastly, while our existing work is centered on Chinese text and market dynamics, we propose exploring other languages with corresponding markets to validate the experiment's outcomes.

References

1. Beltagy, I., Peters, M.E., Cohan, A.: Longformer: the long-document transformer. arXiv preprint arXiv:2004.05150 (2020)
2. Cui, Y., Che, W., Liu, T., Qin, B., Wang, S., Hu, G.: Revisiting pre-trained models for chinese natural language processing. arXiv preprint arXiv:2004.13922 (2020)
3. Cui, Y., Che, W., Wang, S., Liu, T.: Lert: a linguistically-motivated pre-trained language model. arXiv preprint arXiv:2211.05344 (2022)
4. Cui, Y., Yang, Z., Liu, T.: Pert: pre-training bert with permuted language model. arXiv preprint arXiv:2203.06906 (2022)
5. Gao, R., Zhang, X., Zhang, H., Zhao, Q., Wang, Y.: Forecasting the overnight return direction of stock market index combining global market indices: a multiple-branch deep learning approach. Expert Syst. Appl. **194**, 116506 (2022)
6. Huang, A.H., Wang, H., Yang, Y.: FinBERT: a large language model for extracting information from financial text. Contemp. Account. Res. **40**(2), 806–841 (2023)
7. Kenton, J.D.M.W.C., Toutanova, L.K.: Bert: pre-training of deep bidirectional transformers for language understanding. In: Proceedings of naacL-HLT, vol. 1, p. 2 (2019)
8. Lewis, M., et al.: Bart: denoising sequence-to-sequence pre-training for natural language generation, translation, and comprehension. arXiv preprint arXiv:1910.13461 (2019)
9. Li, W., Bao, R., Harimoto, K., Chen, D., Xu, J., Su, Q.: Modeling the stock relation with graph network for overnight stock movement prediction. In: Proceedings of the Twenty-Ninth International Conference on International Joint Conferences on Artificial Intelligence, pp. 4541–4547 (2021)
10. Liu, Y., et al.: Roberta: a robustly optimized BERT pretraining approach. arXiv preprint arXiv:1907.11692 (2019)
11. Lopez-Lira, A., Tang, Y.: Can Chatgpt forecast stock price movements? return predictability and large language models. arXiv preprint arXiv:2304.07619 (2023)
12. Lu, D., et al.: BBT-FIN: comprehensive construction of Chinese financial domain pre-trained language model, corpus and benchmark. arXiv preprint arXiv:2302.09432 (2023)
13. OpenAI: Gpt-4 technical report (2023)
14. Radford, A., Narasimhan, K., Salimans, T., Sutskever, I., et al.: Improving language understanding by generative pre-training (2018)
15. Shao, Y., et al.: CPT: a pre-trained unbalanced transformer for both Chinese language understanding and generation. arXiv preprint arXiv:2109.05729 (2021)
16. Wu, S., et al.: Bloomberggpt: a large language model for finance. arXiv preprint arXiv:2303.17564 (2023)
17. Xie, Q., Han, W., Lai, Y., Peng, M., Huang, J.: The wall street neophyte: a zero-shot analysis of chatgpt over multimodal stock movement prediction challenges. arXiv preprint arXiv:2304.05351 (2023)
18. Yang, H., Liu, X.Y., Wang, C.D.: FinGPT: open-source financial large language models. arXiv preprint arXiv:2306.06031 (2023)

19. Zaheer, M., et al.: Big bird: transformers for longer sequences. Adv. Neural. Inf. Process. Syst. **33**, 17283–17297 (2020)
20. Zhang, J., et al.: Fengshenbang 1.0: being the foundation of Chinese cognitive intelligence. arXiv preprint arXiv:2209.02970 (2022)
21. Zhang, Z., et al.: Mengzi: towards lightweight yet ingenious pre-trained models for chinese. arXiv preprint arXiv:2110.06696 (2021)

A Practical Byzantine Fault Tolerance Algorithms Based on Randomized Mean Clustering, Trust and Credibility

Haonan Zhai⊙ and Xiangrong Tong$^{(\boxtimes)}$⊙

Yantai University, College of Computer and Control Engineering, Yantai, China
`txr@ytu.edu.cn`

Abstract. The Practical Byzantine Fault Tolerance (PBFT) consensus protocol, while robust, faces efficiency challenges with the escalating number of network nodes. Various enhancement algorithms employ grouping strategies to bolster performance in large-scale networks. However, as nodes consolidate into smaller clusters, their capacity to accommodate Byzantine nodes diminishes markedly, prompting the need for a systematic approach to distributing Byzantine nodes evenly across consensus regions. In order to address the above issues, this paper proposes a Practical Byzantine fault tolerant algorithm based on Randomized Mean Clustering, Trust, and Credibility (CTPBFT). Nodes possess two key attributes: trust and credibility. Trust determines the priority of node cluster allocation, while credibility evaluations ensure cluster uniformity. A customized random equalization algorithm assigns nodes within the federated chain to diverse clusters. Post-partitioning, the consensus process is streamlined, with each cluster autonomously conducting consensus activities. A well-designed reward function incentivizes nodes to execute the consensus protocol, aiding the system's smooth and efficient operation.

Keywords: PBFT · Clusters · Trust · Credibility · Reward functions

1 Introduction

Blockchain, originating from Bitcoin, is a decentralized protocol. Integrates distributed data storage, cryptographic algorithms, consensus mechanisms, and programmable smart contracts, forming a distributed system [1]. The consensus mechanism is a critical component, ensuring node coherence in a distributed environment [2]. This mechanism significantly impacts the performance and

Supported by the National Natural Science Foundation of China (62072392,61972360), the Major Innovation Project of Science and Technology of Shandong Province (2019522Y020131), the Natural Science Foundation of Shandong Province (ZR2020QF113) and the Yantai Key Laboratory: intelligent technology of high-end marine engineering equipment.

Y. Tan and Y. Shi (Eds.): DMBD 2023, CCIS 2017, pp. 63–77, 2024.
https://doi.org/10.1007/978-981-97-0837-6_5

security of the blockchain system, ultimately shaping its potential for large-scale implementation [3]. Blockchain, renowned for its decentralized architecture [4], mandates consensus confirmation by all nodes for each transaction [5,6]. However, the increasing node count results in a significant drop in blockchain performance [7,8]. It involves dividing consensus-involved nodes into distinct regions [9], enabling concurrent transaction processing [10]. Traditional PBFT lacks trust attributes for node behavior evaluation, neglecting the issue of malicious Byzantine nodes [11]. Additionally, prior PBFT lacks a predefined reward function, which is essential for incentivizing accurate consensus participation.

However, integrating partitioning methods and trust into PBFT presents a significant challenge. As the capacity to handle erroneous or malicious nodes diminishes when nodes are grouped into clusters [12]. Addressing this challenge requires a novel algorithm to distribute Byzantine nodes across consensus regions uniformly. Post-partitioning assessments are proposed to validate the accuracy and rationality of the process. The current limitations of the trust evaluation strategy in accounting for historical behavior and mutual evaluation subjectivity call for a more comprehensive trust mechanism. This mechanism should encompass diverse facets, including inter-node evaluations and the potential integration of a dual trust attribute. Additionally, PBFT lacks a predefined or fixed reward function, which is crucial for incentivizing node participation while mitigating risks of excessive rewards or biases. The design of the reward function must ensure fairness and reasonableness, aligning with both the consensus algorithm and system objectives while factoring in resource costs and system sustainability.

In order to address the above issues, this paper proposes a Practical Byzantine Fault Tolerance Algorithm based on Randomized Mean Clustering, Trust, and Credibility(CTPBFT). Two critical attributes, trust and credibility, are assigned to nodes. The trust value represents the dynamic evaluation by other nodes within the cluster, influencing the prioritization of nodes during cluster assignment. Regulated by a Sigmoid function, trust remains within the recognizable range of 0 to 1. After allocation, the overall cluster credibility is checked for balance, and if the difference is small, the allocation is deemed reasonable; otherwise, reallocation is necessary. The randomized balancing algorithm further refines the consensus process by judiciously clustering nodes based on their trust. Importantly, consensus takes place only within the respective clusters, significantly reducing the number of communications between nodes by simplifying the preparation and commit phases. Additionally, the reward mechanism, contingent on computational resources, network bandwidth, and storage consumption, incentivizes nodes to adhere to the consensus protocol through tokens. The reward framework aligns with the consensus algorithm and system goals, considering resource costs and ensuring system sustainability. The main contributions of this research are as follows:

1. Two credit assessment attributes, trust, and credibility, are introduced to evaluate node performance. Trust reflects the dynamic assessment of nodes, while credibility is influenced by the historical behavior of nodes and is determined by the number of consecutive correct consensuses. Trust determines

the priority of cluster division, while credibility acts as a litmus test to assess the reasonableness of cluster division. This combination of dynamic and static credit assessment mechanisms is realized.

2. Designing a Random Equalization Algorithm aimed at distributing normal and Byzantine nodes evenly across clusters, ensuring the availability of each cluster. The algorithm streamlines and enhances the consensus process by confining consensus activities within individual clusters. This refinement significantly reduces inter-node communications, thereby augmenting consensus efficiency.

3. Designing a Reward Function tailored to compensate nodes based on their consumption of computational resources, network bandwidth, and storage space during the consensus process. This strategic approach serves to motivate nodes towards accurate consensus completion, bolstering positive reinforcement and enhancing the stability of the system's consensus mechanism.

After experimental verification, CTPBFT outperforms the PBFT, GPBFT [13] and CPBFT [14] algorithms in terms of delay, information throughput and communication overhead.

2   Related Works

The Byzantine Fault Tolerance Algorithm constitutes a pivotal avenue of research within the realm of distributed systems, with the overarching objective of guaranteeing consensus attainment even in the face of faulty nodes [15,16]. The PBFT algorithm accentuates the pivotal aspects of trustworthiness and security within distributed systems, holding notable implications for the domains of blockchain technology and other related fields [17,18]. By introducing a consensus mechanism, blockchain technology effectively addresses the intricate concerns surrounding trust and security within decentralized networks [19].

Castro and Liskov invented PBFT, the first broadly used Byzantine fault-tolerant algorithm, in 1999 [20]. However, the PBFT algorithm for solving the Byzantine common question demands network communication with a time complexity of $O(N^2)$ [21]. To tackle this issue, many scholars have optimized the PBFT. RBFT improves the performance of the system under the worst conditions by reducing the performance of the system under optimal conditions, thus improving the robustness of the whole system [22]. However, RBFT is better than PBFT in terms of delays and communication overheads, mainly because it has more consensus phases than PBFT [23,24]. Zyzzyva optimizes the consensus process of PBFT when there is no Byzantine node in the system, reducing the time complexity from $O(N^2)$ to $O(N)$ [25]. The literature [13] proposes GPBFT to reach consensus using geographical information of fixed IoT devices, which reduces the overhead of verification and recording transactions. The literature [14] proposes CPBFT, which introduces credit attributes and changes the architecture to reduce the consensus steps, thus reducing the amount of data transfer and increasing the throughput.

3   CTPBFT Algorithm Design and Implementation

3.1   Node Trust Assessment

In order to solve the consistency problem of nodes in a distributed environment, it is crucial to introduce trust attributes in improving the consensus mechanism [26,27]. The incorporation of trust attributes significantly fortifies system security and reliability [28]. The first evaluation during the node initialization process establishes a direct correlation between superior server configurations, robust network environments, and higher initial credit values. Subsequent consensus rounds update the nodes' credit values in a timely manner to ensure real-time adaptability and accuracy.

The trust value evaluation formula (1) of node i is shown as follows:

$$Trust_i = \beta TD_i^t . \tag{1}$$

where, $Trust_i$ denotes the current trust value of node i. The trust value is determined by the dynamic evaluation of node i. TD_i^t is the interaction behavior between node i and other nodes for evaluation. β is the weight corresponding to the dynamic evaluation. It should be noted that the range of node dynamic evaluation is within the cluster in which it is divided.

The dynamic evaluation of node i is a mutual evaluation between nodes. The dynamic evaluation of node i can be expressed as Eq. (2):

$$TD_i^t = \begin{cases} \dfrac{\sum_{J=1}^{\frac{N}{G}} \dfrac{\sum_{m=l}^{l} f(m) TD_{ij}^{t_m}}{l}}{\dfrac{N}{G}} & l \neq 0 \\[4ex] 0 & l = 0 . \end{cases} \tag{2}$$

where node i is not equal to node j, N is the total number of nodes in the system, G is the number of clusters, and $\frac{N}{G}$ denotes the number of nodes in a single cluster, which indicates that dynamic evaluation is performed only within a cluster. t denotes the period of request messages sent by the client, l denotes the number of consensuses in period t, m is the mth consensus. $TD_{ij}^{t_m}$ is the mth consensus in which both node i and node j belong to the same cluster, and node j and node i After performing the interaction, the rating of node j to node i. $f(m)$ denoted as the time decay factor, which can be expressed as Eq. (3):

$$f(m) = \sigma^{1-m}(0 < \sigma < 1, 1 \leq m \leq l) . \tag{3}$$

where $f(m)$ represents the distance between the number of consensus and the current consensus round. And the farther the distance from the current consensus round, the larger the time decay and the smaller the impact on the dynamic evaluation of nodes.

3.2   CTPBFT Divided Cluster Strategy

In order to solve the problem that the consensus mechanism decreases the consensus efficiency in a large number of nodes, CTPBFT adopts the strategy of dividing the nodes into clusters so that the interconnection communication between nodes is performed only in the clusters. The structural model diagram (1) of its divided clusters is shown below:

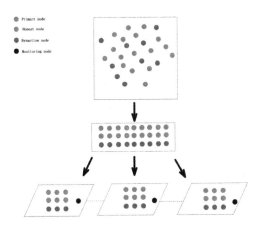

Fig. 1. Schematic diagram of CTPBFT structural model

Algorithm 1 Randomized Average Distribution Algorithm

Input:
A system time t and random number generator Rg() to get random set;
The node Trust $\{Trust_1, Trust_2, ..., Trust_N\}$
Output:
G clusters $C = \{C_1, C_2, ..., C_G\}$;
1: Initialize all nodes;
2: Get radom set $R = \{r_1, r_2, ..., r_N\}$;
3: Sort the Trust=sort(Trust);
4: **for** $Trust_i$ in Trust **do**
5: Get reasonable clusters $C' = \{C'_1, C'_2, ..., C'_j\}$
6: To be selected which $|C'| = \min \{C_1, C_2, ..., C_G\}$ and j is the number of $|C'|$;
7: Get $r_i = $ Rg(t_i);
8: Select clusters C'_G as the clusters of node i which $c = r_i$ %j;
9: **if** The sum of Credibility does not differ much between clusters **then**
10: **else**   Randomized Average Distribution Algorithm()
11: END

Figure 1 shows how 27 nodes are assigned to 3 clusters, the top three nodes in trust value are appointed as primary nodes in each cluster, and Byzantine nodes are all equally divided into different clusters to ensure that each cluster reaches consensus. Given N nodes and G clusters denoted as C, an allocation procedure is established. Initially, nodes are sorted in descending order based on their trust values. Nodes ranked from 1 to G are then randomly assigned to G clusters. Notably, clusters that have already been assigned nodes will not be considered in subsequent allocations. Subsequently, nodes ranked G+1 to 2G are systematically distributed across the G clusters. This process continues until the final allocation is achieved, with nodes ranked N-G to N being assigned to the G clusters, thereby completing the allocation process. Algorithm (1) for CTPBFT random assignment is shown above:

3.3 Node Credibility and Reward Curves

In this section, we explore the pivotal role of trust and credibility in the CTPBFT algorithm's cluster allocation process. Maintaining balanced cluster distribution is a fundamental objective achieved by ensuring that the total credibility of nodes within a single cluster closely aligns with other clusters. As the consensus process unfolds, node trust values expand, resulting in larger trust differentials, which can complicate cluster allocation validation. In contrast, node credibility values, ranging from 0 to 1, offer a more straightforward means of rationalizing cluster assignments. Consequently, CTPBFT employs trust for node cluster allocation and harnesses credibility for cluster validation [29]. For honest nodes, we adopt the strategy of starting carefully, rewarding quickly, and ending smoothly. We elect the Sigmoid reward curve as the incentive model for honest nodes (see Fig. 2).

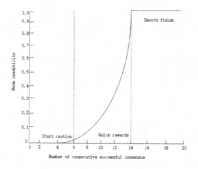

Fig. 2. Node-credibility curves

When a node completes consensus after the first few times, it is only partially certain that it is an honest and credible node, so the accretion of credibility will be slow at the beginning. However, suppose the number of consecutive consensus counts for that node exceeds the value of the threshold we set. In that case, we can determine its credibility virtually and reward it with quick credibility to perform an essential function in the following consensus. However, if it does not maintain it in the subsequent consensus, We will instantly clear its credibility score to zero. When a node's credibility gains enough value, we use a "smooth end" approach for its award to prevent honest nodes from scoring too high and causing power imbalance. Therefore, Eq. (4) is used as the credibility score rewarding strategy for honest nodes.

$$Cs_i = \omega * Sigmoid(\phi * T_i) \,. \tag{4}$$

where Cs_i denotes the credibility score of node i;ω is the maximum credibility score, which in our scheme $\omega = 1$.ϕ is the fast reward start adjustment parameter, which is set according to the actual need. T_i is the number of consecutive honest Consensus of node i. From the above credibility value calculation method, the credibility score of each node can be calculated using the historical job information. We can give a threshold of $omega$ and phi, $omega$, and phi. We can incorporate the probability of performing various behaviors based on correct and failed nodes into the formula for calculating the credibility values. $omega$ is the credibility score of honest nodes when they work correctly continuously, and the value of $omega$ can be adjusted to control the threshold of fast rewards.

3.4   Improved Consensus Process

1. Request Stage
   Client c sends an execution request <REQUEST,m,c,t > to the primary node of each cluster. REQUEST denotes the message sent by the client, m is the specific message, c is the client address, and t is the timestamp.
2. Pre-preparation stage
   After the client sends the request, the pre-preparation phase is executed. The primary node sends a pre-preparation message to the rest of the nodes in the cluster. The message format is <PRE-PREPARE,v_G,n,d,m,p_G >. Where v_G is the view number of the current cluster, n is the sequence number of the requested message, d is the hash value of m, m is the specific message, and p denotes the primary node of the current cluster.
3. Preparation Stage
   All nodes in the cluster receive a pre-preparation message broadcast by the primary node and check it. After the verification is complete, each node forwards the message to the other nodes in the group. And writes the readiness message to the local message log. The nodes will enter the preparation phase. The message format <PREPARE,v_G,n,d,i >. Where v_G is the current view number, n is the serial number of request m in the current view, d is the summary of m, i is the node serial number, and p_G is the primary node.
4. Response Stage
   When the node checks that the ready message is true, it enters the acknowledgment phase. At the beginning of the acknowledgment phase, the node verifies the message and returns the result to the primary node.
5. Reply Stage
   Consensus is deemed to be achieved when the primary node collects a sufficient number of acknowledgments from the cluster. The primary node will deliver the result of the confirmation to the client and update the scores of all nodes as well as the credibility at the same time.

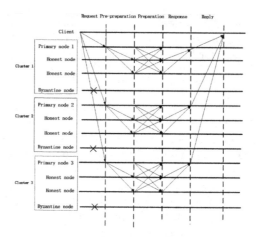

Fig. 3. CTPBFT consensus process

Figure 3 shows the consensus flow of CTPBFT simulated with 12 nodes and 3 clusters. The specific algorithm flow and the common notations are shown in Algorithm 2.

Algorithm 2 CTPBFT algorithm
___
1: While <REQUEST,o,t,c >= TRUE do
2: broadcast «PREPREPARE,$v_G,n,d,$>σ_G,m>
3: **if** <PREPREPARE>= TRUE **then**
4:     broadcast <PREPARE,v_G,n,d,i>σ_i;
5:     receive <PREPARE,v_G,n,d,i>σ_n;
6: **else** do nothing;
7: **if** prepared(m,v_G,n,i)=TRUE **then**
8:     $result\{\} = result\{\} \cup result\{i\}\ \sigma_m$
9: **else** do nothing;
10: **if** $\exists \sum (result\{i\} \in result\{\})$>$2f + 1/G$ **then**
11:     Primary node broadcast the result to client.
12: **else** do nothing;
13: UpdateConNodes() and ReGroup();
14: END

---

4 Reward Functions

4.1 Feasibility Analysis of the Reward Function

The reward function takes into account the computational resources, network bandwidth, and storage space of the nodes:

Suppose there are n nodes, of which f are Byzantine nodes. In each consensus cycle, each node can receive a base bonus of B. The length of the consensus cycle is T.

The workload W_i of node i can be calculated by the following Eq. (5):

$$W\_i = w\_c * C\_i + w\_b * B\_i + w\_s * S\_i. \tag{5}$$

Among them, w_c, w_b, and w_s are weighting coefficients, which indicate the weight of computational resources, network bandwidth, and storage space in the total workload, respectively. These coefficients can be adjusted according to the actual demand. C_i denotes the computational resources provided by node i in the consensus process, B_i denotes the network bandwidth provided by node i in the consensus process, and S_i denotes the storage space provided by node i in the consensus process.

The total contribution P_i of node i in the consensus process can be calculated by the ratio of its workload W_i to the total workload W of all nodes. Eq. (6) is as follows:

$$P\_i = W\_i \sum_{1}^{n} W\_n. \tag{6}$$

The bonus R_i of node i in each consensus cycle can be calculated by the following Eq. (7):

$$R\_i = B * P\_i * (1 - f/n)/T. \tag{7}$$

where B is the base bonus, f is the number of Byzantine nodes, and n is the total number of nodes. The more honest nodes in the system out of proportion, the more generous the reward.

5   Experiment

We simulated the performance of PBFT, GPBFT, CPBFT, and CTPBFT algorithms using Python language with all consensus nodes running on the same host. The hardware configuration of the host is i5-9300H, and the graphics card is GTX1660 Ti. The nodes are divided into PBFT nodes, CTPBFT nodes, and CPBFT and GPBFT nodes by writing different node behavior codes. There can be any number of consensus nodes in the network. Since the number of clusters in CTPBFT can be unlimited, 3 clusters are used when there are less than 300 nodes, 4 clusters when there are 300–400 nodes, and 5 clusters when there are 400–500 nodes. In the next experiments, the performance of PBFT, CPBFT, GPBFT, and CTPBFT is compared in the following three aspects.

5.1   Algorithm Complexity Analysis

The communication overhead of the PBFT protocol is proportional to the number of nodes in the network and the number of messages. In PBFT, each node needs to communicate with other nodes by sending a total of $2f + 1$ messages, where f is the maximum number of Byzantine nodes allowed. Since each node has to communicate with other nodes, when the number of nodes increases, the communication overhead increases accordingly. In addition, in PBFT, nodes need to go through three phases to reach a consensus among themselves, and each phase requires message exchange. So, the number of messages also increases with the number of phases, further increasing the communication overhead.

In order to reduce the communication overhead of the PBFT protocol, the submission phase of the consensus process is simplified, and the reply phase is improved. The phase that originally required confirmation from each node was changed to require confirmation from the primary node only. This can greatly reduce the amount of communication and computation between nodes and improve the efficiency and scalability of the system (Fig. 4).

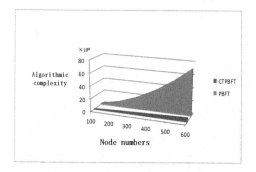

Fig. 4. Algorithmic Complexity

For the merit of PBFT in terms of communication costs, the four algorithms are compared and calculated. The concrete algorithm flow of PBFT is divided into three stages. In the pre-preparation phase, number of connections in the consensus system in this phase is $(N - 1)$. In the preparation phase, number of connections in the consensus system in this phase is $(N - 1) * (N - 1)$ times. In the commit phase, all nodes validate the received preparation messages. When the confirmation result is true, the node sends a confirmation message to all nodes but its own. In this phase, number of connections in the consensus system is $N * (N - 1)$. Thus, the count of exchanges in the consensus process of the conventional PBFT consensus algorithm is $2N * (N - 1)$.

As can be seen from Fig. 3, the specific calculation process of the CTPBFT consensus algorithm is divided into three stages. Assume that N is the total number of nodes in the system, and G is the number of clusters. In the pre-preparation phase, the primary node broadcasts a pre-preparation message to all other nodes in the cluster. In this phase, number of connections in the consensus system is $(N/G - 1) * G$. In the preparation phase, after verifying that the pre-preparation message sent by the primary node is passed, the nodes in the cluster send the preparation message to other consensus nodes. In this phase, number of connections in the consensus system is $(N/G - 1) * (N/G - 1) * G$. In the response phase, the primary node accepts the validation message from the nodes in the cluster and performs the validation. In this phase, number of connections in the consensus system is $(N/G - 1) * G$. Thus, the count of exchanges to complete a procedure for the improved CTPBFT consensus algorithm is $N^2/G - G$.

5.2 Communication Overhead

The communication overhead is the communication traffic generated by the consensus of the nodes in the system. The Communication expenses of the PBFT are one of the important performance metrics. Since PBFT uses the solution of the Byzantine General problem, it is an algorithm with very frequent communication between nodes, and message delivery, processing, and verification are required at each stage. Hence, the communication overhead is very high [30].

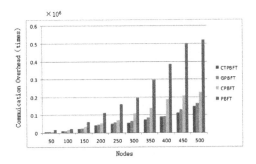

Fig. 5. Communication overhead

The communication overhead of PBFT consists of two main components: the overhead of sending and receiving messages and the overhead of message verification and processing. Specifically, nodes need to send and receive different kinds of messages in the PBFT algorithm, such as pre-prepared messages, prepared messages, source messages, commit messages, etc., and each message contains several data items, such as sequence number, view number, signature, etc., and the size of these data items affects the communication overhead. At the same time, when verifying and processing messages, nodes need to perform complex operations such as public key encryption, decryption, signature verification, etc. These operations also take up large processing and computing resources, increasing the communication overhead. In this experiment, the transaction traffic of each algorithm is tested separately. As can be seen from Fig. 5, the communication overhead of the algorithms all tend to increase as the number of nodes increases. The more nodes there are, the more obvious the advantage of the scheme becomes.

5.3 Message Throughput

Throughput is defined as the number of transactions executed by the system per unit of time. The level of the system's ability to process transactions relies on the size of the throughput, which is usually indicated in terms of transactions per second (TPS). Information throughput depends on the bandwidth of the network and the processing capacity of the nodes [30].

The Eq. (8) for the calculation of information throughput is shown below:

$$TPS = \frac{transaction \Delta t}{time} . \tag{8}$$

where $transaction \Delta t$ is the number of transactions processed by the system during the consensus process, and $time$ is the time necessary for the system to deal with the trade.

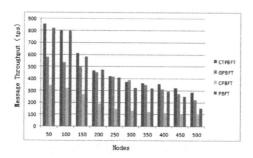

Fig. 6. Message Throughput

In this experiment, The client is set to issue 30 claims and record the number of trades performed per second at various From Fig. 6. The throughput of the CTPBFT consensus algorithm is higher than the other three consensus algorithms. At the same time, the throughput of the algorithm decreases as the number of nodes increases. The advantages of CTPBFT are still evident.

The stability of CTPBFT also impacts its consensus equality as the system operates due to its divisional clusters and credit mechanisms. If a malicious node is employed as a primary node, it will significantly reduce the consensus efficiency. The emulation outcome shows that due to the credit mechanism, the likelihood of malicious nodes participating in consensus is significantly reduced, and the incorrect selection probability of primary nodes is also reduced. In terms of long-term operation, CTPBFT dramatically increases the throughput of the system.

5.4   Transaction Delay

Transaction latency is the time required for a client node to send a transaction request to the primary node until the client receives a transaction receipt confirmation message [31].

The CTPBFT algorithm is optimized in terms of transaction latency compared to the original PBFT algorithm. The CTPBFT algorithm simplifies and improves the submission and reply phases, thus reducing the communication overhead and transaction latency. At the same time, the CTPBFT algorithm uses a reward mechanism based on nodes' computing resources, network bandwidth, and storage space to encourage nodes to participate in consensus correctly, thus increasing the transaction processing speed of the system (Fig. 7).

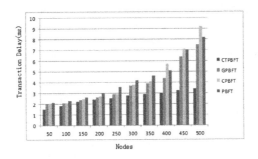

Fig. 7. Transaction Delay

The CTPBFT algorithm is optimized in the consensus process to simplify the submission and reply phases, reducing the communication overhead and transaction latency between nodes. In the commit phase, the CTPBFT algorithm adopts a fast commit mechanism, which only needs to wait for the reply from the primary node to upload the transaction to the chain, thus improving the transaction processing speed.

Two hundred tests were conducted, and the average of every 10 transaction latencies was taken as the experimental data. The experimental outcomes show that CTPBFT significantly outperforms the other three algorithms in terms of transaction latency.

6   Conclusion

In this paper, a practical Byzantine fault-tolerant algorithm (CTPBFT) based on randomized mean clustering and trust and credibility is proposed. The algorithm introduces the dual trust property, stochastic equalization algorithm, and a reward function. It effectively addresses the challenge of equitable distribution of Byzantine nodes through dynamic evaluation and consideration of nodes' historical behavior. By confining consensus activities to individual clusters, inter-node communication is significantly minimized. The implemented reward mechanism incentivizes accurate and swift consensus completion. Experimental results consistently demonstrate improved system throughput, reduced latency, and minimized communication overhead compared to the PBFT algorithm. This highlights the algorithm's enhanced performance.

References

1. Banerjee, M., Lee, J., Choo, K.K.R.: A blockchain future for internet of things security: a position paper. Digit. Commun. Netw. **4**(3), 149–160 (2018)
2. Zbierski, M.: Iwazaru: the byzantine sequencer. In: Kubátová, H., Hochberger, C., Daněk, M., Sick, B. (eds.) ARCS 2013. LNCS, vol. 7767, pp. 38–49. Springer, Heidelberg (2013). https://doi.org/10.1007/978-3-642-36424-2_4
3. Chondros, N., Kokordelis, K., Roussopoulos, M.: On the practicality of practical byzantine fault tolerance. In: Narasimhan, P., Triantafillou, P. (eds.) Middleware 2012. LNCS, vol. 7662, pp. 436–455. Springer, Heidelberg (2012). https://doi.org/10.1007/978-3-642-35170-9_22
4. Watanabe, H., Fujimura, S., Nakadaira, A., Miyazaki, Y., Akutsu, A., Kishigami, J.: Blockchain contract: securing a blockchain applied to smart contracts. IEEE International Conference on Consumer Electronics (2016)
5. Alwabe, M., Kwon, Y.: Blockchain consistency check protocol for improved reliability Int. J. Comput. Syst. Sci. Eng. (2), 36 (2021)
6. Bhat, P., Thankachan, R., Chandrasekaran, K.: Sharding distributed social databases using social network analysis. Soci. Netw. Anal. Min. **5**(1), 1–11 (2015)
7. Chen, Z., Fiandrino, C., Kantarci, B.: On blockchain integration into mobile crowdsensing via smart embedded devices: a comprehensive survey. J. Syst. Architecture **115**, 102011 (2021)
8. Liang, K., et al.: A secure and efficient ciphertext-policy attribute-based proxy re-encryption for cloud data sharing. Future Gener. Comput. Syst. **52**, 95–108 (2015)
9. Wang, J., et al.: Distributed secure storage scheme based on sharding blockchain Comput. Mater. the Continuum, no. 3, pp. 18 (2022)
10. Kokoris-Kogias, E., et al.: OmniLedger: a secure, scale-out, decentralized ledger via sharding (2017)
11. Li, A., et al.: An improved distributed query for large-scale RDF data. Big Data Mag. **2**(4), 002 (2020)
12. Yuvaraju, M., Mansingh, P.: A secure data sharing scheme based on blockchain for industrial internet of things using consensus algorithm. Industry 4.0 Interoperability, Analytics, Security, and Case Studies. N.p.: CRC Press (2021)
13. Lao, L., et al.: G-PBFT: a location-based and scalable consensus protocol for IoT-Blockchain applications. In: 2020 IEEE International Parallel and Distributed Processing Symposium (IPDPS) (2020)
14. Wang, Y., Song, Z., Cheng, T.: Improvement research of PBFT consensus algorithm based on credit. In: Zheng, Z., Dai, H.N., Tang, M., Chen, X. (eds.) BlockSys 2019. CCIS, vol. 1156, pp. 47–59. Springer, Singapore (2019). https://doi.org/10.1007/978-981-15-2777-7_4
15. Luu, L., et al.: A secure sharding protocol for open blockchains. In: the 2016 ACM SIGSAC Conference (2016)D
16. Zhai, S., Li, X., Wang, Y.: Research on the storage and sharing model of electronic license based on blockchain. In: Xie, Q., Zhao, L., Li, K., Yadav, A., Wang, L. (eds.) ICNC-FSKD 2021. LNCS, vol. 89, pp. 1321–1330. Springer, Cham (2022). https://doi.org/10.1007/978-3-030-89698-0_136
17. Team, Z., et al.: The zilliqa technical whitepaper, vol. 16 (2019). Accessed Sept
18. Syta, E., et al.: Scalable bias-resistant distributed randomness. In: 2017 IEEE Symposium on Security and Privacy (SP) (2017)
19. Zamani, M., Movahedi, M., Raykova, M.: RapidChain: scaling blockchain via full sharding (2018)

20. Liu, F., et al.: Regulated and unregulated emissions from a spark-ignition engine fuelled with low-blend ethanol-gasoline mixtures. In: Proceedings of the Institution of Mechanical Engineers, Part D: Journal of Automobile Engineering (2012)
21. Aublin, P., Mokhtar, S., Quema, V.: RBFT: redundant byzantine fault tolerance. In: IEEE International Conference on Distributed Computing Systems (2013)
22. Liu, J., et al.: Scalable byzantine consensus via hardware-assisted secret sharing. IEEE Trans. Comput. **68**(1), 139–151 (2019)
23. Crain, T., et al.: DBFT: efficient leaderless byzantine consensus and its application to blockchains. In: 2018 IEEE 17th International Symposium on Network Computing and Applications (NCA) (2018)
24. Saad, S., Radzi, R.: Comparative review of the blockchain consensus algorithm between proof of stake (POS) and delegated proof of stake (DPOS). Penerbit UTM Press (2020)
25. Chinnakotla, S., et al.: Intraportal islet autotransplantation independently improves quality of life after total pancreatectomy in patients with chronic refractory pancreatitis. Ann. Surg. **276**(3), 441–449 (2022)
26. Yin, M., et al.: HotStuff: BFT consensus with linearity and responsiveness. In: the 2019 ACM Symposium (2019)
27. Wang, Z., et al.: Reinforcement-mining: protecting reward in selfish mining. In: International Conference on Provable Security (2022)
28. Shen, T.: Reputation-driven dynamic node consensus and reliability sharding model in IoT blockchain. Algorithms, **15** (2022)
29. Ren, X., Tong, X., Zhang, W.: Improved PBFT consensus algorithm based on node role division. Comput. Commun. **11**(2), 19 (2023)
30. Frauenthaler, P., et al.: ETH relay: a cost-efficient relay for ethereum-based blockchains. In: 2020 IEEE International Conference on Blockchain (Blockchain) (2020)
31. Zegers, F., et al.: Event-triggered formation control and leader tracking with resilience to byzantine adversaries: a reputation-based approach. IEEE Trans. Control Netw. Syst. **99**, 1–1 (2021)

Improved Joint Distribution Adaptation for Fault Diagnosis

Dali Gao$^{(\boxtimes)}$, Xiaobin Mao, Long Sheng, and Shuangling Wang

Science and Technology on Information System Engineering Laboratory, Nanjing 210023, China
gao_personal@163.com

Abstract. In the blast furnace (BF) ironmaking process, it is difficult to obtain labeled fault samples and the probability distribution drifts significantly. Therefore, transfer learning has been introduced to fault diagnosis of BF. Most of the existing transfer learning methods achieve domain adaptation by reducing the marginal and conditional distribution discrepancies, without considering the prior distribution. To address this issue, this paper provides a theoretical derivation of the effect of the prior distribution discrepancies on knowledge transfer, and proposes a new method called Improved Joint Distribution Adaptation (IJDA). The model performs reconstruction of the weighted source data to offset the discrepancies of prior distribution, and extracts domain-invariant features by aligning joint distribution to achieve knowledge transfer. In the transfer BF fault diagnosis experiments, the proposed method achieves promising performance improvement.

Keywords: Transfer learning · fault diagnosis · domain adaptation

1 Introduction

Blast furnace (BF) ironmaking is the key unit of iron and steel manufacturing, BF follows the sintering, pelletizing and other pre-processes, the main redox reaction in the furnace, i.e., under high temperature and pressure conditions, sintered ore, pelletized ore react with carbon monoxide to produce molten iron.

Figure 1 illustrates the process of blast furnace ironmaking. The procedure involves the continuous feeding of iron ore (which may include sintered ore, pellets, and other forms of iron ore), fuel (such as coke and coke powder), and a solvent (typically limestone) into the furnace in a predetermined ratio. Simultaneously, hot air at approximately 1200 °C, along with coal powder, is injected from the tuyere located at the bottom of the blast furnace. Under the high-temperature and high-pressure conditions, the combustion of coke generates carbon monoxide, which reacts with the iron ore in the presence of hydrogen to produce liquid pig iron. This pig iron is then discharged from the iron tap.

The safe and stable operation of the blast furnace directly affects the quantity and quality of steel products, which has significant economic value [1–3]. Constructing a timely and accurate fault diagnosis model is crucial for realizing energy saving, emission reduction, and improving production quality and efficiency. However, due to the

Y. Tan and Y. Shi (Eds.): DMBD 2023, CCIS 2017, pp. 78–92, 2024.
https://doi.org/10.1007/978-981-97-0837-6_6

extremely complex physical and chemical reactions involved in the BF ironmaking process, there is still no complete and accurate mechanism model. Meanwhile, in the harsh environment of high temperature and pressure, the actual condition of the reactions inside the BF is difficult to be directly measured and sensed. All these bring great challenges to the fault diagnosis of BF.

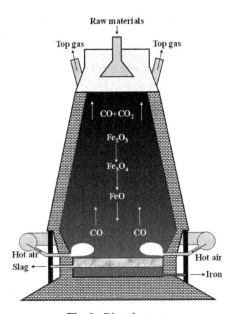

Fig. 1. Blast furnace.

With the wide application of distributed control system and various types of sensors, the massive amount of process data has led to the significant development of data-driven fault diagnosis methods.Zhou et al. proposed a combination of principal component analysis (PCA) and independent component analysis (ICA) to identify abnormal furnace conditions in the BF ironmaking process, and verified its validity in experiments on BF production data [4].Bangalore et al. proposed a method based on artificial neural network (ANN) for early fault detection of gearbox bearings [5]. Wang et al. proposed a novel multitasking attentional convolutional neural network for rolling bearing fault diagnosis, and the proposed method was validated with multiple bearing datasets [6].

The successful application of the above traditional data-driven methods relies on two latent assumptions: a large number of labeled samples are available for training, the training and test data have to obey the same distribution [7–9]. However, it is difficult to fulfill these assumptions in the BF production process due to the following reasons.

1) There is a scarcity of labeled samples, and when there is an abnormal tendency in the operating state of the BF, the operator will intervene artificially in the furnace condition, which makes it impossible to obtain fault samples.

2) Time-varying and multi-condition characteristics, due to the adjustment of the production plan and changes in the type and quality of the feed ore, the probability distribution of the BF production data drifts significantly.

Compared with traditional data-driven methods, transfer learning can learn transferable knowledge from different but related source domains to improve the generalization performance of the model in the target domain [10–12]. In addition, it is worth noting that transfer learning does not require that the training and test data obey the same distribution. These advantages make transfer learning effective in handling complex data with time-varying and multi-condition characteristics.

Feature-based method is a popular and challenging topic in transfer learning. Pan et al. proposed transfer component analysis (TCA) in 2011 [13], TCA maps the original data into the reproducing kernel Hilbert space (RKHS) by kernel method and using maximum mean discrepancy (MMD) to measure the discrepancy between the features of data in different domains. Duan et al. improved the MMD to a multi-kernel maximum mean discrepancy to improve the nonlinear handling of the model. Later, Long et al. proposed joint distribution adaptation (JDA) [14] based on TCA, which adapts the conditional distributions in addition to the marginal distribution to improve the domain adaptation performance of the model. Wang et al. noticed that the marginal and conditional distributions are not equally important in the process of domain adaptation, and thus proposed the balanced distribution adaptation (BDA), which calculates the overall and local domain discriminative loss from different domains by A-distance to adjust the weights of the two distributions [15].

In recent years, transfer learning has also been gradually introduced into fault diagnosis in industry [16, 17]. Xie et al. proposed a fault diagnosis method based on TCA and experimentally evaluated the diagnostic effect of choosing different kernel functions [18]. Li et al. proposed a fault diagnosis algorithm with domain adaptation capability by combining MK-MMD with deep neural network for the problem of distributional discrepancy of rolling bearing data [19]. Wen et al. used a three-layer sparse self-encoder for feature extraction and achieved feature alignment by reducing MMD, and the proposed method was tested on a well-known bearing dataset from Case Western Reserve University and showed promising improvements [20].

Most of the existing transfer learning methods achieve domain adaptation by reducing the marginal and conditional distribution discrepancies, without considering the impact of the prior distribution or the category weight discrepancies on the domain adaptation performance. However, the occurrence of various types of faults varies significantly with the operating state of the BF, thus showing obvious a prior distribution discrepancy, and it will be more obvious when the selection criteria of the samples are different. Weiss et al. used a lot of transfer learning methods to conduct experiments on datasets with obvious discrepancies in the prior distributions, and their experimental results show that the effect of the transfer learning will gradually decrease when the discrepancy in the prior distributions increases [21].

The application of transfer learning in BF fault diagnosis belongs to the typical unsupervised transfer learning, and there has been relatively little research on prior distribution discrepancy. Aiming at this problem, this paper gives a theoretical derivation of the effect of the prior distribution difference on transfer fault diagnosis, and proposes a new method based on improved joint distribution adaptation (IJDA) for fault diagnosis. The model weights the source domain data to offset the discrepancy of the prior distributions, and extracts domain-invariant features by reducing the joint distribution discrepancy to realize knowledge transfer. The proposed method achieves good results on actual BF datasets and achieves performance improvement compared with other transfer learning methods.

The main innovations of the paper are as follows:

1) A new fault diagnosis method, Improved Joint Distribution Adaptation (IJDA), which can simultaneously perform domain adaptation to both the prior and joint distribution, is proposed to improve the fault diagnosis accuracy.
2) A weighting operator for offsetting the discrepancy of a prior distributions is defined, and the domain adaptation performance can be improved by iterative updating.

The rest of this paper is organized as follows. Section 2 details the transfer learning problem. Section 3 includes the proposed method. In Sect. 4, transfer fault diagnosis experiments are conducted with actual BF data. Finally, conclusions are drawn in Sect. 5.

2   Transfer Learning Problems

As shown in Fig. 2, transfer learning aims to extract the transferable knowledge in the relevant source domain to improve the performance of the model in the target domain,

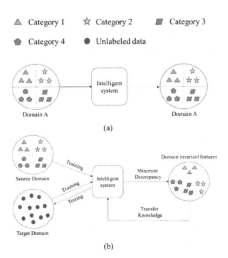

Fig. 2. Comparison of traditional data-driven method and transfer learning (a) Traditional data-driven method. (b) Transfer-learning.

Compared with other methods such as transductive learning [22] and active learning [23] which target the scarcity of labeled samples, the biggest difference between transfer learning is that it doesn't require that the training and testing data obey the same distribution. In recent years, transfer learning has gradually become a research hot topic in artificial intelligence, and has been widely used in computer vision, healthcare, natural language processing and many other fields.

In BF fault diagnosis, n_s labeled historical data are usually used as the source domain $\mathcal{D}_s = (X_s, Y_s)$, and n_t unlabeled data from the test are used as the target domain $\mathcal{D}_t = X_t$. Due to the adjustments of the production plan and the variations of the types and qualities of the feed ores, $\mathcal{D}_s$, and $\mathcal{D}_t$ sampled from different times do not obey the same distribution. Therefore, it is a typical transfer learning problem to utilize historical data to achieve effective recognition of unlabeled test data by the model.

Since the source and target domains only differ in their respective data probability distributions including class prior distribution P(y) and joint distribution composed of marginal distribution P(x) and conditional distribution P(y|x), learning domain-invariant features which are subject to the almost the same distribution is a critical process. Based on domain-invariant features, the model trained on the source domain data can also classify the features learned from the target domain. Considering the fault types and monitoring variables of historical and test data are the same, and only differ in data distribution, the key to realizing knowledge transfer is to extract domain invariant features to achieve approximate uniform distribution in feature space, and the diagnosis problem can be further summarized as a domain adaptation problem.

In practical applications, the distribution of class priors, or class weights, can vary significantly across different domains. Ignoring these class weight biases can lead to a decrease in domain adaptation performance. In the case of class weight bias, distribution difference can be minimized by learning a domain-invariant representation or preserving class weights in the source domain. However, it is not reasonable to expect that the class weights in the target domain will remain identical to those in the source domain when there is a class weight bias. Our empirical experiments have demonstrated the superior capability of IJDA in handling class weight bias.

3 Proposed Method

In this section, we describe the construction and solution process of the proposed method in detail.

3.1 Reconstruction with Weighted Source Domain

The probability distributions of the source domain data x_s and the target domain data x_t are denoted as: $p(x_s)$ and $p(x_t)$, respectively, which can be expanded according to the full probability formula as:

$$p(x_u) = \sum_{c=1}^{C} p(y_u = c)\, p(x_u|y_u = c) = \sum_{c=1}^{C} w_u^c p(x_u|y_u = c), u \in \{s, t\} \quad (1)$$

where $w_s^c = p(y_s = c) = \frac{n_s^c}{n_s}$, $w_t^c = p(y_t = c) = \frac{n_t^c}{n_t}$ denote the prior distribution of the source and target domains, respectively. n_s and n_t denote the number of samples in the source and target domains respectively, C is the number of fault categories, n_s^c and

n_t^c denote the number of samples belonging to fault category c in the source and target domains respectively, and y_s and y_t denote the labels of the samples in the source and target domains respectively. It is worth noting that since the target domain samples are usually unlabeled, y_t generally consists of pseudo-labels, and the specific generation process will be described later.

From Eq. (1), only when $w_s^c = w_t^c$, the discrepancies between domains can be approximated by the differences between $p(x_u | y_u = c)$ instead. However, the occurrence of various types of faults varies significantly with the operating state of the BF, thus showing obvious prior distribution discrepancies, and it will be more obvious when the selection criteria of the samples are different. Therefore, it is difficult to satisfy the assumption that $w_s^c = w_t^c$ in practical applications, and ignoring the prior distribution will result in an inaccurate measure of the discrepancies between domains, making the model's classification results closer to the source domain than to the target domain, which affects the model's domain-adaptive performance and fault diagnosis accuracy.

3.2 Modeling and Solving

A complete procedure of IJDA is summarized in Algorithm 1. After solving the transformation matrix, the discrepancy between domains is significantly reduced. Based on the learned domain invariant features, the classifier can achieve accurate recognition of unlabeled samples in the target domain.

Algorithm 1: Improved Joint Distribution Adaptation (IJDA)

Input: Source data X_s, target data X_t, labels of source data Y_s, regularization parameter λ

Output: adaptive classifier f.

Begin:

> Train an initial classifier with (X_s, Y_s) until convergence.
> Utilize the classifier to classify X_t and generate the pseudo-label $\widehat{Y}_t$.
> **Repeat**:
>> Calculate the auxiliary weight **W**, and perform a weighted reconstruction of the source domain data according to the equation (2).
>> Construct the M_c according to the equation (5) and (6).
>> Obtain the transformation matrix A according to the eigen decomposition of equation (8).
>> Train the classier f on $\{A^T X_s, Y_s\}$
>> Update $\widehat{Y}_t$ according to f.
> **Until**: $\widehat{Y}_t$ no longer changes

End: Return an adaptive classifier f

As shown in Fig. 3, to reduce the prior distribution discrepancy and improve the generalization capability of the model in the target domain, this paper proposes Improved Joint Distribution Adaptation (IJDA) to construct a new distribution $p_w(x_s)$ of the source domain with the same prior distribution as that of the target domain.

Due to the lack of labels of the target samples, the number of target samples belonging to the fault category c n_t^c usually cannot be obtained directly, so this paper uses a self-training method in the solution process, using the labeled source samples (X_s, Y_s) to train an initial classifier (e.g., such as support vector machine, SoftMax, etc.), and the result of the classifier's recognition of x_t is used as the pseudo-label y_t for computing n_t^c, and the accuracy of the pseudo-labels are gradually improved through iterative updating.

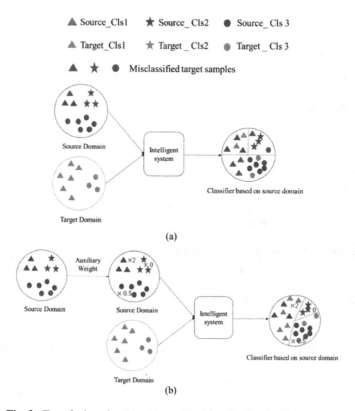

Fig. 3. Transfer learning (a) without (b) with prior distribution adaptation

Let $w_c = \frac{w_t^c}{w_s^c}$, $\mathbf{W} = [w_1, w_2, \cdots, w_C]^T$, then it can be introduced:

$$p_w(x_s) = \sum_{c=1}^{C} w_c w_s^c p(x_s|y_s = c) = \sum_{c=1}^{C} w_t^c p(x_t|y_t = c) \qquad (2)$$

By introducing auxiliary weights $\mathbf{W}$, the model weights and reconstructs the source samples, so that the class prior distribution of the source domain is closer to the target domain, thus reducing the discrepancy between the prior distributions of different domains. In addition, in the BF production process where the occurrence of various types of faults is not balanced, the weighted reconstruction helps to accurately recognize faults with fewer samples.

After completing the prior distribution alignment, the model employs MMD to measure the distributional discrepancy between domains and needs to find a suitable transformation matrix A to enable approximate unification of the probability distributions of the source and target samples in the feature space, then there is:

$$
\begin{aligned}
D &= \left\| \frac{1}{n_s} \sum_{i=1}^{n_s} A^T w_c x_i - \frac{1}{n_t} \sum_{j=1}^{n_t} A^T x_j \right\|_H^2 \\
&= tr\left[A^T \left(\frac{1}{n_s^2} WW^T X_s^T X_s + \frac{1}{n_t^2} 11^T X_t^T X_t - \frac{1}{n_s n_t} W1^T X_s^T X_t - \frac{1}{n_s n_t} 1W^T X_t^T X_s \right) A \right] \\
&= tr\left(A^T [X_s\ X_t] \begin{bmatrix} \frac{1}{n_s^2} WW^T & -\frac{1}{n_s n_t} W^T 1 \\ -\frac{1}{n_s n_t} 1^T W & \frac{1}{n_t^2} 11^T \end{bmatrix} \begin{bmatrix} X_s^T \\ X_t^T \end{bmatrix} A \right) \\
&= tr\left(A^T X M_c X^T A \right)
\end{aligned}
\tag{3}
$$

For the nonlinear characteristics in process data, MMD is usually combined with a kernel function to solve for A in a high-dimensional space, which can be obtained by combining the kernel trick:

$$
\begin{aligned}
D &= \left\| \frac{1}{n_s} \sum_{i=1}^{n_s} A^T w_c \emptyset(x_i) - \frac{1}{n_t} \sum_{j=1}^{n_t} A^T \emptyset(x_j) \right\|_H^2 \\
&= tr\left(A^T [\emptyset(X_s)\ \emptyset(X_t)] \begin{bmatrix} \frac{1}{n_s^2} WW^T & -\frac{1}{n_s n_t} W^T 1 \\ -\frac{1}{n_s n_t} 1^T W & \frac{1}{n_t^2} 11^T \end{bmatrix} \begin{bmatrix} \emptyset(X_s)^T \\ \emptyset(X_t)^T \end{bmatrix} A \right) \\
&= tr\left(A^T \begin{bmatrix} \emptyset(X_s)^T \\ \emptyset(X_t)^T \end{bmatrix} [\emptyset(X_s)\ \emptyset(X_t)] \begin{bmatrix} \frac{1}{n_s^2} WW^T & -\frac{1}{n_s n_t} W^T 1 \\ -\frac{1}{n_s n_t} 1^T W & \frac{1}{n_t^2} 11^T \end{bmatrix} A \right) \\
&= tr\left(A^T \begin{bmatrix} \langle \emptyset(X_s), \emptyset(X_s) \rangle & \langle \emptyset(X_s), \emptyset(X_t) \rangle \\ \langle \emptyset(X_t), \emptyset(X_s) \rangle & \langle \emptyset(X_t), \emptyset(X_t) \rangle \end{bmatrix} M_c A \right) \\
&= tr\left(A^T \begin{bmatrix} K_{s,s} & K_{s,t} \\ K_{t,s} & K_{st,t} \end{bmatrix} M_c A \right) \\
&= tr\left(A^T K M_c K^T A \right)
\end{aligned}
\tag{4}
$$

where $tr((A^T K M_c K^T A)$ denotes the marginal distribution discrepancy between domains when c = 0 and M_c takes the value:

$$
M_c = \begin{cases} \frac{w_c w_{c'}}{n_s^2}, & x_i \in D_s^c, x_j \in D_s^{c'} \\ \frac{1}{n_t^2}, & x_i, x_j \in D_t \\ -\frac{w_c}{n_s n_t}, & \text{otherwise} \end{cases}
\tag{5}
$$

When c $\in (1, C)$, tr$((\mathbf{A}^{\mathrm{T}}\mathbf{KM_cK}^{\mathrm{T}}\mathbf{A})$ denotes the conditional distribution discrepancy between domains, and $\mathbf{M_c}$ takes the value of

$$M_c = \begin{cases} \frac{w_c^2}{(n_s^c)^2}, & x_i, x_j \in D_s^c \\ \frac{1}{(n_t^c)^2}, & x_i, x_j \in D_t^c \\ -\frac{w_c}{n_s^c n_t^c}, & \begin{cases} x_i \in D_s^c, x_j \in D_t^c \\ x_i \in D_t^c, x_j \in D_s^c \end{cases} \\ 0, & otherwise \end{cases} \quad (6)$$

D_s^c and D_t^c denote the source and the target dataset belonging to fault category c, respectively. In summary, IJDA can be uniformly represented as:

$$\underset{A}{\text{argmin}} \sum_{c=0}^{C} \text{tr}((\mathbf{A}^{\mathrm{T}}\mathbf{KM_cK}^{\mathrm{T}}\mathbf{A}) + \lambda \|A^2\| \quad (7)$$
$$\text{s.t.} \mathbf{A}^{\mathrm{T}}\mathbf{KHK}^{\mathrm{T}}\mathbf{A} = \mathbf{I}$$

where $\lambda \in (0, 1)$ is the hyperparameter and $\|A\|^2$ is the regular term of the model complexity to avoid the overfitting, meanwhile, to maintain the internal properties of the transformed data, we set the constraints $\mathbf{A}^{\mathrm{T}}\mathbf{KHK}^{\mathrm{T}}\mathbf{A} = \mathbf{I}$, where $\mathbf{H}$ is the central function, i.e., $\mathbf{H} = I_{n_s+n_t} - 1/n_s + n_t 11^T$

By means of Lagrange multipliers, Eq. (7) can be reduced to a general problem of eigen-decomposition:

$$(\mathbf{KHK}^{\mathrm{T}})^{-1}(\mathbf{K}\sum_{c=0}^{C}\mathbf{M_cK}^{\mathrm{T}} + \lambda\mathbf{I})\mathbf{A} = \Phi\mathbf{A} \quad (8)$$

where Φ is the introduced Lagrange operator, after the feature decomposition, the transformation matrix A can be represented by the d smallest eigenvectors obtained, and d denotes the dimensions of the feature after dimensionality reduction.

4 Experiment Results and Comparison

In this section, transfer fault diagnosis experiments are conducted on the actual BF dataset and the superiority of the proposed method is verified by comparison with other transfer learning methods.

4.1 Dataset

In this paper, the actual BF data of an ironmaking plant in October and November 2017 are used for experimental validation. The data contains two common abnormal furnace conditions, namely channeling and hanging.

1. Channeling is the phenomenon of excessive development of gas flow in a certain area of cross-section. Channeling is often preceded by a decrease in wind pressure, a higher spike in top pressure, and a relative increase in gas flow and permeability index. Possible causes of channeling are: poor quality of the raw material, incompatibility of the gas flow with the permeability, large fluctuations in furnace temperature, etc.

2. Hanging is a phenomenon in which the charge stops falling and two consecutive batches of material abnormally stagnate. Before the occurrence of hanging, the furnace condition will generally appear, the top pressure is reduced, the gas flow is reduced, the permeability index is significantly reduced and other signs. The main reasons that may lead to hanging are: increased powder resulting in a decrease in permeability, large fluctuations in furnace temperature, etc.

The BF data, totaling 35 key observed variables, are listed in Table 1. The frequency of observation is once every 10 s. To take advantage of the temporal correlation information and to minimize the effects of noise on the data, a sample consists of a matrix of 35 consecutive moments of BF data.

Table 1. Variable list

No.	Variable (unit)	No.	Variable (unit)
1	Oxygen enrichment rate (%)	19	Hot blast pressure (MPa)
2	Blast furnace permeability index	20	Actual blast velocity (m/s)
3	CO volume (%)	21	Hot blast temperature (1) (°C)
4	H_2 volume (%)	22	Hot blast temperature (2) (°C)
5	CO_2 volume (%)	23	Top temperature (1) (°C)
6	Blast velocity at tuyere of blast furnace (m/s)	24	Top temperature (2) (°C)
7	Enriching oxygen flow (m3/h)	25	Top temperature (3) (°C)
8	Cold blast flow (104 m3/h)	26	Top temperature (4) (°C)
9	Blast momentum (KJ)	27	Coal injection set value (T/h)
10	Blast furnace bosh gas volume (m3)	28	Actual coal injection rate (T/h)
11	BF bosh gas index	29	Actual coal injection in last hour (T)
12	Theoretical combustion temperature (°C)	30	Enriching oxygen pressure (MPa)
13	Blast furnace top gas pressure (1) (°C)	31	Total pressure drop (Kpa)
14	Blast furnace top gas pressure (2) (°C)	32	Drag coefficient
15	Blast furnace top gas pressure (3) (°C)	33	Cold blast temperature (1) (°C)
16	Blast furnace top gas pressure (4) (°C)	34	Cold blast temperature (2) (°C)
17	Cold blast pressure (1) (MPa)	35	Blast humidity g/m
18	Cold blast pressure (2) (MPa)		

The production data in October and November are represented as dataset Oct and dataset Nov, respectively. Dataset Oct consists of 632 channeling samples, 412 hanging samples, and 1391 normal samples for a total of 2435 samples. There are 1288 normal samples, 923 channeling samples, 118 hanging samples, and 2329 total samples in the dataset Nov.

4.2 Results of Data Experiments

Due to the adjustments of the production plan and the changes in the type and quality of the feed ore, there are obvious discrepancies in the distribution of BF data between dataset Oct and Nov. To visualize this discrepancy, we use the t-distributed stochastic neighbor embedding (t-SNE) technique to map the high-dimensional features into a 3-D space. As shown in Fig. 4, there is a significant discrepancy in the distribution of data between the source and target domains.

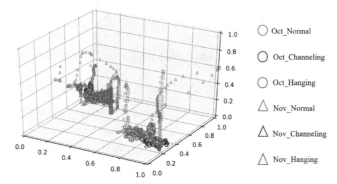

Fig. 4. Visualization of discrepancy between domains

To further illustrate the effectiveness of the proposed method, IJDA is compared with the following seven methods, convolutional neural networks (CNN) trained using only source samples, transfer component analysis (TCA), joint distribution adaptation (JDA), balanced distribution adaptation (BDA), deep domain confusion (DDC) [24], multi-adversarial domain adaptation network (DAN) [25], domain adaptive neural network (DANN) [26]. In each experiment, the parts before and after the arrow indicate the source and target domain, respectively. The experiments follow the evaluation criteria of the unsupervised transfer learning task, all labeled source samples and half of the unlabeled target samples are involved in the model training, while the other half of the unlabeled target samples are used for test, and each experiment is repeated ten times, and the final average is taken as the result of the experiment.

From the Table 2, we can see that the proposed method obviously improves the accuracy of fault diagnosis. Specifically, we can get the following conclusions:

1) Due to the obvious drift of distribution in different time periods, models based on transfer learning are significantly better than CNN, which indicates that compared with traditional intelligent algorithms, transfer learning can effectively handle classification tasks where data obeys different distributions, and it has a broad application prospect in the application scenarios with time-varying, multi-conditions and other complex characteristics.

2) Compared with TCA and JDA, IJDA shows a promising accuracy improvement, which may be attributed to the fact that IJDA aligns the data distribution more comprehensively. Due to the alignment of conditional probability distributions, JDA achieves

Table 2. Recognition results of methods

Method	Testing accuracy ± STD (%)		Average accuracy
	Oct → Nov	Nov → Oct	
CNN	0.422 ± 0.037	0.472 ± 0.024	0.447
TCA [13]	0.498 ± 0.043	0.475 ± 0.056	0.487
DDC [24]	0.517 ± 0.064	0.583 ± 0.088	0.550
DAN [25]	0.674 ± 0.069	0.642 ± 0.051	0.658
JDA [14]	0.793 ± 0.014	0.637 ± 0.088	0.715
DANN [26]	0.732 ± 0.032	0.745 ± 0.014	0.739
BDA [15]	0.806 ± 0.013	0.728 ± 0.025	0.767
IJDA (ours)	0.849 ± 0.062	0.764 ± 0.059	0.807

better domain adaptation than TCA. Based on JDA, IJDA analyzes the effect of the discrepancy in the prior distribution on knowledge transfer and realizes the adaptation of the prior distribution by weighted reconstruction of the source domain. This shows that in the BF ironmaking process where the occurrence of various types of faults varies significantly, considering prior distribution of data can effectively reduce the discrepancy between domains to improve the accuracy of fault diagnosis.

3) Compared with BDA, the improved accuracy of IJDA is limited, probably because BDA adjusts the weights of the marginal and conditional distributions by adjusting the hyperparameters, which improves the model's domain adaptation performance to a certain extent. IJDA doesn't set the relative weights to leverage the different importance of distributions, because there is no definite formula for calculating the relative importance of the marginal and conditional distributions. The parameter generally needs to be set artificially in advance, but it is difficult to determine the appropriate hyperparameters.

4) Compared with the three widely used deep feature-based transfer learning methods (DDC, DAN, DANN), the proposed IJDA achieved a higher recognition accuracy. This verifies that IJDA reduces the distribution difference between domains more effectively than the three widely used transfer learning methods. The possible reason is that the class prior distributions are usually caused by changes in sample selection criteria and application scenarios, considering the change of the class prior distribution is conducive to domain adaptation. In addition, under the condition of aligning only the marginal distribution, the deep transfer learning method still achieves favourable classification results, which demonstrates the effectiveness of deep learning, and combining IJDA with deep learning may be an effective way to subsequently improve the performance.

We take the experiment Oct → Nov as an example and visualize the features extracted by various methods, the results are shown in Fig. 5. In Fig. 5(a)−(d), compared with the original data distribution, the distance between the features extracted from different domains is significantly reduced. Almost all methods can distinguish normal samples from fault samples, but there is a difference in the effect of distinguishing various types of fault samples. Compared with Fig. 5(a)−(c), the clustering effects of samples belonging to same fault category from different domains have all achieved significant improvement in Fig. 5(d), which shows that reducing the discrepancy of prior distribution can effectively improve the model's domain adaptation performance.

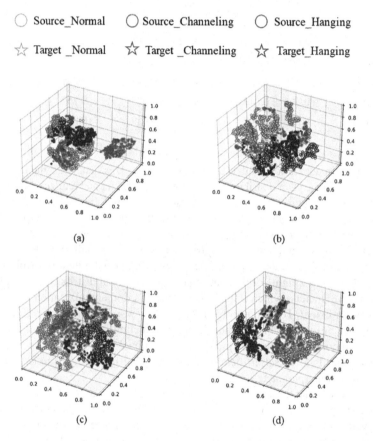

Fig. 5. t-SNE visualization of learned features. (a) TCA. (b) JDA. (c) BDA. (d) IJDA.

5   Conclusion

To address the time-varying and multi-condition characteristics of the BF production process, transfer learning is introduced into the BF fault diagnosis by extracting the domain invariant features for knowledge transfer, and gives a theoretical derivation of the discrepancy in prior distributions affecting diagnostic effects and proposes a new fault diagnosis method namely improved joint distribution adaptation (IJDA), to align the probability distributions comprehensively.

Through the weighted reconstruction of the source domain, IJDA takes the prior distribution and the joint distribution into domain adaptation, and further explores the practical application of intelligent fault diagnosis under different data distributions. A fault diagnosis model that can effectively deal with the drift of probability distribution is constructed, and the effectiveness of the method is verified on the actual BF production dataset.

However, most of the current researches require that the category spaces of the source and target domains are identical, but it is often difficult to meet this requirement in practical applications. When a novel fault not covered in the source domain appear in the target domain, the model will have classification errors. How to deal with unknown faults effectively in transfer learning is an important research direction in the future.

References

1. Zhou, P., Li, H., Shi, P., et al.: Simulation of the transfer process in the blast furnace shaft with layered burden. Appl. Therm. Eng. **95**, 296–302 (2016)
2. Saxen, H., Gao, C., Gao, Z.: Data-driven time discrete models for dynamic prediction of the hot metal silicon content in the blast furnace—a review. IEEE Trans. Industr. Inf. **9**(4), 2213–2225 (2012)
3. Zhou, P., Guo, D., Wang, H., et al.: Data-driven robust M-LS-SVR-based NARX modeling for estimation and control of molten iron quality indices in blast furnace ironmaking. IEEE Trans. Neural Netw. Learn. Syst. **29**(9), 4007–4021 (2017)
4. Zhou, P., Zhang, R., Xie, J., et al.: Data-driven monitoring and diagnosing of abnormal furnace conditions in blast furnace ironmaking: an integrated PCA-ICA method. IEEE Trans. Industr. Electron. **68**(1), 622–631 (2020)
5. Bangalore, P., Tjernberg, L.B.: An artificial neural network approach for early fault detection of gearbox bearings. IEEE Trans. Smart Grid **6**(2), 980–987 (2015)
6. Wang, H., Liu, Z., Peng, D., et al.: Feature-level attention-guided multitask CNN for fault diagnosis and working conditions identification of rolling bearing. IEEE Trans. Neural Networks Learn. Syst. **33**(9), 4757–4769 (2021)
7. Chen, X.: Research on a network fault diagnosis expert system based on machine learning. Command Inf. Syst. Technol. **2**(01), 41–44 (2011)
8. Zhang, C.: Design and realization of fault diagnosis expert system in complex information system. Command Inf. Syst. Technol. **4**(04), 27–32 (2013)
9. Zhang, C., Chen, N., Zhang, X., et al.: Server status monitoring and fault diagnosis system based on NB-IoT. Command Inf. Syst. Technol. **12**(03), 96–100 (2021)
10. Long, M., Wang, J., Cao, Y., et al.: Deep learning of transferable representation for scalable domain adaptation. IEEE Trans. Knowl. Data Eng. **28**(8), 2027–2040 (2016)
11. Lu, W., Liang, B., Cheng, Y., et al.: Deep model based domain adaptation for fault diagnosis. IEEE Trans. Industr. Electron. **64**(3), 2296–2305 (2016)
12. Duan, L., Tsang, I.W., Xu, D.: Domain transfer multiple kernel learning. IEEE Trans. Pattern Anal. Mach. Intell. **34**(3), 465–479 (2012)
13. Pan, S.J., Tsang, I.W., Kwok, J.T., et al.: Domain adaptation via transfer component analysis. IEEE Trans. Neural Networks **22**(2), 199–210 (2010)
14. Long, M., Wang, J., Ding, G., et al.: Transfer feature learning with joint distribution adaptation. In: Proceedings of the IEEE International Conference on Computer Vision, pp. 2200–2207 (2013)
15. Wang, J., Chen, Y., Hao, S., et al.L Balanced distribution adaptation for transfer learning. In: 2017 IEEE International Conference on Data Mining (ICDM), pp. 1129–1134. IEEE (2017)

16. Gao D, zhuo Zhu X, Yang C, et al. Deep weighted joint distribution adaption network for fault diagnosis of blast furnace ironmaking process. Comput. Chem. Eng. **162**, 107797 (2022)
17. Gao, D., Yang, C., Yang, B., Chen, Y., Deng, R.: Minimax entropy-based co-training for fault diagnosis of blast furnace. Chinese J. Chem. Eng. **162**, 107797 (2023)
18. Xie, J., Zhang, L., Duan, L., et al.: On cross-domain feature fusion in gearbox fault diagnosis under various operating conditions based on transfer component analysis. In: 2016 IEEE International Conference on Prognostics and Health Management (ICPHM), pp. 1–6. IEEE (2016)
19. Li, X., Zhang, W., Ding, Q., et al.: Multi-layer domain adaptation method for rolling bearing fault diagnosis. Signal Process. **157**, 180–197 (2019)
20. Wen, L., Gao, L., Li, X.: A new deep transfer learning based on sparse auto-encoder for fault diagnosis. IEEE Trans. Syst. Man, Cybern. Syst. **49**(1), 136–144 (2017)
21. Tzeng, E., Hoffman, J., Saenko, K., et al.: Adversarial discriminative domain adaptation. In: Proceedings of the IEEE Conference on Computer Vision and Pattern Recognition, pp. 7167–7176 (2017)
22. Shen, Z., Chen, X., Zhang, X., et al.: A novel intelligent gear fault diagnosis model based on EMD and multi-class TSVM. Measurement **45**(1), 30–40 (2012)
23. Jin, Y., Qin, C., Huang, Y., et al.: Actual bearing compound fault diagnosis based on active learning and decoupling attentional residual network. Measurement **173**, 108500 (2021)
24. Tzeng, E., Hoffman, J., Zhang, N., et al.: Deep domain confusion: Maximizing for domain invariance. ArXiv preprint arXiv:1412.3474 (2014)
25. Long, M., Cao, Y., Wang, J., et al.: Learning transferable features with deep adaptation networks. In: International Conference on Machine Learning, pp. 97–105. PMLR (2015)
26. Ganin, Y., Ustinova, E., Ajakan, H., et al.: Domain-adversarial training of neural networks. J. Mach. Learn. Res. **17**(1), 2096–2030 (2016)

Pretrained Language Models
and Applications

A Unified Recombination and Adversarial Framework for Machine Reading Comprehension

Jinzhi Liao, Yipeng Wu[✉], Yong Su, and Zhixiao Dong

Academy of Military Sciences, Beijing, China
927063622@qq.com

Abstract. The ability of the machine to conduct reading comprehension plays a vital role in artificial intelligence. Multi-choice machine reading comprehension requires the machine to understand the semantics better, since most of its corresponding candidates are paraphrases of the references. State-of-the-art methods concentrate on the single type question and design ad-hoc models. Nevertheless, in practical reading comprehension scenarios, given a passage, there are usually various angles to examine students. This leads to the challenges of multi-type questions and uncertain number of associated candidates. It is evident that existing methods cannot cope with these real-life scenarios since they merely focus on the single type question. To address the aforementioned challenges, we propose a unified machine reading comprehension framework via recombination and adversarial learning, which can handle these issues in a single model. First, we introduce the recombination layer to recombine candidates, which converts all types of questions into the same form. Next, to enrich the information contained by the representations of candidates, we design the encoding and the fusion layers to achieve the interaction between the passage and combined candidates. Finally, the adversarial learning mechanism is employed to add stochastic disturbance to the training procedure, which can help the model avoid the convergence problem and produce discriminative representations. Experimental results on the real-world reading comprehension datasets from the high school science textbooks validate the superiority of our method, particularly in tackling the challenges of multi-type question and uncertain number of candidates.

Keywords: Multi-choice machine reading comprehension · Unified framework · Multi-type question · Recombination of candidate

1 Introduction

Machine reading comprehension (MRC) is an important fundamental task in natural language processing that helps to further improve machine intelligence [8].

This work was supported by NSFC under grants (Nos. 72301284).

In this task, a machine needs to answer a specific question based on a full understanding of the provided reference text (sentence, paragraph or article). MRC can be further categorized into two types: extractive machine reading comprehension (EMRC) and multi-choice machine reading comprehension (MCMRC), based on whether the answer appears in the relevant document or not. EMRC is the most common type of MRC[1]. EMRC requires extracting text spans from the reference to answer a given question, and some tasks provide additional candidates [7]. Unlike the former, candidates in MCMRC are mostly paraphrases or summaries of the original text [18], so it puts more stringent requirements on the machine's comprehension ability. The research in this paper focuses on the related problems of MCMRC.

Existing studies on MCMRC can be roughly categorized into three types: the first class designs attention mechanism to achieve interaction between text, questions, and candidates, and then promote information discovery and fusion to make the model more accurate in predicting results [2,3,5,13,19,26,31,32]. The second class is based on pre-trained language models, which are pre-trained on large corpus in the first stage, and fine-tuned in a specific MCMRC task downstream in the second stage [14,15,26,28]. Besides the two categories mentioned above, technical tools such as cognitive sciences [22], evidence sentence filtering [25], and graph neural networks [10] have been proposed into MCMRC to achieve better results.

Notice that in real-life reading comprehension scenarios, the same context is usually examined from different perspectives, which leads to a possible mix of question types, such as multiple-choice, judgment and matching. The diversity of question types makes uncertain number of candidates, which may range from two for positive and negative judgments, to four traditional four-choice questions, to a variable number of candidates for matching questions. For example, the reading comprehension dataset TQA [11], derived from science textbooks for middle school students, contains 1,076 reference texts with 26,260 questions, with an average of 24 questions per text. In order to fully examine students' mastery of the text, the types of post-text questions involve multiple dimensions, such as judgment, multiple choice, and matching questions, and are interspersed with questions without any clear segmentation in their distribution.

Therefore, how to make the model adaptive for solving mixed-type reading comprehension tasks remains a challenging problem. Previous methods need to design the combined input pattern of text, questions, and candidates based on the question type when encoding, e.g., multiple-choice questions need to concatenate all of them as inputs, whereas judgment questions only need to match text and questions. In addition, the output form of the classifier needs to be designed based on the number of candidates, when making the final probability prediction. Although these problems can be mitigated to some extent by introducing additional type discriminators to determine the problem type and then

---

[1] Multiple-choice reading comprehension refers primarily to the provision of candidates in the form of each question, with specific question types including, but not limited to, judgmental, multiple-choice, and matching questions.

classify the processing, the model framework under this design needs to be customized and constructed according to the problem type as well as the number of candidates. This fails to cope with dynamically changing real-world scenarios. Therefore, real scenario-driven hybrid reading comprehension tasks are in dire need of specialized further research.

To this end, this paper investigates a unified modeling framework for hybrid machine reading comprehension and proposes a Recombination Adversarial Model (RAM) to cope with reading comprehension scenarios with multiple types of questions and uncertain number of candidates. To address the mentioned problem, RAM uniformly transforms all the problems into single-choice decisions, and solves multiple-choice and matching by determining the correctness of each option.

Specifically, RAM first splits the candidates and combines them with the questions one by one to form a questionnaire. Subsequently, the reference text is combined with the newly generated candidates, thus transforming different types of questions into judgment form to predict the probability of their correctness. This transformation overcomes the difficulty of existing research in not being able to perform reading comprehension of multiple types of questions in a uniform manner. In order to further enrich the information capacity in the candidates, RAM incorporates the results of the reference text's attentional interactions with the candidates in the vector representation space after completing the encoding, which makes the judgment of the probability of establishment more reliable. In addition, in this framework, the inclusion of the same component in the new candidates under the given question may make the content from original candidates to be smoothed during the encoding process. This in turn leads to the problem of convergence of the vector representations of the new candidates. For this reason, we propose to use an adversarial learning approach in the training phase to expand the variability of the representations by randomly perturbing and forcing them to pay more attention to the different parts in the new candidates during the learning process. Finally, experiments on public datasets prove RAM's superior performance.

Briefly, the main contributions of this paper include the following three aspects.

- We identify the deficiencies in the traditional MCMRC task setting, and propose a new reading comprehension task to approach the real-word scenarios, containing multiple types of questions and uncertain number of candidates;
- A model RAM is designed to solve the above problems in a unified way, including a recombination layer to unify different types of questions, an encoding layer to achieve semantic representation of long text, an attention fusion layer to enrich the information of candidates, an adversarial training module to expand the variability of the semantic representation, and a prediction layer;
- The performance of RAM is evaluated using a new dataset, TTQA, which is different from the traditional task and possesses the above two characteristics.

2   Related Work

This section focuses on existing models for solving MCMRC, which can be categorized into three categories based on the design ideas: attention mechanism based, pre-trained language model based, and other models.

2.1   Attention Mechanism Based Methods

The traditional studies selects the optimal answer by collecting and summarizing evidence (text spans) from the context relevant to the question, followed by matching the evidence with candidates [2,13]. Zhu et al. argue that this simple matching retrieval model does not fully utilize the information in the text [32]. Thus, a hierarchical neural network-based attention streaming framework is designed to fully utilize the candidates to represent word-level and sentence-level interactions between the reference text, the question, and the candidates. Wang et al. regard the question and candidate as two sequences, and calculate attention weighted representations based on each character in the reference text [26]. The reference text, questions and candidates are first encoded into word representations enhanced by additional POS tags and matching features [3]. Then the candidate representations are enriched by combining the reference text and question. A convolutional neural network is further applied to dynamically extract spatial correlation information between neighboring regions under different window sizes to form spatial attention. When obtaining the comprehensive semantics of contexts and questions, on the basis of four commonly used attentions, namely, splicing, bilinear, dot product, and difference set, the attentions of query2context and context2query are fused in two directions to strengthen the key information of the reference and questions, and weaken the irrelevant information [5]. Comparison networks explicitly compare candidates at the character level, where the candidates are first encoded as representations via BERT [19]. Then, for each candidate, it is compared one by one with other candidates at the word level using an attention based mechanism in embedding space to identify their relevance. Literature. Zhang et al. propose bicollinear matching network using BERT as an encoder, which bi-directionally merges all pairwise relations between the <Reference Text, Question, Candidate> triplet [26], and utilize a gating mechanism to fuse representations from both directions. In addition, two reading strategies commonly used by humans are integrated. One is text-sentence selection, which helps extract evidence from the reference text and then matches the evidence with candidates. The other is candidate interaction, which encodes comparison information into each candidate.

These approaches focus on designing attention mechanism to reveal associations between the reference text, the question, and the candidates. However, different types of questions have different characteristics that require targeted design, for example, in judgment questions it is not necessary to design the interaction of the candidate ("right" or "wrong") with the reference text and the question.

2.2   Pre-trained Language Model Based Methods

As mentioned above, with the emergence of BERT, the development of natural language processing moves into the era of pre-trained language models. In addition to serving as the encoding module of the overall model, the pre-trained language model can also be directly fine-tuned to the representation applied to the downstream tasks of MCMRC.

Devlin et al. propose a self-encoding language model BERT [4]. The overall framework is based on a 12-layer transformer encoder, and two self-supervised tasks of random mask and predicting the corresponding positional characters and sentence continuity prediction are designed to pre-train the model on a general-purpose corpus. Finally, the probability of each candidate is predicted by a classifier with the same number of candidates. Yang et al. argue that the mask mechanism in BERT leads to non-uniform data inputs in both training and fine-tuning phases [28]. Thus, they discard the mask mechanism and propose a two-stream self-attention mechanism, namely XLNET, to combine the strengths of both auto-encoding and auto-regressive structure. Inside the transformer, from the above and below words of a selected word, $n - 1$ are randomly selected and put into the above position of that word, hiding the inputs of other words through an attention mask. RoBERTa improves BERT in three main ways: 1) the sentence continuity prediction task is removed after experimental validation; 2) a dynamic MASK scheme is proposed, where sentence input to the model is followed by a random MASK; and 3) the size of the batch-size for each round of training was enlarged [15]. ALBERT aims to make the model lighter, faster training and better results [14], and a matrix decomposition maps the one-hot vectors to the low-dimensional space first. Then to the hidden layer, ALBERT shares parameters among all encoding layers, and finally a self-supervised task is introduced based on the associations of the topics to predict whether the two sentences switched their order.

Although these methods have achieved good results on the MCMRCs, fine-tuning requires specific input and output forms according to the given downstream task, which makes it impossible to directly use pre-trained language models in scenarios with variable options.

3   Methods

This section first gives a definition of the MCMRC task, followed by details of the proposed model and its training and prediction process.

Definition 1 Mixed-choice reading comprehension: The MCMRC task can be represented as providing the $<P, Q, A>$ triplet, where P denotes the reference text, which can be in the form of a sentence, paragraph, or entire article; Q denotes the natural language form of the question, and there may be more than one question under the same reference text, with a variety of question types; $A = \{a^1, a^2, ..., a^n\}$ denotes the set of candidates corresponding to a particular question; and n denotes the number of candidates, of which there is and is not a single correct answer. There is only one correct answer. The machine is required to read and understand the question based on the reference text and finally select the correct result from the candidates.

The model consists of a recombination layer, an encoding layer, a fusion layer, an adversarial training module, and a prediction layer. The framework is shown in Fig. 1.

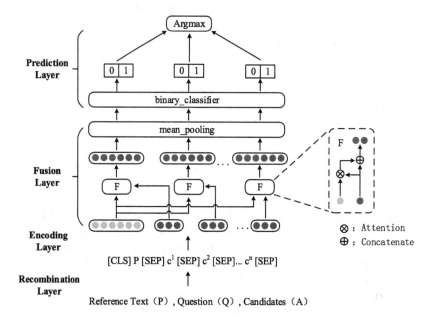

Fig. 1. A sketch of the proposed framework.

3.1   Recombination Layer

In existing studies, the data input and probability prediction classifier of the model need to be customized according to the type of question and the number of candidates. Specifically for judgment questions, only the text and the question need to be input, followed by a binary classification judgment based on the resulting text vector. For multiple-choice questions, all the texts might be concatenated as inputs after combining the reference text, the question, and the candidates, in a specific way through the internal interactions of the model.

For making the model not change with the specific type of the given question and the certain number of corresponding candidates, RAM first converts all questions uniformly into single-choice decision form. For any question, the candidates are split and concatenated to the question to build a new candidate with the same number of original candidates, which is denoted as:

$$C = \{c^1, c^2, ..., c^n\} = \{Q + a^1, Q + a^2, ..., Q + a^n\}. \tag{1}$$

where C denotes the set of recombined candidates. For the sake of concise description, "candidates" are referred to the "recombined candidates" in the following parts.

Subsequently, the reference text P is combined with the candidates as background knowledge for the machine to determine whether the factual statements in the candidates are valid, in the following combination form:

$$P, c^1, c^2, ..., c^n.$$

The reason for concatenation is that RAM should not only consider the information contained in the reference text P when encoding candidates, but also need to pay attention to the key information in other candidates. This will help the model to find out the relationship between different candidates to make a more reasonable prediction.

After completing the internal interaction of the model, distinguishing from the existing work, RAM will make the judgment of whether the binary classification holds for each candidate individually. The details of which will be elaborated in Sect. 3.5.

3.2   Encoding Layer

Neural networks cannot directly process discrete natural language symbolic information, and thus need to map word vectors to natural language through a encoding layer. We first use the pre-trained language model RoBERTa [15] as a disambiguator for text disambiguation and word list mapping, the specific input form is as follows:

$$[CLS]P[SEP]c^1[SEP]c^2[SEP]...[SEP]c^n[SEP],$$

where $[CLS]$ denotes the special character in RoBERTa that marks the starting position of the input text, and $[SEP]$ denotes the spacing character between different texts in RoBERTa.

In the reading comprehension of real scenarios, there is the phenomenon that the length of reference texts are generally long. Following the BERT setting, RoBERTa applies self-attention mechanism where each character is encoded with all the characters in the input. However, there is an upper length constraint of 512 characters when encoding word vectors. To overcome this problem, we adopt Longformer [1], which is capable of handling long text, as the encoding mechanism. Longformer improves the traditional self-attention mechanism, where each character only computes local attention for other characters near a fixed window size and raises the upper limit of the length of encoded text to 4096. In addition, BigBird [30] also achieves to reduce the complexity in BERT to linear by designing and combining random attention, window attention, and global attention, which in turn expands the upper input limit to 4096. In the paper, we will test and analyze the two long sequence encoding mechanisms will be tested and analyzed in Sect. 4.

At this point, the word vector representations of the reference text and the candidates are available:

$$\mathbf{E} = (\mathbf{e}^1, \mathbf{e}^2, ..., \mathbf{e}^m) \in R^{m \times d},$$

where $\mathbf{E}$ denotes the word vector encoding of the input text sequence, $\mathbf{e}^i$ denotes the word vector of the ith character in the sequence, R denotes the real number space, m denotes the length of the text, and d denotes the dimension size.

3.3 Fusion Layer

After encoding layer, we acquire the reference text representation $\mathbf{E}_p \in R^{x \times d}$ and the candidate representation $\mathbf{E}_c^j \in R^{y^j \times d}$, where x denotes the length of the reference text and y^j denotes the length of the jth candidate.

For further capturing the association relationship between candidates and reference texts, we design an attention mechanism between texts and candidates:

$$\mathbf{a} = tanh(\mathbf{E}_p \mathbf{W}_{pc} \mathbf{E}_c^j + \mathbf{b}_{pc}), \tag{2}$$

$$\mathbf{s} = softmax(\mathbf{a}), \tag{3}$$

$$\mathbf{E}_{cp}^j = \mathbf{s} \times \mathbf{E}_p, \tag{4}$$

where $tanh$ denotes the nonlinear activation function to achieve nonlinear mapping, $\mathbf{W}_{pc}$ denotes the learnable weight matrix, $\mathbf{b}_{pc}$ denotes the bias term, and $softmax$ implements the values within the matrix normalized on $[0, 1]$. The final candidate $\mathbf{c}^j$ is obtained as an attention vector representation of the reference text $\mathbf{E}_{cp}^j$.

Subsequently, we use $mean\_pooling$ to obtain the mean vector representation of each candidate, i.e.:

$$\mathbf{C}^j = mean\_pooling(\mathbf{E}_c^j) = \frac{1}{|y^j|} sum(\mathbf{E}_c^j), \tag{5}$$

where $| \cdot ||$ denotes the number of specific objects and sum denotes the linear sum. The candidate average vector representation $\mathbf{C}^j \in R^d$ will be used for information fusion as well as final probabilistic prediction. After obtaining the attention representation, we apply the highway network mechanism [6] to realize the fusion of information as follows:

$$\widehat{\mathbf{C}}_p^j = relu(\mathbf{W}_r[\mathbf{C}^j; \mathbf{C}_p^j; \mathbf{C}^j - \mathbf{C}_p^j; \mathbf{C}^j \circ \mathbf{C}_p^j]), \tag{6}$$

$$\mathbf{G} = sigmoid(\mathbf{W}_g[\mathbf{C}^j; \mathbf{C}_p^j; \mathbf{C}^j - \mathbf{C}_p^j; \mathbf{C}^j \circ \mathbf{C}_p^j]), \tag{7}$$

$$\mathbf{O}^j = \mathbf{g} \circ \widehat{\mathbf{C}}_p^j + (1 - \mathbf{g}) \circ \mathbf{C}^j, \tag{8}$$

where $\mathbf{W}_r$ and $\mathbf{W}_g$ denote the learnable weight matrices, $[;]$ denotes the vectors of the series input, $\circ$ denotes the multiplication of the corresponding positional elements of the two matrices, and $relu$ denotes the nonlinear activation function.

$\mathbf{O}^j$ denotes the linear interpolation of the input vectors with the intermediate vector $\widehat{\mathbf{C}}_p^j$, and $\mathbf{g}$ denotes the gating threshold to control the adjustment of the weights of the components in the linear interpolation.

The final representation of the candidate obtained after the fusion layer can be computed by linear splicing $\mathbf{M}^j \in R^{2d}$:

$$\mathbf{M}^j = [\mathbf{E}_c^j; \mathbf{O}^j].$$

3.4 Adversarial Learning

Although the attention fusion mechanism in Sect. 3.3 enables the RAM to partially distinguish the key information in the candidates, it can be seen from Eq. (1) that the question text accounts for a large portion of the recombined result. This may cause the model to learn the candidate representation due to too many identical components between different candidates smoothing the original candidate information. The final representation obtained from learning has a high degree of similarity, which in turn affects the prediction results.

Adversarial learning aims to improve the model's ability to recognize original samples and adversarial samples. Adversarial samples are samples generated by adding small random perturbations to the input original samples [23]. However, adversarial perturbation in text classification does not act on natural language because discrete symbolic inputs cannot satisfy the continuity requirement for perturbation insertion. Thus, we act on continuous word vector representations [16].

Therefore, we draw on the idea of adversarial learning in training, and actively introduce random perturbations in training to increase the data volatility during model training. This will force the model to focus on the difference between different candidate representations. In adversarial training, $\mathbf{E}$ is used to denote the input, θ denotes the parameters of the model, and adversarial training adds the following loss to the loss function of the original classifier:

$$\mathbf{r}_{adv} = \arg\min_{\|r\| \leq \varepsilon} \mathcal{L}(\mathbf{E} + \mathbf{r}, \theta), \tag{9}$$

where $\mathbf{r}_{adv}$ denotes the final input random perturbation, $\mathbf{r}$ denotes the random perturbation, $\|\cdot\|$ denotes the second paradigm, ε denotes the hyper-parameters, and $\mathcal{L}$ denotes the loss function.

RAM employs the linear approximation [30] to realize the above equation in the neural network as follows:

$$\mathbf{r}_{adv} = -\varepsilon g / \|g\|, \tag{10}$$

$$g = \nabla_E \mathcal{L}(f_\theta(\mathbf{E}), y), \tag{11}$$

where g denotes the gradient of the loss function $\mathcal{L}$ over the input word vector denoted $\mathbf{E}$, ∇_E denotes the gradient operation, f denotes the model operation, and y denotes the sample labeling.

3.5   Model Training and Prediction

After being processed by the above procedure, the model treats each candidate as a separate sample and makes a probabilistic determination. Through this operation, RAM achieves uniform prediction for different types of questions with uncertain numbers of candidates. Specifically, the model concludes with a probabilistic prediction of the candidate between [0, 1] by means of a binary classifier:

$$\mathbf{P} = sigmoid(f_p(\mathbf{M})), \tag{12}$$

where $\mathbf{P}$ denotes the probabilistic output of candidates, is used to smooth the neural network output to between [0, 1], and f_p denotes a binary fully connected prediction network with output dimension 1.

During training, unlike the multi-categorical cross entropy loss calculation in traditional models, RAM predicts the probability of each candidate and calculates the loss value one by one. The operation follows the binary cross entropy loss function (BCE). The mathematical publicity is:

$$\mathcal{L}_p(\mathbf{P}, \mathbf{L}) = \frac{1}{|N|} \sum_{k \in N} BCE(p^k, l^k), \tag{13}$$

where $\mathcal{L}_p$ denotes the loss value calculated by BCE, $\mathbf{L}$ denotes the set of true labels, k denotes the kth candidate, N denotes the set of all candidates in the current batch_size, and $|\cdot|$ denotes the number of specific objects.

Similar to the regular loss value computation process, the training process of adversarial learning only requires the addition of a random perturbation $\mathbf{r}_{adv}$ to the vector input, which is operated as follows:

$$\mathbf{P}_{adv} = sigmoid(f_p(\mathbf{C} + \mathbf{r}_{adv})), \tag{14}$$

$$L_{adv}(\mathbf{P}_{adv}, \mathbf{L}) = \frac{1}{|N|} \sum_{k \in N} BCE(p^k_{adv}, l^k). \tag{15}$$

Combining the two, the final loss function for RAM training is:

$$\mathcal{L} = \mathcal{L}_p + \mathcal{L}_{adv}. \tag{16}$$

In testing, the prediction result $\mathbf{P}$ in Eq. 12 is directly used as the probabilistic prediction of the candidates, and the candidate with the largest probability value is selected as the final prediction.

4   Experiment

This section first describes the details of the experimental setup such as dataset, model, and parameters designed in the experiments, followed by testing the overall effectiveness of RAM on TTQA, analyzing the results for different types of questions and uncertain number of candidates, followed by ablation experiments and case studies.

Table 1. Table on statistics of MCMRC datasets. "#" denotes the number, "–" represents that the corresponding dataset does not exist in this category of samples, and T/F denotes the number of judgment question.

Datasets	# of context	# of question	# of choice	Context length	Question length	Choice length	T/F rate
ReCLor [29]	6,138	6,138	4	73.6	17.0	23.4	–
DREAM [21]	6,444	10,197	3	85.9	8.6	5.3	–
RACE [13]	27,933	97,687	4	321.9	10.0	5.3	–
MCTest [26]	660	2,640	4	210.1	7.8	3.4	–
MultiRC [12]	871	9,872	–	263.1	10.9	5.4	27.6%
TTQA	1,073	13,049	2/4/7	743.0	9.8	2.6	41.4%

4.1   Experimental Setup

Data Setup. In order to reflect the characteristics of multiple types of questions and uncertain number of candidates in real reading comprehension scenarios, the experiment uses the text-only QA dataset of TQA (referred as TQA² from which only relevant data involving the text QA part are extracted, and the pictures and noise data involved in the text are eliminated. Finally, 1,073 documents and 13,049 questions and corresponding candidates are acquired, and the specific statistics of the data features are shown in Table 1. Following the original training set/validation set/test set data division in TQA, 663 documents are similarly used for training, 200 documents for validation, and 210 documents for testing in TTQA. Compared to the dataset of traditional MCMRC, two types of judgment questions and multiple-choice questions are included in TTQA, and there exist three numbers (2, 4, and 7) of candidates, and the average length of the text is longer, and the ratio of the average length of the questions to the average length of the candidates is higher.

Model Setup. Since this type of task is the first one proposed in this paper, it is difficult for the existing methods to solve the related problems in TTQA with a unified model. Thus, we experimentally analyze the RAM with random selection as the baseline model and 3 different settings.

- Random selection (RANDOM). Use a random function to randomly generate predictions of outcomes for different questions;
- RAM (Bi-LSTM [9]). Bi-LSTM is utilized to replace the encoding layer in the model and the rest of the model is run as modeled;

---

² TQA is a multimodal textbook question dataset, which contains 13,693 text-only questions and 12,567 image-text questions. To fully evaluate the effectiveness of the model, this paper uses the plain text question answering part of TQA as the experimental data set, referred to as TTQA. Dataset link: https://allenai.org/data/tqa.

- RAM (BigBird [30]). Big Bird is used as a word vector encoder in the encoding layer, and the rest of the process runs according to the model;
- RAM (Longformer [1]). Longformer is used as a word vector encoder in the encoding layer, and the rest of the process runs according to the model.

Table 2. Table on overall results. "All" denotes the total results for all questions in TTQA.

Method	All (%)
Random	25.04
RAM (Bi-LSTM)	42.30
RAM (BigBird)	51.84
RAM (Longformer)	69.56

Parameter Setup. RoBERTa, BigBird and Longformer used in this paper all adopt the versions encapsulated in the official open-source transformers [27] package from huggingface. In Bi-LSTM, BigBird and Longformer, the maximum text length is set to 2500.

- In Bi-LSTM, batch_size=64, hidden_dim=100, and GoLve [17] is used as the initial word vector.
- In BigBird, batch_size=9, word vector dimension d=768, block_size=64, and the number of random attention blocks is num_random_blocks=3.
- In BigBird Longformer, batch_size=9, attention window size is 256, and the candidate text sequence is selected as the global attention object.

Hyper-parameters in Adversarial Learning. The model testing environment is a 3*Tesla V100 32G memory server. The experiment uses precision as the evaluation index, which is the proportion of correct predictions among all the questions.

4.2 Overall Results

As shown in Table 2, in general, the results of RAM are not satisfactory. In the best setting (Longformer), RAM has done 69.56% of the questions correctly, and there is still a large room for improvement compared with the top students in humans. In addition, it can be seen from the table that different encoding structures have a great impact on the results, and Bi-LSTM has a poor effect in long texts because it is difficult to capture the context information in long sequences [24]. The reason why the effect of Longformer exceeds that of Big Bird17.72% may be that the setting of sliding window expands the boundary of attention, so that RAM learns more semantic associations during training. At the same time, setting the candidate as the object of global attention is more helpful to model the interaction between the candidate and the reference text.

In order to investigate the performance of RAM in solving multi-type questions with uncertain numbers of candidates, the dataset is also refined and split, and experiments are carried out on different settings. The detailed analysis will be given below.

4.3 Multi-type Problem Analysis

Since the matching questions are also to select the correct one from multiple choices, we also include them in multiple choice questions to be analyzed uniformly, and the final results are shown in Table 3.

Table 3. Table on multiple types of questions results. T/F denotes judgment questions (true or false), and MC denotes multiple choice questions.

Method	T/F (%)	MC (%)
random	35.09	19.00
RAM (Bi-LSTM)	58.22	32.72
RAM (Big Bird)	63.93	47.10
RAM (Longformer)	74.56	66.56

In general, the accuracy of the judgment questions is higher than that of the multiple choice questions. However, compared with the correct rate of judgment questions in random selection is twice that of multiple choice questions, the gap between the two sides in RAM is significantly reduced. This proves that the structure proposed in this paper is effective in dealing with multi-type questions. Besides, in addition to the difference in the number of candidates (see Sect. 4.4 for a detailed analysis), another possible reason is that RAM's framework is essentially a structure that converts MCMRC into single-choice true or false decisions. Thus, it is naturally suitable for solving judgment problems.

4.4 Analysis of Different Numbers of Candidates

Since there are no double choice questions in the multiple choice questions of TTQA, the results with the number of candidates being 2 are quoted from the judgment question column, and the results are shown in Table 4.

As shown in the table, with the increase of the number of candidates, the accuracy of model prediction decreases accordingly, which is in line with the real situation of human beings in reading comprehension tests. The increase of the number often means the increase of interference items, which will further affect human judgment. However, for RAM, increasing the number of candidates means that it is more difficult for the model to learn the differences between different candidate representations.

Table 4. Table on different numbers of choices results.

Method	#2 (%)	#4 (%)	#7 (%)
random	35.09	16.16	2.84
RAM (Bi-LSTM)	58.22	29.22	3.50
RAM (Big Bird)	63.93	38.26	8.84
RAM (Longformer)	74.56	50.40	16.16

Specifically, the model tends to distinguish the positions of positive and negative samples in the vector space during learning. The candidate length (2.6) in TTQA is short compared with the average length of the question (9.8), which easily leads to a large overlap part of the results generated by Eq. 1. At this time, the increase of the number of candidates means that the number of training negative samples increases, and the overlap degree between these negative samples with the same label is high, making their positions in the vector space closer. This will lead to the convergence of the representation of different candidates, and further increases the difficulty of the model to distinguish the key information in different candidates. To solve this problem, this paper designs two modules, attention fusion and adversarial learning.

5   Conclusion

Aiming at the problem that there are multiple types of questions and uncertain number of candidates in multi-choice reading comprehension, we design a unified single-choice decision model RAM, converting the multi-choice problem into the true or false judgment of candidate one by one. In addition, in order to improve RAM's ability to distinguish between different candidates, we propose two novel modules, i.e., fusion layer and adversarial learning. Experiments demonstrate the effectiveness of RAM in solving the above problems through a unified framework, as well as the reasonableness of the design of different components.

Follow-up work will consider how research can incorporate external common-sense knowledge, such as knowledge graphs, to enrich the contextual information when the model learns to train, and thus make better predictions [20].

References

1. Beltagy, I., Peters, M.E., Cohan, A.: LongFormer: the long-document transformer. CoRR abs/2004.05150 (2020)
2. Chen, D., Bolton, J., Manning, C.D.: A thorough examination of the CNN/daily mail reading comprehension task. In: ACL (2016)
3. Chen, Z., Cui, Y., Ma, W., Wang, S., Hu, G.: Convolutional spatial attention model for reading comprehension with multiple-choice questions. In: AAAI, pp. 6276–6283 (2019)

4. Devlin, J., Chang, M., Lee, K., Toutanova, K.: BERT: pre-training of deep bidirectional transformers for language understanding. In: NAACL-HLT, pp. 4171–4186 (2019)
5. Duan, L., Gao, J., Li, A.: A study on solution strategy of option-problems in machine reading comprehension. J. Chin. Inf. Process. **33**(10), 81–89 (2019)
6. Greff, K., Srivastava, R.K., Schmidhuber, J.: Highway and residual networks learn unrolled iterative estimation. In: ICLR (2017)
7. Gu, Y., Gui, X., Li, D., Shen, Y., Liao, D.: Survey of machine reading comprehension based on neural network. J. Softw. **31**(7), 2095–2126 (2020)
8. Hermann, K.M., et al.: Teaching machines to read and comprehend. In: NeurIPS, pp. 1693–1701 (2015)
9. Hochreiter, S., Schmidhuber, J.: Long short-term memory. Neural Comput. **9**(8), 1735–1780 (1997)
10. Huang, Y., Fang, M., Cao, Y., Wang, L., Liang, X.: DAGN: discourse-aware graph network for logical reasoning. In: NAACL-HLT, pp. 5848–5855 (2021)
11. Kembhavi, A., Seo, M.J., Schwenk, D., Choi, J., Farhadi, A., Hajishirzi, H.: Are you smarter than a sixth grader? Textbook question answering for multimodal machine comprehension. In: CVPR, pp. 5376–5384 (2017)
12. Khashabi, D., Chaturvedi, S., Roth, M., Upadhyay, S., Roth, D.: Looking beyond the surface: a challenge set for reading comprehension over multiple sentences. In: NAACL-HLT, pp. 252–262 (2018)
13. Lai, G., Xie, Q., Liu, H., Yang, Y., Hovy, E.H.: RACE: large-scale reading comprehension dataset from examinations. In: EMNLP, pp. 785–794 (2017)
14. Lan, Z., Chen, M., Goodman, S., Gimpel, K., Sharma, P., Soricut, R.: ALBERT: a lite BERT for self-supervised learning of language representations. In: ICLR (2020)
15. Liu, Y., et al.: RoBERTa: a robustly optimized BERT pretraining approach. CoRR abs/1907.11692 (2019)
16. Miyato, T., Dai, A.M., Goodfellow, I.J.: Adversarial training methods for semi-supervised text classification. In: ICLR (2017)
17. Pennington, J., Socher, R., Manning, C.D.: Glove: global vectors for word representation. In: EMNLP, pp. 1532–1543 (2014)
18. Rajpurkar, P., Zhang, J., Lopyrev, K., Liang, P.: Squad: 100, 000+ questions for machine comprehension of text. In: EMNLP, pp. 2383–2392 (2016)
19. Ran, Q., Li, P., Hu, W., Zhou, J.: Option comparison network for multiple-choice reading comprehension. CoRR abs/1903.03033 (2019)
20. Sun, K., Yu, D., Chen, J., Yu, D., Cardie, C.: Improving machine reading comprehension with contextualized commonsense knowledge. In: ACL, pp. 8736–8747 (2022)
21. Sun, K., Yu, D., Chen, J., Yu, D., Choi, Y., Cardie, C.: DREAM: a challenge dataset and models for dialogue-based reading comprehension. Trans. Assoc. Comput. Linguistics **7**, 217–231 (2019)
22. Sun, K., Yu, D., Yu, D., Cardie, C.: Improving machine reading comprehension with general reading strategies. In: NAACL-HLT, pp. 2633–2643 (2019)
23. Szegedy, C., et al.: Going deeper with convolutions. In: CVPR, pp. 1–9 (2015)
24. Vaswani, A., et al.: Attention is all you need. In: NeurIPS, pp. 5998–6008 (2017)
25. Wang, H., et al.: Evidence sentence extraction for machine reading comprehension. In: CoNLL, pp. 696–707 (2019)
26. Wang, S., Yu, M., Jiang, J., Chang, S.: A co-matching model for multi-choice reading comprehension. In: ACL, pp. 746–751 (2018)
27. Wolf, T., et al.: Transformers: state-of-the-art natural language processing, In: EMNLP, pp. 38–45 (2020)

28. Yang, Z., Dai, Z., Yang, Y., Carbonell, J.G., Salakhutdinov, R., Le, Q.V.: XLNet: generalized autoregressive pretraining for language understanding. In: NeurIPS, pp. 5754–5764 (2019)
29. Yu, W., Jiang, Z., Dong, Y., Feng, J.: ReClor: a reading comprehension dataset requiring logical reasoning. In: ICLR (2020)
30. Zaheer, M., et al.: Big bird: transformers for longer sequences. In: NeurIPS (2020)
31. Zhang, S., Zhao, H., Wu, Y., Zhang, Z., Zhou, X., Zhou, X.: DCMN+: dual co-matching network for multi-choice reading comprehension. In: AAAI, pp. 9563–9570 (2020)
32. Zhu, H., Wei, F., Qin, B., Liu, T.: Hierarchical attention flow for multiple-choice reading comprehension. In: AAAI, pp. 6077–6085 (2018)

Research on Data Mining Methods in the Field of Quality Problem Analysis Based on BERT Model

Zihuan Ding[✉] and Guangyan Zhao

Beihang University, Beijing 100191, China
dingzihuan@buaa.edu.cn

Abstract. In the current quality problem analysis work, there are problems such as large amount of data with scattered distribution, isolated data and difficult machine understanding. Most of the current data mining work in the field is based on deep learning models, which is difficult to be integrated into the characteristics of the data in the field. Also, there are still some deficiencies in its accuracy rate and training speed. Therefore, this paper carries out the research of data mining methods in the field of quality problem analysis and incorporates the characteristics of data in the field on the basis of the existing model construction research. Focusing on the named entity recognition task and the relationship extraction task, the data are preprocessed by sequence annotation method to form the data sets of the two tasks. For the first task, a BERT-based recognition method is adopted, where the input is processed by word-level segmentation and the meaning features are learned. For the second task, a method also based on the BERT model is used. The models trained by the two tasks are used to achieve data mining work in the field of quality problem analysis. Comparative analysis by examples shows that the training results based on BERT model are better than those based on LSTM model in both tasks.

Keywords: Quality Issues · Data Mining · Named Entity Recognition · Relation Extraction

1 Introduction

In the era of big data, units at all levels generate a large amount of data, information and expert knowledge in all aspects related to the general quality characteristics of equipment, such as equipment development, testing, production and maintenance. However, in the current equipment quality problem analysis work, there are problems such as large amount of data with scattered distribution, data stored in the management system without association, data mostly described in the form of natural language which is difficult to be understood by the machine and so on. The valuable information behind the data cannot be effectively integrated at the semantic level. Research on data mining methods in the field of quality problem analysis is a major direction to solve these problems.

© The Author(s), under exclusive license to Springer Nature Singapore Pte Ltd. 2024
Y. Tan and Y. Shi (Eds.): DMBD 2023, CCIS 2017, pp. 111–123, 2024.
https://doi.org/10.1007/978-981-97-0837-6_8

One of the major tasks in data mining is the named entity recognition task, which is currently biased towards the study of how to achieve the ability to automatically identify and extract potential target entities from a raw corpus. The two main research hotspots focus on the study of text vectorisation representation algorithms and the study of how to automatically and quickly complete the task based on deep learning algorithms and other advanced intelligent technologies. At the same time, research on the relationship extraction task is also needed to extract potential links between entity pairs from the original corpus. The hot research directions are relation extraction models based on attention mechanism [1, 2], models based on graph convolutional networks [3, 4], models based on adversarial machine learning [5], models based on deep residual networks [6], models based on migration learning [7–9] and so on. Most of the current data mining work in the field of quality problem analysis is based on deep learning models, which is difficult to be integrated into the characteristics of the data in the field. Also, there are still some deficiencies in its accuracy rate and training speed.

Therefore, this paper carries out the research on these problems to incorporate the characteristics of the field into the training model and improve the accuracy of model. Focusing on the named entity recognition task and relationship extraction task in the field of quality problem analysis, the data in the field are preprocessed through sequence annotation methods to form the data sets for the two tasks. The named entity recognition method and relationship extraction method based on BERT model are adopted to integrate the data characteristics of the quality problem analysis domain into the model construction research which can improve the accuracy and training speed of the data mining work. Finally, an example is used to compare the training results of BERT-based model and LSTM-based model.

2   Related Work

2.1   Data Related to Quality Problem Analysis

Overall, the data related to quality problem are closely related to the product with faults as the core, covering multiple aspects of fault discovery, problem analysis, problem solving and design improvement, including multiple descriptions of fault phenomena, fault causes, occurrence locations, fault mechanisms, improvement programs, maintenance measures and so on, which are carried out throughout many aspects of the equipment life cycle.

Direct and potential relationships between data related to quality problem include as follows:

(1) In the description of the basic information of the product, data related to quality problem usually include product name, model number and other attributes, describing the faulty parts which have problems.
(2) In the description of the basic information about the failure, data related to quality problem usually contain attributes such as failure phenomena and causes, describing the failure problem that occurred.
(3) In the description of the corrective action/repair task, data related to quality problem usually include a description of the fault repair method, describing the solution to the faulty issue.

(4) Overall, data related to quality problem are connected with the basic descriptive information about the faults, which is reflected in the descriptions of the fault phenomena and failure mode attributes used within different phases and tasks.

2.2 BERT Model

The pre-trained language model BERT is varied from the Transformer model. Its neural network structure uses the Encoder structure of Transformer, as shown in Fig. 1, which is able to learn the contextual features of the input sequences based on the attention mechanism. It is also suitable for completing the sequence labelling task.

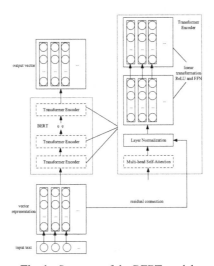

Fig. 1. Structure of the BERT model

The input to the model is a sequence of initial word vector representations corresponding to the original text, which is learnt through stacked Multi-Head Self-Attention layers to obtain a feature vector Z that hides the feature information of the input sequence. The feature vector Z is input to FFN (Feed Forward Neural Network) and output to the neural network after going through the ReLU activation function layer and the linear activation function layer.

$$ReLU = \max(0, ZW + b) \tag{1}$$

$$FFN = \max(ZW_1 + b_1)W_2 + b_2 \tag{2}$$

This output is a sequence of word vector representations corresponding to the original text of higher quality obtained after BERT model learning.

The application of the BERT model consists of two parts: pre-training and fine-tuning. Firstly, the model is trained to learn the vector representation of words using unsupervised learning on a large-scale corpus. After that, the pre-trained language model is plugged into the task. A small number of neural network layers for solving the task are added to the model. And the model is trained using supervised learning on a new corpus of quality problem analysis for the specified task as shown in Fig. 2.

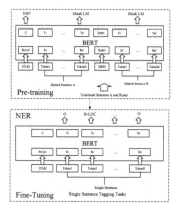

Fig. 2. Training approach of BERT model applied to downstream tasks

3 Method

3.1 Pre-processing of Data

The pre-processing of the raw data involves the construction of the dataset for training the algorithmic model for performing the named entity recognition task and the relationship extraction task.

Named entity recognition is a sub-task of NLP whose goal is to identify potential entities in a given sentence. It includes two tasks, entity recognition and entity classification.

In this paper, a sequence labelling approach is used to deal with the entity recognition task. The sequence annotation approach treats the named entity recognition task as a sequence labelling task, thus transforming it into a multi-classification problem with a supervised learning approach for model training. During training, a corresponding label is designed for each word in the sentence, and the label represents the category to which the word belongs. Through model training, the words in the sentence are classified to the correct category, and the named entities are obtained after result processing.

When the entity recognition task is executed as a sequence annotation task, suitable classification labels need to be designed for the elements in the sequence. The classification labels should typically reflect two types of information:

(1) Word position information: reflect the position of the word in the entity and identify the entity boundary.
(2) Entity type information: reflect the corresponding entity category of the entity to which the word belongs.

In this paper, the BIOES method is chosen to design sequence annotation labels as shown in Fig. 3. The BIOES method expands the entity end position information and individual vocabulary information on the basis of the BIO method, which enriches the information content, but also increases the number of labels to be predicted.

BIOES/ BILOU/ BMEWO	B stands for **beginning** (signifies beginning of an NE) I stands for **inside** (signifies that the word is inside an Named Entity) O stands for **outside** (signifies that the word is just a regular word outside an NE) E stands for **end** (signifies that the word is the end of an NE) S stands for **singleton** (signifies that the single word is an NE)

Fig. 3. Sequence labelling method BIOES

Sequence annotation labels for the task are usually divided into two parts. The first part is the word position label, which identifies the entities in the text by stating the entity boundaries. The second part is the entity category label, which indicates the entity category corresponding to the entity to which the word belongs. The two parts are connected by "-", which takes the form of:

$$<Entity\ Position\ Label\text{-}Entity\ Type\ Label> \tag{3}$$

The BIOES method is chosen to annotate word positions while entity categories are labelled with prescribed classes and attributes to form sequential annotation labels:

$$<B - Tag, I - Tag, O, E - Tag, S - Tag> \tag{4}$$

The purpose of relationship extraction task is to extract potential semantic relationships between pairs of entities present in a text. The quality problem analysis field relationship extraction task analysed in this paper belongs to the restricted domain relationship extraction task, where the set of relationship types is given in advance. At that point the relationship extraction task is transformed into a relationship classification task, which essentially classifies the relationships that may exist between candidate entity pairs. This type of relationship extraction is capable of identifying relationships that exist between entity pairs that are not expressed in the form of relationship trigger words.

Since the essence of the restricted domain relational extraction task is relational classification, the data input to the model should typically reflect three types of information when performing training relational classification models using supervised learning methods:

(1) Entities or pairs of entities present in the sentence.
(2) Semantic relations between pairs of entities.
(3) Raw text where entities and relationships are located.

Based on the task requirements, the labelling form of the design relationship extraction task is as follows:

$$<Entity1, Entity2, relation, text> \tag{5}$$

Figure 4 shows a specific description of the labels used.

116   Z. Ding and G. Zhao

Entity1 signifies **Head entity in An entity pair** (Entity pairs exist in the given text)
Entity2 signifies **Tail entity in An entity pair** (Entity pairs exist in the given text)
relation signifies **Relationship between entity pairs** (Relationships are defined by the Schema of KG)
text signifies **the given text** (Entity pairs exist in the given text)

Fig. 4. Design of annotation labels for the relationship extraction task

3.2 Named Entity Recognition Task

A core task when carrying out data mining for the field of quality problem analysis is to extract knowledge triples from the raw text. First, the algorithmic model for performing the named entity recognition task is trained. In this paper, the task is regarded as a sequence labelling task. Since the Transformer structure is suitable for dealing with problems where the inputs are sequences, this paper carries out the research on named entity recognition methods based on the BERT model structure.

The training process of BERT-based named entity recognition model is shown in Fig. 5. The pre-processed annotated sequences used to train the model are fed into the network structure. The inputs are processed at the word level to construct the embedded representations of the inputs. And the stacked Multi-Head Self-attention layers in BERT is used to map the words to different spaces, to learn the meaning features in depth and to be able to control the model to learn the local features or global features of the input sequences by the attention scores. The output of BERT is downscaled by a linear layer to obtain the predicted labels corresponding to the input words. The output of BERT is dimensionality reduced by a linear layer to obtain the predicted labels corresponding to the input words.

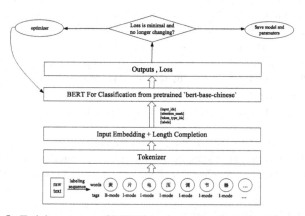

Fig. 5. Training process of BERT-based named entity recognition model

In the model, the Tokenizer layer processes the input training data in terms of disambiguation and the disambiguated result is fed into the embedding layer, which transforms the string into its corresponding embedded representation at the word level. The output of the embedding layer is a tensor:

$$tensor = \{['input\_id'], ['attention\_mask'], ['token\_type\_ids'], ['labels']\} \quad (6)$$

The length of each element in the tensor is the maximum length of the input sequence. For sequences with insufficient length, their lengths need to be complemented.

The BERT layer is inherited from the pre-trained bert-base-chinese model, which accepts the embedded representation of the input sequence and fine-tunes it on the target task. Its output is downgraded by a linear layer to obtain the predicted classification result corresponding to each word in the input sequence.

3.3 Relationship Extraction Task

After obtaining the entities in the text, it is also necessary to establish the relationship between the entities to form knowledge triples, so as to complete the task of data mining. After analysis, facing the original corpus with different features, this paper regards the relationship extraction task as a sequence labelling task as well. The Transformer structure can also be used to deal with the relationship extraction problem. Meanwhile, the relational classification task needs to obtain the positional features of entities in a sentence, and the model input of BERT contains Position Embedding, whose composition structure contains Multi-Head Self-Attention structure. So, this paper carries out the research on the relational extraction method based on the structure of BERT model.

The training process of the BERT-based relation extraction model is shown in Fig. 6. The spliced head entity, tail entity and the vector representation of the statement in which they are located are directly fed into the BERT model to learn the sequence features of the input sequences in the high-dimensional space. The predictive classification of relations is obtained by dimensionality reduction of the learnt feature vectors.

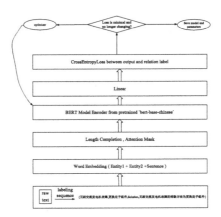

Fig. 6. Training process of BERT-based relational extraction model

In the model, on the basis of Self-Attention, the Multi-Head Self-Attention mechanism linearly combines multiple augmented semantic representation vectors for each word, through which it further learns the different meanings expressed by the same words in different contexts. The introduction of the Multi-Head Attention mechanism layer enables the model to better learn richer textual semantic features.

4   Experiments

4.1   Construction of Dataset

In this paper, the publicly available fault disposal manual of a power supply system is used as the raw text to construct the training dataset. The raw text contains the description of the knowledge of the fault part, the fault phenomenon, the possible causes of the fault, and the measures to solve the problem. The format of the raw text used in the experiment is shown in Fig. 7.

如在使用中的发电机发生故障，在作出发电机故障最后结论前必须首先确定载流线路以及与发电机配套的各设备都是良好的。

1. 电源参数显示系统显示发电机输出电压为 0V 或只有几伏电压

可能原因：（1）副励磁机绕组短路。使用万用表检查绕组电阻为 0，或者用兆欧表检查绝缘电阻为 0。（2）主发电机激磁绕组断路。

排除方法：（1）将发电机从发动机上取下来，送往修理厂修理，更换副励磁机定子组件。（2）将发电机从发动机上取下来，送往修理

Fig. 7. Example of raw text

When constructing the dataset, the text after the clauses is firstly labelled to get the ANN file as shown in Fig. 8. The file contains five columns of data. The first column is the entity serial number. The second column is the label corresponding to the entity. The third column is the corresponding position number of the first word of the entity in the whole document. The fourth column is the next number to the corresponding position number of the last word of the entity in the positive document. And the fifth column is the labelled entity.

```
28   T28 symptom 459 465  调压输出为0
29   T29 problem 467 479  交流发电机控制保护器故障
30   T30 cause 485 490     连接器松动
31   T31 problem 492 504  交流发电机控制保护器故障
32   T32 cause 510 515     调压板故障
33   T33 problem 517 529  交流发电机控制保护器故障
34   T34 cause 535 540     接口板故障
35   T35 cause 560 565     电源板故障
36   T36 problem 542 554  交流发电机控制保护器故障
37   T37 problem 567 579  交流发电机控制保护器故障
38   T38 cause 585 590     微机板故障
39   T39 problem 592 604  交流发电机控制保护器故障
```

Fig. 8. Example of entity labelling results

The above labelling results need to be further processed for use in BIOES format. Firstly, the list of labels is initialized by setting the label for each word in the document to O. Next, number by the position of the first characters of the entity recorded in the ANN document. The labels on the corresponding positions are replaced with 'B-' and entity type. Similarly, number by the position of the last character of the entity. The label on the corresponding position is replaced with 'E-' and entity type. For the character located between these two kinds of position numbering, the label on the corresponding position is replaced with 'I-' and entity type. Thus, completing the conversion of labelling results. The characters in the document and their corresponding BIOES labels are output to the specified file in the prescribed format, forming a training data set that meets the task requirements.

Finally, the format of the dataset that can be used to perform the training of the algorithm for the named entity recognition task is obtained as shown in Fig. 9. The dataset is divided into two columns. The first column is the characters in the document and the second column is the labels corresponding to the characters. The two columns are separated by a space character.

```
的 O
旋 B-cause
转 I-cause
整 I-cause
流 I-cause
器 I-cause
整 I-cause
流 I-cause
管 I-cause
有 I-cause
击 I-cause
穿 I-cause
现 I-cause
象 E-cause
。 O
```

Fig. 9. Example of training dataset for named entity recognition task

The input corpus used to construct the training dataset for the relationship extraction task is the same as that for the named entity recognition task. After the annotation of the relationships is completed, the exported results are also in ANN file format, and the contents of the file are shown in Fig. 10. The file contains four columns of data. The first column is the relationship serial number. The second column is the label corresponding to the relationship. The third column is the corresponding serial number of the head entity in the entity relationship pair <HeadEntity, rel, TailEntity> in the output entity document. The fourth column is the corresponding serial number of the tail entity in the entity pair in the output entity document.

```
R1  PerformLike Arg1:T1 Arg2:T2
R2  BecauseOf Arg1:T3 Arg2:T4
R3  BecauseOf Arg1:T5 Arg2:T6
R4  SolveBy Arg1:T7 Arg2:T8
R5  SolveBy Arg1:T9 Arg2:T10
R6  PerformLike Arg1:T11 Arg2:T12
R7  SolveBy Arg1:T228 Arg2:T229
R8  BecauseOf Arg1:T226 Arg2:T227
R9  SolveBy Arg1:T224 Arg2:T225
R10 SolveBy Arg1:T222 Arg2:T223
R11 BecauseOf Arg1:T220 Arg2:T221
R12 BecauseOf Arg1:T218 Arg2:T219
```

Fig. 10. Example of relationship labelling results

Next, process the results into the required format. First of all, get the entity number in the relationship file, find the entity name pointed by the number in the corresponding entity file and replace the entity number in the relationship file with the entity name. Then find out the original statement where the entity relationship pair is located in the source document and output the result to the specified file according to the specified format, so as to form a training dataset that meets the requirements of the task.

Finally, the format of the dataset that can be used to perform the training of the algorithm for relational extraction task is shown in Fig. 11. The dataset is divided into four columns. The first column is the head entity. The second column is the tail entity. The third column is the type of relationship. And the fourth column is the original statement in which the entity-relationship pairs are located. Each column is separated by a comma.

```
11  无刷交流发电机故障,主电机输出绕组断路,Reason,无刷交流发电机故障的可能原因为主电机输出绕组断路。
12  无刷交流发电机故障,更换转子组件,Solution,无刷交流发电机故障的排除方法为更换转子组件。
13  无刷交流发电机故障,更换定子组件,Solution,无刷交流发电机故障的排除方法为更换定子组件。
14  交流发电机控制保护器故障,调压输出为0,Model,交流发电机控制保护器故障的故障表现为调压输出为0。
15  交流发电机控制保护器故障,连接器松动,Reason,交流发电机控制保护器故障的可能原因为连接器松动。
16  交流发电机控制保护器故障,调压板故障,Reason,交流发电机控制保护器故障的可能原因为调压板故障。
17  交流发电机控制保护器故障,接口板故障,Reason,交流发电机控制保护器故障的可能原因为接口板故障。
18  交流发电机控制保护器故障,电源板故障,Reason,交流发电机控制保护器故障的可能原因为电源板故障。
19  交流发电机控制保护器故障,微机板故障,Reason,交流发电机控制保护器故障的可能原因为微机板故障。
```

Fig. 11. Example of training dataset for relational extraction task

4.2 Named Entity Recognition Task

The dataset obtained to perform the named entity recognition task is used for model training. The labelled dataset is divided into training set, development set and test set in 8:1:1. The training model is based on BERT structure for performing named entity recognition task. The model training results are shown in Table 1.

Table 1. Training results of BERT-based named entity recognition model

	Precision	Recall	F1-Score	Support
I-problem	1.0000	1.0000	1.0000	75
E-measurement	1.0000	0.1667	0.2857	6
E-problem	1.0000	1.0000	1.0000	11
B-problem	0.5238	1.0000	1.0000	11
I-measurement	0.7250	1.0000	0.8406	29
B-cause	1.0000	1.0000	1.0000	4
B-symptom	0.0000	0.0000	0.0000	1
E-cause	1.0000	0.5000	0.6667	4
I-cause	0.9048	1.0000	0.9500	19
I-symptom	0.3333	1.0000	0.5000	1
E-symptom	0.0000	0.0000	0.0000	1
B-measurement	1.0000	0.5000	0.6667	6
O	0.9875	0.9581	0.9693	83
Avg/Total	0.9463	0.9363	0.9273	251

In the table, Precious is used to evaluate the rate of correct predictions among the outcomes predicted by the model. Recall is used to evaluate the rate of correctly identifying all potentially possible outcomes by the model. F1-score is used to combine the evaluation of Precious and Recall. The Support column indicates the total number of corresponding labels in the test set.

Then, compare with the results of model training for the named entity recognition task based on the LSTM structural model as shown in Table 2.

Table 2. Training results of LSTM-based named entity recognition model

	Precision	Recall	F1-Score	Support
I-problem	1.0000	0.8667	0.9286	75
E-measurement	1.0000	0.3333	0.5000	6
E-problem	1.0000	1.0000	1.0000	11
B-problem	0.5238	1.0000	1.0000	11
I-measurement	0.7436	1.0000	0.8529	29
B-cause	1.0000	0.7500	0.8571	4
B-symptom	0.0000	0.0000	0.0000	1
E-cause	1.0000	0.5000	0.6667	4
I-cause	0.8636	1.0000	0.9268	19
I-symptom	0.3333	1.0000	0.5000	1
E-symptom	0.0000	0.0000	0.0000	1
B-measurement	1.0000	0.5000	0.6667	6
O	0.9750	0.9368	0.9571	83
Avg/Total	0.9203	0.8924	0.8908	251

Judging from the results, overall, the recognition accuracy and recall of the BERT-based model on the test set are better than the LSTM-based model. From this point of view, the BERT-based model is more suitable for performing the target task.

4.3 Relationship Extraction Task

The dataset obtained to perform the relationship extraction task is used for model training. The labelled dataset is divided into training set, development set and test set in 8:1:1.

Relational extraction experiments are performed using the BERT-based model and the results are shown in Fig. 12. The model is able to learn the features of the training data fully when the training is carried out to about 2 rounds. The model was trained for a total of 5 rounds, and the total duration of training was 17.8739s, with an average duration of 3.5748s per round.

Then, compare with the results of the experiments on relationship extraction based on LSTM model as shown in Fig. 13. To achieve the effect of being able to learn the features of the training data more adequately, it requires the training to be carried out up to about 50 rounds.

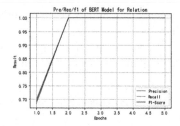

Fig. 12. Training results of BERT-based relational extraction model

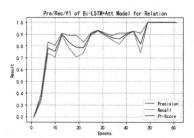

Fig. 13. Training results of LSTM-based relational extraction model

Judging from the results, the BERT-based model can have good recognition accuracy and recall on the test set. And only few training rounds are needed to learn the features of the training data.

5 Conclusion

This paper introduces a data mining method based on BERT model in the field of quality problem analysis, which integrates the characteristics of data in the field into the research of model construction, solves the problems such as large amount of data in the field with scattered distribution, isolated data and difficult to be understood by machines, and compares the results with the training results based on LSTM model.

Firstly, a method of preprocessing data related to quality problem analysis by sequence annotation method is given to form a dataset for two tasks of named entity recognition and relationship extraction. Then, for the two tasks, a BERT-based model training method is used to achieve data mining in the field. Finally, an example is used for comparison. The training effect of the BERT model in both tasks is better than that of the LSTM model.

However, there are still some limitations of the study. The analysis time of training based on BERT model in the field of quality problem is longer and the training process consumes a lot of GPU performance. Follow-up work needs to be carried out to address these issues for model improvement and optimization research.

References

1. Chang, L., Lihu, P.: Multi-feature fusion-based extraction of word-level attentional relations. J. Taiyuan Univ. Sci. Technol. **43**(05), 389–395 (2022)
2. Lee, J., Seo, S., Choi, Y.S.: Semantic relation classification via bidirectional LSTM networks with entity-aware attention using latent entity typing (2019)
3. Lin, M., Yinjun, Z., et al.: Joint entity relationship extraction based on graph neural networks. Appl. Res. Comput. **39**(02), 424–431 (2022)
4. Wang, S., Zhang, Y., Che, W., et al.: Joint extraction of entities and relations based on a novel graph scheme. In: Proceedings of the IJCAI, pp. 4461–4467 (2018)
5. Wang, Z., Chang, B., Sui, Z.: Distantly supervised neural network model for relation extraction. In: Sun, M., Liu, Z., Zhang, M., Liu, Y. (eds.) CCL/NLP-NABD -2015. LNCS (LNAI), vol. 9427, pp. 253–266. Springer, Cham (2015). https://doi.org/10.1007/978-3-319-25816-4_21
6. Quan, Y., Shuxin, X.: Relationship extraction algorithm based on residual shrinkage networks. J. Comput. Appl. **42**(10), 3040–3045 (2022)
7. Lishuang, L., Rui, G., et al.: Protein interaction extraction based on migration learning. J. Chin. Inf. Process. **30**(02), 160–167 (2016)
8. Yunpeng, C.: A study of relationship extraction based on deep learning. Jilin University (2021)
9. Chuanzhi, Z., Xiaolong, J., et al.: A review of deep learning-based relational extraction research. J. Chin. Inf. Process. **33**(12), 1–18 (2019)

Cross-Language Text Search Algorithm Based on Context-Compatible Algorithms

Jianqiao Sheng[1]([✉]), Liang Zhang[1], Xiyin Wang[1], Run Xu[1], and Jiaqi Wu[2]

[1] Information and Communication Branch, State Grid Anhui Electric Power Co., Ltd., Hefei, China
cambridgeace@sina.com.cn

[2] State Grid Anhui Electric Power Co., Ltd., Huainan Power Supply Company, Beijing, China

Abstract. In this era of knowledge explosion, the Internet is filled with a flood of information; however, complex and various. With the increasing close exchanges of technical at home and abroad, cross-lingual searching algorithm becomes particularly important. This article studied on the cross-lingual text searching algorithm based on context compatibility. In this article, context was integrated into searching, to some extent of which ensures the accurate interpretation of words of cross-lingual and is able to search for relevant text more accurately at the same time, which can avoid complex syntax analysis of various language, and find a multilingual common as well as feasible way in searching. In addition, IK and kuromoji was chosen as the Chinese and Japanese word segmentation device respectively with the use of massive subtitles to create a corpus and then searching in the context of word co-frequency analogue sentence relationship. Based on the context compatibility algorithm to study on the cross-lingual text searching, we designed the preliminary experiment and carried it out with some distinction effect.

Keywords: Context · Word segmentation · Frequency statistics of words in common · Corpus linguistics

1 Introduction

In the last century, human knowledge has expanded at an unprecedented rate, and information has been stored in increasingly rich ways, making fast and accurate retrieval especially important in the massive amount of data and information. As a result, the concept of automatic retrieval technology was born. It has also given rise to the efforts of a wide range of researchers.

Text search technology, after the rapid development in recent times, also quickly reached a bottleneck in some fields and some aspects [1]. In terms of language, there are problems such as insufficiently clear expression of search intent; fuzzy localization; cumbersome and ineffective information data. In terms of information sources, there are problems such as different information sources; inconsistent systems and storage formats; and contradictions between heterogeneous resource integration and unified user access for retrieval. In addition to the above problems, in this era of frequent exchanges between China and foreign countries, cross-language text search algorithms are urgently on the stage [2]. The so-called cross-language is to switch between different languages, and the conventional translation by dictionary is not only large, but also because of the different language habits often produce ambiguity, and, it is not easy to recognize some similar meanings.

This paper makes a bold attempt on the basis of theoretical research. The contextual context in contextual research is taken as the main point of analysis, and a quantifiable context is constructed by simulating the contextual context model with the word co-sentence frequency relationship. A corpus with subtitles as raw material is created. The main work done in this paper are:

Corpus design. In this paper, we innovatively take the vast amount of subtitles available on the internet, i.e. .ass files and .rst files, and preprocess them. Then it is filtered, categorized, integrated, and computed to get the parts of interest, which are stored in the corpus. This process is fully automated and does not require human intervention [3]. And there is a guarantee of volume. Furthermore, it does not require any cost and is economically feasible.

1) Contextual Model Simulation. In the study of linguistic environment, it is found that contextual contexts constrain each other and can characterize semantics well. And this kind of constraint relationship is relatively easy to transform and realize in computer science. Thus, this paper adopts the interaction relationship between words, i.e., the frequency distribution of co-sentences, to simulate the contextual language environment. The abstract context is operated concretely to facilitate the operation of the search algorithm.

2) Context-Based Cross-Language Search. In this paper, the input sentence is subjected to a segmentation process, and the obtained segmentation is filtered to obtain the keywords of the sentence. At this point, the keywords are subjected to contextual simulation, i.e., finding the corpus index of the co-sentences between every two words in order to find the corresponding corpus. The participles of the requested language in it are taken out and filtered again, then the keywords of the requested language are obtained. The method utilizes the copula relationship, which reduces the frequency of ambiguity to some extent. It is also based on context, so it is easy to extend the correspondence of similar semantics, which makes the search more comprehensive. Because context is an abstraction common to all languages, the context-based search algorithm is more compatible, and when adding more languages, it does not need to change its search structure and has good robustness.

2   Research Status

2.1   Overview of the Linguistic Contextual Representation Model

2.1.1   A Model of Intra-sentential Syntactic Constraints

Syntactically, there are some simple constraints in each statement:

1) Predicate + Object
2) Subject + Predicate + Object

3) Subject + Predicate + Epithet
4) Subject + Predicate + Object + Object Complement

Where the predicate is usually a verb or a gerund, the object, object complement and subject are nouns, and the epithet is mostly an adjective. In addition to these, in English grammar there are:

1) Verb + Noun
2) Gerund + Adjective
3) Adjective + Noun
4) Verb + Adverb
5) Preposition + Noun

We explore lexical properties in order to facilitate further accurate and quick understanding of the connotations of words later on, so as to explore the general thrust of what that text is trying to convey [4, 5]. Secondly, with mutual constraints, that is, things have interactions with things, i.e., things themselves are factors of change, but without physical things, then there is not a trigger for change, which cannot be calculated. For example: the equation x + y = 10 is known; find the value of x, y. When there are no other conditions, x, y still has an infinite number of solutions. This is mainly due to the fact that there are fewer constraining equations than there are unknowns. Thus it is unsolvable in the absence of any other known conditions, not that there are no solutions here, but that there is no narrowing down of the connotations of the word for the text [6]. Whether the model works or not is then determined by whether we can find some known conditions. Very thankfully, many words are actually lexically certain. For example, you, me, and he, as pronouns, are all nouns; in English, with, by, via, etc. are prepositions that are mostly followed by the noun gender. Having found some words with known lexical properties, the lexical properties before and after will be slowly determined under mutual constraints [7, 8]. The rough relationship is shown in Fig. 1 below:

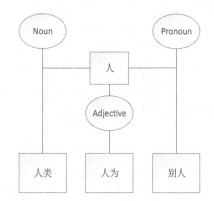

Fig. 1. The part-of-speech constraint of "man"

2.1.2 Model of Homophily Constraints

From the model above, the lexical properties of each word can basically be derived. However, only knowing the lexical properties is still not enough. It is well known that most words have multiple meanings, i.e., each word may have different lexical properties, and each lexical property may also have multiple meanings [9].

For example, in the explanation of the word "man" mentioned in the previous section, it is the same noun but with different interpretations. This requires the recording of some fixed collocations. In Chinese, it is mainly manifested in the expansion of words, such as "人类", and the word "类", most of the collocations indicate the attributes, and "人" in this context can also determine its basic meaning [10].

Then "play badminton", "play ping-pong" and "play basketball", in which "play" is followed by the word the word for "ball". Then the word "play" indicates the meaning of competition and match.

2.1.3 Contextual Constraints Model

With the two models above, you can basically determine the connotation of a word. Still, many times it's not perfect, especially for some pronouns. "He's a great basketball player!" It can be concluded that "he" denotes a person. So the question is, who is he? Is "he" in this text a protagonist, i.e. complementary to the understanding of the text, or is it just a supporting character, i.e. not contributing to the general idea of the text [11].

This is where we use contextual constraints. Pronouns of this type, for the most part, take over with the subject of the preceding sentence. The method we use is roughly to go back up and find a subject that is not a pronoun, then roughly determine its inner meaning. Note: We are talking about approximation here, which can only be said to be accurate in most cases, because the contexts themselves are very complex, and even if we only look at narrow contextual cases, there are many constraints that we can't take into account in all of them.

2.2 Context-Compatible Algorithm

2.2.1 Computable Context Modeling Concepts

The above contextual research results are mainly located in the field of linguistic research, so most of the results are qualitative analyses, which are difficult to be expressed using computer algorithms, and this paper proposes computable context models. As mentioned earlier, the context model is also the co-sentence relationship between words, taking the sentence as the unit [12].

Therefore, the statistical word co-sentence frequency can reflect part of the context in the above sentence, thus providing some sense of contextual analysis support for cross-language search. The details are shown as follows:

If the existing corpus contains only five words a, b, c, d, e. The sentences in the corpus have:

(1) a b c (2) a c e (3) a d e (4) b d e (5) b c d e

In this example, we can obtain the frequency relation about the word a as shown in Fig. 2.

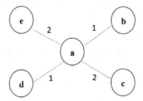

Fig. 2. Frequency relationship of word a

By analogy, the word relationships contained in the entire corpus can be obtained, as shown in Fig. 3.

#	a	b	c	d	e
a	#	1	2	1	2
b	#	#	2	2	2
c	#	#	#	1	2
d	#	#	#	#	3
e	#	#	#	#	#

Fig. 3. Thesaurus co-sentence relationship table

After obtaining the above lexicon co-sentence relation table, when retrieving, if there is a sentence containing a, b, c, since the frequency of a, c co-sentence is greater than that of a, b, the context of the sentence should be biased to a, c.

2.2.2 Context-Compatible Algorithm

With the previous foundation, we can basically grasp the basic connotation of words. On this basis, the context construction algorithm based on word connotation compatibility is proposed. That is, the word connotation compatibility algorithm is one of the core of the research of this topic, which is mainly to study the whole sentence's context based on the sentence as a unit of participle, through the word connotation compatibility judgment of the neighboring words [13], and the research includes the formal definition of the context, the neighboring word connotation compatibility and incompatibility judgment, and the sentence as a unit of the context construction, and so on. Also proposed a sentence context construction method based on word connotation compatibility: this paper achieves the compatibility of neighboring word connotations by counting word connotations instead of semantics, and constructs the context of the sentence through the compatible context, which serves as a more stable and structured semantic definition as a basis for cross-language text retrieval and categorization.

In this process, the first step is to disambiguate the given sentence, however, not all of the obtained disambiguities are semantically meaningful, therefore, filtering is performed. The resulting participles are modeled according to the computable context model above to obtain a context model [14]. Based on this context, the corpus is expanded, searched, and associated corpus is identified, and cross-language correspondences are found from the corpus, which leads to the desired set of language words. Similarly, words that interfere with semantics or are redundant are filtered out, and what remains is the set of keywords for the desired language.

2.3 Participle Algorithm

Words are the smallest linguistic units containing meaning that can move independently, and to break down a sentence into individual words, we need to use a word-splitting algorithm. And before that, we must also figure out the structural laws of language [11].

To get the keywords, first of all, we need to separate the words. For English, words are separated by spaces. As for Chinese, it is a language based on characters, and there is no obvious distinction between words, so the basis and key to information processing in Chinese is the analysis of words.

The following are a few commonly used methods.

Word-by-word traversal. Word by word traversal method is, from the beginning of the article, word by word traversal, and all the words in the dictionary in accordance with the longest to the shortest order of their matching search, until the end of the article. That is, no matter how short the article is, even if it is only one sentence, and how large the dictionary is, as large as a million entries, the entire dictionary must be traversed. Its inefficiency is obvious, generally large systems will not be considered.

Mechanical lexicography. The string of Chinese characters to be parsed is somehow matched with the words in a "large enough" dictionary, and if the corresponding string can be found in the dictionary, the match is successful, otherwise, the match fails. In the process of recognizing a word, there can be different scanning directions, different lengths of preferred matches, and whether or not it is combined with the lexical annotation process to perform different patterns of matches.

The full cut segmentation method. First, the sentence to be retrieved is fully cut into keywords. Then, after getting the keywords, a backward index is built. It is important to know not only in which articles the keywords appear, but also where they are located in the articles.

3   Core Algorithm Implementation

3.1 Segmentation Algorithm Implementation

In this paper, the Chinese and Japanese word separation algorithms are IKAnalyzer and Kuromoji respectively. IK Analyzer is an open source Chinese word separation toolkit based on the java language. And it is lightweight. Nowadays, IKAnalyzer has been turned into a direct Java-oriented utility component, and is independent of the Lucene project. IK Analyzer also provides an implementation of Lucene's default optimizations, and IK has implemented a simple algorithm for eliminating disambiguation through participle disambiguation. Kuromoji is an open source Java-based Japanese word splitter. It is built into Lucene and Solr as the default Japanese lexer. But he also does not rely on Lucene or Solr, can be used alone. It is an application of the Viterbi algorithm and uses the IPA dictionary by default.

In this paper, IK is used as the Chinese lexer and Kuromoji is used as the Japanese lexer. When using the IK Analyzer. First, instantiate an IKAnalyzer disambiguator and create an in-memory index object. Create an index instance to associate to memory. Create a document, add a field of type String, length 1000, named ID and a field of type Text, named fileName, where fieldName has been previously assigned, to the document and write it to the index. Next is the search process, first of all, instantiate a searcher, and then use the QueryParser query analyzer to construct the Query object, and set the default search conditions, set the conditions of the search, AND_OPERATOR means "with". Search for the 10 records with the highest similarity, and store the search results in an array.

When using the Kuromoji splitter, note that there are three split modes, Normal, Search and Extends, and the results are different (Table 1):

Table 1. Table of three patterns of word splitting

Sample	ジャイ子っていってたなぁ
Normal mode	ジャイ｜子｜って｜いっ｜て｜た｜なぁ
Search mode	ジャイ｜子｜って｜いっ｜て｜た｜なぁ
Extends mode	ジ｜ャ｜イ｜子｜って｜いっ｜て｜た｜なぁ

3.2 Word Co-sentence Algorithm Implementation

The clauses obtained earlier contain bi-directional indexes which point to the corpus where the clause is located and its position. In this paper, it is necessary to count the frequency with which each word is co-sentenced with other words, i.e., the number of times it is co-sentenced with a particular word / the total number of words in the lexicon.

Taking out the bi-directional index chain of the participle is really counting the indexes that are the same in it. Intuitively, comparing strings in two generic arrays requires M × N comparisons, but thankfully, at the time of insertion, dichotomization is used, which means that the entire index chain is ordered, i.e., as long as we compare the sizes starting from the head of the table, and if equal, then they are selected and each is moved back by one index, and when they don't want to be equal, then the smaller ones are moved back by one index.

3.3 Context-Based Cross-Context Search Algorithm Implementation

The so-called cross-language is a group of different languages that express the same or similar meanings. With the variety of meanings of words and the complexity of the syntax of various languages, it is quite difficult to search and match all the sentences with the same or similar meanings directly from the connotation of the words. Moreover, as the number of languages increases, all languages have to be syntactically analyzed, in other words, the complexity is directly linked to the number of languages. In other words, the complexity is directly related to the number of languages. The increase in complexity and computation for each additional language is quite significant.

After previous research, it can be noted that no matter which language, every sentence has a context, and the context, in a sense, can directly represent the connotation of the sentence. This gives another way of thinking, starting from the context, to find sentences or keywords with the same or similar connotation in different languages.

It is worth mentioning that some words appear too frequently in sentences, such as pronouns, conjunctions, names, etc., and do not have really valid connotations. Although some semantically irrelevant words have been removed during word separation, some of them cannot be checked. This requires us to filter the words first.

In this paper, we have described the card structure of the corpus, in which Chinese and Japanese correspondences already exist. Therefore, we directly find out, the Japanese equivalent of the given Chinese sentence and vice versa.

So let's boil down the whole search process to, for example, querying Japanese in Chinese:

1) The given sentences are disambiguated to obtain a collection of Chinese disambiguators;

2) The resulting set of partitioned words is filtered to remove words that have no semantic meaning or interfere with the semantics, such as those that occur too frequently; in this paper, a Gaussian low-pass filter is invoked here to filter out words with too high a frequency. The Gaussian kernel function used is:

$$k(||x - xc||) = \exp\{-||x - xc||^2 \div (2 \times \sigma)^2)\} \qquad (1)$$

where xc is the center of the kernel function and σ is the width parameter of the function, which controls the radial range of action of the function.

3) Iterate through the words in the set so that each word finds out the corpus sentences that co-occur with other words, i.e., find out the shortID of the corpus that is common to two and two and record it in map as <corpus number, corresponding count>.

4) Search in the corpus, find the corresponding corpus according to shortID, take out the participle of its corresponding Japanese corpus, and count the number of references.

5) Iterate over the corresponding Japanese participles and count the co-sentence relations of each Japanese participle with other words.

6) Filtering is performed with Gaussian filtering using three criteria; the first is by frequency of occurrence; the second by frequency of co-sentence; and the third is by word length. The resulting set is the key set of the corresponding Japanese text. It should be noted that some of the words obtained are very chopped up and not meaningful, so this is used as a criterion.

It is also not difficult to realize that all correspondences are based on the corpus, and thus the requirement of richness of the corpus is extremely important. This also reflects the fact that the previous direct search for corpora on the Internet, whether paid or free, inevitably lacks richness. It also confirms the innovation, superiority and necessity of building a corpus with bilingual subtitles.

4   Experiments

4.1   Experimentation with Segmentation Algorithms

4.1.1   Experimental Effects of the IK Lexer

In order to ensure the effectiveness of the splitter effect, we conducted several sets of experiments before the application, and the input strings and the returned results are shown in Table 2.

Table 2. Segmentation return results

input	IKAnalyzer 是开源的，基于 java 开发的轻量级的中文分词工具包。
output	ikanalyzer|开源|基于| java|开发|轻量级|中文|分词|工具包
input	好的，然后使用这一函数将以字符串全部转成大写。
output	好|这一|函数|将以|字符串|转成|大写

4.1.2   Experimental Effects of the Kuromoji Segmenter

The experiments are as follows:

When entering a sample sentence: ジャイ子っていっててたなぁ, and use three separate split-phrase modes. The inputs are shown in Table 3 below.

Table 3. Segmentation return results

Normal mode	Search mode	Extends mode
Start: 0, word: ジャイ	Start: 0, word: ジャイ	Start: 0, word: ジャイ
Start: 3, word: 子	Start: 3, word: 子	Start: 3, word: 子
Start: 4, word: って	Start: 4, word: って	Start: 4, word: って
Start: 6, word: いっ	Start: 6, word: いっ	Start: 6, word: いっ
Start: 8, word: て	Start: 8, word: て	Start: 8, word: て
Start: 9, word: た	Start: 9, word: た	Start: 9, word: た
Start: 10, word: なぁ	Start: 10, word: なぁ	Start: 10, word: なぁ

4.2   Corpus Realization

4.2.1   Preparation of the Corpus

The corpus we need is a Japanese text corresponding to a synonymous Chinese text, which makes it easy to think of subtitles. There are a lot of Japanese comics and dramas on the Internet, and some of them have been subtitled by some subtitle enthusiasts with bilingual characters subtitles. These bilingual subtitles exist in the form of .ass or .srt files in some subtitle platforms, which certainly gives us a direction.

Resourcefulness: there are quite a few lines in an episode of a Japanese drama, and the amount of lines in one of them is already significant, reaching orders of magnitude of ten thousand. This is only a relatively small number of episodes of Japanese drama. And like the King of Thieves, Naruto, hundreds of episodes of Japanese manga, the amount of lines is countless. In this way, for the richness of the resource is no longer a problem.

Economic feasibility: most of these bilingual subtitles are translated and organized by Japanese language interest enthusiasts, and the non-profit texture facilitates others to watch classic movie and television works, so they are free and open source to the public on the Internet. This solves a problem of funding.

4.2.2 Corpus Generation

The basic structure of the data has been defined, on the basis of which the execution logic is considered. The steps for building a corpus are shown as following:

- Preprocessing a subtitle file;
- Reading by line;
- Taking out timestamps;
- Take out the corpus again;
- Determine whether it is Japanese or Chinese, and use the corresponding word splitter to split the words;
- Encapsulate the timestamp, the Chinese and Japanese corpus, and the Chinese and Japanese participles into a phrase card and pass it into the database.

The specific implementation process is as follows:

1. Collect .ass or .srt files with Chinese and Japanese subtitles. As shown in Fig. 4 below. Due to the large number of resources, only some of them are cut out to give readers a more visual representation.

[zmk.tw][渚神&青翼][王牌投手...	2016/5/4 21:41	WinRAR ZIP 圧縮...	367 KB
[zmk.tw][渚神&异域][刀语][Kat...	2016/5/4 21:29	WinRAR ZIP 圧縮...	509 KB
[zmk.tw][渚神字幕组][圣斗士星矢冥...	2016/5/4 21:42	WinRAR ZIP 圧縮...	751 KB
[zmk.tw][渚神字幕组][夏威夷男孩][中...	2016/5/4 21:43	WinRAR 圧縮文件	233 KB
[zmk.tw]Log Horizon.rar	2016/5/4 21:30	WinRAR 圧縮文件	480 KB
[zmk.tw]The Pacific Part 9.[1080i 7...	2016/5/4 21:43	WinRAR 圧縮文件	339 KB
[zmk.tw]The.Pacific.Pt.IX.720p.HDT...	2016/5/4 21:44	WinRAR 圧縮文件	172 KB
[zmk.tw]The.Pacific.Pt.VII.[1080i 72...	2016/5/4 21:43	WinRAR 圧縮文件	271 KB
[zmk.tw]境界的彼方[渚神中日双语字...	2016/5/4 21:42	WinRAR 圧縮文件	210 KB
[zmk.tw]空之境界 1-8字幕(中日双语...	2016/5/4 21:41	WinRAR 圧縮文件	208 KB
[zmk.tw]来自风之明日[渚神中日双语...	2016/5/4 21:43	WinRAR 圧縮文件	272 KB
[zmk.tw]胜者即是正义2 リーガルハ...	2016/5/4 17:30	WinRAR ZIP 圧縮...	233 KB
[zmk.tw]嫌な女 S01E01-E06 HDTV.r...	2016/5/5 17:42	WinRAR 圧縮文件	188 KB
[zmk.tw]幸福洋蒸 Koufuku Graffiti.2...	2016/5/5 17:41	WinRAR 圧縮文件	977 KB
[zmk.tw]中二病也要谈恋爱！恋 中二...	2016/5/5 17:43	WinRAR ZIP 圧縮...	179 KB
[zmk.tw]幸福洋葱 常里工程 最终整理[...	2016/5/4 21:30	WinRAR ZIP 圧縮...	322 KB

Fig. 4. Chinese and Japanese Bilingual Subtitle Catalog

2. As an example, open the 73e56b26f7708dec768c6f1a54b2e438.ass file and take out the section of interest in the .ass file. The relevant Japanese corpus information and the relevant Chinese corpus information in the document are shown in Fig. 5.

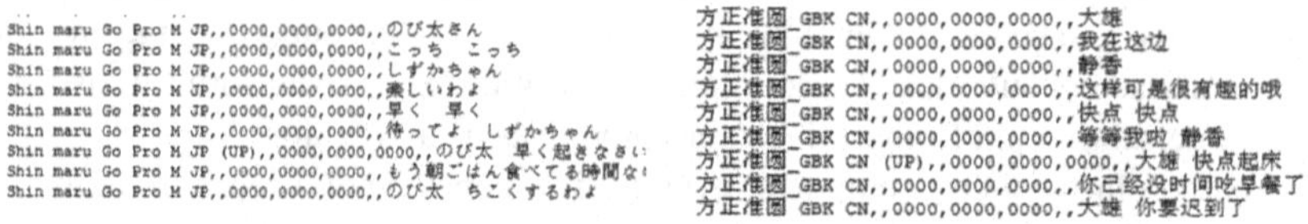

```
Shin maru Go Pro M JP,,0000,0000,0000,,のび太さん          方正准圆_GBK CN,,0000,0000,0000,,大雄
Shin maru Go Pro M JP,,0000,0000,0000,,こっち  こっち         方正准圆_GBK CN,,0000,0000,0000,,我在这边
Shin maru Go Pro M JP,,0000,0000,0000,,しずかちゃん           方正准圆_GBK CN,,0000,0000,0000,,静香
Shin maru Go Pro M JP,,0000,0000,0000,,楽しいわよ             方正准圆_GBK CN,,0000,0000,0000,,这样可是很有趣的哦
Shin maru Go Pro M JP,,0000,0000,0000,,早く  早く            方正准圆_GBK CN,,0000,0000,0000,,快点 快点
Shin maru Go Pro M JP,,0000,0000,0000,,待ってよ  しずかちゃん   方正准圆_GBK CN (UP),,0000,0000,0000,,大雄 快点起床
Shin maru Go Pro M JP (UP),,0000,0000,0000,,のび太  早く起きなさい！  方正准圆_GBK CN,,0000,0000,0000,,你已经没时间吃早餐了
Shin maru Go Pro M JP,,0000,0000,0000,,もう朝ごはん食べてる時間な！  方正准圆_GBK CN,,0000,0000,0000,,大雄 你要迟到了
Shin maru Go Pro M JP,,0000,0000,0000,,のび太  ちこくするわよ
```

Fig. 5. Relevant Japanese corpus information and relevant Chinese corpus information

As you can see, the first part is some configuration stuff that doesn't do much for us; the second part is Japanese lines, so we just need to intercept their timestamps and Japanese statements; the third part is the same as the second part, and what we're interested in making is their timestamps and Chinese statements. Here we will start by choosing the ninth line as a sample (Table 4):

Table 4. Chinese and Japanese corpus

	timestamp	line
Japanese Sample	0:00:42.50,0:00:43.78	もう朝ごはん食べてる時間ないわよ
Chinese Sample	0:00:42.50,0:00:43.78	你已经没时间吃早餐了

3. The obtained Chinese and Japanese texts are respectively subjected to the respective lexer segmentation. The sliced Chinese and Japanese corpus is obtained, as shown in Table 5.

Table 5. Sliced Chinese-Japanese corpus

participle	post-lexical result
IK	你|已经|没|时间|吃|早餐|了
kuromoji	もう|朝ごはん|食べてる|時間|ない|わよ

4.3 Implementation of Cross-Language Search Algorithms

In order to test the search effect, experiments are conducted in this paper. Due to the limitation of time and materials, the corpus designed in this paper favors Japanese manga, and the search effect on Japanese manga style statements is relatively good. Therefore, we take "The highest vote-getter is Hokuto Shinken, which has been finished for dozens of years" as an example sentence, and conduct experiments on the implementation code provided in Chapter Three. The frequency of occurrence and co-sentence relationship statistics are shown in Fig. 6.

```
加载扩展停止词典：stopword.dic
total words size:124
Max wave Occurs :40
Min wave Occurs :2
Avg wave Occurs :3.596774193548387
Max wave ConsenLen :105660
Min wave ConsenLen :2200
Avg wave ConsenLen :31542.25806451613
```

Fig. 6. Statistical relationships

The results of the three ways of filtering are shown in Table 6.

Table 6. Filtering results of the three ways

Filter by occurs	Filter by relateCorpus	Filter by word' length
token1: で	token1: で	token1: ヴオイドテク
token2: て	token2: て	token2: ジャージー
token3: だ	token3: だ	token3: プレイヤー
token4: しか	token4: しか	token4: とかいう
token5: は	token5: は	token5: リーダー

These are the three different sets of Japanese keywords that correspond to the phrase "The Hokuto Shinken, which has been finished for decades, received the highest number of votes".

5 Summarize

In this paper, in the process of conducting research on cross-language text search algorithms based on context-compatible algorithms, a new idea of building a corpus is proposed, i.e., using subtitles to automate the expansion of the corpus through a program. This approach is widely sourced, highly productive, easily accessible and contains basically no economic burden. Of course, most of the words appearing in subtitles are common words, which is enough to solve the cross-language search of some common sentences, however, for universalization, traditional translation corpus such as dictionaries have to be added. Based on the self-built corpus, the cross-lingual text search algorithm based on context-compatible algorithm studied in this paper has the following three main advantages over other search algorithms:

First, in terms of semantic localization, under simple contextual constraints, it is possible to narrow down the semantic scope of words to a certain extent, and more accurately enable inter-conversion between languages, as can be demonstrated by the apple theory in the text.

Second, in the search depth, the usual search algorithms, just intercept the simple keywords to search, while the text used in the context of the search can be expanded, can also be searched for its near-synonymous words. Because of the similar context, the meaning of the sentence expression is similar.

Finally, in terms of complexity, because context is an attribute of each language, and in this paper is expressed in terms of co-sentence frequency, then each additional language does not increase its complexity, as long as the respective participle, and then unified processing; whereas the conventional cross-language search, there is also the consideration of the respective language grammars, i.e., for each additional language, a considerable increase in complexity ensues, and the cost is too high.

This cross-language search algorithm based on context compatibility proposes a more feasible solution for cross-language search, and it does prove to be feasible. And in this algorithm, the filtering effect on the clauses becomes a key to determine the performance. Ideally, the filter should filter out components that do not affect the meaning of the sentence, such as some pronouns, names, places, conjunctions, etc., or, can be a variety of names, addresses, etc. into a single word. In addition, in different professions, the same word will have different interpretations, which also affects the search effect to a certain extent, therefore, in the later stage, it should be added to the professional classification. And in this paper, not to study.

References

1. Zobel, J., Moffat, A.: Inverted files for text search engines. ACM Comput. Surv. (CSUR) **38**(2), 6-es (2006)
2. Wang, J.H.: On the function and realization of context. Rhetorical Learn. (2) (2003)
3. Chen, J.: The nature of context and its characteristics. J. Xi'an Foreign Lang. Inst. (4) (1997)
4. Li, H., Qu, Y.: A review of research on keyword-based data querying on the semantic web. Comput. Sci. (07) (2011)
5. Jin, Y., Wang, Z.: Research on semantic web retrieval model and key technology based on reasoning. Comput. Eng. Des. (07) (2013)
6. Lu, Y., Li, Y.: Improvement of TF. IDF algorithm for calculating weights of text feature items. Book Intell. Work **57**(3), 89–94 (2013)
7. Lu, N.: Research on knowledge association cueing and its application for knowledge discovery. (11), 1187–1189
8. Chen, T., Su, W.: A technique for analyzing textual information association relationship based on semantic reasoning. Telecommun. Technol. **54**(1), 67–73 (2014)
9. Wang, L.: Research on search engines and their relevance ranking. Wuhan University (2004)
10. Li, M., Wang, Q.: Research and realization of Chinese full-text search technology. J. Intell. **22**(1), 10–17 (2003)
11. Liang, N.: Automatic participles in written Chinese and an automatic participle system– CDWS. J. Beijing Univ. Aeronaut. Astronaut. **4**, 009 (1984)
12. Hirsch, J.E.: An index to quantify an individual's scientific research output. Proc. Natl. Acad. Sci. U.S.A. **102**(46), 16569–16572 (2005)
13. Newman, M.E.J.: Scientific collaboration networks I: network construction and fundamental result. Phys. Rev. E **64**(1), 1–23 (2001)
14. Newman, M.E.J.: Scientific collaboration networks II: shortest paths, weightednetworks, and centrality. Phys. Rev. E **64**(1), 24–60 (2001)

PEKD: Joint Prompt-Tuning and Ensemble Knowledge Distillation Framework for Causal Event Detection from Biomedical Literature

Xiaoyu Li[1,2], Haonan Liu[1,2], Li Jin[1,2(✉)], Gege Li[3], and Shichang Guan[1,2]

[1] Aerospace Information Research Institute, Chinese Academy of Sciences, Beijing 100190, China
[2] Key Laboratory of Network Information System Technology (NIST), Aerospace Information Research Institute, Chinese Academy of Sciences, Beijing 100190, China
jinlimails@gmail.com
[3] School of Mechanical, Electronic and Control Engineering, Beijing Jiaotong University, Beijing 100044, China

Abstract. Identifying causal precedence relations among chemical interactions in biomedical literature is crucial for comprehending the underlying biological mechanisms. However, several issues persist, including the scarcity of labeled data, the complexity of domain transfer, and limited computing resources in this field. To tackle these challenges, we present a novel approach called Prompt-Ensemble Knowledge Distillation (PEKD). The PEKD model employs a BERT encoder combined with prompt templates to extract causal relationships between events. Additionally, model compression is achieved through a knowledge distillation framework that incorporates loss function regularization constraints, reducing resource overhead and computational time. To enhance the performance of knowledge distillation, an ensemble method with multiple teachers is utilized. Experimental results demonstrate that the proposed approach achieves a significant improvement in macro-F1 compared to the direct distillation methods. Importantly, it exhibits commendable performance when trained on few-shot datasets and compact models.

Keywords: Prompt Learning · Knowledge Distillation · Multi-teacher Ensemble · Event Relationship Extraction · Biomedical Cause-Effect

1 Introduction

With the rapid growth of biomedical big data, there has been a significant expansion in the size of text-based databases holding professional papers. These repositories contain a wealth of untapped professional knowledge. Particularly valuable are the hidden sets of causal precedence relationships within biochemical reactions, establishing a link between consecutive events, where one event acts as a prerequisite for another. This knowledge encompasses the intricate interplay among biochemical events, complex processes, and underlying mechanisms in the realm of biochemical reactions. Such reactions span a broad spectrum, ranging from protein signaling pathways to phosphorylation reactions. Causal events within biochemical reactions can assist doctors in encoding the relational characteristics of reaction mechanisms, aiding inference when evidence is insufficient [1]. However, extracting comprehensive causal mechanisms from the extensive existing data in the field of biomedical research still presents numerous challenges.

The continuous progression of natural language processing, breakthroughs in critical technologies, and the ongoing development and enhancement of systematic applications are all unfolding dynamically. The purpose of event relation extraction is to automatically extract the logical relationships that precede events, which serve as the fundamental semantic units, from a piece of text and store them in a knowledge database. Among them, causal precedence is an important type of event relation. Figure 1 provides several task examples.

Corpus Example in Biomedical Domain	Event Relation
AMPK directly phosphorylates Raptor in an LKB1 dependent manner *leading to* the binding of 14-3-3 proteins to Raptor and subsequent inhibition of mTORC1.	E1 **Precedes** E2
In this regard, neurofibromin negatively regulates RAS activity *by* accelerating the hydrolysis of active GTP bound RAS to inactive GDP bound RAS.	E2 **Precedes** E1
They found that Nedd4 requires Mnk2 dependent phosphorylation of Ser112 and Ser121 for its interaction with Spry2.	**None**

Fig. 1. Examples of relations in event pairs in the causal precedence dataset

Recently, large-scale pre-trained language models (LLMs) have greatly enhanced the state-of-the-art performance across various natural language processing tasks. However, there are still challenges in utilizing LLM-based extraction methods in the field of biomedicine. On one hand, there is a scarcity of annotated data in the biomedical domain, leading to an insufficient number of samples for neural network learning. For instance, the Pathway Commons database aims to facilitate research on causal mechanisms; however, it currently covers only 1% of the literature with annotated data [2]. To address this issue, several methods have been proposed for training on few-shot learning [3]. However, the prevailing approach involves fine-tuning pre-trained models obtained from general language corpora using a limited number of expert samples. These methods lack prompt methods with prior knowledge, making it challenging for the models to rapidly acquire domain-specific knowledge for adaptation to downstream tasks [4]. On the other hand, the increasing depth and dimensionality of neural networks, coupled with the introduction of numerous large-scale language models, have resulted in substantial CPU and GPU costs, as well as significant memory consumption when performing computations with these complex and extensive models. However, deploying these complex models on resource-constrained devices has become a formidable challenge as portable intelligent terminal devices continue to advance. Model compression techniques based on pruning algorithms and knowledge distillation are necessary to accommodate the limited memory and lower computational capacity of such devices [5]. Based on the research background mentioned above, we propose the PEKD method to improve the performance of causal event relation extraction on few-shot datasets in the field of biomedicine. Our main contributions of this paper are as follows:

1. In the context of few-shot dataset scenarios, general benchmark models encounter difficulties in rapidly adapting to the biomedical domain. To tackle this issue, we propose an innovative approach of incorporating prior knowledge through prompt instructions. This approach enhances the model's rapid understanding in specific domains and accelerates the fine-tuning training on few-shot datasets.
2. To address the limitations posed by computational resources and parameter scale on practical intelligent terminal devices in the biomedical field, it is necessary to compress the model. We propose an innovative knowledge distillation framework called prompt-tuning. This framework involves training a teacher model with full parameters and then training a student model with compressed parameters to fulfill the model compression requirements.
3. To overcome the challenges of large learning biases and overfitting in single teacher-student knowledge distillation training frameworks, we propose a novel multi-teacher ensemble learning paradigm. This strategy significantly mitigates variance and bias during the training of teacher networks and knowledge transfer processes, facilitating model compression while simultaneously enhancing knowledge distillation performance.

2 Related Work

2.1 Event Relation Extraction Approach Based on Neural Network

There are two primary frameworks for neural network-based event relation extraction tasks: pipeline-based event relation extraction and joint extraction-based event relation extraction. The pipeline-based event relationship extraction method, which divides the extraction task into upstream task (event detection) and downstream task(relation classification). Chen et al. [6] employed a Dynamic Multi-pooling Convolutional Neural Network (DMCNN) to identify trigger words and event elements in the text. For the downstream relationship classification task, Zeng et al. [7] proposed a deep convolutional neural network based on positional features. The joint extraction approach, which mitigates the issue of error transfer between upstream and downstream tasks by uniformly modeling them. Zheng et al. [8] employed a hybrid modeling approach for named entity recognition and relationship classification tasks.

2.2 Few-Shot Learning Methods for Neural Network Models

Prominent methods in this regard encompass model fine-tuning, data enhancement, and migration learning. Few-shot learning is a technique that involves model fine-tuning, where a neural network model is initially pre-trained on a large-scale dataset and then fine-tuned using few-shot datasets. Howard et al. [9] introduced a generalized method for fine-tuning language models, which dynamically adjusts the learning rate during fine-tuning. Few-shot learning based on data augmentation, which aims to enhance sample diversity through auxiliary expansion and feature enhancement, particularly in scenarios with limited samples. Wang et al. [10] employed semi-supervised learning to motivate the top-level unit of a CNN to learn features from unlabelled data, going beyond the constraints of small sample data. Few-shot learning based on transfer learning, which is an emerging learning framework that transfers existing knowledge from one domain to another. Vinyals et al. [11] introduced a matching network based on metric learning to address the single-sample migration learning problem. This network utilizes a kernel function to calculate the distance between the labeled samples and the unlabeled samples, ensuring alignment of the distributional features between the training set and the query set.

2.3 Compression Methods for Neural Network Models

Contemporary model compression techniques for neural networks encompass various methods, such as pruning, parameter sharing, quantization, decomposition, lightweight network design, and knowledge distillation. The purpose of the pruning algorithm is to selectively remove nodes, connections, or convolutional kernels from the model based on computation. Gao et al. [12] proposed a dynamic pruning algorithm that enables the trained model to dynamically assess the significance of the convolution kernel's output feature maps and make decisions on whether to skip specific convolution channels. Knowledge distillation involves training small models using a large model, commonly known as the teacher model for the large model and the student model for the small models. The initial distillation method proposed by Hinton et al. [13] is based on information transfer from logits in a neural network. To mitigate the impact of structural and scale differences between the student model and the teacher model, Mirzadeh et al. [14] introduced the concept of a helper model. The teacher model is utilized to distill the helper model, which, in turn, is employed to distill the student model.

3   Main Method

we perform experiments on causal relationship extraction (CRE) using domain-specific corpora in the field of biomedicine [15]. Given the practical application scenarios for causal relationship extraction, such as rapid information processing, frequent question answering, and client-side deployment, we also conduct experiments to reduce the size of neural network models.

3.1   Problem Definition

Causal Relationship Extraction: Given a text corpus sequence $s = s_1, s_2, ..., s_L$, which is achieving word embedding, feature extraction, and relationship classification by utilizing a model M. Finally, we will get a 1×3 relationship vector $v_{re} = (r_1, r_2, r_3)$, which represents the logits for three types of relationships: **Cause-Effect, Effect-Cause, and No-Causality**. Knowledge distillation-based model compression task is to equip the student model, acting as a compact network, with accuracy and recall levels approaching those of the teacher model when performing the task of causal relationship extraction. Specifically, given a text corpus sequence $s = s_1 s_2 ... s_L$, a teacher model M_T is employed to produce logits: $v_{re-t} = (t_1, t_2, t_3)$. Subsequently, through the process of knowledge distillation, we train the student model M_S to obtain output logits: $v_{re-s} = (z_1, z_2, z_3)$.

3.2   Framework

We introduce a multi-teacher ensemble knowledge distillation model, as illustrated in Fig. 2, which integrates prompt tuning, effectively addressing both the tasks of causal relationship extraction and model compression simultaneously.

Next, given a text corpus sequence $s = s_1 s_2 ... s_L$ and a supplementary prefix $p = p_1 p_2 ... p_Q$, we construct a fused prompt text sequence $\bar{s} = p_1 p_2 ... p_Q s_1 s_2 ... s_L$. By using teacher models M_T^1, M_T^2, ..., M_T^n, we can obtain logits $v_{re-t} = (t_1, t_2, t_3)$. Subsequently, we train a student model M_S through knowledge distillation to produce output logits $v_{re-s} = (z_1, z_2, z_3)$ for classification.

For convenience, we label the proposed model as the "Main Model", consisting of three modules: the prompt-tuning-based meta-extraction module, which handles basic causal relationship extraction tasks; the knowledge distillation module for training the compact network; and the multi-teacher ensemble module, which reduces variance and improves model performance. Let's introduce each module individually:

Causal Relation Extraction Model Based on BERT. We initially investigate the meta-extraction module, which utilizes a neural network to perform the fundamental task of causal relation extraction. It primarily comprises two components: the prompt-tuning BERT encoder [5] and an MLP classifier, as depicted in Fig. 3. Prompt-tuning represents a novel paradigm in NLP tasks [16]. It entails

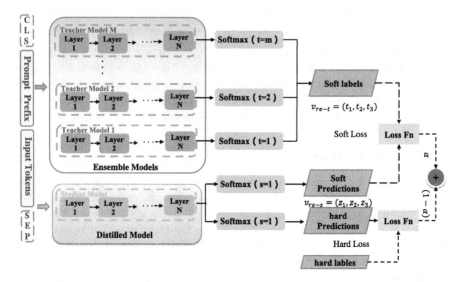

Fig. 2. Framework of multi-teacher Knowledge distillation model with prompt-tuning

incorporating additional prompt information into the text to facilitate easier fine-tuning for downstream tasks. In contrast to the traditional 'pre-training + fine-tuning' paradigm, which often exhibits a substantial gap between pre-training and the specific downstream task, prompt-tuning tackles the downstream task by manually or automatically designing template prompts and expected text responses. This approach narrows the gap between pre-training and downstream tasks.

In the context of causal relation extraction on the Causal Priority dataset, the training sample size is relatively small. Based on the findings of Scao and Rush [17], a single prompt can be considered equivalent to approximately 100 regular data points, resulting in a significant improvement in sample efficiency. For the dataset utilized in this experiment, when considering utilizing 64% of the total samples for training (equivalent to approximately 512 samples), incorporating a single prompt is akin to augmenting the training data by approximately 20%. Building upon this, we devised a series of prompt templates to augment the data samples. This process entails appending a prefix $p = p_1 p_2 ... p_Q$ to the sequence $s = s_1 s_2 ... s_L$, yielding a merged prompt text sequence denoted as $\bar{s} = p_1 p_2 ... p_Q s_1 s_2 ... s_L$, which serves as the input for the sample sequence. To ensure compatibility with the BERT network, it must be extended with specific tokens to create the sequence $s_{in} = [CLS] \, p_1 p_2 ... p_Q \, [SEP] \, s_1 s_2 ... s_L \, [SEP]$, where $[CLS]$ denotes the usage of this sequence for classification tasks, and $[SEP]$ serves as a sentence separator.

BERT initially encodes the input sequence s_{in} into one-hot encoding using dictionary mapping, thereby transforming s_{in} into the original word vectors $X_{one-hot}$. Subsequently, it acquires the word embedding vector X_e, which serves

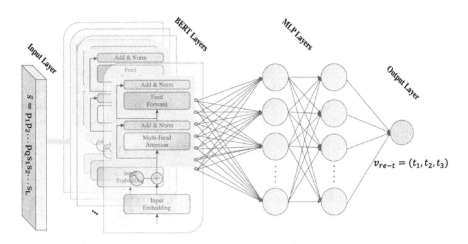

Fig. 3. Structure of causal relation extraction model based on BERT

as the input to the encoding block, by integrating token embeddings, positional embeddings, and segment embeddings. This process is represented by the following equation:

$$X_e = Embedding\left(s_{in}\right) \tag{1}$$

The encoding block consists of multiple stacked Transformer Encoder layers, which incorporate a multi-head self-attention mechanism for aggregating contextually relevant information. The attention mechanism, denoted as A, calculates the similarity between the query Q and the keys K to derive the corresponding values V, as shown in Eq. 2. Self-attention is a mechanism where both the keys and values are set to the sequence itself. Multi-head self-attention is achieved by concatenating multiple distinct self-attention mechanisms using the contact-function, enabling the capture of more comprehensive representation capabilities.

$$A\left(Q, K, V\right) = softmax\left(\frac{QK^T}{\sqrt{d}}\right) V \tag{2}$$

In the $i - th$ Encoder layer, Q_i represents the query, while K_i and V_i represent the key-value pairs. $H_{i,j}$ denotes the $j - th$ attention head within the layer, and MH_i refers to the multi-head self-attention mechanism within the same layer. $W_{i,j}^Q$, $W_{i,j}^K$, and $W_{i,j}^V$ represents the weight matrices for the $j - th$ attention head in the layer, and W_i^o represents the output mapping matrix within the layer. Then, $H_{i,j}$ and MH_i can be represented as Eq. 3 and Eq. 4, respectively:

$$H_{i,j}\left(Q_i, K_i, V_i\right) = A\left(W_{i,j}^Q Q_i^T, \ W_{i,j}^K K_i^T, \ W_{i,j}^V V_i^T\right) \tag{3}$$

$$MH_i\left(Q_i, K_i, V_i\right) = Concat\left(H_{i,1}\left(Q_i, K_i, V_i\right), \ldots\ldots, H_{i,h}\left(Q_i, K_i, V_i\right)\right) W_i^o \tag{4}$$

In the $i-th$ Encoder layer, if we denote the input as X_i, it serves as both the query and the key-value pairs within that layer:

$$Q_i = K_i = V_i = X_i \tag{5}$$

Let Y_i represent the output of this layer, which is obtained from the attention encoding of the input X_i in this layer. This is achieved through residual connections and layer normalization (LayerNorm function), as described in Eq. 6:

$$
\begin{aligned}
Y_i &= LayerNorm\left(X_i + MH_i\left(Q_i, K_i, V_i\right)\right) \\
&= LayerNorm\left(X_i + MH_i\left(X_i, X_i, X_i\right)\right)
\end{aligned}
\tag{6}
$$

The input to the first layer is the word embedding vector X_e. Subsequently, the input for each layer is the output from the previous layer, as expressed in Eq. 6 and Eq. 7:

$$
\begin{aligned}
X_1 &= X_e \\
X_{i+1} &= Y_i
\end{aligned}
\tag{7}
$$

Based on Eq. 6 and Eq. 7, the output vector for each layer can be computed. The output vector from the $C-th$ layer is then passed through a $two-layer$ MLP with weights and biases denoted as W_1, W_2, b_1, and b_2. This MLP produces the v_{re} vector and determines the causal relationship category, as shown in Eq. 8:

$$v_{re} = ERE\_Bert_{model}\left(s_{in}\right) \tag{8}$$

Model Compression Module Based on Knowledge Distillation. In practical application scenarios, there is often a need to restrict the size of model parameters, lower model training costs, reduce the required computational resources (such as GPUs), and save computation time. Therefore, this experiment aims to compress the model for these reasons. Generally, training compact models directly leads to substantial performance gaps compared to large models. Therefore, this experiment considers utilizing the training results of a large model to guide the training of a compact model. Specifically, in this experiment, the knowledge distillation method is employed to transfer the knowledge acquired by a large language model during training to a compact model. The process commences with training a teacher network using the cross-entropy loss, which compares the model's predicted results with the data labels. Subsequently, the teacher network generates predictions, which serve as labels to guide the training of the student network, in addition to the original data labels. The student network produces the final prediction results.

Let v_{re} vectors be calculated according to Eq. 1–Eq. 8 for both the teacher model and the student model, denoted as v_{re-t} and v_{re-s} respectively. These vectors can be expressed as shown in Eq. 9:

$$
\begin{aligned}
v_{re-t} &= ERE\_Bert_{teacher}\left(s_{in}\right) \\
v_{re-s} &= ERE\_Bert_{student}\left(s_{in}\right)
\end{aligned}
\tag{9}
$$

The loss L_{st} during the training of the student network is represented by Eq. 10:

$$L_{st} = \alpha L_{soft} + (1 - \alpha) L_{hard} \tag{10}$$

where, α is a parameter ranging from 0 to 1. L_{soft} represents the mean squared error between the logits of the three categories predicted by the teacher network and those predicted by the student network for the three categories, as depicted in Eq. 11:

$$L_{soft} = \|v_{re-s} - v_{re-t}\|_2^2, \tag{11}$$

where L_{hard} represents the cross-entropy between the predicted results of the student network and the one-hot vector representation v_{re-l} of the original data labels, as illustrated in Eq. 12:

$$L_{hard} = v_{re-s} \cdot log\,(v_{re-l}) + (1 - v_{re-s}) \cdot log\,(1 - v_{re-l}) \tag{12}$$

The experiment explores three approaches for guiding the student network using the predicted labels from the teacher network and the original data labels:

- $\alpha = 0$: The student network is trained solely using the original data labels, resulting in fine-tuning of the student model.
- $\alpha \in \{0, 1\}$: The student network is trained by combining both the original data labels and the teacher network's predictions. The parameter α controls the balance between the two sources of guidance.
- $\alpha = 1$: The student network is directly trained using only the results of training the teacher network.

Knowledge Distillation Module Utilizing Multiple Teacher Ensembles. In the aforementioned knowledge distillation process, fine-tuning the teacher network during training is prone to overfitting, resulting in an increase in the variance of the teacher network. This characteristic is subsequently transferred as knowledge to the student network. Therefore, in this experiment, we consider splitting the dataset multiple times while maintaining the size of the student network unchanged. Consequently, multiple teacher networks are fine-tuned through training, and an ensemble strategy is employed to leverage the collective knowledge of these teacher networks.

An approach involves training the student network by utilizing the average logits predicted by multiple teacher networks. This process entails rewriting v_{re-t} in Eq. 9 based on the formulation provided in Eq. 13:

$$v_{re-t} = \frac{1}{n} \sum_{i=1}^{n} v_{re-t}^i \tag{13}$$

The second approach utilizes the Adaboost algorithm, known for its ability to simultaneously reduce both variance and bias in a classification model. Therefore, in the experiment, the Adaboost method is employed to enhance the performance of the teacher model. This achievement is accomplished by resampling the original dataset using a technique that assigns higher weights to misclassified samples. Subsequently, the logits predicted by the teacher model are employed to distill the knowledge into the student network.

A crucial aspect of the Adaboost-based ensemble method is the maintenance of a sample weight table, denoted as W_s. During the $k-th$ round, the weight of the $i-th$ sample is denoted as w_k^i, and the corresponding classifier is represented as β_k. Let x_i and y_i represent the sample and class label, respectively. The weighted error e_k for this round on the training set and the corresponding learning weight β_k are computed as shown in Eq. 14. The update of w_k^i is performed based on Eq. 15.

$$
\begin{aligned}
e_k &= \sum_{i=1}^{n} w_k^i I\left(max\left(B_k\left(x_i\right)\right) \neq y_i\right) \\
\beta_k &= \frac{1}{2} log\left(\frac{1-e_k}{e_k}\right)
\end{aligned}
\tag{14}
$$

$$
w_{k+1}^i = \frac{w_k^i}{Z_k} exp\left(\beta_k Sn\left(B_k\left(x_i\right), y_i\right)\right)
\tag{15}
$$

where $I(x)$ is the indicator function, Z_k is the weight normalization factor. And $Sn\left(B_k\left(x_i\right), y_i\right) = -1$ when the classification is correct and $Sn\left(B_k\left(x_i\right), y_i\right) = 1$ otherwise.

The final step involves taking the weighted average of the logits output from Eq. 16 by the classifier:

$$
v_{re-t} = \sum_{k=1}^{n} \beta_k B_k(x)
\tag{16}
$$

4   Datasets and Experiments

4.1   Datasets

The dataset utilized in this experiment is the Causal Priority Dataset [15], extensively annotated by domain experts with a wealth of knowledge in the field of biochemistry. This dataset serves as a valuable resource for both studying event extraction in the biochemistry domain and researching the causal relationships between these biochemical events. In other words, it aids in determining the inevitability of one event leading to the occurrence of another event.

The dataset comprises 858 pairs of annotated biochemical reaction events, labeled as "E1" or "E2" according to their order of appearance in the text. Each event pair can exhibit one of three causal relationships: E1 causing E2, E2 causing E1, or no causal relationship. These event pair relationships consist of 109 instances of E1 causing E2, 27 instances of E2 causing E1, and 722 instances with no relationship.

4.2   Evaluation Metric

As discussed in the preceding section, the Causal Priority Dataset suffers from a class imbalance issue. In this experiment, we adopt the widely used machine learning approach and employ macro-F1 as the primary evaluation metric, which calculations are presented in Eq. 17–Eq. 18.

$$\textbf{Pre} = \frac{TP}{TP + FP} \qquad \textbf{Rec} = \frac{TP}{TP + FN} \qquad (17)$$

$$\textbf{marco-F1} = \frac{2 \times \textbf{Pre} \times \textbf{Rec}}{\textbf{Pre} + \textbf{Rec}} \qquad (18)$$

4.3   Hyper-Parameters

BERT as the Meta-model. In this experiment, various versions of the BERT model were selected to obtain and compare the performance of pre-trained models on downstream causal relation extraction tasks. The selection considered different model parameter sizes and training corpora. The pre-trained models were obtained from the Huggingface library.

- **bert-base-uncased model**: It is a pre-trained model on general text corpora with an approximate parameter size of 110 million.
- **biobert-base model**: This model is specific to biomedical language, with an approximate parameter size of 110 million.
- **tiny-bert model**: This model has the same pre-training data as the bert model but a smaller parameter size of approximately 5.5 million.
- **mini-bert model**: This model is similar to the bert model in terms of pre-training data but has a smaller parameter size of approximately 11 million.

The dataset was divided into an 80% training set and a 20% test set. For all models, this experiment employed 5-fold cross-validation, with each fold undergoing 20 rounds of training. The learning rate was set to 1e-4.

Knowledge Distillation Experiment. Based on the performance of different meta-models, biobert-base was selected as the teacher network, and mini-bert was chosen as the student network for subsequent experiments. To mitigate overfitting of the teacher network during fine-tuning, the fine-tuning stage consisted of only 8 rounds of training. Experiments were performed using various values of α, ranging from 0.00 to 1.00 with increments of 0.25. To evaluate the impact of different templates on the performance of knowledge distillation under the prompt-tuning paradigm, four types of prefix templates were designed, as described in the following:

- **Template A: "Which one precedes the other?"**
- **Template B: "Which tokens causally precede?"**
- **Template C: "Find the preceding tokens:"**
- **Template D: "Do leading tokens causally precede?"**

Meta-model Comparative Experiments. Table 1 presents the experimental results of different models score on the validation and test sets. The results show that using domain-specific word embedding models improves the F1 score of BiLSTM models, particularly with larger hidden layer dimensions. Various BERT models outperformed BiLSTM in terms of extraction performance, with the larger-parameter BERT models performing significantly better than the two compact models. Among the compact models, the larger-parameter mini-bert model showed slightly superior performance compared to tiny-bert. When comparing the basic models, the biobert-base model, which underwent extensive pre-training with domain-specific corpora, achieved better performance than the bert-base-uncased model.

Table 1. Performance of different BERT and LSTM models

Types		Validation			Test		
Models	Submodels	Acc	Rec	F1	Acc	Rec	F1
BiLSTM	lstm-general-300	0.273	0.406	0.326	0.246	0.413	0.308
	lstm-general-700	0.288	0.531	0.373	0.291	0.426	0.345
	lstm-specified-300	0.262	0.551	0.355	0.275	0.583	0.383
	lstm-specified-700	0.385	0.610	0.472	0.402	0.546	0.462
BERT	bert-base	0.415	0.588	0.486	0.510	0.521	0.515
	tiny-bert	0.329	0.631	0.433	0.390	0.531	0.449
	miny-bert	0.337	0.552	0.419	0.424	0.505	0.460
	biobert	**0.442**	**0.656**	**0.528**	**0.532**	**0.574**	**0.553**

Table 2 presents the results of the knowledge distillation experiment with varying α values for the student network on both the validation and test sets. The results clearly indicate that as the value of α increases, there is a discernible trend of higher F1 scores on the test set; however, the relationship is not strictly linear. This initial observation implies that, in the context of causal relation extraction tasks on the causal priority datasets, the student network's performance improves when it acquires knowledge directly from the teacher network, rather than relying solely on the original data labels.

4.4   Overall Performance

Table 3 presents the results obtained for the student network on both the validation and test sets using the prompt template of prefix **D** and employing the Adaboost algorithm for multiple teacher ensemble.

From the experimental results, the performance of the main model on the test set demonstrates a significant improvement. This improvement can be attributed to the following reasons: Firstly, the dataset's class imbalance tends to bias the model towards predicting the absence of causality. By employing the Adaboost

Table 2. Performance of knowledge distillation models with different α

Parameter α Values	Validation			Test		
	Acc	Rec	F1	Acc	Rec	F1
0.00	0.337	0.552	0.419	0.424	0.505	0.460
0.25	0.362	0.530	0.444	0.426	0.507	0.464
0.50	0.341	0.552	0.422	0.426	0.518	0.469
0.75	0.355	**0.564**	**0.438**	0.421	0.525	0.467
1.00	**0.359**	0.560	0.437	**0.434**	**0.532**	**0.479**

algorithm for multiple teacher ensembles, the weights of samples with potential causality, even if they were misclassified, are increased, thereby improving the model's recall. Secondly, implementing prompt tuning for both the student and teacher models enhances the effectiveness of the self-attention mechanism by minimizing the vector distance between the word embeddings related to causality and the phrase 'causally precede'.

Table 3. Student models' performance via knowledge distillation of main model

Models	Validation			Test		
	Acc	Rec	F1	Acc	Rec	F1
Directly Distillation	0.353	0.560	0.439	0.436	0.532	0.479
Our Main Model	**0.419**	**0.571**	**0.484**	**0.444**	**0.569**	**0.498**

Table 4. Student models' performance with identical prompt-tuning template

Prompt Templates	Validation			Test		
	Acc	Rec	F1	Acc	Rec	F1
A	0.318	0.560	0.405	0.426	0.525	0.470
B	0.410	**0.565**	0.474	0.423	**0.557**	0.480
C	0.335	0.536	0.412	0.426	0.537	0.475
D	**0.423**	0.560	**0.482**	**0.449**	0.545	**0.492**

4.5   Ablation Study

Single-Teacher Fusion with Prompt Tuning Knowledge Distillation.
Table 4 presents the performance of student networks achieved through knowledge distillation with a single teacher. Incorporating prompt tuning in the distillation process results in a certain improvement of the student network compared to the direct distillation method. This improvement can be attributed to the use of prefix prompt templates, which serve as anchors for the model in downstream tasks. However, the enhancement is not substantial compared to the main model, likely due to the impact of overfitting during teacher network training and the lack of variance reduction through ensemble methods.

Knowledge Distillation with Multiple Teachers Ensemble Without Prompt Tuning. The F1 scores of student networks trained using a multiple teachers ensemble, with the prompt-tuning component removed, in the verification and test sets are 0.456 and 0.494, respectively. These scores show an improvement of 0.10 and 0.14 compared to direct distillation. However, the improvement is not substantial compared to the main model. The primary reason, based on the result analysis, is the theoretical foundation for error reduction through ensemble learning. The result indicates that as the variance of predictions from different models increases, reflecting greater diversity among the models, the generalization error of the ensemble model decreases.

5   Conclusion

This paper presents a novel PEKD framework designed to tackle the challenge of extracting causal event relations in the field of biomedical sciences. In order to address the needs of scenarios with limited samples, we propose a fine-tuning approach that significantly improves the baseline model's adaptability in the biomedical sciences. Moreover, due to the widespread adoption of next-generation intelligent terminals, there is a need to compress and deploy pre-trained models. Hence, we propose a method for compressing knowledge distillation models based on constraints from loss function regularization, enabling the generation of compact neural networks. Lastly, to address the performance degradation bottleneck in compressed pre-trained models, we propose an innovative strategy that integrates multiple teachers to optimize the effectiveness of knowledge distillation. Our devised strategies, validated through various ablative experiments, demonstrate their capability to enhance the performance of the baseline model. This exploration aims to propose more efficient methods to advance domain-specific technologies.

Acknowledgements. The work is supported by the National Natural Science Foundation of China (62206267).

References

1. Li, Z., Li, Q., Zou, X., Ren, J.: Causality extraction based on self-attentive BiLSTM-CRF with transferred embeddings. Neurocomputing **423**, 207–219 (2021)
2. Rodchenkov, I., et al.: Pathway commons 2019 update: integration, analysis and exploration of pathway data. Nucleic Acids Res. **48**(D1), D489–D497 (2020)
3. Frisoni, G., Moro, G., Carbonaro, A.: A survey on event extraction for natural language understanding: riding the biomedical literature wave. IEEE Access **9**, 160721–160757 (2021)
4. Kang, H., et al.: TSPNet: translation supervised prototype network via residual learning for multimodal social relation extraction. Neurocomputing **507**, 166–179 (2022)
5. Liang, Z., Noriega-Atala, E., Morrison, C., Surdeanu, M.: Low resource causal event detection from biomedical literature. In: Proceedings of the 21st Workshop on Biomedical Language Processing, Dublin, Ireland, pp. 252–263 (2022)
6. Chen, Y., Xu, L., Liu, K., Zeng, D., Zhao, J.: Event extraction via dynamic multi-pooling convolutional neural networks. In: Proceedings of the 53rd Annual Meeting of the Association for Computational Linguistics and the 7th International Joint Conference on Natural Language Processing, Beijing, China, pp. 167–176 (2015)
7. Zeng, D., Liu, K., Lai, S., Zhou, G., Zhao, J.: Relation classification via convolutional deep neural network. In: Proceedings of COLING 2014, the 25th International Conference on Computational Linguistics: Technical Papers, Dublin, Ireland, pp. 2335–2344 (2014)
8. Zheng, S., et al.: Joint entity and relation extraction based on a hybrid neural network. Neurocomputing **257**, 59–66 (2017)
9. Howard, J., Ruder, S.: Universal language model fine-tuning for text classification. arXiv preprint arXiv:1801.06146 (2018)
10. Wang, Y.-X., Hebert, M.: Learning from small sample sets by combining unsupervised meta-training with CNNs. In: The 30th Conference on Neural Information Processing Systems, Barcelona, Spain, pp. 244–252 (2016)
11. Vinyals, O., Blundell, C., Lillicrap, T., Wierstra, D., et al.: Matching networks for one shot learning. In: The 30th Conference on Neural Information Processing Systems, Barcelona, Spain, vol. 29 (2016)
12. Gao, X., Zhao, Y., Dudziak, Ł., Mullins, R., Xu, C.-Z.: Dynamic channel pruning: feature boosting and suppression. arXiv preprint arXiv:1810.05331 (2018)
13. Hinton, G., Vinyals, O., Dean, J.: Distilling the knowledge in a neural network. arXiv preprint arXiv:1503.02531 (2015)
14. Mirza, P.: Extracting temporal and causal relations between events. In: Proceedings of the ACL 2014 Student Research Workshop, Baltimore, Maryland, pp. 10–17 (2014)
15. Hahn-Powell, G., Bell, D., Valenzuela-Escárcega, M.A., Surdeanu, M.: This before that: causal precedence in the biomedical domain. arXiv preprint arXiv:1606.08089 (2016)
16. Li, X., Wang, W., Fang, J., Jin, L., Kang, H., Liu, C.: PEINet: joint prompt and evidence inference network via language family policy for zero-shot multilingual fact checking. Appl. Sci. **12**(19), 9688–9709 (2022)
17. Scao, T.L., Rush, A.M.: How many data points is a prompt worth?. arXiv preprint arXiv:2103.08493 (2021)

Empirical Analysis on the Effectiveness of Pre-trained Models in the Identification of Physical Violence Against Women in Videos for a Multi-class Approach

I. Abundez[1], G. Miranda-Piña[1(✉)], R. Alejo[1], E. E. Granda-Gutiérrez[2], A. Cisniega[1], and O. Portillo-Rodríguez[3]

[1] Division of Postgraduate Studies and Research, National Institute of Technology of Mexico (TecNM) Campus Toluca, Av. Tecnológico s/n, Agrícola Bellavista, 52149 Metepec, Mexico
{iabundezb,mm22280266,ralejoe,mm22281243}@toluca.tecnm.mx

[2] UAEM University Center at Atlacomulco, Universidad Autónoma del Estado de México, Carretera Toluca-Atlacomulco Km. 60, 50450 Atlacomulco, Mexico
eegrandag@uaemex.mx

[3] Faculty of Engineering, Universidad Autónoma del Estado de México, Cerro de Coatepec s/n, Ciudad Universitaria, 50100 Toluca, Mexico
oportillor@uaemex.mx

Abstract. Violence against women captured in videos and surveillance systems necessitates effective identification to enable appropriate reactions for controlling and mitigating of its effects in public spaces and the potential apprehension of aggressors. While several algorithms have been developed for violence detection, their evaluation has primarily focused on controlled scenarios with clear differentiation between violent and non-violent scenes, representing two-class identification problems. However, real-world situations often present challenges where specific actions, such as hugs or effusive greetings, fall into an ambiguous class that is difficult to classify. Consequently, this transforms into a multi-class identification problem. In this study, we assess the performance of three pre-trained models, namely VGG16, ResNet50, and InceptionV3, to evaluate their efficacy in addressing the multi-class identification challenges. Furthermore, we compare their performance against datasets consisting of two-class classifications, where the models generally exhibit satisfactory results. Our analysis reveals that the models struggle to differentiate the ambiguous scenes effectively, with Inception V3 achieving a 0% correct detection rate for this class. Notably, VGG16 outperforms the other models, attaining accurate detections of 48% for the ambiguous class, 75% for non-violence scenes, and 54% for violence scenes. This research sheds light on the limitations of current classification models when confronted with the complexity of real-world scenarios. The findings emphasize the importance of developing improved algorithms capable of accurately distinguishing ambiguous situations and enhancing the performance of violence detection systems.

TecNM has partially supported this investigation with project 13816.22-P.

Keywords: Artificial Neural Networks · Deep learning · Physical-violence against women · Transfer learning · VGG16 · ResNet50 · InceptionV3

1 Introduction

In Mexico, The National Institute of Statistics Geography and Informatics has reported that 34.7% of women experience physical violence. The states with violence reports are the State of Mexico (78.7%), Mexico City (76.2%), and Queretaro (75.2%). In those states, women aged 15 years and older have experienced some gender violence in their lifetime. According to data from the 2021 National Survey on the Dynamics of Relationships in Households, violence against women in Mexico remains a significant concern. The survey findings indicate that women residing in urban areas experience a higher prevalence of violence, accounting for 73% of reported cases. Additionally, women between the ages of 25 and 34 face a particularly heightened risk, with a prevalence rate of 75%. The study also reveals that women with lower education levels are disproportionately affected, with 78% reporting incidents of violence. Furthermore, women who are separated, divorced, or widowed are significantly impacted, comprising 74% of reported cases [1]. In many cases, women victims of violence are part of a group already in precarious or vulnerable conditions, such as indigenous women and inhabitants of rural communities. Physical violence is one of the most severe problems in our society, and the efforts to mitigate it should be focused on the worrying consequences that can lead to death or permanent physical and emotional injuries [2].

Additionally to these facts, already severe, another complex factor that makes their containment even more complicated is the amount of economic, technological, and human resources required to provide care and response to the victims of violence. However, with the new technologies that appear every day, there are more tools to help the victims; such is the case that arises [3], who presents an architecture developed for the detection of criminal activities based on real-time analysis using a deep learning technique called Faster R-CNN, which has the function of detecting robberies and thefts. This application could return erroneous data if the offender's modus-operandi changes or the event unfolds differently than those used to train the network. Another example is shown in [4], where different deep learning models were studied to identify violence in images using pre-trained models exhibiting success rates of approximately 90 % using the public datasets MoviesFight and HockeyFight.

In the same context, in [5] the authors present a comparison of pre-trained models (such as VGG16, ResNet, InceptionV3 and MobileNet) in the detection of physical violence in video. Their experiments were conducted using a public dataset with recorded videos of students acting out the scenes with violent and non-violent behaviors. The results of these models showed that the MobileNet architecture gave the best result in terms of accuracy, while InceptionV3 came in second place.

Also, in [6], a neural network model for violence detection based on separating frames into three stages is proposed. This method is known as an end-to-end deep learning framework. An outstanding feature of this method is that frames that could slow down the network's learning process are removed in the first stage, resulting in much faster training.

One way to identify violence is through the posture taken by the aggressor. In [7], an algorithm capable of identifying fights by estimating the posture that someone adopts just before starting a fight was presented. Its outcome was achieved mainly by using a deep neural network called Open Pose, which detects silhouettes or outlines of people in video and images. This network comprises multiple layers of convolutional neural networks that process an image to obtain the body posture of the people in that image.

A different approach to treating the problem is presented in [8] to detect a person's state of mind through convolutional neural networks, which could anticipate a violent action. It is an antecedent for women's differentiation in video images. This uses image separation using the Stochastic Gradient Descent method that seeks to minimize an objective function written as the sum of differentiated functions and solves the problem of high computational cost using the Principal Component Analysis (PCA) technique. This work resulted in a robust algorithm capable of identifying human emotions through facial expressions with a high level of effectiveness.

In [9] is proposed a neural network capable of distinguishing attacks with bladed weapons and firearms through the labeling of images and objects that involves thousands of photo frames of different types of weapons, ranging from the most common (such as pistols) to the most destructive (such as shotguns or assault rifles), to carry out later training that gives the algorithm the ability to identify firearms in real-time. On the other hand, in [10] is presented a SELayer-C3D violence detection model addressing the problem primarily in local regions, obtaining an accuracy of 99%.

Other problems to consider in identifying violence or similar tasks are false positives and error rates, which could be the difference between life and death. In [11], a neural network model that significantly reduces false positives and the error rate is proposed by changing the neural network approach. The challenge is to detect falls in older adults at their homes; because the camera does not see some falls in some cases, instead of focusing on detecting falls, the authors seek to train the algorithm to detect when the person is on the floor. In this way, higher percentages of effectiveness were achieved.

Much of the work aimed at detecting violence on video presents the problem that once violence has been identified, it is impossible to know who has attacked whom, that is, who is the victim and who is the perpetrator. So, in [12], the authors focused on developing a neural network that can provide additional data about the detected aggression. It is achieved by an Acceleration Measure Vector (AMV) composed of direction and magnitude of motion where the temporal derivative of AMV can detect abrupt movements. In this sense, if it is a kick or a punch, the algorithm detects who has initiated the attack.

Usually, videos used to train neural network models for detecting violent events use collections of pre-fabricated or acted scenes that could undoubtedly represent an inconvenience when facing actual acts of violence. Therefore, [13] proposed a network model based on ResNet50, which was trained with real videos from video surveillance cameras using different environments to detect violence and to classify it into three categories, the first of which involves violence with firearms and the remaining two only violent or inappropriate behaviors. The result is a truly more efficient model since its training was more precise and punctual and, therefore, could give better results if applied to real surveillance videos.

Despite the significant advances that have been made in detecting violence on video, there are still efforts aimed at treating the problem in a general way, and their study has not focused on violence against women. For this reason, in this work, we focus on physical violence against women and address the problem of false positives. For that, we built a dataset with three classes that contain images (obtained from video) related to violence against women: a) violent scenes, b) non-violence, and c) scenes that could be difficult to classify or cause false positives. The effectiveness of three popular deep learning neural network models: VGG16, ResNet50, and Inception V3, are studied in this multi-class context.

2   Theoretical Foundations

One of the most common neural network architectures is Feed-Forward, comprised of at least three neuron layers (one input, one output, and one hidden) [14]. In deep learning versions, Feed-Forward Neural Networks have two or more hidden layers, reducing the number of nodes per layer and using fewer parameters. Although it implies a more complex optimization problem [15], the availability of modern frameworks like TensorFlow or Apache-Spark (characterized by new technological approaches like Graphical Processing Units (GPUs) or cluster computing), makes this drawback less restrictive. Similarly, recurrent neural networks allow more efficient processing of long and variable-length data sequences [16].

Convolutional Neural Networks (CNN) is a trendy architecture that combines a fully connected layer (similar to multilayer perceptron or another linear classifier like support vector machines) with one or more convolutional layers to build a map that has the function of extracting key features (see Fig. 1). This architecture implements pooling to reduce the dimensionality of the features vector and save only the relevant features [17]. Consequently, abstract features can be extracted by the convolutional layers, where convolutional kernels behave as local filters for unprocessed sequential data and produce non-variant local features. Succeeding pooling layers extract the essential features within fixed-length windows [18]. CNNs are powerful extractors of meaningful features [19] and are effective in problems related to modeling image data, summarization, and classification [20]. VGG16, ResNet50, and InceptionV3 are very popular pre-trained CNN models in classification tasks with promising results.

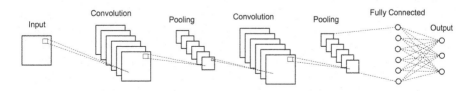

Fig. 1. Typical CNN is comprised of convolutional layers interleaved with pooling layers.

2.1 VGG16

It is the first deep neural architecture successor of the AlexNet model, also called VGGNet, which comprises multiple convolutions of fully connected layers, and many image recognition parameters [21]. The main difference between the previous models and VGG16 is that its creators proposed using considerably small 3×3 receptive fields that can also be called filters and a stride of just one pixel. It is important to note that the receptive field or filter in the first layer in the AlexNet had an 11×11 with stride 4. It also involves fewer weight parameters and reduces the over-fitting in the training process.

At the 2014 ImageNet Large Scale Visual Recognition Challenge (ILSVRC), which is an annual competition where the new CNN models of image classification are presented, the VGG16 model with 16 layers achieved a test accuracy of 92.7%, leading the top 5 on ImageNet classification with an error of 7.3% [21]. Although the model did not win the event, its performance was so good that it caught the attention of researchers, scientists, and developers, enabling further innovations.

2.2 ResNet50

ResNet50 model is part of the ResNet family, whose architecture was introduced to avoid dead connections and reduce the effect of layers on performance. The number of deep layers depends on its version; then, ResNet50 has 50 deep layers. It is a residual CNN model that has produced ground-breaking performances in image recognition, object detection, face recognition, and image classification. The architecture has four stages that fix the degradation problem in deeper CNNs [22] and was designed with a convolution of 7×7 kernels, a max pooling with a stride of size 2, and the kernel increment in each layer. This configuration obtains very high accuracy and efficiency values. Therefore, this model can be used for artificial or non-artificial vision tasks. In addition, to perform a faster training process, it uses the "bottleneck" concept to reduce the number of parameters and the number of matrix operations.

2.3 InceptionV3

InceptionV3 is a CNN of the Inception family which aims to improve computational efficiency and reduce the number of parameters compared to its predecessor, using computation added in the most efficient way possible through factored convolutions and aggressive regularization [23]. The InceptionV3 version has 42 layers, with which it has demonstrated that it can achieve an accuracy of over 78.1%. This model consists of symmetric, non-symmetric, and convolution compilation blocks, as well as average reduction, maximum reduction, concatenations, and fully connected layers. Its most important feature is the consumption of fewer computer resources, which requires fewer optimization techniques, fewer parameters, and processes fewer convolutions, thus increasing speed and resources in training.

3   Experimental Set-Up

3.1   Dataset

The images used for this investigation are based on the videos in the public GitHub repository "airtlab"[1]. This repository contains 350 video clips labeled as non-violent and violent, which were simulated by non-professional actors, and are available for educational and research purposes [24].

Our modified dataset includes three classes of images related to physical violence against women: a) violence, b) no violence, and c) scenes where it is to hard distinguish between violence or non-violence (ambiguous), i.e., those situations where differentiating violence from a non-violence scene could be too difficult to an automatic classifier (for example, a strong hug or a very warm greeting, among others). Figure 2 shows an example of a scene with violence against the woman (left), a non-violence scene (center), and a scenario that could be difficult to classify or ambiguous (right). It is worth mentioning that for situations of violence we selected videos in which the male actor was the perpetrator and the female actress was the victim.

Fig. 2. Examples of images for the three classes involved in the classification of scenes: violence against a woman (left), a non-violence scene (center), and image hard to be classified as violence or non-violence or ambiguous(right).

Each frame of the selected videos was extracted using the Python programming language and the OpenCV library (open-source) [25]. Next, each video frame was manually labeled according to where violence was evident, where it was not, and where it was hard to identify (ambiguous). Finally, we created a dataset (D) of 2100 images with 700 violence (where the male actor was the perpetrator), 700 non-violence, and 700 ambiguous images. The images were normalized in size (224×224 pixels) to match the requested input shape of the pre-trained models selected as classifiers, and then the images were converted to grayscale.

To study the impact of images that are hard to be identified in the classifier performance, we set two datasets D_i, where D_1 contains only violence and non-violence images and D_2 violence, non-violence, and ambiguous images.

Dataset $D_i = \{x_1, x_2, \ldots, x_Q\}$ was split randomly in three disjoints sets: TR_i to train the model, TV_i to validate it, and TE_i to test its generalized ability, $D_i = TR_i \cup TV_i \cup TE_i$; and $TR_i \cap TV_i \cap TE = \oslash$, and x_q corresponds to q-th image in D_i. TR_i contains 50% of the samples of D_i, while TV_i and TE_i contains the remaining 50% (25% for each one).

---

[1] https://github.com/airtlab/A-Dataset-for-Automatic-Violence-Detection-in-Videos.

3.2 Free Parameters Specification

The classification models selected for comparison are pre-trained on large data sets, so only fine tuning is required for their implementation in more specific tasks, such as ours in detecting physical violence against women. Considering this, to carry out the fine tuning for each model we freeze the last 3 layers of each one, to later connect it to the layers of a new model. The model structure to connect with the output of the pre-trained model was found by testing different configurations and selecting the best one for each model based on the performance shown.

For the VGG16 and ResNet50 models, their outputs were connected to a flattened layer, two dense layers with 128 nodes, and the ReLu (rectified linear unit) activation function. The lost function used was categorical cross-entropy, which classifies the data by predicting the probability of whether the data belongs to one class or the other class. It is also worth mentioning that categorical cross-entropy is a measurement tool commonly used to evaluate the precision of probabilistic predictions. Adam optimizer was used to train the models due to its utility as a stochastic gradient descent method. The size of the batch was set to 25, and the number of epochs to 50.

Finally, for the InceptionV3 model, a flattened layer was also considered, but this model differs from the others because its dense layer has 4096 nodes. InceptionV3 uses a ReLu activation function, a 0.2 dropout layer, and a softmax layer with n neurons. As in the previous models, n changes when the number of classes changes. In addition, the trial-and-error method found all the parameters selected for fine-tuning, where these values gave the best results for the classification tasks using the pre-trained weights of ImageNet.

We used the Linux operating system (Ubuntu distribution), where Anaconda software was installed as a development environment for the Python programming language. The TensorFlow framework was used with Keras as a programming interface to design, configure, and train the studied models. All tests were carried out on a computer that had a 4 GB NVIDIA GeForce GTX 1650TI graphics card with CUDA (Unified Computing Device Architecture) support.

3.3 Performance of the Deep Learning Models

The confusion matrix is one way to visualize the performance of any classifier. It is generally used in binary classification problems [26]; nevertheless, it also could be applied to multi-class problems [27]. The confusion matrix is a cross table that records the number of occurrences between two raters, the true/actual classification, and the predicted classification, as shown in Table 1. In this paper, we use a confusion matrix with three columns for the predicted category and three rows for the actual occurrences (which correspond to three classes: violence, non-violence, and ambiguous) to test the performance of the studied models.

Table 1 presents three classes (A, B, and C), with 16, 22, and 18 samples in each one, of which only 5, 6, and 7 (respectively) are classified correctly, the rest are misclassified. In addition, we use the *accuracy* (Eq. 1) to know the global performance of each classifier, which is obtained directly from the confusion matrix as follows:

Table 1. Example of confusion matrix for a multi-class problem.

		\multicolumn{4}{c}{**Predicted class**}
		Class A	Class B	Class C	**Total**
	Class A	5	7	4	**16**
True class	Class B	9	6	7	**22**
	Class C	8	5	5	**18**
	Total	**22**	**18**	**16**	**56**

$$accuracy = \frac{\sum_i^N c_{i,i}}{\sum_i^N \sum_j^N c_{i,j}}, \tag{1}$$

where N is the total number of samples, i corresponds to the number of classes and $c_{i,j}$ corresponds to the value at position (i, j) of the confusion matrix.

4 Results and Discussion

This section presents the experimental results of the pre-trained models used to detect physical violence against women in videos. VGG16, ResNet50, and InceptionV3 were tested on two different datasets: a two-class dataset, and a three-class dataset with ambiguous images. To evaluate the performance of such models, the confusion matrix was used as a metric to visualize how many images in the dataset were correctly classified based on their actual labels. The number of correctly classified images is in bold in all matrices presented.

4.1 VGG16 Model

Regarding this model, Table 2 shows a high level of classification for the non-violence class, and the number of violence images correctly classified that the VGG16 model performed well in the binary classification test (two-classes dataset).

Table 2. Confusion matrix for binary classification with VGG16 model.

		\multicolumn{2}{c}{**Predicted class**}
		Non-violence	Violence
True class	Non-violence	**174**	1
	Violence	40	**135**

In contrast, Table 3 shows that in the multi-class classification task, this classifier still distinguishes the non-violence class best, followed by the violence class, while it shows the worst classification performance for the ambiguous class. However, the model could not perform well for all the classes involved. This could be explained due to the complexity of the third class, where the movements in the images used can be mistaken as violence against women when it could be a greeting, a hug, or something related.

Table 3. Confusion matrix for multi-class classification with VGG16 model.

		Predicted class		
		Ambiguous	Non-violence	Violence
	Ambiguous	**84**	79	12
True class	Non violence	36	**131**	8
	Violence	60	20	**95**

4.2 ResNet50 Model

To evaluate the performance of this model, Table 4 presents the number of correctly classified and misclassified images for the binary classification task, where the violence class showed the best classification, with 82% of the 175 violence images used for the test data. In contrast, only 24% of the non-violence images were correctly classified. This shows that the ResNet50 model could not learn how to differentiate violence from non-violence scenes.

Table 4. Confusion matrix for binary classification with ResNet50 model.

		Predicted class	
		Non-violence	Violence
	Non-violence	**42**	133
True class			
	Violence	31	**144**

In the multi-class scenario test for ResNet50, Table 5 shows a better classification performance for the non-violence class, and most images are classified in this class. Thus, ResNet50 exhibited a low overall performance in a multi-class task, obtaining the lowest number of images classified for the violence class, which is the area of interest. Moreover, as can be observed, both VGG16 and ResNet obtained the same number of correctly classified non-violence images.

Table 5. Confusion matrix for multi-class classification with ResNet50 model.

		Predicted class		
		Ambiguous	Non-violence	Violence
	Ambiguous	**33**	135	7
True class	Non-violence	30	**131**	14
	Violence	49	107	**19**

4.3 InceptionV3 Model

Finally, the last pre-trained model used to detect physical violence against women in video images showed a low performance for the class of interest in the two-class test. It showed similar behavior to the other two models for the binary classification, tending to classify better the non-violence images, as can be observed in Table 6, where only 91 images (about 50%) of the violence class were well classified. In contrast, 93% of the non-violence images were correctly classified.

Table 6. Confusion matrix for binary classification with InceptionV3 model.

		Predicted class	
		Non-violence	Violence
	Non-violence	**163**	12
True class			
	Violence	84	**91**

Table 7 evidences a low performance of the InceptionV3 model for the multi-class task. The network could not classify images of the ambiguous class in this scenario; instead, most of the images were classified as non-violent. This could be explained by the fact that most of the images were extracted from non-violent video clips, where the behavior shown in the scene appears to be confusing in determining whether raising the hand will be a punch or simply a greeting. On the other hand, InceptionV3 only classified 39 images (about 20%) for the interest class, while the non-violence class performed well with 171 images correctly classified.

Furthermore, to support the results of the confusion matrices, accuracy values were calculated for each test. These values are shown in Table 8, where it is observed how VGG16 continues to rank as the best classification algorithm in both approaches, with 88% accuracy 59% accuracy in the multiclass approach. However, these values indicate that the algorithms' learning and the classification level are poor. The latter could be associated with the number of images used for this task and the complexity of determining when an act of violence against women occurs.

Table 7. Confusion matrix for multi-class classification with InceptionV3 model.

		Predicted class		
		Ambiguous	Non-violence	Violence
	Ambiguous	**0**	167	8
True class	Non-violence	0	**171**	4
	Violence	0	136	**39**

Table 8. Accuracy values of the selected pre-trained models. Values in bold are the best precision values for each scenario.

	VGG16	ResNet50	InceptionV3
Binary	**0.8829**	0.5314	0.7257
Multiclass	**0.5905**	0.3486	0.4000

Based on the results obtained with the selected hyperparameter configuration, VGG16 emerged as the most effective model in both: binary and multi-class scenarios, consistently demonstrating relatively strong performance, as evident from the previously presented confusion matrices. InceptionV3 followed as the second-best model, exhibiting satisfactory results in binary classification but struggling significantly in the multi-class setting. On the other hand, ResNet50 initially performed poorly in binary classification but surpassed InceptionV3 in multi-class classification. Although InceptionV3 achieved higher accuracy values than ResNet50, it failed to classify any images from the ambiguous class correctly.

Notably, the accuracy values were obtained considering only two categories, underscoring the model's limited performance in the multi-class approach. Consequently, the results highlight the challenges faced by the classifiers in learning classes other than non-violence, suggesting that non-violence class was learned more effectively by all models tested. These findings underscore the need for further research and model development to improve the classifiers' ability to classify complex classes, particularly in multi-class scenarios, accurately. By addressing these limitations, enhanced models can contribute to more robust violence detection systems that effectively identify and distinguish between various classes, ultimately fostering safer environments for women.

5   Conclusions and Future Research

This study examined the performance of popular pre-trained models for binary image classification in multi-class scenarios, specifically in identifying violence against women. The presence of an ambiguous class, which is challenging to distinguish from the typical binary classes of violence or non-violence scenes, complicates the accurate classification of violence in real video captures.

The findings highlight the limitations of models that perform well in controlled scenarios and two-class classification problems but struggle to respond effectively when faced with the ambiguity inherent in real-life situations, such as frames depicting hugs or effusive greetings that may be misclassified as violence.

Analyzing the confusion matrices, it was observed that the ResNet50 model achieved an 82% correct identification rate for violence scenes (the most significant class) in a two-class dataset. However, when the dataset included ambiguous scenes as a third class, this model could only identify 10% of the violence images and 18% of the ambiguous class.

Similarly, the InceptionV3 model demonstrated a 52% correct detection rate for violence images in the two-class dataset but surprisingly failed to identify any scenes from the ambiguous class (0%) in the three-class approach. Furthermore, it was considered that since it is a deeper architecture, the gradients may not flow efficiently to the shallower layers in the established epochs, and therefore their learning capacity could be affected.

On the other hand, the VGG16 model exhibited the best performance in identifying ambiguous images. It correctly recognized 77% of violence images in the two-class problem, and it achieved 54% correct identification for violence scenes, 75% for non-violence scenes, and 48% for the ambiguous class in the three-class context. These results can be attributed to the architecture of this model, because by having more parameters the network has a greater capacity to easily fit the new data, therefore it learns the features better.

Future research should focus on developing or fine-tuning models capable of accurately predicting classes that can potentially confuse automatic classifiers. This is essential to avoid false positives and prevent misinterpretation of potentially dangerous scenes. Additionally, exploring more realistic multi-class problems instead of binary classification would facilitate a more comprehensive evaluation of proposed models. These efforts will contribute to advancing violence detection systems and improve their effectiveness in real-world scenarios.

References

1. INEGI. Violencia contra las mujeres en méxico (2022). https://www.inegi.org.mx/tablerosestadisticos/vcmm/
2. Moctezuma-Navarro, D., Narro-Robles, J., Orozco-Hernandez, L.: La mujer en méxico: inequidad, pobreza y violencia. Rev. mex. cienc. polít. soc 117–146 (2014)
3. Suárez Páez, J.E.: Arquitectura de detección de actividades criminales basada en análisis de vídeo en tiempo real. PhD thesis, Universitat Politècnica de València (2020)
4. Bisbé, E.L.: Detección de escenas de violencia con modelos deep learning. B.S. thesis, Universidad Autonoma de Madrid (2020)
5. Victor, E.D.S., Lacerda, T.B., Miranda, P.B.C., Nascimento, A.C.A., Furtado, A.P.C.: Federated learning for physical violence detection in videos. In: 2022 International Joint Conference on Neural Networks (IJCNN), pp. 1–8. IEEE (2022)
6. Min Ullah, F.U., Ullah, A., Muhammad, K., Ul Haq, I., Baik, S.W.: Violence detection using spatiotemporal features with 3D convolutional neural network. Sensors **19**(11), 2472 (2019)
7. Powell González, J.E., et al.: Detección de peleas en videos usando estimación de postura y bi-lstm. Master's thesis, Benemérita Universidad Autónoma de Puebla (2021)
8. Rodriguez, P.S.: Reconocimiento de expresiones faciales mediante el uso de redes neuronales convolucionales. B.S. thesis, Universitat Politécnica de Catalunya (2017)

9. Sánchez, J., Campos, M.A.: Red neuronal artificial para detección de armas de fuego y armas blancas en video vigilancia. Revista de Iniciación Científica **7**(2), 83–88 (2021)

10. Jiang, B., Xu, F., Tu, W., Yang, C.: Channel-wise attention in 3d convolutional networks for violence detection. In: 2019 International Conference on Intelligent Computing and its Emerging Applications (ICEA), pp. 59–64. IEEE (2019)

11. El Kaid, A., Baïna, K., Baïna, J.: Reduce false positive alerts for elderly person fall video-detection algorithm by convolutional neural network model. Procedia Comput. Sci. **148**, 2–11 (2019)

12. Datta, A., Shah, M., Da Vitoria Lobo, N.: Person-on-person violence detection in video data. In: 2002 International Conference on Pattern Recognition, vol. 1, pp. 433–438. IEEE (2002)

13. Vosta, S., Yow, K.-C.: A CNN-RNN combined structure for real-world violence detection in surveillance cameras. Appl. Sci. **12**(3), 1021 (2022)

14. LeCun, Y., Bengio, Y., Hinton, G.: Deep learning. Nature **521**(7553), 436–444 (2015)

15. Goodfellow, I., Bengio, Y., Courville, A.: Deep Learning. MIT Press, Cambridge (2016)

16. Yu, Y., Si, X., Hu, C., Zhang, J.: A review of recurrent neural networks: LSTM cells and network architectures. Neural Comput. **31**(7), 1235–1270 (2019)

17. Bengfort, B., Bilbro, R., Ojeda, T.: Applied Text Analysis with Python. O'Reilly Media Inc. (2018)

18. Zhao, R., Yan, R., Wang, J., Mao, K.: Learning to monitor machine health with convolutional bi-directional LSTM networks. Sensors **17**(2) (2017)

19. Wu, J.-L., He, Y., Yu, L.-C., Robert Lai, K.: Identifying emotion labels from psychiatric social texts using a bi-directional LSTM-CNN model. IEEE Access **8**, 66638–66646 (2020)

20. Kattenborn, T., Leitloff, J., Schiefer, F., Hinz, S.: Review on convolutional neural networks (CNN) in vegetation remote sensing. ISPRS J. Photogramm. Remote. Sens. **173**, 24–49 (2021)

21. Yang, H., Ni, J., Gao, J., Han, Z., Luan, T.: A novel method for peanut variety identification and classification by improved VGG16. Sci. Rep. **11**, 15756 (2021)

22. Theckedath, D., Sedamkar, R.R.: Detecting affect states using VGG16, ResNet50 and SE-ResNet50 networks. SN Comput. Sci. **1**(2), 1–7 (2020)

23. Szegedy, C., Vanhoucke, V., Ioffe, S., Shlens, J., Wojna, Z.: Rethinking the inception architecture for computer vision. In: 2016 IEEE Conference on Computer Vision and Pattern Recognition (CVPR), pp. 2818–2826 (2016)

24. Bianculli, M., et al.: A dataset for automatic violence detection in videos. Data Brief **33**, 106587 (2020)

25. Bradski, G.: The OpenCV library. Dr. Dobb's J.: Softw. Tools Prof. Program. **25**, 120–123 (2000)

26. Luque, A., Carrasco, A., Martin, A., De-Las-Heras, A.: The impact of class imbalance in classification performance metrics based on the binary confusion matrix. Pattern Recogn. **91**, 216–231 (2019)

27. Grandini, M., Bagli, E., Visani, G.: Metrics for multi-class classification: an overview (2020)

Assessing GPT-4 Generated Abstracts: Text Relevance and Detectors Based on Faithfulness, Expressiveness, and Elegance Principle

Bixuan Li, Qifu Chen, Jinlin Lin, Sai Li, and Jerome Yen[✉]

University of Macau, Avenida da Universidade, Taipa, Macau, China
{MC36529,MC35690,MC25602,MC36627,jeromeyen}@um.edu.mo

Abstract. In recent years, the advancement of Artificial Intelligence (AI) technology has brought both convenience and panic. One of the most notable AI systems in recent years was ChatGPT in 2022. In 2023, GPT-4 was released as the latest version. Scholars are increasingly investigating the potential of ChatGPT/GPT-4 for text generation and summarization. Inspired by the principle of "Faithfulness, Expressiveness, and Elegance" in translation, this study investigates the writing and summarizing capabilities of GPT-4, one of the latest AI chatbots. For this purpose, we collected 60 articles from top financial and technology journals, extracted the abstract part, and fed it into GPT-4 to generate abstracts. Three evaluation metrics were created for evaluation: the Text Relevance Score, the AI Detector Score, and the Plagiarism Detector Score. Our findings indicate that abstracts generated by GPT-4 closely resemble the original abstracts without being detected by the plagiarism detector Turnitin in most cases. This implies that GPT-4 can produce logical and reasonable abstracts of articles on its own. Also, we conducted a cross-temporal analysis of GPT-4's effectiveness and observed continuous and significant improvement. Nevertheless, with the advancement of AI detectors, the abstracts generated by GPT-4 can broadly be recognized as AI-generated. Furthermore, this paper also discusses ethical concerns and future research directions.

Keywords: Artificial Intelligence · Large Language Models · GPT-4 · Chatbot · Abstract Generation

1 Introduction

The father of artificial intelligence (AI), John McCarthy, defines it as "the science and engineering of making intelligent machines." The evolution of AI has had a lengthy historical trajectory. The term "artificial intelligence" was officially coined in 1956 by the Dartmouth Summer Research Project on Artificial Intelligence (DSRPAI) at Dartmouth College [1]. Beginning in August 1956, the development of artificial intelligence has ebbed and flowed over 70 years. In 1966, Joseph Weizenbaum at MIT developed the well-known computer program ELIZA, a natural language processing (NLP) program that could mimic a conversation with a person [2]. Nevertheless, the initial "AI winter" arose

© The Author(s), under exclusive license to Springer Nature Singapore Pte Ltd. 2024
Y. Tan and Y. Shi (Eds.): DMBD 2023, CCIS 2017, pp. 165–180, 2024.
https://doi.org/10.1007/978-981-97-0837-6_12

after government funding ceased in 1974. A few years later, the Japanese government sponsored AI for the Fifth Generation Computer project in 1980 [3]. The boom did not last long, and AI encountered its second winter from 1987 to 1993. A remarkable turning point in AI occurred when Garry Kasparov, the world chess champion, was defeated by IBM's chess machine "Deep Blue" on May 11, 1997 [4]. Since then, artificial intelligence has garnered increased attention and continued to evolve. Various new AI robots and systems have been developed, such as MIT's Kismet [5], Google's driverless car, IBM's Watson [6], and Google DeepMind's AlphaGo [7].

In 2017, the Transformer, a novel network architecture designed by the Google Machine Translation Team [8], provided the foundation for developing OpenAI's GPT. In 2018, inspired by Google's research [9], OpenAI released the first Generative Pre-trained Transformer, GPT-1. After just eight months, GPT-1 was improved upon with the release of GPT-2 [10]. The GPT series continued to evolve, leading to the release of GPT-3 in 2020 [11], InstructGPT in January 2022 [12], and ChatGPT in November 2022 [13]. ChatGPT, an AI-based language model, sparked an explosion of interest in AI. ChatGPT reached 57 million users in its first month in just five days and 100 million users in January 2023 [14].

As an innovative AI technology, ChatGPT is expected to impact the way researchers work significantly. Researchers have already utilized ChatGPT to generate articles, literature summaries, and computer code [15]. Nevertheless, there are still conflicting opinions about the potential of ChatGPT for writing and summarizing. The editor-in-chief of Nature and Science argues that ChatGPT does not meet the authorship standard [16]. The editor-in-chief of the Science, Holden Thorp, says "We are now updating our license and Editorial Policies to specify that text generated by ChatGPT (or any other AI tools) cannot be used in the work" [17]. Meanwhile, many scholars have begun to explore ChatGPT's ability to write in various fields. For example, Gao et al. use ChatGPT to generate 50 abstracts based on top medical journals and evaluate them. They find that ChatGPT can generate abstracts without plagiarism but identified as AI-generated [18]. Likewise, Dowling has also experimented with ChatGPT's potential to assist in writing a research study by involving 32 reviewers to evaluate ChatGPT's output [19]. Cascella has concluded that ChatGPT could summarize and draw conclusions from an abstract's background, methods, and results [20].

Since the release of GPT-4 by OpenAI on March 14, 2023 [21], there have been several articles investigating its performance. According to reports, GPT-4 surpasses the passing score on official USMLE exam questions by over 20 points [22]. Additionally, GPT-4 ranks in the top 10% on a simulated bar exam, while its predecessor, GPT-3.5, ranked in the bottom 10%. OpenAI describes GPT-4 as containing human-level performance on academic standards [21]. GPT-4 can accomplish complex tasks within multiple fields, such as mathematics, coding, vision, medicine, law, psychology, and more [23].

Continuing but distinct from previous research, we aim to evaluate GPT-4's writing and summarizing capabilities objectively. To this end, we conducted structured tests to evaluate GPT-4's ability to generate academic abstracts, prioritizing the financial and technology fields. Inspired by the principles of "Faithfulness, Expressiveness, and Elegance" in Translation (Yan Fu) [24], we developed three evaluation metrics to assess the quality of text generated by GPT-4 systematically. We selected 60 articles from leading financial and technology journals and utilized GPT-4 to generate abstracts. We assessed the accuracy of the generated abstracts by comparing them to those written by humans, similar to evaluating "faithfulness" in translation. Moreover, we implemented an AI detector and plagiarism detector to assess the quality of the abstracts generated by GPT-4 and determine whether they can be recognized as plagiarized or AI-generated. The last, "Elegance" calls for human reviewers to identify which would be our future research.

This article provides insights into the performance of large language models, particularly GPT-4, in text generation and contributes to the advancement of research and application in the text generation domain. Consistent with prior studies, our experiments indicate that GPT-4 generated abstracts achieve high relevance scores when compared to the original abstracts without being identified as plagiarized. However, such generated abstracts are easily recognized as being generated by AI. Different from prior studies, we carried out a cross-temporal analysis of GPT-4's efficacy and noted continuous and substantial enhancement. This implies that GPT-4 can more efficiently acquire textual and visual data. Additionally, we introduced two novel terms, "All in One Conversation" and "Individual Conversations", to distinguish whether abstract generation occurs in a single or multiple windows. It can be found from the comparison results that using individual windows improves performance, but after the enhancements of GPT-4, this advantage has shrunk. This also reflects the improved consistency in GPT-4's performance. In addition, the proper use of GPT-4 requires the implementation of adequate safeguards to prevent data breaches and to strike a balance between the continuity of GPT-4 and human beings. These issues are of concern to many people.

Section 2 introduces why GPT-4 outperforms other large language models (LLM). It also outlines the evolution of GPT-4 and discusses related research on GPT-4's writing proficiency. Section 3 illustrates our methodology in detail. Section 4 demonstrates our findings from experiments. Section 5 discusses limitations, ethical concerns, and future research topics. Finally, Sect. 6 provides the conclusion.

2 Literature Review

2.1 Comparison of GPT-4 to Other Large Language Models (LLMs)

When it comes to the field of natural language processing (NLP), mainstream large-scale language models are one of the important breakthroughs. GPTs, LaMDA, GLM/ChatGLM, and PaLM/Flan-PaLM are mainstream models. Models such as BERT and GPT have very powerful functions. BERT is developed based on the concept of transfer learning and is primarily used to address language understanding tasks, such as question answering and semantic relationship extraction. In contrast, GPT is created using the idea of generative pre-training and is mainly utilized for language generation duties, such as text generation and carrying out machine translation [25].

ChatGLM is a large-scale language model for Chinese-English bilingual pre-training. It uses 130 billion parameters and 400 billion tokens for training and combines the model structures of GPT and BERT [26]. In English, it performs better than GPT-3; while in Chinese, it performs better than ERNIE TITAN 3.0 with 260 billion parameters. LaMDA is built by fine-tuning a transformer-based neural language model specifically designed for dialogue. It has up to 137 billion parameters and can use external knowledge sources for conversation [27].PaLM model is a super-large model trained by Google based on the PathWay distributed training architecture, with 540 billion parameters and 780 billion tokens [28].

Compared with other language models such as BERT, GLM, and PaLM, Chat-GPT and GPT-4 have several advantages. GPT-4 possesses a significant edge as it boasts an expansive capacity, enabling exceptional precision in executing a diverse array of language-based assignments. Its extensive applicability allows for meticulous customization towards various tasks like translation, summarization, and question answering. Another important advantage of GPT-4 is that it can achieve a high level of proficiency in generating human language that is difficult to distinguish from text written by humans. While other language models may have similar goals, none can achieve the same level of proficiency in these areas as GPT-4, and therefore it is used in this experiment (Table 1).

Table 1. GPT series vs. other models

Model	Parameters	Primary Use Case
GPT-4	1 quadrillion	Conversational ability and multimodal support
GPT-3	175 billion	Text generation, conversational ability
ChatGLM	130 billion	Conversational ability and mathematical logic
LaMDA	137 billion	Conversational ability and multimodal support
PaLM/Flan-PaLM	540 billion	Conversational ability and mathematical logic

By looking at the evolution of GPT-4 and its comparison with other LLMs, we can see the superior performance of GPT-4 in various domain tasks. This provides a basis for us to conduct the next experiments and stimulates our interest in exploring the potential and application value of GPT-4 for academic abstract generation.

2.2 The Evolution of GPT from GPT-1 to GPT-4

The GPT (Generative Pre-trained Transformer) family of models is a series of language models designed to facilitate natural language processing (NLP) tasks by pre-training large language models. Different versions of GPT models have different design ideas and performances, as shown in Fig. 1. For example, GPT-1 combines supervised and unsupervised learning and performs better on specific language tasks [9]; GPT-2 aims to train word vector models with more generalization ability, and demonstrates its versatility by increasing the network parameters and expanding the dataset [10]; however, the improvement of GPT-2's generalization ability also creates the problem of mediocre results; GPT-3 solves the problem of GPT-2's mediocre results by introducing few-shot learning and employs sparse attention module [11]. Sparse-attention module i.e., when computing self-attention, only some of the words in the input sequence are considered instead of all the words. This reduces the computation and memory footprint and significantly increases the number of references to a mega language model. InstructGPT uses a reinforcement learning scheme based on GPT-3 to further improve performance [12]. ChatGPT is optimized for conversational tasks based on the GPT-3.5 model and can carry out natural and fluent conversations and demonstrate abilities such as coherent thinking and logical reasoning. In comparison, GPT-4 demonstrates the ability to be more reliable and creative when the task is more complex and can handle more detailed instructions [29]. GPT-4 also has strong multimodal capabilities, representing the first step in the evolution from a large-scale language model to a multimodal model. GPT-4-All-Tools is an updated version of the GPT-4, providing access to additional tools, including image generation with DALL-E, web browsing, and a Python environment.

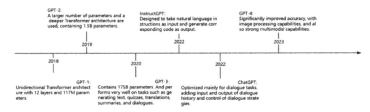

Fig. 1. GPT series development process

The new paradigm of prompting in the GPT-4/GPT-3 model can be summarized as "Pre-train + Prompt + Predict". This model adapts various downstream tasks to resemble pre-training tasks for effective prompt selection. By selecting appropriate prompts, the user can control the model to predict the output so that a fully pre-trained model can be used to solve diverse downstream tasks. In this case, the principle of text generation is as follows: Step 1: Input processing: transform the input into vectors. Step 2: Capture features: pass the vectors to the Transformer model and the neural network captures their features and relationships. Step 3: Understanding Context: Self-attention mechanism that allows the model to focus on different parts of the input and understand the relationships between them. Step 4: Generate content: generate the most probable words based on the already generated text and input. After that the generated text is passed will the RM model for further training as well as further optimization of the model through the PPO algorithm.

2.3 Writing Capabilities in GPT-4

Although GPT-4 was released in March 2023, pertinent research has already been published. Sanderson states that GPT-4 can produce writing that is close to human writing and can analyze graphics, which is exciting for researchers, but also disappointing for its security [30]. Bubeck also explores the language, vision, coding, and mathematics abilities of the early version of GPT-4. By tasking GPT-4 to write a proof in the style of Shakespeare, they suggest that GPT-4 can not only learn the general concepts and patterns of many fields but also synthesize them in creative ways [23]. Lee proves that GPT-4 can produce a medical note and scrutinize a suggested medical note in the medical field [31]. Furthermore, Ufuk utilizes GPT-4 to produce radiology abstracts and demonstrate its effectiveness in scientific writing within the radiology field [32]. Meanwhile, Li highlights GPT-4's impressive performance on numerical reasoning tasks for financial text analysis, but its limitations in sentiment analysis and named entity recognition [33]. Unlike previous studies, inspired by "Faithfulness, Expressiveness, and Elegance" in Translation [24], we would explore the writing and summarizing ability of the GPT-4 with structured tests.

3 Methods

3.1 Datasets

Given that finance and technology are influential fields in modern society, and the literature in these areas typically contains ample data, graphs, and terminology, this is particularly representative and valuable for evaluating GPT-4's ability to generate abstractions. Considering the future fields of application, finance and technology are undoubtedly two of the most influential areas in society. As a result, we elected to investigate finance and technology fields for this study.

Due to the rapid advancement of artificial intelligence (AI) technology and the iterative nature of OpenAI's products, a step-by-step research approach has been implemented. We initially delved into the financial sector, which is characterized by intricate concepts that could help us evaluate GPT-4's accuracy in comprehending and specializing content. Within the next two months, we conducted research on the technology field at GPT-4-All-Tools. GPT-4-All-Tools is a version of GPT-4, equipped with additional tools to enhance its capabilities, including DALL-E, python environment, and browsing tool. This update and advancement of GPT-4 offer a temporal side-by-side comparison of its ability to generate abstracts, providing us with a unique research perspective on its impact.

After selecting the fields, our objective was to identify the leading academic journals in each industry and select articles with high citations from them. Therefore, we shortlisted six journals in each sector as our sample source, based on their impact factor (IF) and SCImago Journal Rank (SJR) (shown in Table 2). The Impact Factor (IF), also referred to as the Journal Impact Factor (JIF), is a scientometric measure created by Clarivate Analytics. It calculates the average annual number of citations received by articles published in a specific journal during the preceding two years. SJR represents the Scimago Journal Rankings, a metric that evaluates journal citations based on their number and quality.

Next, we chose five articles from each journal according to our selection principle. This principle involves selecting articles published within the past decade, sorting them by number of citations (highest to lowest), and ensuring they do not exceed 80 pages in length. In general, except for the minimum number of citations for articles in the past three years, which has been relaxed to about 100 times, the number of citations for articles in other years is around 300–60,000.

We downloaded articles from Google Scholar or the official publication website, removing any existing abstracts to avoid interference. We used the AskYourPDF plug-in to upload articles in the finance field in GPT-4 when GPT-4 could not upload PDFs

Table 2. Journal's impact factor from IF/JIF&SJR (2022)

Field	Journal/Impact Factor (2022)	IF/JIF	SJR↓
Finance	Journal of Finance	8.0	15.5
Finance	Review of Financial Studies	8.2	12.2
Finance	Journal of Financial Economics	8.9	10.6
Finance	Journal of Accounting and Economics	5.9	6.1
Finance	Review of Finance	4.4	5.7
Finance	Journal of Financial and Quantitative Analysis	3.9	3.7
Technology	IEEE Journal on Selected Areas in Communications	13.1	7.7
Technology	IEEE Wireless Communications	12.9	6.6
Technology	Science Robotics	27.5	6.5
Technology	Nature Machine Intelligence	25.9	6.2
Technology	IEEE Transactions on Pattern Analysis and Machine Intelligence	24.3	4.4
Technology	IEEE Transactions on Neural Networks and Learning Systems	10.4	3.4

directly, as shown in Fig. 2. However, for experiments in the technology field, GPT-4 has the capability to upload PDFs directly as depicted in Fig. 2.

Fig. 2. Using AskYourPDF plug-in vs uploading PDF files directly into GPT-4

3.2 Prompting

One major consideration when utilizing GPT-4 is designing effective prompts. We gradually improved the prompting based on the answers, GPT-4 prompting experimental process as shown in Fig. 3.

Pre-designed question: "Generates an abstract in only one paragraph".

In the first step, to make the abstracts generated by GPT-4 more professional, a preset scenario was added to GPT-4 when asking questions. The guidebook "How to Write a Good Scientific Paper" [34], outlines the procedures and techniques for crafting an effective abstract. Based on this, we asked GPT-4 to generate abstracts with the following prompt:

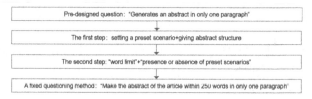

Fig. 3. GPT-4 prompting experimental process

"Act as an expert Academic writer specializing in finance, please generate the abstract part based on the content of the article I have given:

The abstract should be a concise, stand-alone summary of the paper that covers the following topics:

- Background/motivation/context,
- Aim/objective(s)/problem statement,
- Approach/method(s)/procedure(s)/materials,
- Results, and Conclusion(s)/implications".

After adding the preset scenarios, GPT-4 focused on given materials and repeatedly read them. It only mechanically produced text and constructed paragraphs based on the provided "keywords composed of the summary". There was no discernible logical coherence or emotional tone between sentences, and some paragraphs were longer or shorter than others.

After identifying problems with the use of the preset scenarios, our second step was to investigate the results of combining textual constraints with the scenarios. It is widely agreed in the academic community that abstracts should be between 100–250 words in length. Most abstracts from the selected twelve journals in the dataset adhere to the established consensus on a maximum word limit of approximately 250 words. Thus, "250 words" will be implemented as one of the experimental scenarios, and two control groups will also be included: "original abstract's word count" and "unlimited word count". The study randomly selected five articles in two different settings: one with no preset scenario and the other with a preset scenario. Then, we used GPT-4 to give corresponding grades (from 0 to 100) from these different perspectives: Accuracy, Clarity, Comprehension, Similarity, etc., as shown in Table 3.

Table 3. GPT-4's grades of generated abstracts with and without preset scenarios

	Without preset scenarios	With preset scenarios	The average grade
Original word count	95	92	93.5
250 words	98	93	95.5
Unlimited	90	91	90.5
The average grade	94.3	92	–

From the perspective of word limit, GPT-4 gives the highest score to abstracts of about 250 words, regardless of whether there is a preset scenario; From the perspective of whether there are preset scenarios, GPT-4's grades for "with preset scenarios" is lower than for "without preset scenarios". Based on the experimental results, we decided to use a fixed prompting method to conduct experiments: "Make the abstract of the article within 250 words in only one paragraph".

Furthermore, this article introduces a novel method for GPT-4, which examines its perpetual production of all abstracts within one single window, versus generating abstracts for each article in an individual window every time. To indicate this approach, we have introduced two new terms, "All in One Conversation" and "Individual Conversations".

3.3 Evaluation Metrics

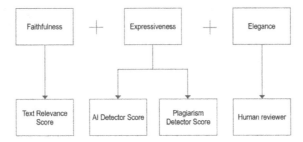

Fig. 4. An indicator system for measuring the performance of GPT-4 generated abstracts

Inspired by "Faithfulness, Expressiveness, and Elegance" in Translation, this article assesses GPT-4 generated abstracts using three distinct metrics: "Text Relevance Score", "AI Detector Score", and "Plagiarism Detector Score", each rated on an scale of 0 to 100. As shown in Fig. 4, Faithfulness is evaluated through the "Text Relevance Score", and Expressiveness is evaluated through the "AI Detector Score" and "Plagiarism Detector Score"; Elegance needs human reviewers to evaluate.

"Text Relevance Score" compares the GPT-4 generated abstracts with the original abstracts to establish the text relevance index. The score is calculated by GPT-4 itself with the prompt: "Please grade the textual relevance of these articles to the original abstract". Based on the answers given by GPT-4, the scores were mainly generated based on the documents' content focus, key discussed technologies, mentioned applications, and overall context. The higher the score, the higher the correlation between the GPT-4 generated abstracts and the original ones.

"AI Detector Score" demonstrates the probability that text is identified as AI-generated. It utilizes the CopyLeaks, one of the most accurate AI detectors, known for its accuracy in identifying AI-generated text. The higher the score of this indicator, the higher the probability the text is AI-generated.

"Plagiarism Detector Score" indicates whether GPT-4 generated abstracts include plagiarism of others' works or achievements. This indicator uses the website "Turnitin" for detection. Turnitin is a well-known website designed for the detection of such plagiarism in papers. The higher the score, the more direct use of original text or other articles is present, and the lower the proportion of text generated by GPT-4 itself.

4 Results

4.1 Text Relevance Scores

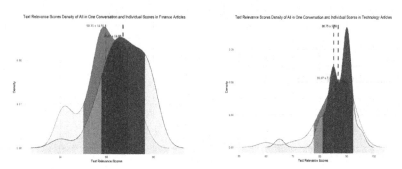

Fig. 5. Text Relevance Scores density of All in One Conversation and Individual Conversations

Table 4. Text Relevance Scores summary statistics

Field	Text Relevance Scores	Min	Max	P25	P75	Mean	Median
Finance	All in One Conversation	30.0	85.0	55.0	70.0	59.3	60.0
	Individual Conversations	30.0	90.0	61.3	83.8	70.7	70.0
Technology	All in One Conversation	60.0	95.0	81.3	90.0	85.1	85.0
	Individual Conversations	65.0	95.0	85.0	90.0	86.8	90.0

Figure 5 displays the density distribution of the Text Relevance Scores for the financial and technology fields. The "Individual Conversations" and "All in One Conversation" are represented by blue and red colors on each graph, respectively. Shown in the Fig. 5, the distribution of GPT-4 text relevance scores is consistent and concentrated within a similar one-standard deviation of these density curves. However, in the Finance field, the standard deviation is larger than that in Technology. This indicates that the stability of the GPT-4 increases with each upgrade.

Table 4 displays density curve statistics for All in One Conversation and Individual Conversations, indicating mean scores, scores above the 25th and 75th percentile, and standard deviations. It is shown that Individual Conversations outperformed All-in-One Conversations above the 25th percentile in both fields. Besides, Individual Conversations achieved higher average scores compared to All in One Conversations in both fields, we can conclude that Individual Conversations have superior Text Relevance Scores when compared to the average scores of All in One Conversations. However, because of the enhancement of GPT-4-All-Tools, the gap between the two conversation types decreases in the technology field. In addition, the performance of GPT-4 is consistently reliable when using the plug-in or uploading the PDF file in GPT-4. An examination of the top scores achieved by both fields - reaching as high as 90 in Finance and 95 in Technology - demonstrates that abstracts generated by GPT-4 can be highly relevant to those generated by human authors.

In conclusion, our analysis of the statistical properties of the density curves and the Text Relevance Scores of abstracts produced by All in One Conversation and Individual Conversations in the finance and technology fields enables us to draw some preliminary findings. Although the text relevance scores are outstanding and largely consistent for both conversation methods, Individual Conversations show superior performance in certain aspects, especially in the mean and percentile values. Moreover, the improvement of GPT-4 All-Tools seems to be obvious, showing that the ability of GPT-4 to capture textual and pictorial information is becoming more consistent and better. The short-term progress has also made us realize its potential and capabilities, and we are also looking forward to his performance in the future.

4.2 AI Detector Scores

Since we conducted experiments sequentially in the financial and tech domains, it should be noted that CopyLeaks only indicated whether the contents were AI or HUMAN-generated without providing the probability in the technology field. Earlier, in our experiments in finance, CopyLeaks provided AI-generated probabilities as AI Detector Scores. Therefore, the analyses presented below apply to the financial field.

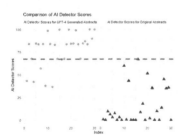
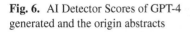
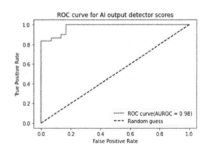

Fig. 6. AI Detector Scores of GPT-4 generated and the origin abstracts

Fig. 7. ROC curve for AI Detector Scores

According to Fig. 6, the AI Detector Scores of the original abstracts peak at approximately 67%. Conversely, the AI Detector Scores for GPT-4 generated abstracts frequently exceed 67%, which indicates a considerable deviation from the AI Detector Scores distribution trend of the original abstracts. The 25th percentile value of AI Detector Scores for GPT-4 generated texts is 67.8. This suggests a high likelihood that GPT-4 generated abstracts can be identified with accuracy.

Based on the AI Detector's ability to accurately detect texts likely written by AI, we have labeled them as either GPT4 (TPR) or human-written (FPR) to create a dummy variable. In Fig. 7, using the ROC (receiver operating characteristic curve) method, we analyzed the performance of our model to better understand its scale. The figure illustrates an AUC of about 0.98, indicating excellent model performance across various thresholds. A ROC curve area near 1 signifies a balanced ratio of True Positive Rate (TPR) to False Positive Rate (FPR). This indicates that present AI detection techniques can differentiate between content generated by humans and AI, which has significant implications for maintaining academic integrity, copyright protection, etc. (Table 5).

Table 5. GLM shows a relationship between the Text Relevance Scores with AI Detector Scores

Variable	Estimate	Std. Error	tvalue	Pr(>|t|)
AI Detector Scores-GPT-4	0.8558	0.05178	16.53	***(2.69e−16)

This paper uses GLM regression to explore the relationship between the Text Relevance Scores and AI Detector Scores. According to the results of the generalized linear regression, an increase of one unit in "AI Detector Scores (GPT-4) [%AI]" corresponds to a corresponding increase of 0.8558 in the mean of the dependent variable. Supported by the standard error and t-value, this coefficient estimate is highly significant (Pr(>|t|) < 2.69e−16), indicating that "AI Detector Scores (GPT-4) [%AI]" has significant predictive power for the dependent variable. Furthermore, in addition to the regression coefficients, the AIC value of the model is 275.44, indicating its relative excellence in interpreting the data. These results show a positive correlation between the Text Relevance Scores of the GPT-4 generated abstracts and their AI Detector Scores. As the relevance of GPT-4-generated texts increases, AI performance improves, and AI Detector Scores rise accordingly. This also demonstrates the consistency of GPT-4's performance at a different level.

4.3 Plagiarism Detector Scores

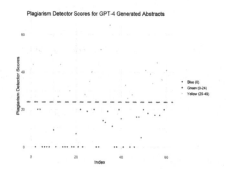
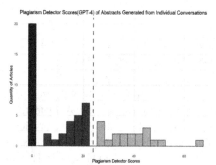

Fig. 8. Scatter gram of Plagiarism Detector Scores for GPT-4 generated abstracts from

Fig. 9. Histogram of Plagiarism Detector Scores for GPT-4 generated abstracts

GPT-4 utilizes advanced NLP technology, machine learning algorithms, and large-scale data processing capabilities. This article examines its capabilities for analyzing and generating original abstracts by exploring issues of plagiarism and content duplication.

In Fig. 8, the Plagiarism Detector Score threshold is set at 24% (according to Turnitin's official website, a score of 24% is marked in the green zone), meaning that if the Plagiarism Detector Score in the text is greater than the threshold, it is considered unacceptable. Using this as a standard, most of the abstracts generated by GPT-4 meet the requirements. Figure 9 shows a left-skewed distribution, which indicates that GPT-4 generates texts through its comprehensive internal mechanisms, with most texts maintaining a relatively low plagiarism rate. Therefore, we can conclude that the summary generated by GPT-4 is generated by itself after understanding, rather than using a large number of original texts or existing sentences on the Internet. However, the use of the GPT4-All-Tools add-on and the search engine's internet connectivity heighten the risk of plagiarism, damaging the authenticity and reliability of text generated by GPT-4.

5 Discussion

One of the main features touted by GPT-4's advancements is its improved accuracy when working with more complex tasks and its ability to analyze images and graphics. In this study, we demonstrated the performance of GPT-4 in generating abstracts of the 60 top journal articles by feeding the entire article without the original abstract. We found that GPT-4 performed better in Individual Conversations than in All in one Conversations. During the experiments in the finance field, we observed that GPT-4 incorrectly generated a few abstracts with the incorrect journal names or author names when all abstracts were generated in one conversation. When generating abstracts in individual conversations, it was observed that GPT-4 first scanned the article to locate the abstract section instead of generating it. However, when conducting experiments in the field of technology at GPT-4-All-Tools, the problems mentioned above basically never occur. Moreover, 41 out of 60 abstracts were not detected as plagiarized using Turnitin. However, 53 out of 60 were recognized as AI-generated using CopyLeaks, which is consistent with the previous research [18, 35]. Different from prior research, our findings indicate that the enhancement of GPT-4 leads to improved Text Relevance Scores in generating abstracts. Previously, Individual Conversations outperformed All in one Conversations, but this advantage has also diminished following the improvements of GPT-4. These prove that the advancement of GPT-4 has enhanced the quality of text generation and improved consistency. In conclusion, GPT-4 has sufficient summarizing and writing capabilities without plagiarism but is most likely to be recognized as AI-generated. As technology advances, its capabilities will continue to grow stronger and more impactful.

The study has several limitations. Firstly, the findings are dependent on the performance of the plagiarism detection tool Turnitin and the AI detector CopyLeaks. Secondly, when conducting experiments in the field of technology, CopyLeaks stopped providing AI-generated probability values, which can potentially impact research outcomes. Thirdly, the dataset utilized in the experiment may not be sufficient. Fourth, the accuracy of the Text Relevance Scores produced by GPT-4 is contingent on the performance of GPT-4. Finally, the result also relies on the prompting design, and there will be improved prompting designs in the future.

Ethical considerations are crucial for successfully implementing this technology. It is important to recognize its impact on society and use it cautiously. In Australia, students have been caught cheating on online exams using an AI chatbot, leading people to think about how to use AI ethically and where to draw the ethical line [36]. On the one hand, we cannot prevent ChatGPT/GPT-4 from generating misleading, inaccurate, or biased information [37]. In our experiments, we observed several errors while utilizing GPT4, including incorrect authors or journal names. Therefore, it is important to evaluate ChatGPT/GPT-4 carefully and prudently. However, our experiments reveal that GPT-4 generated text is largely identifiable as AI. Although there are some minor flaws, they still provide some reassurance on the ethical side. On the other hand, we cannot prevent people from relying on ChatGPT/GPT-4 and engaging in academic dishonesty. It will be difficult to ban the use of ChatGPT/GPT-4 in scientific publications, but we have the responsibility to use it properly as "co-authors" [38]. The essential components necessary to advance human knowledge remain human thinking, analyzing, verifying, and testing.

We hope this research will inspire further research on these interesting topics. In future studies, we recommend including more fields such as medicine, education, and psychology to conduct experiments with more fields. The future study can also evaluate the summarizing and writing ability of GPT-4 by using financial news, financial statements, or technology reports as sample data. Additionally, future research can also expand the sample size and expand the evaluation metrics. Furthermore, we suggest that future studies involve human reviewers to measure the quality of the texts generated by GPT-4. Further experiments can explore how GPT-4 reacts differently to different emotional prompts. Additionally, with the launch of GPT-5 and other advanced LLMs, future experiments and comparisons can be conducted.

6 Conclusion

Inspired by the principle of "Faithfulness, Expressiveness, and Elegance" in translation [24], we designed the above experiments to evaluate the writing and summarizing capabilities of large-scale language models (particularly GPT-4). Our findings indicate that GPT-4 can generate abstracts with up to a 95 Text Relevance Score that resembles those created by human authors. However, it is easy to detect that the abstracts were generated by artificial intelligence, even though plagiarism detection is less likely to be detected. In addition, we found some interesting findings during the experiments. For example, GPT-4 first scanned the abstract part of the article instead of summarizing the abstract itself, and GPT-4's performance in Individual Conversations outperforms its performance in All in One Conversation. However, as GPT-4 evolved, it made progress in both conversation methods resulting in improved scores and a shortened gap. This also reveals the rapid improvement of GPT-4. The findings of this article will contribute to the text generation capabilities of large language models and the advancement of research and applications in the field of text generation.

Ethical concerns inevitably remain one of the main priorities of GPT-4. In the future, we should focus on how to use it sensibly and legally rather than ignoring its presence. Although our experiments have some limitations, we still hope to inspire future researchers. We hope that in the future it will be possible to show that GPT-4 or other LLMs can generate texts that can achieve not only "Faithfulness" and "Expressiveness", but also "Elegance" in the text generation in the future. We aspire to a future where technology fulfills ethical obligations and maximizes its potential for advancing humanity toward a better future.

Acknowledgments. This research was funded by The Science and Technology Development Fund, Macau SAR (File no. 0091/2020/A2).

References

1. Haenlein, M., Kaplan, A.: A brief history of artificial intelligence: on the past, present, and future of artificial intelligence. Calif. Manage. Rev. **61**, 5–14 (2019)
2. Weizenbaum, J.: ELIZA—a computer program for the study of natural language communication between man and machine. Commun. ACM **9**, 36–45 (1966)
3. Swinbanks, D., Anderson, C.: Japan stubs its toes on fifth-generation computer. Nature **356**, 273–274 (1992)
4. Campbell, M., Hoane, A.J., Hsu, F.: Deep blue. Artif. Intell. **134**, 57–83 (2002)
5. Breazeal, C.: Toward sociable robots. Robot. Auton. Syst. **42**, 167–175 (2003)
6. Ferrucci, D.A.: Introduction to "this is watson." IBM J. Res. Dev. **56**, 1:1–1:15 (2012)
7. Silver, D., et al.: Mastering the game of Go with deep neural networks and tree search. Nature **529**, 484–489 (2016)
8. Vaswani, A., et al.: Attention is all you need. In: Advances in Neural Information Processing Systems, vol. 30 (2017)
9. Radford, A., Narasimhan, K.: Improving language understanding by generative pre-training (2018)
10. Radford, A., Wu, J., Child, R., Luan, D., Amodei, D., Sutskever, I.: Language models are unsupervised multitask learners (2019)
11. Brown, T., et al.: Language models are few-shot learners. arXiv (Cornell University) (2020)
12. Ouyang, L., et al.: Training language models to follow instructions with human feedback. arXiv (Cornell University) (2022)
13. Natalie: ChatGPT—Release Notes. https://help.openai.com/en/articles/6825453-chatgpt-release-notes. Accessed 28 Aug 2023
14. Baruffati, A.: Chat GPT statistics 2023: trends and the future perspectives GITNUX. https://blog.gitnux.com/chat-gpt-statistics/. Accessed 27 Sept 2023
15. van Dis, E.A.M., Bollen, J., Zuidema, W., van Rooij, R., Bockting, C.L.: ChatGPT: five priorities for research. Nature **614**, 224–226 (2023)
16. Stokel-Walker, C.: ChatGPT listed as author on research papers: many scientists disapprove. Nature **613** (2023)
17. Thorp, H.H.: ChatGPT is fun, but not an author. Science **379**, 313 (2023)
18. Gao, C.A., et al.: Comparing scientific abstracts generated by ChatGPT to original abstracts using an artificial intelligence output detector, plagiarism detector, and blinded human reviewers. bioRxiv (2022)
19. Dowling, M., Lucey, B.: ChatGPT for (finance) research: the Bananarama conjecture. Financ. Res. Lett. **53**, 103662 (2023)
20. Cascella, M., Montomoli, J., Bellini, V., Bignami, E.: Evaluating the feasibility of ChatGPT in healthcare: an analysis of multiple clinical and research scenarios. J. Med. Syst. **47** (2023)
21. OpenAI: GPT-4 technical report. arXiv (Cornell University). (2023)

22. Nori, H., King, N., McKinney, S.M., Carignan, D., Horvitz, E.: Capabilities of GPT-4 on medical challenge problems. arXiv (2023)
23. Bubeck, S., et al.: Sparks of artificial general intelligence: early experiments with GPT-4. arXiv (Cornell University) (2023)
24. Fu, Y.: Tianyan Lun yi liyan [Preface to the evolution and ethics]. In: Luo, X. (ed.) Fanyi Lunji [An Anthology of Chinese Translation Theories]. Commercial Press, Beijing (1898)
25. Liu, Y., et al: Summary of ChatGPT-related research and perspective towards the future of large language models. arXiv (Cornell University) (2023)
26. Zeng, A., et al.: GLM-130B: an open bilingual pre-trained model. arXiv (Cornell University) (2022)
27. Thoppilan, R., et al.: LaMDA: language models for dialog applications. arXiv (2022)
28. Chowdhery, A., Narang, S., Devlin, J., Bosma, M., Mishra, G., et al.: PaLM: scaling language modeling with pathways. arXiv (Cornell University) (2022)
29. Katz, D.M., Bommarito, M.J., Gao, S., Arredondo, P.: GPT-4 passes the bar exam. SSRN Electron. J. (2023)
30. Sanderson, K.: GPT-4 is here: what scientists think. Nature (2023)
31. Lee, P., Bubeck, S., Petro, J.: Benefits, limits, and risks of GPT-4 as an AI chatbot for medicine. N. Engl. J. Med. **388**, 1233–1239 (2023)
32. Ufuk, F., Peker, H., Sagtas, E., Yagci, A.B.: Distinguishing GPT-4-generated radiology abstracts from original abstracts: performance of blinded human observers and AI content detector. medRxiv (2023)
33. Li, X., Zhu, X., Ma, Z., Liu, X., Shah, S.: Are ChatGPT and GPT-4 general-purpose solvers for financial text analytics? An examination on several typical tasks. arXiv (Cornell University) (2023)
34. Mack, C.A.: How to Write a Good Scientific Paper. Washington, Usa Spie Press, Bellingham (2018)
35. Khalil, M., Er, E.: Will ChatGPT get you caught? Rethinking of plagiarism detection. arXiv (Cornell University) (2023)
36. Dwivedi, Y.K., et al.: "So what if ChatGPT wrote it?" Multidisciplinary perspectives on opportunities, challenges and implications of generative conversational AI for research, practice and policy. Int. J. Inf. Manage. **71**, 102642 (2023)
37. Liebrenz, M., Schleifer, R., Buadze, A., Bhugra, D., Smith, A.: Generating scholarly content with ChatGPT: ethical challenges for medical publishing. Lancet Digit. Health **5** (2023)
38. Rahimi, F., Talebi Bezmin Abadi, A.: ChatGPT and publication ethics. Arch. Med. Res. **54** (2023)

Financial Text Sentiment Analysis Based on ChatGPT—Taking the Real Estate Industry as an Example

Jinlin Lin, Qifu Chen, Sai Li, Bixuan Li, and Jerome Yen[✉]

University of Macau, Macau SAR, China
{mc25602,mc35690,mc36627,mc36529,jeromeyen}@um.edu.mo

Abstract. In the era of artificial intelligence technology, it has become a trend to combine artificial intelligence technology with other industries. As an emerging force in artificial intelligence, ChatGPT provides new ideas for the combination of the financial industry and artificial intelligence. This paper focuses on whether it is feasible to apply ChatGPT to analyze text sentiment in financial markets. We collected three types of financial texts from different information sources, designed two rounds of experiments based on the subjectivity of the texts, "Industry Emotional Training" and "Enterprise Emotional Training", and compared the performance of ChatGPT3.5 and ChatGPT4.0 horizontally. Experimental results show that it is feasible to use the ChatGPT tool to analyze text sentiment in financial markets. Based on the differences in the performance of different versions of ChatGPT, ChatGPT4.0 is better than ChatGPT3.5 in analyzing financial market text sentiment. These findings provide support for the development of ChatGPT in the financial industry. This paper further explores how ChatGPT can be applied to a wider range of financial scenarios in the future, allowing AI technology to better assist the digital transformation of the traditional financial industry.

Keywords: ChatGPT · Artificial Intelligence · Sentiment Analysis · Financial Market

1   Introduction

With the rapid development of information technology, the financial sector has begun to see an influx of financial texts such as listed enterprise information announcements, social media, and news media. Nowadays financial practitioners and researchers pay more attention to the sentiment and tone expressed in the content of texts from these information sources [1]. Sentiment in financial market is generally defined as a biased expectation of overly optimistic or pessimistic in future cash flows or discount rates of listed companies [2], also as the general emotions of market participants towards the financial markets. There are many factors that lead to fluctuations and changes in the financial market, especially the personal emotions of investors mentioned. Many personal emotions constitute the overall market sentiment of the financial market.

SS1: Prof. Ben Niu

In the past, people often used dictionary sentiment analysis, machine learning methods, natural language processing technology, etc. to conduct sentiment analysis of financial market texts. Since ChatGPT was introduced, researchers have also been exploring its potential applications and future development in different fields. In the educational field, ChatGPT can be used for personalized tutoring, article grading, language translation, etc. [3]. It confirms that the integration of AI and education will open new opportunities to vastly improve the quality of teaching and learning [4]. In the healthcare field, AI can be used in healthcare education, scientific research in the healthcare industry, healthcare practice, etc. [5]. In the financial field, the application scenarios of ChatGPT include, but are not limited to financial public opinion monitoring, financial market sentiment analysis, financial risk management, etc. [6].

However, ChatGPT provides a new idea, which is to perform Fine-tuning on the basis of a general large language model to build a dedicated model for financial text sentiment analysis tasks. Many scholars have applied ChatGPT as a role research tool in sentiment analysis. However, there are few applications in the financial field, and a handful of text sentiment analyses using ChatGPT for the Chinese financial market. Therefore, this paper mainly conducts text sentiment analysis on the Chinese financial market. Using ChatGPT as a research tool, horizontally compare the differences between ChatGPT3.5 and ChatGPT4.0. Explore the impact and analysis of information from different text emotional sources on emotions. At the same time, we focus on the impact of text subjectivity on sentiment analysis.

This paper's objective is to discuss whether ChatGPT can accurately and stably analyze financial text sentiment. In this paper, we will analyze the past methods of financial market text sentiment analysis and explore how to apply ChatGPT to financial market text sentiment analysis. The framework of this paper is as follows: Part II discusses the research methods used in the past for financial market text sentiment analysis; The third part analyzes the factors affecting ChatGPT sentiment changes from the bottom level; the fourth part introduces the experimental framework of this paper; the fifth part conducts experiments and result analysis; the last part summarizes the experimental conclusions and formulates future work plans.

2 Literature Review

In the past few years, text sentiment analysis methods in the financial field can be divided into dictionary-based methods, machine learning-based methods, and sentiment dictionary-machine learning combination methods [7–9].

2.1 Dictionary-Based Methods

More influential foreign English text sentiment dictionaries such as: Loughran and Mc Donald dictionary (LM dictionary), Henry dictionary, Harvard IV-4 dictionary, etc. Since there is no more authoritative Chinese financial sentiment dictionary, although the Chinese translations of these English dictionaries can be used, due to translation limitations and language and cultural differences, the use effect will be greatly reduced [10].

Common Chinese dictionaries for sentiment analysis in China include the following: Dalian University of Technology Sentiment Vocabulary Ontology Database, China National Knowledge Infrastructure Sentiment Dictionary (How Net), Tsinghua University Praise and Derogation Dictionary, National Taiwan University Simplified Chinese Sentiment Polarity Dictionary, etc.; These dictionary corpora are derived from Chinese dictionaries and popular literature works, and are not specially created for texts in the financial field [11]; However, text sentiment analysis methods based on dictionaries also have shortcomings: dictionaries are manually compiled and cannot be updated in a timely manner, resulting in lag; In addition, it ignores the order of word appearance and grammatical structure, causing deviations or even deviations in the understanding of text content [12].

2.2 Machine Learning-Based Methods

Sentiment analysis methods based on machine learning use statistical machine learning algorithms to extract features from a large amount of labeled or unlabeled corpus and perform sentiment analysis to output the results. Sprenger et al. (2013) analyzed about 250,000 stock-related messages (so-called tweets) using a naive Bayesian approach, found associations between tweet sentiment and stock returns, message and transaction volumes, and divergence and volatility [13]. However, this type of method usually fails to understand contextual information, leading to the problem of ignoring contextual semantics; Furthermore, the disadvantage of machine learning is the need to build a sufficiently large library of documents labeled for sentiment polarity.

2.3 Emotion Lexicon - Machine Learning Combination Methods

This method combines the above two methods. Its basic mechanism is to first use the emotional dictionary to optimize feature representation (equivalent to playing the role of a training set) or use the dictionary to generate a training set. On this basis, a machine learning model with better performance is trained for text sentiment analysis [12]. For example, Li et al. (2019) used traditional dictionary methods based on customized word lists and supervised machine learning methods (Support Vector Machines and Convolutional Neural Networks) for sentiment extraction [10]; However, Mishev et al. (2020) conducted research showing that the performance of the sentiment dictionary-machine learning combination method in financial field research is far inferior to methods based solely on machine learning [14].

2.4 Using ChatGPT Tool as an Analysis Method

The use of ChatGPT, a large language model, overcomes the limitations of traditional methods and has good application prospects. Fatouros (2023) adopted a zero-sample prompting approach and examined multiple ChatGPT prompts on a curated dataset of foreign exchange-related news headlines, highlighting the potential of ChatGPT to significantly improve sentiment analysis in financial applications [15]; Belal et al. (2023) used ChatGPT as a data labeling tool for different sentiment analysis tasks. Compared to the best-performing vocabulary-based algorithm, ChatGPT significantly improves accuracy by 20% on the tweet's dataset and ~25% on the Amazon reviews dataset [16].

3 Overview of ChatGPT Technology Process

In 2017, Google proposed the Transformer model, a model that became the basic unit of systems such as ChatGPT, pioneering the introduction of a method for building deep neural networks based on the attention mechanism, thus marking an important turning point in the development of artificial intelligence [17].

In the large language model, both the encoder and the decoder are assembled from multiple Transformer components [18]. GPT uses Decoders. The training process for these models is to randomly remove some words from hundreds of millions of text samples and continuously learn how to fill in these blanks. This requires the collection of large amounts of data to train supervised policy models. The training and learning of language models mean learning complex contextual connections from large amounts of data [19]. From OpenAI's data source diagram (see Fig. 1) [20], OpenAI trained ChatGPT using approximately 13 trillion tokens, sourced from Wikipedia, books, journals, Reddit links, Common Crawl, and other datasets. These big data advantages better enable ChatGPT to train and carry out market sentiment analysis work.

Dataset	Quantity (tokens)	Weight in training mix	Epochs elapsed when training for 300B tokens
Common Crawl (filtered)	410 billion	60%	0.44
WebText2	19 billion	22%	2.9
Books1	12 billion	8%	1.9
Books2	55 billion	8%	0.43
Wikipedia	3 billion	3%	3.4

Fig. 1. Map of data sources for the GPT-3.5 model (OpenAI official website).

The data dimensions of ChatGPT's interaction with users include three aspects: Original Training Data, Users Feed Data, and ChatGPT Answer Data (see Fig. 2). Original Training Data is the data for initial training of ChatGPT; Users Feed Data and ChatGPT Answer Data, which are information input and generated by users during interaction with ChatGPT. From the left half of the figure, we can see the mutual influence between ChatGPT and Data. At the same time, Users and Data in the right half also influence and interact with each other to achieve the interaction between ChatGPT and Users. It can be speculated that since the launch of ChatGPT, Users Feed Data and ChatGPT Answer Data will increase as users engage in conversations with ChatGPT, resulting in a higher proportion of conversation-based tasks in the data collection process. This shift may involve more question-and-answer-style prompts rather than just prompts, leading to increased external interference and potential impact on ChatGPT's performance. Therefore, the emotions of both ChatGPT and Users may be affected.

With the development of artificial intelligence and financial technology, large language models have been continuously improved, updated and developed over time. The data set of the latest version of the ChatGPT series, ChatGPT4.0, has been updated to 2023. From a technical perspective, ChatGPT4.0 version retains the same architecture of the predecessor of the ChatGPT series, but it has shown significant progress in scale. The OpenAI official website provides a comprehensive description and evaluation of the

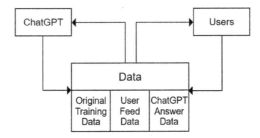

Fig. 2. Relationship of ChatGPT & Users & Data.

Table 1. Comparison of ChatGPT4.0 and ChatGPT3.5.

Features	ChatGPT4.0	ChatGPT3.5
Model Size	170 trillion	175 billion
Modality	Text, Images	Text
Context Window Length	8192 to 32768	2048

technology and performance of ChatGPT4.0 [21], as shown in Table 1: The parameters of ChatGPT4.0 reach 170 trillion, which is 1,000 times the parameters of ChatGPT3.5; ChatGPT4.0 supports multi-modal input, including text and images; the context length of ChatGPT4.0 is 4–16 times larger than ChatGPT3.5.Through the comparison of data set dimensions and technical dimensions, ChatGPT4.0 is indeed better than ChatGPT3.5 in many aspects.

4   Research Methodology

4.1   Workflow of the Experiments

This paper collects financial texts of the target analysis objects (see Fig. 3). Design two rounds of experiments: "industry experiment" and "enterprise experiment". Emotional perception is guided through Prompting, and the corresponding label emotional value (positive or negative) is assigned to the event corresponding to each type of financial text. In addition, compare the differences between ChatGPT3.5 and ChatGPT4.0 for sentiment value analysis. Originally, we used ChatGPT3.5 version for experiments in August, and now we have experiments on ChatGPT4.0 version in November.

The ChatGPT Prompt approach used in this paper: on a scale of -1 to 1, where -1 is the most negative and 1 is the most positive, what is the sentiment value of the following whose (Evergrande Group, Country Garden) text (news media, information announcements, social media): Text_Requiring_Sentiment_Analysis [22].

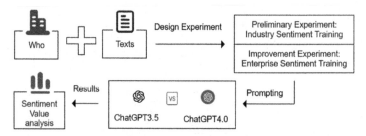

Fig. 3. Workflow of the Experiments.

4.2 Datasets

Table 2. Description of different Text Sentiment Sources.

Categories	Sources	Representative	Subjectivity
Information announcements	Donation Stock, Update of Financial Information, Clarification Information, Inside Information	Enterprise Sentiment	Weak
News Media	Securities Daily, China Philanthropy Times, Shanghai Securities News, Securities Times	Official Sentiment	Weak
Social Media	Wechat Official Account (Reads 100k+)	Personal Emotions	Strong

The sources of financial text emotions can be divided into three categories: information announcements, news media and social media, as shown in Table 2. The sources of these texts are diverse, as are the strengths and weaknesses of the perspectives, and subjectivities of different groups of people they represent. This paper selects two typical representatives of the real estate industry, "Evergrande Group" and "Country Garden", as the entry point for analyzing the sentiment value of the industry.

4.3 Preliminary Experiment: Industry Sentiment Training

The industry experiment design is as follows: as shown in Table 3, select representative events in the real estate industry, control the number of texts of each type to 2, initial samples to 6, and conduct 10 times experiments. To avoid the intervention of the strong subjectivity of social media, first place the less subjective text before the more subjective text in the order of Q1-Q6. Then, Prompt is performed according to the chronological order of events, 10 rounds of real estate industry sentiment value sequences are obtained and completed the initial training environment in the real estate industry.

Table 3. Order of Industry Prompt and sources in single round.

Order	Date	Sources	Title of Financial text
Q1	2021-12-3	Information announcements	Inside Information [23]
Q2	2023-7-31	News Media	Yang Huiyan Donated 20% stock equity of Country Garden Services [24]
Q3	2023-7-31 Later	Information announcements	Update of Financial Information [25]
Q4	2023-8-19	News Media	Evergrande Group responded to "filing for bankruptcy protection in the United States": A normal overseas reorganization process without involving bankruptcy applications [26]
Q5	2023-7-31	Social Media	Breaking news	Yang Huiyan donated her majority stake in Country Garden services WeChat official account "property explosion") [27]
Q6	2023-8-16	Social Media	Divorce! Xu Jiayin wants to run? (WeChat official account "Zheng Shitang 2019") [28]

(Later: The latter text occurs at the same date)

4.4 Improvement Experiment: Enterprise Sentiment Training

The improved enterprise experimental design is as follows: As shown in Table 4 and Table 5, it is based on the industry sentiment of the preliminary experiment, with Evergrande Group and Country Garden as the experimental subjects. Using social media factors as an intervention, two types of texts with weak subjectivity were placed before and after the text with strong subjectivity (E3 and C3) to form a controlled experiment. Use Prompting to perform sentiment analysis on the same research object based on the sequence of events. Finally, the changes and differences in the text emotion index before and after the intervention were obtained.

Table 4. Order of Evergrande Group Prompt and sources.

Order	Sources	Date	Title of Financial text	Environment
E1	Information announcements	2021-12-3	Inside Information [23]	before intervention
E2	News Media	2023-8-16	Evergrande Group was suddenly investigated by the CSRC, Xu Jiayin Ding Yumei identity change what is the mystery? [29]	before intervention
E3	Social Media	2023-8-16 Later	Divorce! Xu Jiayin wants to run? [28]	intervention
E4	Information announcements	2023-8-18	Clarification Information [30]	after intervention
E5	News Media	2023-8-19	Evergrande Group responded to "filing for bankruptcy protection in the United States": A normal overseas reorganization process without involving bankruptcy applications [26]	after intervention

Table 5. Order of Country Garden Prompt and sources.

Order	Sources	Date	Title of Financial text	Environment
C1	Information announcements	2023-7-30	Donation Stock of the Chairman of the Board of directors and Controlling Shareholder [31]	before intervention
C2	News Media	2023-7-31	Yang Huiyan donated 20 percent stock equity of Country Garden Services [24]	before intervention
C3	Social Media	2023-7-31 Later	Breaking news	Yang Huiyan donated her majority stake in Country Garden Services [27]	intervention
C4	News Media	2023-8-1	Country Garden pre-loss results in the first half of the year which said it would ensure cash flow security [32]	after intervention
C5	Information announcements	2023-8-10	Profit warning [33]	after intervention

(Later: The latter text occurs at the same date)

5   Experiment and Results

5.1   Preliminary Experiment: Industry Sentiment Training

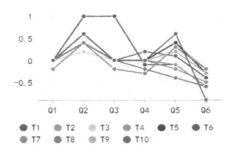

Fig. 4. Industry sentiment value fluctuations.

Table 6. Order of Industry Prompt and sources in single round.

	T1	T2	T3	T4	T5	T6	T7	T8	T9	T10	Variance01	Variance02	Range01	Range02
Q1	0	0	0	0	0	0	−0.2	0	0	0	0.00	0.00	0.2	0.2
Q2	1	0.6	0.2	0.4	0.4	0.4	0.4	0.4	0.6	0.6	0.05	0.02	0.8	0.4
Q3	1	0	0	0	0	0	−0.2	0	0	0	0.11	0.00	1.2	0.2
Q4	−0.1	0	0	0	0	0.2	−0.3	−0.2	0	0	0.02	0.02	0.5	0.5
Q5	−0.1	−0.1	0.4	−0.2	0.4	0.1	0.3	−0.4	0.2	0.6	0.10	0.11	1	1
Q6	−0.6	−0.6	−0.2	−0.5	−0.3	−0.4	−0.2	−0.6	−0.3	−0.9	0.05	0.05	1.1	1.1
Variance	0.43	0.15	0.04	0.09	0.07	0.07	0.09	0.12	0.09	0.30	–	0.0015	–	–
mean	0.20	-0.02	0.07	-0.05	0.08	0.05	-0.03	-0.13	0.08	0.05	0.03 (mean)			

Variance01: before adjustment variance; Variance02: after adjustment variance (exclude T1).
Range01: before adjustment range; Range02: after adjustment range (exclude T1); (Range = Highest Value – Lowest Value)

T (Turn) in Fig. 4 denotes the test rounds of industry sentiment, Q (Question) denotes the order of questions for industry representative companies, and the cross matrix in Table 6 corresponds to the ChatGPT sentiment value of different questions under different rounds, and the analysis results are as follows:

From the perspective of Question Q, the sentiment value of the less subjective texts Q1, Q3, and Q4 in the T2, T3, T4, T5, T9, and T10 rounds are all 0. The score of Q2 is also maintained at around 0.4, indicating that even the less subjective messages defined in this paper may carry a stronger emotional coloring, and the sentiment value of Q1-Q4 are all maintained in a more stable range, with the extreme deviations generally low. At the same time, ChatGPT made more obvious emotional responses to the more subjective texts Q5 and Q6, with a more discrete distribution of sentiment value in all rounds, with large extreme deviations, all reaching more than 1.

From the point of view of round T, compared with other sequences, the first round of sentiment value has the greatest deviation from the average trend. The T1 line segment demonstrates the greatest degree of fluctuation (see Fig. 4). The first round of the mean shown in Table 6 is 0.20, the variance of 0.43, is also more than the average. At the same time, the process of sentiment value of Q1-Q3 from 0 to 1 rapidly, indicating that ChatGPT in the first round of the experiments needs to adapt to the sentiment of the text and may have the problem of overreacting to changes in industry information.

Therefore, if we exclude the "adaptation factor" of T1 in the first round and observe again. For the text with weak subjective emotion, the range of Q2 changed from 0.8 to 0.4, Q3 changed from 1.2 to 0.2. The change of Q3's range well illustrates the problem of the "adaptation factor". For Q4, Q5 and Q6 with strong subjective emotions, the range did not change before and after removing T1. Probably because ChatGPT itself has already adapted to the industry information and started to make corresponding sentiment value to the financial texts. On the other hand, the performance difference between Q5 and Q6 is most obvious in different experimental rounds. The variance of Q5 is 0.11, the range is 1, the variance of Q6 is 0.05, the range is 1.1. The variance and range of the two are larger than those of other questions, indicating that ChatGPT's recognition of highly subjective text sentiment scores are more scattered.

Table 7. 10 rounds of Industry Experiment Sentiment Values (Using ChatGPT4.0 in November).

	T1	T2	T3	T4	T5	T6	T7	T8	T9	T10
Q1	−0.5~−1	~−1	−0.5~−0.8	−0.6~−0.7	~−0.7	~−1	−0.8or−0.9	−0.7	−0.6~−0.8	−0.6~−0.7
Q2	0.5~1	~1	0.5~0.8	0.8~0.9	~0.7	~1	0.8 or 0.9	0.8	0.7~0.9	0.7~0.8
Q3	−0.5~−1	~−1	−0.5~−0.8	−0.6~−0.7	~−0.6	~0	−0.3or−0.4	−0.6	−0.4~−0.6	−0.6~−0.7
Q4	−0.5~0	~0	0.1~0.4	−0.2~0.2	~−0.3	~0	0.2or0.3	0.3	−0.2~0.2	0.2~0.3
Q5	−0.5~0	~0	−0.2~0.2	−0.3~0.1	~−0.2	~0	0.1or0.2	0.1	−0.2~0.2	~0
Q6	−0.5~0	~−1	−0.5~−0.8	−0.8~−0.9	~−0.7	~−1	−0.6or−0.7	−0.8	−0.7~−0.9	~−0.8

(~: means "closer to"/"around" XX to XX)

Table 7 shows the experimental results of ChatGPT4.0 version, which tends to give a range of values rather than a specific value. The sentiment value for the same question is stable from T1 to T10, although there are small fluctuations in the middle, and gradually transitions from a rough range to a detailed range. For answers in the same round, ChatGPT gave answers with similar formats, such as "closer to", "around XX to XX". In summary, the sentiment value of ChatGPT4.0 version is not affected by initial adaptation factors and becomes stable after gradual training, making it a feasible sentiment analysis tool.

To sum up, the two versions of ChatGPT have basically consistent changes in sentiment value for the real estate industry in the 10 rounds of text, indicating that the expectations for the real estate industry are consistent. For ChatGPT3.5, it does require an emotional pre-adaptation step. In addition, it recognizes less subjective text with less obvious but more concentrated responses. It responds significantly but discretely when identifying highly subjective texts. ChatGPT4.0 version performs stably and has an even distribution of sentiment values.

5.2 Improvement Experiment: Enterprise Sentiment Training

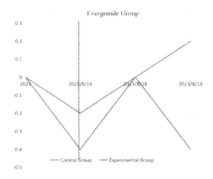
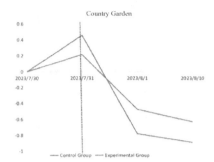

Fig. 5. Evergrande Group Sentiment Value (Using ChatGPT3.5 in August).

Fig. 6. Country Garden Sentiment Value (Using ChatGPT3.5 in August).

The enterprise sentiment value is obtained using ChatGPT3.5 version (see Fig. 5 and Fig. 6). The dotted line represents the change in text sentiment value before and after intervention. The turning part shows that strong subjective text emotional involvement will have an impact on later text emotions.

As shown in Table 8, the enterprise sentiment value is obtained using ChatGPT4.0 version. The analysis results are divided into two parts: sentiment and value. Compared with ChatGPT3.5, the analysis of ChatGPT4.0 version is more detailed and cautious, including not only qualitative but also quantitative analysis.

The different categories of text sentiment value of Evergrande Group and Country Garden were analyzed by ChatGPT, to explore the sentiment value changes of weakly subjective texts (information announcements, news media) before and after the intervention of strongly subjective texts (social media). The results of the improvement experiment show that.

(1) under market information asymmetry (limited database), ChatGPT as a participant is still limitedly rational, and there are significant differences in the changes of weakly subjective text sentiment value with different events, such as the K-shape of two-level Evergrande Group polarization.

(2) Based on the limited ability of information processing, ChatGPT generates differences in the sentiment value of different textual sources, and produces psychological phenomena when making sentiment judgments biased, and the performance of information announcements with weaker subjectivity scatters more concentrated. From the perspective of overall volatility, pessimistic expectations make the reflections of text sentiment value lower after subjectivity interventions than before interventions, such as Country Garden.

Table 8. Enterprise Sentiment Training (Using ChatGPT4.0 in November).

Evergrande Group			Country Garden		
Prompting	Sentiment	Value	Prompting	Sentiment	Value
E1	negative	closer to −1	C1	skewing more towards the positive side	likely between 0.5 and 1
E2	negative	closer to −1	C2	positive	range of 0.7 to 1
E3	Closer to middle	closer to −1	C3	neutral to slightly positive or negative	around 0
E4	closer to the middle, possibly leaning slightly positive side	lean towards the positive side	C4	predominantly negative	around −0.6 to −0.8
E5	closer to the middle, possibly leaning slightly positive side	lean towards the positive side	C5	generally negative	around −0.5 to −0.7

6 Conclusion and Future Work

6.1 Conclusion

This paper designed two experiments, from industry sentiment research to enterprise sentiment research, selected typical representative companies in the real estate industry, "Evergrande Group" and "Country Garden". Used ChatGPT3.5 and ChatGPT4.0 versions to carry out analysis of financial text sentiment.

For ChatGPT3.5 version:

(1) Combining the findings of two experiments, ChatGPT does require an emotional pre-adaptation step.
(2) There are differences in the sentiment indicators generated by ChatGPT from different text sources, which may lead to psychological bias when making sentiment judgments.
(3) ChatGPT may have an insignificant response but a concentrated distribution when identifying text sentiments with weak subjectivity (information announcements, news media), and an obvious response but discrete distribution when identifying text sentiments with strong subjectivity (social media).
(4) In addition, when ChatGPT was interfered with by the emotions of highly subjective texts, its analysis of weakly subjective texts would have obvious emotional fluctuations.

For ChatGPT4.0 version:

(1) Emotional values are not affected by initial adaptation factors and become stable after gradual training.
(2) Tend to give a range value rather than a specific value, sentiment analysis and gradually transition from a coarse range to a detailed range
(3) The analysis is more detailed and cautious, including not only qualitative(sentiment) but also quantitative(values) analysis.

Taking all aspects into account, ChatGPT4.0 version is indeed better than Chat-GPT3.5 version for financial market text sentiment analysis.

6.2 Future Work

Regarding text research, we believe that there are still many areas worthy of improvement. Firstly, based on ChatGPT itself. Its mistakes in financial text sentiment analysis may stem from the large differences between the corpus data learned by ChatGPT and the financial field, which is also a huge barrier to its commercial application in the financial field. In addition, based on other sentiment analysis methods, we comparatively analyze the differences between ChatGPT and dictionaries, artificial intelligence, different machine learning algorithms, etc., and explore whether the combination of different methods will produce better results. These are questions worthy of our thinking and discussion.

Secondly, based on the application level of the ChatGPT function, we will use more examples to further demonstrate the feasibility of applying ChatGPT to text sentiment analysis in the financial market; if feasible, ChatGPT can be applied to a wider range of financial scenarios in the future, such as:

(1) Market sentiment forecasting, forecasting future market trends, etc.
(2) Select information and topics that less people pay attention to in the market to conduct experiments, and explore ChatGPT's emotional response to such financial texts, and the effect may be more obvious.
(3) In addition to text-based sentiment analysis, it can also be applied to various forms of scene analysis such as sound and images.
(4) Aiming at the Chinese financial market, in the future, we can also build a corpus with Chinese characteristics, unique rules and expressions of the Chinese market, etc., and use this to train ChatGPT to train a large language model that is more in line with China's national conditions and help China's financial market.

Acknowledgment. This research was funded by University of Macau Internal Fund, Macau SAR (File No. CPG2023-00013-FST).

References

1. 姚加权, 冯绪, 王赞钧, 纪荣嵘, 张维: 语调, 情绪及市场影响: 基于金融情绪词典. 管理科学学报 **24**(05), 26–46 (2021). https://doi.org/10.19920/j.cnki.jmsc.2021.05.002
2. 唐国豪, 姜富伟, 张定胜: 金融市场文本情绪研究进展. 经济学动态 (11), 137–147 (2016)
3. Baidoo-Anu, D., Owusu, Ansah, L.: Education in the era of generative artificial intelligence (AI): understanding the potential benefits of ChatGPT in promoting teaching and learning. SSRN Electron. J. (2023)
4. Hwang, G.J., Xie, H., Wah, B.W., Gašević, D.: Vision, challenges, roles and research issues of Artificial Intelligence in Education. Comput. Educ.: Artif. Intell. **1** (2020)
5. Sallam, M.: ChatGPT utility in healthcare education, research, and practice: systematic review on the promising perspectives and valid concerns. Healthcare. **11**(6) (2023)
6. 汪寿阳, 李明琛, 杨昆, 林文灿, 姜尚荣, 魏云捷:ChatGPT+金融: 八个值得关注的研究方向与问题[J].管理评论 **35**(04), 3–11 (2023). https://doi.org/10.14120/j.cnki.cn11-5057/f.2023.04.007
7. Johnman, M., Vanstone, B.J., Gepp, A.: Predicting FTSE 100 returns and volatility using sentiment analysis. Account. Financ. **58**, 253–274 (2018)
8. Singh, N.K., Tomar, D.S., Sangaiah, A.K.: Sentiment analysis: a review and comparative analysis over social media. J. Ambient Intell. Human. Comput. **11**, 97–117 (2020)
9. Zucco, C., Calabrese, B., Agapito, G., et al.: Sentiment analysis for mining texts and social networks data: Methods and tools. Wiley Interdisc. Rev.: Data Min. Knowl. Discov. **10**(1), e1333 (2020)
10. Li, J., Chen, Y, Shen, Y, et al.: Measuring China's stock market sentiment. Available at SSRN 3377684 (2019)
11. 范小云, 王业东, 王道平, 郭文璇, 胡煊翊: 不同来源金融文本信息含量的异质性分析—基于混合式文本情绪测度方法. 管理世界 **38**(10), 78–101 (2022). https://doi.org/10.19744/j.cnki.11-1235/f.2022.0145
12. 李合龙, 任昌松, 柳欣茹 汪存华. 金融市场文本情绪研究综述. 数据分析与知识发现1–25 (2023)
13. Sprenger, T.O., Tumasjan, A., Sandner, P.G., Welpe, I.M.: Tweets and trades: the information content of stock microb-logs. Eur. Financ. Manage. **20**(5), 926–957 (2014)
14. Mishev, K., Gjorgjevikj, A., Vodenska, I., et al.: Evaluation of sentiment analysis in finance: from lexicons to transformers. IEEE Access **8**, 131662–131682 (2020)
15. Fatouros, G., Soldatos, J., Kouroumali, K., et al.: Transforming sentiment analysis in the financial domain with ChatGPT. arXiv preprint arXiv:2308.07935 (2023)
16. Belal, M., She, J., Wong, S.: Leveraging ChatGPT as text annotation tool for sentiment analysis. arXiv preprint arXiv:2306.17177 (2023)
17. Dowling, M., Brian, L.: ChatGPT for (finance) research: the Bananarama conjecture. Financ. Res. Lett. **53** (2023)
18. Devika, M.D., Sunitha, C., Ganesh, A.: Sentiment analysis: a comparative study on different approaches. Procedia Comput. Sci. **87**, 44–49 (2016)
19. Susnjak, T.: ChatGPT: the end of online exam integrity?. arXiv preprint arXiv:2212.09292 (2022)
20. Brown, T., Mann, B., Ryder, N., et al.: Language models are few-shot learners. In: Advances in Neural Information Processing Systems, vol. 33, pp. 1877–1901 (2020)
21. OpenAI. GPT-4technicalreport (2023). https://cdn.openai.com/papers/gpt-4.pdf
22. Cao, Y., Zhai, J.: Bridging the gap–the impact of ChatGPT on financial research. J. Chin. Econ. Bus. Stud. (2023)
23. CHINA EVERGRANDE GROUP: Inside Information (2021). https://doc.irasia.com/listco/hk/evergrande/announcement/ca211203.pdf

24. Gongyishibao: Yang Huiyan Donated 20% stock equity of Country Garden Services (2023). http://www.gongyishibao.com/html/redian/2023/07/24585.html
25. COUNTRY GARDEN HOLDINGS COMPANY LIMITED: Information announcements Update of Financial Information (2023). https://www.bgy.com.cn/upload/file/2023-07-31/17d3613e-98e9-4c97-897b-ae40e58f00c3.pdf
26. Xu, J., Chen, X.: Evergrande Group responded to "filing for bankruptcy protection in the United States": a normal overseas reorganization process without involving bankruptcy applications (2023). https://finance.china.com.cn/industry/company/20230819/6022917.shtml
27. Wuyedabaozha: Breaking news | Yang Huiyan donated her majority stake in Country Garden Services (2023). https://mp.weixin.qq.com/s/D7zXqU5uunw325x41Ga2zQ
28. Zhengshitang2019: Divorce! Xu Jiayin wants to run? (2023). https://mp.weixin.qq.com/s/ozcoXXAdk1SGuQZApP4pNA
29. Li L., Zhang, L.: Evergrande Group was suddenly investigated by the CSRC, Xu Jiayin Ding Yumei identity change what is the mystery? (2023). https://www.stcn.com/article/detail/949619.html
30. CHINA EVERGRANDE GROUP: Clarification Information (2023). https://doc.irasia.com/listco/hk/evergrande/announcement/ca230818.pdf
31. COUNTRY GARDEN SERVICES HOLDINGS COMPANY LIMITED: Donation Stock of the Chairman of the Board of directors and Controlling Shareholder (2023). https://www1.hkexnews.hk/listedco/listconews/sehk/2023/0730/2023073000072_c.pdf
32. Zhang, Y.: Country Garden pre-loss results in the first half of the year which said it would ensure cash flow security (2023). http://www.xinhuanet.com/2023-08/01/c_1212250964.htm
33. COUNTRY GARDEN HOLDINGS COMPANY LIMITED: Information announcements Profit warning (2023). https://www.bgy.com.cn/upload/file/2023-08-10/132c46a4-5577-4245-b7e9-f88329949e0d.pdf

Reinforcement Learning Approaches

A New Deep Reinforcement Learning Algorithm for UAV Swarm Confrontation Game

Laicai Xie[1], Wanpeng Ma[2], Liping Wang[2], and Liangjun Ke[1,3](✉)

[1] School of Automation Science and Engineering, Xi'an Jiaotong University,
Xi'an 710049, China
`keljxjtu@xjtu.edu.cn`
[2] Army Aviation Research Institute, Beijing 101121, China
`wanglp14@tsinghua.org.cn`
[3] State Key Laboratory for Manufacturing Systems Engineering, Xi'an 710049, China

Abstract. UAV swarm confrontation game is a type of intelligent game problem. Multi-agent reinforcement learning theory provides an effective solution for this game. However, when using common multi-agent deep reinforcement learning algorithms, such as the multi-agent deep deterministic policy gradient (MADDPG) algorithm, to train the strategy of UAV swarm, there are issues such as slow convergence speed and weak generalization ability on similar tasks. To address these issues, this paper combines the model-agnostic meta-learning (MAML) algorithm in few-shot learning with the original MADDPG algorithm, and proposes an improved MB-MADDPG algorithm, which is applied to the strategy optimization of a UAV swarm confrontation task. Experimental results show that compared with the original algorithm, the improved algorithm can accelerate the convergence while maintaining the training effect, and the success rate of defense after training with both algorithms exceeds 50%.

Keywords: Multi-agent Reinforcement Learning · UAV Swarm Confrontation · Few-shot Learning · MADDPG · MAML

1 Introduction

Recently, research on UAV swarm has been a hot topic in the field of artificial intelligence [1]. With the advancements in deep reinforcement learning (DRL), it has become the most popular tool for the strategy optimization of UAV swarm [2]. However, when using classic multi-agent deep reinforcement learning algorithms such as multi-agent deep deterministic policy gradient (MADDPG) [3] to train the strategy of UAV swarm, there are problems such as slow convergence speed and weak generalization ability of agents when the distribution of tasks is similar. Achieving acceptable results often requires a significant number of time steps and training data, and when facing different but similar confrontation tasks, retraining becomes necessary, which fails to take advantage of the similarity between tasks. Consequently, it is crucial to effectively utilize the task similarities to accelerate training, reduce the required training data, and ensure the training effect in the strategy optimization process of UAV swarm.

To address the aforementioned problem, this paper combines the model-agnostic meta-learning (MAML) [4] algorithm in few-shot learning with the MADDPG algorithm to propose an improved algorithm named MB-MADDPG. The key idea is to train on a set of tasks similar to the target task to acquire a better set of initialization parameters, which in turn improves the convergence speed during formal training and reduce the amount of training data required. The paper introduces both the original MADDPG algorithm and the improved algorithm to the strategy optimization problem of a UAV swarm confrontation task. Then compares and analyzes their convergence speed and effect, verifying the efficacy of the improved algorithm.

2   Related Work

2.1   UAV Swarm Confrontation Strategy

The mainstream research on UAV swarm confrontation decision-making methods currently focuses on three main directions: swarm intelligence-based methods, neural network-based methods and reinforcement learning-based methods.

The UAV swarm confrontation strategy based on swarm intelligence aims to realize the strategy optimization of UAV swarm by imitating the cooperative behavior observed in ant colonies, bee colonies, wolf packs and other groups [5]. In [6], a dynamic ant colony division model is proposed to address the task allocation problem in the dynamic environment of UAV swarm confrontation.

Neural network-based methods employ neural network as a decision-making unit to realize the decision-making process of UAV swarm. Paper [7] combines expert systems and neural networks, leveraging the characteristics of neural networks to expand existing expert knowledge and achieve robust and adaptable UAV decision-making.

In contrast to other methods, reinforcement learning-based methods utilize the concept of reinforcement learning, enabling agents to continuously optimize their strategies through interactions with the environment to better accomplish the corresponding tasks. This makes them particularly suitable for tackling difficult and complex problems such as UAV swarm decision-making. In [8], a research method for maneuvering decision-making of air combat UAVs based on deterministic policy gradient is proposed. Through autonomous reinforcement learning training, UAVs are able to learn their strategies without prior knowledge.

2.2   Multi-agent Deep Reinforcement Learning

In general, common multi-agent deep reinforcement learning (MADRL) algorithms can be categorized into four types: independent learning, communication-based learning, collaborative learning and modeling-based learning.

In independent learning MADRL algorithms, single-agent deep reinforcement learning algorithms are simply applied to the multi-agent environment. Each agent learns independently based on its own experiences and rewards, without considering the influence of other agents. In [9], three deep reinforcement learning algorithms are extended to a multi-agent environment. By introducing parameter sharing and course learning mechanism in this process, the trained strategies perform well in different scenarios.

Different from independent learning MADRL algorithms, communication-based learning algorithms allow agents to communicate with each other, and their communication mechanism can be dynamically adjusted during the learning process, so that each agent can use the information obtained from the communication to make better decisions. The communication network model [10] is a classic algorithm of this type. In this model, each agent has a channel capable of transmitting continuous information for communication, and the information communicated between agents is learned along with their policies at training time.

Collaborative learning MADRL algorithms do not involve direct communication between agents, but the relevant theories from the field of multi-agent are used during training to enable the agents to learn cooperative strategies. A typical example of this type is the counterfactual multi-agent policy gradients (COMA) [11] algorithm. In COMA, there is a global critic to evaluate each agent's actions for the entire system, while distributed actors are used to optimize the strategy of each agent. So there is no need for communication between agents during task execution.

The idea of modeling-based learning MADRL algorithms is to let the agent predict the behaviors of other agents by modeling them, and then make its own decisions accordingly. An example of this type is the self-predictive modeling [12] algorithm, which allows the agent to learn a better strategy by predicting the goals of other agents.

3   The UAV Swarm Confrontation Problem and the Algorithms

In this section, the UAV swarm confrontation task is described and the algorithms are introduced, including the implementation of the original MADDPG algorithm on this task and the design of the proposed MB-MADDPG algorithm.

3.1   Task Description

The following will describe a territorial defense UAV swarm confrontation task, and imagine the task scenario for the situation of the enemy UAV swarm attack, specifically described as follows:

There are swarms of offensive and defensive UAVs. The defensive UAVs are initially deployed in fixed positions around the base, with the goal of protecting the base and intercept incoming offensive UAVs, preventing them from entering the defensive area. The offensive UAVs departs from a certain distance from the base, and the goal is to approach the target area above the base. During this process, they can also attack the intercepting defensive UAVs. If the offensive UAVs successfully enter the target area or destroy all the defensive ones, the attacking side wins; If all the offensive UAVs are destroyed by the defensive ones before they enter the target area, the defending side wins; If both the offensive and defensive UAVs are destroyed by each other simultaneously, it is counted as a draw.

Each UAV in the confrontation scene carries 4 attack missiles, and has a designated attack range, when an enemy is within the attack range, the UAV will automatically launch an attack using its corresponding automatic attack program. Considering that environmental factors such as wind direction and wind speed on the battlefield will have an impact on the launch and hit of missiles, the attack of each UAV is not necessarily hit, but will have a certain hit rate.

The top view of the designed visual scene is depicted in Fig. 1, where the offensive and defensive UAVs are respectively represented by red and blue cubes, while the defender's base, located at the coordinate origin, is represented by a cone with a colored texture.

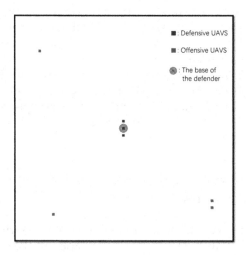

Fig. 1. The top view of the designed visual scene of the task. (Color figure online)

3.2   Reward Function

For the UAV swarm confrontation task described before, the reward function for the defensive UAVs can be designed as follows:

R_t: **The Threat Reward of Offensive UAVs.** Expressed as a penalty when offensive UAVs get too close to the target area. The specific formula of R_t is:

$$R_t = \sum_{n=1}^{N} R_{tn} \qquad (1)$$

In this equation, N is the number of surviving offensive UAVs, R_{tn} is the threat item of offensive UAV n, which can be calculated by:

$$R_{tn} = \begin{cases} 0, & dis_n < 15 \\ (dis_n - 15) \times 0.2, & dis_n \geq 15 \end{cases} \qquad (2)$$

where dis_n is the distance from the offensive UAV n to the target point with coordinates (0, 0, 10).

R_d: **The Distance Reward for Defensive UAVs.** The purpose of setting this item is to prevent defensive UAVs from being too far away from the defensive area. The formula of R_d is:

$$R_d = (dis - 10) \times 0.2 \qquad (3)$$

where dis is the distance from each surviving defensive UAV to the target point with coordinates (0, 0, 10).

R_a: **The Reward of Destroying Enemies.** When a defensive UAV destroys an enemy, a reward of +20 is awarded.

R_e: **The Reward for Settlement.** At the end of an episode, a penalty of -100 is given if offensive UAVs enter the target area or destroys all defensive UAVs. A reward of +100 is given if the defensive UAVs destroy all offensive UAVs, and in the case of a draw, no reward is attached.

The total reward R is the sum of all the above reward:

$$R = R_t + R_d + R_a + R_e \qquad (4)$$

3.3 The Implementation of MADDPG on the Task

Design of Observation Space. During the confrontation, each UAV selects the corresponding action according to its observation, which includes not only its own state information but also the information of the environment. The observation space of a UAV is designed as

$$obs = \{P, Dis, Bul, P_{self}, Dis_{self}, P_{enemy}, Dis_{enemy}\}$$

where the meaning of each element is as follows:

P: The absolute position of the UAV relative to the base (coordinate origin).
Dis: The distance of the UAV to the base.
Bul: The amount of ammunition left on the UAV, $Bul \in \{0, 1, 2, 3, 4\}$.

P_{self}: The position of the nearest surviving friendly UAV relative to the UAV itself.

Dis_{self}: The distance from the nearest surviving friendly UAV to the base.

P_{enemy}: Relative position of the nearest surviving enemy UAV to the UAV itself.

Dis_{enemy}: The distance from the nearest surviving enemy UAV to the base.

Training Process of MADDPG. In the confrontation task described previously, all the defensive UAVs are isomorphic and have the same observation and action space, indicating that they can use a shared actor network for decision-making. So only one actor and critic network need to be optimized during training. The specific training process is shown as Algorithm 1.

Training Parameter Settings. After several adjustments, a set of training parameters that perform well on this task is obtained, with the specific settings shown in Table 1.

3.4   The Description of MB-MADDPG

The MAML algorithm is capable of acquiring a set of network parameters with robust generalization ability through a set of priori tasks as a way to accelerate the training process on new tasks. Accordingly, this paper applies its framework to the MADDPG algorithm and proposes the improved MAML-Based MADDPG (MB-MADDPG) algorithm. While maintaining a fixed number of 3 defensive UAVs, the number of offensive UAVs is varied to 2, 3, and 4, constructing confrontation scenarios of 3 vs. 2, 3 vs. 3, and 3 vs. 4, respectively. The 3 vs. 2 and 3 vs. 3 confrontation scenarios are taken as the priori training tasks, while the 3 vs. 4 confrontation scenario serves as the target task. The overall algorithm is divided into two stages: pre-training and formal training. In the pre-training stage, following the principles of MAML, the training method of MADDPG is employed to train on the two priori training tasks individually, with the objective of obtaining an initialization parameter exhibiting strong generalization ability. The specific process is delineated in Algorithm 2.

The pre-training stage consists of two loops: the inner loop and the outer loop. In the inner loop, agents interact with the environment using the network parameter θ for M episodes on each training task T_i individually. The experiences gained from these interactions are then utilized for training to obtain an updated parameter θ_i on task T_i. Following this, K episodes of testing are conducted on task T_i using θ_i, and the testing loss $L_{T_i}(\theta_i)$ is calculated and recorded. In the outer loop, the gradients of the testing loss $L_{T_i}(\theta_i)$ with respect to θ_i are computed and summed across all tasks, and θ is updated based on the summed gradient. In this paper, $M = K = 1$, indicating that there is only one episode of interaction with the environment during training and testing on each task in the inner loop. The learning rates for the Critic and Actor networks in the inner and outer loops are $\alpha_{in} = \beta_{in} = 0.1$ and $\alpha_{out} = \beta_{out} = 0.001$, respectively.

Algorithm 1: Training process of MADDPG algorithm

---

1 Randomly initialize the Critic and Actor network parameters θ_c and θ_a, and the Critic-target network and Actor-target network parameters $\theta_c^t = \theta_c$ and $\theta_a^t = \theta_a$;

2 **while** *not done* **do**

3   Receive the initial state x;

4   **for** $t = 1$ *to maximum episode length* **do**

5   For each agent n, select the action $a_n = \mu(o_n) + N_t$ according to the existing strategy and exploration;

6   Execute the action $a = (a_1, \cdots, a_N)$ while observing the resulting reward r and the new state x';

7   Store experience $(x, a, r, x', done)$ into replaybuffer D;

8          $x \leftarrow x'$;

9   **end**

10   Sample one batch of S training data $(x^j, a^j, r^j, x'^j, done^j)$ from the replaybuffer D;

11   Calculate TD target

$$y^j = r^j + (1 - done^j) \times \gamma \times Q^{\mu^t}(x'^j, a_1', \cdots, a_N') \big|_{a_k' = \mu^t(o_k'^j)};$$

12   Calculate the updated Critic network parameters using gradient descent:

$$\theta_c = \theta_c - \alpha \frac{1}{S} \nabla_{\theta_c} \sum_j (y^j - Q^\mu(x^j, a_1^j, \cdots, a_N^j))^2$$

13   Calculate the updated Actor network parameters using gradient ascent:

$$\theta_a = \theta_a + \beta \frac{1}{S} \sum_j \nabla_{\theta_a} \mu(o_n^j) \nabla_{a_n} Q^\mu(x^j, a_1^j, \cdots, a_n, \cdots, a_N^j) \big|_{a_n = \mu(o_n^j)}$$

14   Softupdate Critic-target network and Actor-target network respectively:

$$\theta_c^t = (1 - \tau)\theta_c^t + \tau\theta_c$$
$$\theta_a^t = (1 - \tau)\theta_a^t + \tau\theta_a$$

15 **end**

Table 1. Training parameter settings.

Parameter name	Value
Total training episodes	10000
Maximum time step per episode	200
Learning rate (Actor)	0.001
Learning rate (Critic)	0.001
Discount factor	0.96
Batch size	128
Replaybuffer size	500000
Update factor of target network	0.01

Algorithm 2: MB-MADDPG algorithm (pre-training stage)

---

1 Randomly initialize the Critic and Actor network parameters θ_c and θ_a;
2 **while** *not done* **do**
3   **for** *each task T_i* **do**
4   **for** *episode = 1 to M* **do**
5   Receive the initial state x;
6   **for** *t = 1 to maximum episode length* **do**
7   For each agent n, select the action $a_n = \mu(o_n) + N_t$ according to the existing strategy and exploration;
8   Execute the action $a = (a_1, \cdots, a_N)$ while observing the resulting reward r and the new state x';
9   Store experience $(x, a, r, x', done)$ into replaybuffer D;
10              $x \leftarrow x'$;
11   **end**
12   Sample one batch of S training data $(x^j, a^j, r^j, x'^j, done^j)$ from the replaybuffer D;
13   Calculate TD target
$y^j = r^j + (1 - done^j) \times \gamma \times Q^\mu(x'^j, a_1', \cdots, a_N')|a_k' = \mu(o_k'^j)$;
14   Calculate the updated Critic network parameters using gradient descent:

$$\theta_{ci} = \theta_c - \alpha_{in}\frac{1}{S}\nabla_{\theta_c}\sum_j (y^j - Q^\mu(x^j, a_1^j, \cdots, a_N^j))^2$$

15   Calculate the updated Actor network parameters using gradient ascent, then clear replaybuffer D:

$$\theta_{ai} = \theta_a + \beta_{in}\frac{1}{S}\sum_j \nabla_{\theta_a}\mu(o_n^j)\nabla_{a_n}Q^\mu(x^j, a_1^j, \cdots, a_n, \cdots, a_N^j)|a_n = \mu(o_n^j)$$

16   **end**
17   Complete new K episodes on task T_i using the updated Actor and Critic network parameters θ_{ci} and θ_{ai}
18   Calculate Critic loss and Actor loss on task T_i using the experience generated in the new K episodes:

$$L_{cT_i}(\theta_{ci}) = \frac{1}{S}\sum_j (y^j - Q^\mu(x^j, a_1^j, \cdots, a_N^j))^2$$

$$L_{aT_i}(\theta_{ai}) = -\frac{1}{S}\sum_j Q^\mu(x^j, a_1^j, \cdots, a_n, \cdots, a_N^j)|a_n = \mu(o_n^j)$$

19   **end**
20   Critic and Actor networks are updated based on the test error L_{cT_i} and L_{aT_i} on each task T_i:

$$\theta_c \leftarrow \theta_c - \alpha_{out}\sum_{T_i \sim T}\nabla_{\theta_{ci}}L_{cT_i}(\theta_{ci})$$

$$\theta_a \leftarrow \theta_a - \beta_{out}\sum_{T_i \sim T}\nabla_{\theta_{ai}}L_{aT_i}(\theta_{ai})$$

21 **end**

During the formal training stage, the parameters obtained from the pre-training stage serve as the initialization parameters for the Actor and Critic networks. Building upon this initialization, the MADDPG algorithm is employed to train and optimize the defensive strategy in the target task. The specific training process is as described in the previous section, with the key distinction that the Actor and Critic network parameters are not initialized randomly but rather utilize the parameters acquired from the pre-training stage. The parameter configurations during training remain consistent with those employed in the preceding MADDPG algorithm.

4   Experiments and Analysis

4.1   Verification of Strategy Optimization Effect

The performance of the defensive UAVs before and after training during the confrontation is depicted in Fig. 2. It can be seen from Fig. 2a that the untrained defensive UAVs lack the notion of returning to defense, even when the offensive UAVs are on the verge of entering the target area. Consequently, the current defensive strategy proves to be unsuitable.

Figure 2b and Fig. 2c exhibit the performance of the defensive UAVs after training with both the MADDPG and MB-MADDPG algorithms, respectively. Now the movement area of the defensive UAVs has been around the base, so that no matter which direction the offensive UAVs attack from, as long as it enters a certain range of the base, the defensive UAVs can intercept them. Additionally, it is noteworthy that the defensive UAVs maintain a relatively close proximity to one another rather than scattering. This strategic arrangement enables them to fully utilize their numerical advantage, concentrate their efforts on the offensive UAVs one by one, and improve the success rate of defense. Consequently, the trained defensive UAVs not only developed the sense of protecting the base but also learn to effectively exploit their own advantages to strike at the offensive UAVs.

4.2   Comparison and Analysis of Algorithms

The average reward curve obtained by the defensive UAVs at each time step after smoothing is shown in Fig. 3, 4. It can be seen that the average reward obtained by the agent shows an overall upward trend as training progresses. In the case of training with the original algorithm, the reward gradually stabilizes when training episode reaches about 3500, although there are fluctuations in the later training process, the overall trend remains stable, suggesting convergence of the algorithm. The final convergence value is about 1.07.

When employing the improved MB-MADDPG algorithm, the reward tends to converge around the 2000th training episode, ultimately reaching a final convergence value of approximately 1.24.

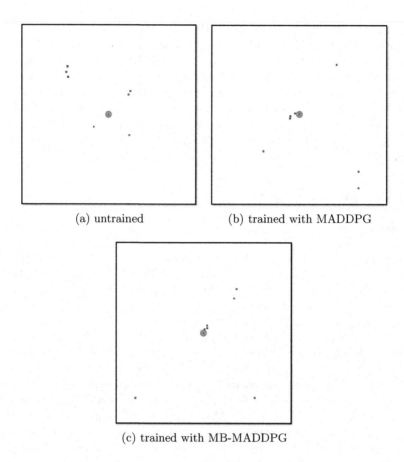

(a) untrained   (b) trained with MADDPG

(c) trained with MB-MADDPG

Fig. 2. Confrontational performance of defensive UAVs before and after training.

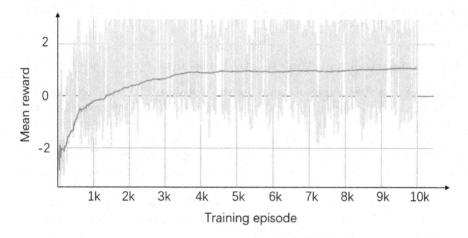

Fig. 3. Reward curve as a function of the training episodes for MADDPG.

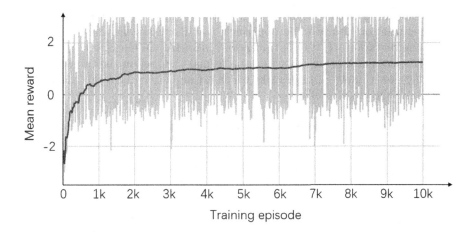

Fig. 4. Reward curve as a function of the training episodes for MB-MADDPG.

Table 2. Summary table of experimental results.

Algorithm	Converge episode	Final convergence value	Win rate in the test
MADDPG	3500	1.07	52%
MB-MADDPG	2000	1.24	55%

Applying the trained defensive strategy for 200 episodes of testing in the identical 3 vs. 4 confrontation scenario, the success rate of defense achieved 52% and 55% respectively. The summarized experimental data is presented in Table 2.

Based on the aforementioned results, it can be seen that the MB-MADDPG algorithm exhibits an improvement in convergence speed compared with the traditional MADDPG algorithm, and can accelerate convergence through priori tasks. The convergence effect of the algorithm, which can be assessed by the final convergence value and test performance, is basically not affected.

The effectiveness of the new algorithm can potentially be attributed to its ability to learn a set of network parameters in the pre-training stage that are more "sensitive" to changes in the task, which means that when a new training task is given, this set of parameters can be quickly adjusted in the direction of the optimal parameter on that task, thereby resulting in accelerated convergence of the training process.

5   Conclusion

This paper proposes a novel algorithm called MB-MADDPG by combining the model-agnostic meta-learning (MAML) algorithm with the multi-agent deep deterministic policy gradient (MADDPG) algorithm. The primary objective is to address the slow convergence speed of the original algorithm and its limited generalization ability when applying to similar tasks. In the task of UAV swarm confrontation strategy optimization, MB-MADDPG exhibits the potential to enhance convergence speed during formal training on the target task by employing pre-training on prior tasks which are similar to the target task, while maintaining the training effect.

Acknowledgments. This work was supported by the National Natural Science Foundation of China (Grant No.61973244, 72001214, and 61573277) and the open fund of CETC Key Laboratory of Data Link Technology.

References

1. Zhou, Y., Rao, B., Wang, W.: UAV swarm intelligence: recent advances and future trends. IEEE Access **8**, 183856–183878 (2020)
2. Xia, Z., et al.: Multi-agent reinforcement learning aided intelligent UAV swarm for target tracking. IEEE Trans. Veh. Technol. **71**(1), 931–945 (2021)
3. Lowe, R., Wu, Y.I., Tamar, A., Harb, J., Pieter Abbeel, O., Mordatch, I.: Multi-agent actor-critic for mixed cooperative-competitive environments. In: Advances in Neural Information Processing Systems, vol. 30 (2017)
4. Finn, C., Abbeel, P., Levine, S.: Model-agnostic meta-learning for fast adaptation of deep networks. In: International Conference on Machine Learning, pp. 1126–1135. PMLR (2017)
5. Tang, J., Duan, H., Lao, S.: Swarm intelligence algorithms for multiple unmanned aerial vehicles collaboration: a comprehensive review. Artif. Intell. Rev. **56**(5), 4295–4327 (2023)
6. Wu, H., Li, H., Xiao, R., Liu, J.: Modeling and simulation of dynamic ant colony's labor division for task allocation of UAV swarm. Phys. A **491**, 127–141 (2018)
7. McMahon, D.C.: A neural network trained to select aircraft maneuvers during air combat: a comparison of network and rule based performance. In: 1990 IJCNN International Joint Conference on Neural Networks, pp. 107–112. IEEE (1990)
8. Guo, J., et al.: Maneuver decision of UAV in air combat based on deterministic policy gradient. In: 2022 IEEE 17th International Conference on Control & Automation (ICCA), pp. 243–248. IEEE (2022)
9. Gupta, J.K., Egorov, M., Kochenderfer, M.: Cooperative multi-agent control using deep reinforcement learning. In: Sukthankar, G., Rodriguez-Aguilar, J.A. (eds.) AAMAS 2017. LNCS (LNAI), vol. 10642, pp. 66–83. Springer, Cham (2017). https://doi.org/10.1007/978-3-319-71682-4_5
10. Sukhbaatar, S., Fergus, R., et al.: Learning multiagent communication with back-propagation. In: Advances in Neural Information Processing Systems, vol. 29 (2016)
11. Foerster, J., Farquhar, G., Afouras, T., Nardelli, N., Whiteson, S.: Counterfactual multi-agent policy gradients. In: Proceedings of the AAAI Conference on Artificial Intelligence, vol. 32 (2018)
12. Raileanu, R., Denton, E., Szlam, A., Fergus, R.: Modeling others using oneself in multi-agent reinforcement learning. In: International Conference on Machine Learning, pp. 4257–4266. PMLR (2018)

Proximal Policy Optimization for Same-Day Delivery with Drones and Vehicles

Meng Li, Kaiquan Cai, and Peng Zhao[✉]

School of Electronic and Information Engineering, Beihang University,
Beijing 100191, China
{limeng021,caikq,pzhao}@buaa.edu.cn

Abstract. With a surge demand for instant gratification in online-shopping, offering same-day delivery with heterogeneous fleets of drones and vehicles provides new insights for decision makers. However, decisions in real-time involving assignment and routing of vehicles and drones suffer "curse of dimensionality", due to stochastic and dynamic orders, huge state spaces as well as associated and diverse decisions. In this paper, a deep reinforcement learning (DRL) based approach is presented to handle this dynamic decision problem. First, a routed-based Markov decision process is formulated to model the problem. Besides, a DRL-based algorithm combining proximal policy optimization and heuristics (PPOh) is developed to decide whether to accept customer requests, how to assign orders and plan routes of fleets. Evaluation on extensive computational experiments shows that PPOh outperforms the extant methods and evidently improves service rates of fleets under the same workload.

Keywords: Same-day Delivery · Proximal Policy Optimization · Route-based MDP · Deep Reinforcement Learning

1 Introduction

Same day delivery (SDD) represents a process of sending products to customers within a shorter time, providing with evident convenience for electronic commerce and shortening the gap on instant gratification between online and brick-and-mortar shopping [19]. To this end, SDD has gained attention and became popular in logistics. In SDD, customer orders arrive dynamically and stochastically from all sides of a city, and they should be served in the same day. Hence, providing SDD service increases cost and brings challenges on operation such as scheduling and route planning.

Vehicles are conventional transportation tools for delivery. Several studies on providing SDD with vehicles focus on routing and scheduling problems [1,4,5]. Customer orders arrive dynamically during a day, and the dispatcher needs to

---

Supported by National Natural Science Foundation of China (Grants No. U213320067).

make decisions in real-time, involving how to schedule vehicles to serve arrived requests and plan traveling routes of vehicles. In recent research, they usually model the dynamic decision process in the SDD as a Markov decision process (MDP) and develop dynamic programming approaches to make decisions [7,8,20]. However, delivery with vehicles has several disadvantages such as traveling slowly and easily being affected by road-traffic conditions. On the other hand, some retailers like Amazon and JD devote to employing drones to deliver packages. Contrary to vehicles, drone delivery benefits from faster travel speed and is not subject to traffic congestion. However, drones can not replace with vehicles, considering their limitation on carrying capacity and battery replacement or charging.

Delivery with a heterogeneous fleet of drones and vehicles seems to a good choice at the sake of improving efficiency. [19] firstly studied on same-day delivery routing problems with heterogeneous fleets of drones and vehicles (SDDPHF), and developed a parametric policy function approximation (PFA) approach to heuristically solve the problem. [3] proposed a Deep Q-network (DQN) approach to make decisions for SDDPHF, and experimental results show that it is superior to PFA in terms of improving service rate during a day with the same workload. However, DQN approach is designed for a fixed fleet size and can not directly generalize to others.

SDDPHF is a complicate dynamic optimization problem and suffers "curse of dimensionality", given that both state and decision spaces are huge, and decisions should be made in real-time. Thus, it is a nontrivial task to design a real-time approach to handle with the problem. Deep reinforcement learning (DRL) is an advanced technique that combining deep learning and reinforcement learning, and becomes popular in fields like game playing [14], robotics [11] and autonomous systems [2]. In recent years, applying DRL to solve optimization problems attracts great interest of researchers, especially for routing problems [13], covering both static [10,12] and dynamic routing [6,18].

In this paper, we develop a route-based MDP [17] to describe the SDDPHF and design a DRL-based approach which combines proximal policy optimization (PPO) and heuristics (abbreviated as PPOh). It improves solution quality compared with state-of-the-art algorithms and can generalize well to different fleet sizes.

In the remaining of this paper, Sect. 2 states the problem with an intuitive example and formulates it with a route-based MDP. Section 3 introduces the proposed solution approach PPOh in detail, and Sect. 4 elaborates computational study and analyzes results. Finally, Sect. 5 draws conclusions and discusses future work.

2   Problem Definition: SDDPHF

In this section, we elaborate SDDPHF defined in [19], and create an intuitive example to illustrate dynamic decision processes in the problem. Next, we design a routed-based MDP to describe the problem, which tunes the conventional MDP by expanding action space with sets of route plans [17].

2.1   Problem Statement

During a working day, stochastic customer orders arrive dynamically from all sides of a city, and the dispatcher does not know where and when a customer order generates until it arrives. A customer order denoted as $c_i = (t_i, l_i, t_i^{end})$ means that an order is recognized with its arriving time t_i, location coordinates l_i and the serving deadline t_i^{end}. Besides, service time for each order is denoted as T_{serve}.

A heterogeneous fleet with multiple vehicles ($v \in V$) and drones ($d \in D$) is responsible for delivery. They are at a depot N at the beginning of a day and will return to the depot at the end of working. We assume working hours of vehicles and drones are T_{vel}^w and T_{dro}^w, respectively. A vehicle travels at a speed V_{vel} and can delivery multiple packages per trip. We follow the previous research [3,19] to set vehicles uncapacitated. On the contrary, a drone travels at a speed V_{dro}, which is faster than a vehicle (i.e., $V_{dro} > V_{vel}$), but it only takes one package per trip and needs to charge after each trip. The charging time is defined as T_{charge}. Further, we suppose the loading time of vehicles and drones at the depot are T_{vel}^l and T_{dro}^l, respectively. A vehicle departs immediately once it finishes loading and is not allowed preemptive depot return, meaning that it does not return to the depot until it finishes service of all loaded packages.

In SDDPHF, as customer orders dynamically arrive, the dispatcher should decide whether to deliver them with vehicles, drones or reject. Rejection represents that the own fleet does not serve the order but sends it to a contractor. Further, the dispatcher should schedule vehicles and drones, as well as plan their routes. The objective is serving as many customer orders as possible under a given workload. It is noted that all decisions in the SDDPHF should be made in real-time.

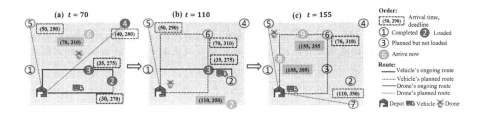

Fig. 1. An intuitive example to illustrate the SDDPHF

For ease of illustration, we construct an intuitive example to describe the SDDPHF. In the example, we assume a fleet of a single vehicle v and a drone d serves customer orders. The vehicle travels on Manhattan-style at a speed of five minutes per grid, and the drone travels in the Euclidean space with a speed of two minutes per grid. The loading time is five minutes, and the charging time for the drone is 20 min. All customer orders should be served within 4 h and the service time of each is $T_{serve} = 5$ min.

As shown in Fig. 1, at $t = 70$ min, customer order c_1 is completed, c_2, c_3 and c_4 are loaded, c_5 is planned to deliver with the drone d and c_6 is a new arriving request at the moment. On the other hand, v and d are both in transit. Assume that v leaves from the depot at $t = 65$ min, and the ongoing route of v is denoted as $\zeta(v) = ((N, 65), (c_2, 100), (c_3, 120), (N, 155))$, meaning that v travels to c_2 at $t = 65 + 7 \times 5 = 100$ min, c_3 at $t = 100 + 5 + 3 \times 5 = 120$ min, and finally returns to the depot at $t = 120 + 5 + 6 \times 5 = 155$ min. The planned route of v is denoted as $\theta(v) = ((N, 155))$, meaning that there is no order to be delivered in its planned route. At the same time, d is traveling to serve c_4 according to its ongoing route $\zeta(d) = [((N, 65), (c_4, 83), (N, 106))]$, where $83 \approx 65 + \sqrt{7^2 + 6^2} \times 2$ and $106 \approx 83 + 5 + \sqrt{7^2 + 6^2} \times 2$. Besides, the planned route of d is $\theta(d) = [((N, 131), (c_5, 143), (N, 160))]$, where $131 = 106 + 20 + 5$, representing that d will travel to serve c_5 after charging and loading. According to states of the fleet and orders, the dispatcher decides to assign c_6 to v and update its planned route to be $\theta(v) = ((N, 160), (c_6, 205), (N, 255))$.

Analogously, c_7 arrives at $t = 110$ min, c_2 and c_4 are successfully served, and d is charging at the depot while v is still in transit at the moment. The dispatcher decides to assign c_7 to d and update its planned route to be $\theta(d) = [((N, 131), (c_5, 143), (N, 160)), ((N, 185), (c_7, 197), (N, 214))]$. Customer orders c_8 and c_9 arrive at $t = 155$ min. c_3 and c_5 are completed at this moment. v returns to the depot and d is in transit. The dispatcher determines to assign both c_8 and c_9 to v and update its planned route to be $\theta(v) = ((N, 160), (c_6, 205), (c_9, 220), (c_8, 245), (N, 265))$.

2.2   Route-Based MDP

The decision process in the SDDPHF is formulated as a route-based MDP, which is firstly presented in [17]. The framework of route-based MDPs is customized for modeling stochastic dynamic vehicle routing problems. The conventional MDP denoted as (S, A, P, R) consists of key components states (S), actions (A), transition probabilities (P) and rewards (R) [16]. Compared to MDP, we incorporate planned routes of vehicles and drones into the action space in our route-based MDP.

Decision Points: A decision point triggers if a new customer order arrives, and thus the ith decision epoch occurs when c_i arrives at t_i.

States: We define states at the ith epoch as S_i, which involves situations of the fleet and customer orders at t_i. The components of states are elaborated as follows.

a. The decision time at the ith decision epoch, that is t_i.
b. The new arriving customer order c_i.
c. The set of planned routes of all vehicles, denoted as $\Theta_V^i = \{\theta(v)|v \in V\}$.
d. The set of planned routes of all drones, denoted as $\Theta_D^i = \{\theta(d)|d \in D\}$

It is noted that information of orders already planned but not loaded, and status on whether vehicles and drones are at the depot or in transit are omitted here, since they can be gained from planned routes. To summary, $S_i = (t_i, c_i, \Theta_V^i, \Theta_D^i)$.

Actions: We define actions at t_i as $x_i = (x_i^1, x_i^2)$, meaning that actions are decomposed into two parts, where x_i^1 associates with assigning c_i to a vehicle, a drone or rejecting (as denoted in Eq. 1), and x_i^2 represents route plans.

$$x_i^1 = \begin{cases} 0, \text{ the order is assigned to a drone} \\ 1, \text{ the order is assigned to a vehicle} \\ 2, \text{ the order is rejected} \end{cases} \quad (1)$$

On the other hand, $x_i^2 = (\Theta_V^{(i,x)}, \Theta_D^{(i,x)})$, where $\Theta_V^{(i,x)}$ and $\Theta_D^{(i,x)}$ represent the updated planning routes of all vehicles and drones.

Rewards: We define rewards at the ith decision epoch as R_i, which is a function of states and actions (i.e., $R_i = f(S_i, x_i)$), and associates with whether a customer order is successfully served.

$$R_i(S_i, x_i) = \begin{cases} 1, \text{ if } x_i^1 \in \{0,1\} \text{ and } a(c_i) \leq t_i^{end} \\ 0, \text{ else} \end{cases} \quad (2)$$

where $a(c_i)$ is the time when the vehicle or the drone responsible for serving c_i arrives to its location l_i. If a customer order can be successfully served by the fleet before its time limit, then set $R_i = 1$ in this decision epoch, otherwise $R_i = 0$. To this end, the accumulated reward of an episode composes to the objective of the SDDPHF.

Transitions: Transitions include converting to a post-decision state and a pre-decision state (i.e., the next state) from the current state S_i, denoted as S_i^x and S_{i+1}, respectively. The post-decision state S_i^x involves the updated information after making the action x_i, and is represented as $S_i^x = (t_i, c_i, \Theta_V^{(i,x)}, \Theta_D^{(i,x)})$. Compared to S_i, S_i^x updates rout plans of vehicles and drones according to the decision. Because of stochastic exogenous information, $S_{i+1} = (t_{i+1}, c_{i+1}, \Theta_V^{i+1}, \Theta_D^{i+1})$ is different from S_i^x. Particularly, a new customer order c_{i+1} arriving naturally leads to changes of the state. Further, if a vehicle or a drone departs between t_i and t_{i+1}, then the planned route of it should be updated. In detail, for a vehicle, the planned routed is updated to $\theta(v) = (N, a(N))$, where $a(N)$ is the time v returns to the depot. For a drone, the planned routed is updated by removing this trip.

Objective: The objective of the SDDPHF is to maximize the number of successfully served orders in a day. Thus, in the route-based MDP, it struggles to find a policy which maximizes the total expected reward, expressed as follows:

$$\pi^* = \arg\max_{\pi \in \Pi} \mathbb{E}[\sum_{i=0}^{|C|} R_i(S_i, X_i^\pi(S_i))|S_0] \quad (3)$$

where C is a set of customer orders, X_i represents the action space and $X_i^\pi(S_i)$ is the selected action according to policy π at the state S_i. Besides, the initial state is $S_0 = (0, 0, \{\theta(v) = (N, 0)|v \in V\}, \{\theta(d) = [(N, 0)]|d \in D\})$.

3   Solution Approach

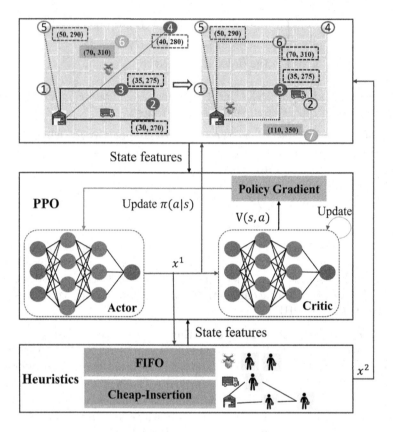

Fig. 2. Algorithm framework of PPOh

In this section, a DRL-based approach combining proximal policy optimization (PPO) and heuristics (abbreviated as PPOh) is presented to solve the SDDPHF. Considering characteristics of actions ($x_i = (x_i^1, x_i^2)$) in the routed-based MDP, the main idea is decomposing the whole task into sub-tasks and tackling them with different but associated algorithms. Visualization of the overall algorithm framework for PPOh is shown in Fig. 2. As interacting with the environment, PPO learns to make decisions on whether assigning orders to vehicles, drones or rejection (x_i^1), and at the same time, two heuristics are designed to create route plans for drones and vehicles (x_i^2). PPO and heuristics are interdependent and communicate with each other. Heuristics provide extracted state features for PPO agent and on the other hand, actions made by PPO also influences route-plans. To this end, the mechanism in the PPOh enables to solve the SDDPHF in real-time.

Proximal policy optimization is a policy gradient optimization algorithm, introduced in [15] and considered state-of-the-art, due to its benefits on having better sample complexity, being simpler to implement and more general. We employ actor-critic style PPO, where both actor and critic functions are parameterized with neural networks. The critic estimates the value function $V_{\phi'}(s_i)$, while the actor network produces actions as interacting with environment and updates policy distribution $\pi(x_i^1|s_i)$ according to the critic suggests [9]. ϕ and ϕ' are parameters of the actor and the critic, and s_i are features extracted from the corresponding state S_i. We design state features at the goal of being informative and easy to generalize, described as follows:

a. t_i: the current decision time.
b. Ds_i: the distance between the depot N and the location of customer order c_i.
c. At_i^D: the earliest available time of drones.
d. At_i^V: the earliest return time among vehicles according to their planned routes.
e. $\Gamma(V, i)$: the feasibility of providing service for c_i with vehicles.
f. $\Gamma(D, i)$: the feasibility of providing service for c_i with drones.
g. δ_i: the increased time-cost of providing service with vehicles, which can be calculated by the cheapest-insertion heuristic.

At_D^i and At_V^i are obtained from the current planned routes of vehicles and drones. $\Gamma(\cdot, i) = 1$ means that it is feasible for drones/vehicles to serve c_i, and $\Gamma(\cdot, i) = 0$ indicates it is infeasible of that. Hence, a state feature can be represented as a seven-dimension vector $s_i = (t_i, Ds_i, At_i^D, At_i^V, \Gamma(V, i), \Gamma(D, i), \delta_i)$.

We redefined rewards r_i in PPOh as Eq. 4. If c_i is successfully served with the fleet before its deadline, then setting $r_i = 1$, otherwise, $r_i = -3$. Definition of action x_i^1 is the same as demonstrated in the route-based MDP.

$$r_i = \begin{cases} 1, \text{ if } x_i^1 \in \{0, 1\} \text{ and } a(c_i) \le t_i^{end} \\ -3, \text{ else} \end{cases} \quad (4)$$

The objective function is calculated according to Eq. 5 - 8, where ω_1 and ω_2 are weight coefficients. $L_i^{CLIP}(\phi)$ is the policy surrogate, $L_i^{VF}(\phi')$ indicates a value function error term (also used for updating the critic network) and $S[\pi_\phi](s_i)$ represents an entropy bonus. $\rho_i(\phi) = \frac{\pi_\phi(x_i^1|s_i)}{\pi_{old}(x_i^1|s_i)}$ is the ratio of the new and the old policies, and $\hat{A}_i$ is the advance function. Parameter ϵ controls the clip degree, and γ is a discount factor.

$$L_i^{combin}(\phi, \phi') = \mathbb{E}_i[L_i^{CLIP}(\phi) - \omega_1 L_i^{VF}(\phi') + \omega_2 S[\pi_\phi](s_i)] \quad (5)$$

$$L_i^{CLIP}(\phi) = \mathbb{E}_i[\min(\rho_i(\phi)\hat{A}_i, \text{clip}(\rho_i(\phi), 1 - \epsilon, 1 + \epsilon)\hat{A}_i)] \quad (6)$$

$$L_i^{VF}(\phi') = \mathbb{E}[\text{MSE}(\sum_i^{|C|} (\gamma)^i r_i, V_{\phi'}(s_i))] \quad (7)$$

$$\hat{A}_i = \sum_i^{|C|} (\gamma)^i r_i - V_{\phi'}(s_i) \tag{8}$$

We refer to [19] and [3] for implementing two heuristics to conduct feasibility check and create route-plans.

First-in-First-Out (FIFO): It is a heuristic to schedule drones. In FIFO, an order c_i is priority to an idle drone which is at the depot and with an empty planning route. If all drones are busy, c_i will be assigned to the earliest available drone. If the drone is able to serve c_i before its deadline t_i^{end}, then it is feasible to assign this order to drones, that is $\Gamma(D, i) = 1$. Otherwise, $\Gamma(D, i) = 0$. On the other hand, drones deliver orders in sequence according to their arrival time, that is orders arriving early will be served first.

Cheapest-Insertion: It is developed on basis of an insertion heuristic in [1]. Main steps for this algorithm are concluded in the following.

a. An idle vehicle at the depot with an empty planning route is the first choice to assign.
b. If all vehicles are busy, traversing all planning routes of vehicles. In detail, for $\theta(v) \in \Theta_V$, traversing to insert c_i before all orders in sequence. An insert-point where both c_i and other customer requests in $\theta(v)$ can be served before their time limits, is a feasible point with an insertion cost (i.e., the additional cost after inserting c_i compared to the original planning route). The best insert point for $\theta(v)$ is one with the least insertion cost (denoted as Δ_v). If it is infeasible for v to serve c_i after traversing $\theta(v)$, then setting $\Delta_v = +\infty$.
c. The best insert cost for c_i is denoted as $\delta_i = \min_{v \in V} \Delta_v$. If $\delta_i = +\infty$, then it is infeasible to serve c_i with vehicles (i.e., $\Gamma(V, i) = 0$). Otherwise, $\Gamma(V, i) = 1$, and we can obtain the updated route by inserting c_i to the corresponding point.

Algorithm 1 displays pseudo-code of the overall training algorithm of PPOh.

4   Computational Results

In this section, we conduct experiments to evaluate performance of the PPOh. We firstly introduce data source and parameter settings in the SDDPHF, as well as hyper-parameters in the PPOh. After that, we compare results of PPOh with other baseline policies/algorithms, to confirm effectiveness of our proposed approach.

Algorithm 1: Training algorithm for PPOh

---

1 Initialize parameters ϕ and ϕ' in neural networks, as well as a trajectory buffer $\mathcal{M}$ to capacity $|C|$;

2 **for** $episode = 1, K$ **do**

3   Initialize the state feature s_0;

4   **for** $i = 1, |C|$ **do**

5   Collect s_i according to the environment and heurictis, and get x_i^1 and r_i by interacting with the policy $\pi_{\phi_{old}}$;

6   Store (s_i, x_i^1, r_i) in $\mathcal{M}$;

7   Obtain updated route-plans (x_i^2) according to heuristics and conduct actions x_i ;

8   **end**

9   Compute advantage estimates $\hat{A}_i$ on the basis of the current $V_{\phi'}(s_i)$ (Equation 8);

10   Sample mini-batches from $\mathcal{M}$ to update the policy by maximizing Equation 5 with N_k epochs;

11   Fit value function by minimizing on mean-square error (Equation 7) with Adam;

12   Update $\pi_{\phi_{old}} : \phi_{old} \leftarrow \phi$;

13 **end**

4.1   Parameter Setting

In the SDDPHF, we suppose that customer orders arrive from 8 am to 6 pm, and each of them should be served within four hours. The fleet also begins their work at 8 am. Other important parameters associated orders and the fleet are described in Table 1. We follow [3] to create data. In detail, we suppose that the arriving time of customer orders is generated from a Poisson process with an arrival rate λ (i.e., number of orders arriving per unit time). In our experiments, we set $\lambda = 1.2$ per minute, and thus it is around 500 orders in a day. On the other hand, spatial locations of customers are created according to an independent and identical normal distribution, with the standard deviation to 3.0km. Hyper-parameters configuration in PPOh is also shown in Table 1. N_h and N_u are numbers of hidden-layers and units, respectively. Illustration of other hyper-parameters can be found in Sect. 3. Besides, Adam optimizer is used to train neural networks.

4.2   Evaluation

All evaluation results are obtained through running on a workstation with 12 i9-8950HK cores, 128 GB RAM and a single Quadro P3200 GPU (6 GB). Codes are implemented with Pytorch in Python 3.10.

Baseline polices/algorithms are introduced as follows. It is noted that all approaches are with the same heuristics to schedule and plan routes, but distinguished on assigning policy.

Table 1. Parameters configuration

SDDPHF		PPOh	
Parameters	Value	Hyper-parameters	Value
T_{vel}^w	600 min	N_h	2
T_{dro}^w	600 min	N_u	64
T_{vel}^l	3 min	N_k	10
T_{dro}^l	3 min	η	0.0003
V_{vel}	30 km/h	η'	0.01
V_{dro}	40 km/h	γ	0.99
T_{charge}	20 min	ω_1	0.5
T_{serve}	3 min	ω_2	0.2

Random policy [19]: A policy randomly assigns orders to drones/vehicles or reject .

Vehicle-first (VF) [19]: VF assigns customer orders to vehicles with priority rather than drones. If it is infeasible for both vehicles and drones, then reject.

Drone-first (RF) [19]: Contrary to the VF policy, RF assigns customer orders to drones with priority. Only if it is infeasible for drones to serve a request, it is considered to be delivered by vehicles.

Policy function approximation (PFA) [19]: In this approach, a geographical threshold β is learned for assigning customer orders. Considering a fact that drones travel faster than vehicles, if a customer locates farther than β, then assigning it to drones in priority. Otherwise, it is assigned to vehicles first. If it is infeasible for both vehicles and drones, then reject it.

Deep Q-Networks (DQN) [3]: In this approach, before agents making decisions, a feasibility-check mechanism based on heuristics is conducted to recognize feasible actions. Hence, according to different action spaces (i.e., $X_i = \{0, 1, 2\}$, $X_i = \{0, 1\}$ and $X_i = \{0, 2\}$), three DQNs are built to make decisions.

It is noted that we embed feasibility in state features of PPOh rather than using a feasibility-check mechanism, leading to the more efficient and stable training networks.

The training and test curves of learning process are shown in Fig. 3. A data set contains 1,000 instances (a set of orders arriving during a day is denoted as an instance, and thus $500 \times 1,000 = 500,000$ orders totally) is created for training, and another set of 100 instances is for test. Besides, we solve all problems in training and test sets under a fleet of two vehicles and three drones ($|V| = 2, |D| = 3$). The maximum training epoch is set to 400,000, and it took around 38 h to train the model. We can observe from Fig. 3 that PPOh improves the optimization objective with training and is capable of converging. It is noted that episode reward in the process of training is negative since we set a penalty ($r_i = -3$) for rejection, but we record the objective (i.e., the expected number of served orders in a day) in the test phase.

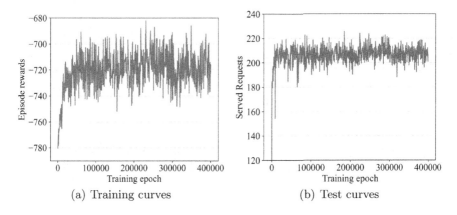

(a) Training curves   (b) Test curves

Fig. 3. Learning process of the PPOh

Table 2. Evaluation and generalization results on the test set

	Random	VF	DF	PFA	DQN	PPOh
$\|V\| = 2, \|D\| = 3$	165.87	185.36	180.56	197.16	187.20	226.41 (+14.8%)
Generalization						
$\|V\| = 2, \|D\| = 2$	149.30	168.20	165.15	176.11	169.98	206.54 (+17.3%)
$\|V\| = 2, \|D\| = 5$	198.01	219.65	212.21	235.22	219.56	264.20 (+12.3%)
$\|V\| = 2, \|D\| = 8$	247.00	269.34	257.46	284.57	275.47	316.91 (+11.4%)
$\|V\| = 1, \|D\| = 3$	110.35	122.46	118.82	127.60	122.55	139.96 (+9.7%)
$\|V\| = 3, \|D\| = 3$	217.76	247.69	243.40	261.42	255.00	311.30 (+19.1%)
$\|V\| = 5, \|D\| = 3$	277.49	363.38	362.91	382.21	365.25	433.19 (+13.3%)

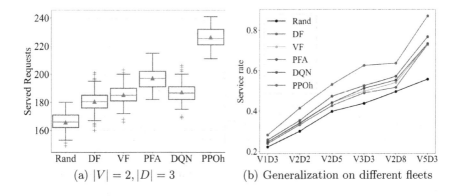

(a) $\|V\| = 2, \|D\| = 3$ (b) Generalization on different fleets

Fig. 4. Visualization of results on the test set

Table 2 shows the test results (the average number of served-customers in a day) of the PPOh and baseline algorithms. Further, we employ the trained model of problems with fleet $|V| = 2, |D| = 3$ to solve SDDDPHF with different fleet sizes, such as $|V| = 2, |D| = 5$ and $|V| = 5, |D| = 3$. The generalization results are also shown in Table 2. However, DQN can not directly generalize to other fleet sizes, given that its input (i.e., state features) of networks is associated with numbers of drones and vehicles. In addition to display the average objective on the test set, we draw a box-plot (Fig. 4(a)) to describe solution distribution of different approaches. In the box-plot, orange triangles are the average values, blue "+" are filters and orange lines in boxes represent the medians. As for different fleet sizes, we also calculate service rates (the ratio of successfully served orders to the total in a day) and compare them in Fig. 4(b). We obtain several observations from results as flows:

a. According to results in Table 2, PPOh evidently improves solution quality and can generalize well to cases with different fleet scales. For most cases, PPOh improves by more than 10%, compared to the best baseline approach. When generalizing to problems with a fleet of three vehicles and three drones, the average objective on the test set even increased by 19.1%.
b. As shown in Fig. 4(a), not only the average is improved, PPOh performs better than other approaches on almost all instances in the test set. Besides, it is robust and performs stably, given that no filters in its box-plot.
c. It is observed from Fig. 4(b) that though PPOh increases service rates in all cases, the improvement under fleet $|V| = 1, |D| = 3$ is slighter than other cases. It states that in the case of excess customer orders and lack of delivery capacity (i.e., service rate is low), the improvement on solutions is very limited.

To summary, PPOh obviously outperforms the extant approaches in terms of solution quality, and is robust to generalize on problems of different fleet sizes.

5   Conclusion

In this paper, we focus on an assignment and routing problem of offering same-day delivery with a heterogeneous fleet of drones and vehicles. Customer orders arrive stochastically and dynamically. Dispatchers should make decisions on how to assign orders, as well as schedule drones and vehicles to deliver packages, at the goal of serving as many customers as possible with a given workload. We formulate the dynamic decision process in this problem with a route-based MDP. To handle this problem, we develop a deep reinforcement learning based approach named PPOh, which combines PPO and two heuristics to make decisions in real-time. Finally, we conduct extensive experiments and compare PPOh with state-of-the-art approaches on test set. Evaluation results show that PPOh is robust to solve problems, outperforms baselines and generalizes well to different fleet sizes.

In the further, we plan to consider more complicated situations in SDD. For example, allowing the preemptive return of vehicles to the depot. On the other hand, instead of employing simple heuristics, more efficient approaches of route planning and scheduling for vehicles and drones should be developed.

References

1. Azi, N., Gendreau, M., Potvin, J.Y.: A dynamic vehicle routing problem with multiple delivery routes. Ann. Oper. Res. **199**, 103–112 (2012)
2. Chen, J., Li, S.E., Tomizuka, M.: Interpretable end-to-end urban autonomous driving with latent deep reinforcement learning. IEEE Trans. Intell. Transp. Syst. **23**(6), 5068–5078 (2021)
3. Chen, X., Ulmer, M.W., Thomas, B.W.: Deep Q-learning for same-day delivery with vehicles and drones. Eur. J. Oper. Res. **298**(3), 939–952 (2022)
4. Ferrucci, F., Bock, S.: Pro-active real-time routing in applications with multiple request patterns. Eur. J. Oper. Res. **253**(2), 356–371 (2016)
5. Ferrucci, F., Bock, S., Gendreau, M.: A pro-active real-time control approach for dynamic vehicle routing problems dealing with the delivery of urgent goods. Eur. J. Oper. Res. **225**(1), 130–141 (2013)
6. Joe, W., Lau, H.C.: Deep reinforcement learning approach to solve dynamic vehicle routing problem with stochastic customers. In: Proceedings of the International Conference on Automated Planning and Scheduling, vol. 30, pp. 394–402 (2020)
7. Klapp, M.A., Erera, A.L., Toriello, A.: The dynamic dispatch waves problem for same-day delivery. Eur. J. Oper. Res. **271**(2), 519–534 (2018)
8. Klapp, M.A., Erera, A.L., Toriello, A.: The one-dimensional dynamic dispatch waves problem. Transp. Sci. **52**(2), 402–415 (2018)
9. Konda, V., Tsitsiklis, J.: Actor-critic algorithms. In: Advances in Neural Information Processing Systems, vol. 12 (1999)
10. Kool, W., Van Hoof, H., Welling, M.: Attention, learn to solve routing problems! arXiv preprint arXiv:1803.08475 (2018)
11. Lillicrap, T.P., et al.: Continuous control with deep reinforcement learning. arXiv preprint arXiv:1509.02971 (2015)
12. Ma, Y., et al.: Learning to iteratively solve routing problems with dual-aspect collaborative transformer. In: Advances in Neural Information Processing Systems, vol. 34, pp. 11096–11107 (2021)
13. Mazyavkina, N., Sviridov, S., Ivanov, S., Burnaev, E.: Reinforcement learning for combinatorial optimization: a survey. Comput. Oper. Res. **134**, 105400 (2021)
14. Mnih, V., et al.: Human-level control through deep reinforcement learning. Nature **518**(7540), 529–533 (2015)
15. Schulman, J., Wolski, F., Dhariwal, P., Radford, A., Klimov, O.: Proximal policy optimization algorithms. arXiv preprint arXiv:1707.06347 (2017)
16. Thrun, S., Littman, M.L.: Reinforcement learning: an introduction. AI Mag. **21**(1), 103 (2000)
17. Ulmer, M.W., Goodson, J.C., Mattfeld, D.C., Thomas, B.W.: On modeling stochastic dynamic vehicle routing problems. EURO J. Transp. Logist. **9**(2), 100008 (2020)
18. Ulmer, M.W., Mattfeld, D.C., Köster, F.: Budgeting time for dynamic vehicle routing with stochastic customer requests. Transp. Sci. **52**(1), 20–37 (2018)

19. Ulmer, M.W., Thomas, B.W.: Same-day delivery with heterogeneous fleets of drones and vehicles. Networks **72**(4), 475–505 (2018)
20. Van Heeswijk, W.J., Mes, M.R., Schutten, J.M.: The delivery dispatching problem with time windows for urban consolidation centers. Transp. Sci. **53**(1), 203–221 (2019)

A Double-Layer Reinforcement Learning Feature Optimization Framework for Evolutionary Computation Based Feature Selection Algorithms

Hong Wang[1,2], Yaofa Su[1,2], Xiaolong Ou[1,2], Jinxin Zhang[3], and Ben Niu[1,2(✉)]

[1] College of Management, Shenzhen University, Shenzhen 518060, China
drniuben@163.com
[2] Greater Bay Area International Institute for Innovation, Shenzhen University, Shenzhen 518060, China
[3] Faculty of Business, Lingnan University, Tuen Mun, Hong Kong

Abstract. Recently, Evolution Computing (EC) has gained widespread use in Feature Selection due to its powerful search capabilities. However, many EC algorithms fail to fully utilize historical combination information between features. Moreover, when faced with ultra-high dimensional data, they often lack the necessary decision-making ability to select a suitable optimization direction. In this paper, we propose a double layer-reinforcement learning framework feature optimizes framework. The framework aids the EC algorithm by continuously obtaining and utilizing combined feedback from features during the iteration process. We leverage the adaptability and decision-making abilities of reinforcement learning to overcome the EC algorithm's limitations. We conducted experiments on 8 datasets from UCI to evaluate the effectiveness of our framework. The experimental results demonstrated that the EC algorithms, optimized by our framework, achieves lower error rates and requires fewer features. Consequently, we posit that reinforcement learning can offer novel methods and ideas for the application of evolutionary computing in feature selection.

Keywords: Reinforcement Learning · Evolution Computing · Feature Selection

1 Introduction

With the continuous development of data analysis and data storage technologies, the collected data in many practical applications has been experienced exponential growth [1]. This has led to an increasing demand for mining and extracting knowledge and patterns from the data. Feature selection (FS) has emerged as a combinatorial optimization problem that aims at selecting the optimal subset of features for downstream prediction tasks. FS offers numerous advantages, enhancing prediction accuracy, reducing feature dimensionality, shortening learning algorithm training times, preventing overfitting, and improving model interpretability [2]. Therefore, FS methods have been widely applied as an important preprocessing step in various fields such as medical data prediction [3], industrial applications [4], and financial investment [5]. This step allows for more representative data, reduces redundant features, and improves the effectiveness and interpretability of models in practical applications.

For an dataset with n features, the task of FS is to select the best subset from the 2^n possible feature subsets. Therefore, the FS problem can be considered as an NP-hard problem [6]. Evolutionary computation has powerful search capabilities, and as a result, many EC algorithms [7–10] have been applied to feature selection in recent years. Although these methods can identify relatively good feature subsets to some extent, many of them tend to get stuck in local optima. To address this problem, several strategies based on the correlation between features and labels, such as relief-based feature correlation guidance strategy [11], correlation-based feature task generation strategy [1] and initialization strategy based on cosine similarity between features and labels [12], have been proposed to guide the algorithm in adding relevant features or removing redundant ones. These strategies explore the potential directions based on the information of correlation between features and label. However, these methods do not fully exploit the combinatorial information among features, leaving room for improvement.

Reinforcement Learning (RL) is a method designed to address decision-making challenges and has found applications in various domains, including game theory [13], combinatorial optimization [14], and multi-agent systems [15]. RL collaborates with the environment, learns from action rewards, maintains a balance between exploitation and exploration, and seeks optimal long-term decisions [16]. To enhance the decision-making capabilities of evolutionary algorithms, studies have integrated RL methods into evolutionary computation. For example, Xu et al. [17] utilized RL's decision-making abilities to guide optimization in Particle Swarm Optimization (PSO) for improving topology communication structure. Additionally, Huynh [18] and Yin [19] introduced adaptive parameter approaches based on RL, implementing them in Differential Evolution (DE) and PSO, respectively. While these strategies enhance the decision-making ability of evolutionary computation algorithms, they lack of exploration of connections between features. Moreover, these reinforcement learning strategies are tailored to specific evolutionary methods, serving as supplements for particular algorithms and lacking universality across all evolutionary computation algorithms.

Evolutionary computation relies on optimizing the positions of individuals and populations to guide optimization. However, it has limitations when applied to combinatorial optimization problems, particularly in extracting combinatory information from feature subsets. Additionally, its decision-making ability in generating new solutions is inadequate, resulting in the production of numerous irrelevant solutions. To address these challenges, we propose a Double-Layer Reinforcement Learning-based Feature Optimization Framework (QLLC) designed for integration into various evolutionary algorithms in this study. Our framework leverages historical information on feature combinations obtained during the iteration process of EC algorithms to guide future optimizations. The framework consists of two layers: the lower layer assesses the merits of features, while the upper layer determines the optimal range of the number of subsets, offering a reference for feature number selection in the lower layer. QLLC utilizes the

Q-Learning algorithm to enhance the evolutionary algorithm's capability in selecting the most suitable feature subset.

2 Background and Related Work

2.1 A Subsection Sample

Feature selection is a vital task in machine learning and data mining, where the objective is to choose the most effective subset of features from a given feature set. Assuming a feature selection issue, a training dataset $X = (x_1, x_2, ..., x_n)$, comprising n features is considered. Feature selection requires choosing k (where $k < n$) features create a selected vector of features F that minimizes the evaluation criterion $fit(F)$. Thus, feature selection can be viewed as an optimization problem:

$$\min \quad fit(F)$$
$$s.t. \quad F = (f_1, f_2, \ldots, f_n), f_i \in \{0, 1\} \forall i \in \{1, 2, \ldots, n\} \tag{1}$$

when $f_i = 1$, it indicates that feature x_i has been selected in F. Conversely, when $f_i = 0$, it indicates that feature x_i has been excluded from the feature subset F.

In the field of feature selection, individuals in EC are typically encoded as numbers ranging from 0 to 1. The individual's position $P = (p_1, p_2, \ldots, p_n)$ is denoted by assuming that each $p_i \in [0, 1], \forall i \in \{1, 2, \ldots, n\}$. Equation (2) shows that to achieve conversion, a threshold value between 0 and 1 is typically selected as θ between P and F.

$$f_i = \begin{cases} 1, \text{ if } p_i > \theta \\ 0, \text{ if } p_i \le \theta \end{cases}, \forall i \in \{1, 2, \ldots, n\} \tag{2}$$

The standard evaluation criteria for feature selection involves assessing the error rate and length of features used in classification algorithms. In this study, we utilize the fitness function displayed in Eq. (3) as our means of evaluating feature subsets:

$$fit(F) = \rho(1 - acc) + (1 - \rho)\frac{L}{n} \tag{3}$$

where acc represents the accuracy of feature subset classification and L represents the number of features selected by the feature subset, ρ is a parameter that balances classification errors with the length of feature subsets. Usually, ρ is set to 0.9.

2.2 Q-Learning

Q-Learning is a reinforcement learning algorithm based on value iteration. The agent learns an action-value function known as the Q-Function, which guides it to make optimal decisions in environments with incomplete information. The core concept of Q-Learning involves representing the value of every state-action pair using a Q-Table. Each entry $Q(s_t, a_t)$ within the Q-Table denotes the expected return or cumulative reward for taking action a_t at state s_t. As the agent interacts with the environment, it learns the optimal policy by updating the Q-Table continuously. Equation (4) demonstrates the update formula for Q-Learning:

$$Q(s_t, a_t) = Q(s_t, a_t) + lr[r + \gamma \ max \ Q(s_{t+1}, a_{t+1}\prime)] \tag{4}$$

where $Q(s_t, a_t)$ represents the Q-Value of taking action a_t in the current state s_t, r represents the immediate reward obtained by the agent after taking action a_t, s_{t+1} represents the transition to the next state, $a_{t+1}\prime$ represents the optimal action in the next state, α is the learning rate, and γ is the discount factor.

The Q-Learning algorithm learns the optimal policy gradually by interacting continuously with the environment and updating the Q-Value. Subsequently, the agent can make optimal decisions in an unknown environment by choosing the best action based on the highest Q-Value in the Q-Table.

2.3 EC-Based Feature Selection Algorithms

Evolutionary computation techniques have gained prominence in feature selection due to their robust global search capabilities. Common EC algorithms in feature selection include genetic algorithms and differential evolution algorithms. These algorithms evolve individuals within a population using mutation, crossover, reproduction, and selection operators, adhering to Darwin's theory of evolution. Representative swarm intelligence algorithms, such as particle swarm optimization [9], ant colony algorithms [15], and bacterial optimization [20], collaboratively explore and converge towards optimal positions through communication mechanisms. Despite their potent optimization capabilities, EC algorithms often grapple with local optima in feature selection, especially in NP-hard combinatorial optimization problems. This challenge intensifies in high-dimensional data, yielding limited outcomes despite substantial computational resources. Numerous researchers have investigated strategies to address this issue.

To improve the convergence speed and performance of genetic algorithms, Zhou [7] recommended employing a precision-first dominance operator and a fast-bit mutation operator. The precision-first dominance operator increases the survival probability of individuals with higher classification accuracy rates in the population, while the fast-bit mutation operator overcomes limitations of traditional bit-string mutation, enhancing efficiency. Despite enhancing the optimization capability and speed of genetic algorithms, these operators do not fully leverage feature combination information, restricting their potential for global optimization.

Currently, Li [9] and Ma [21] partition feature selection into two stages. Initially, features undergo scoring using correlation measures, and subsequently, low-scoring features are discarded. Then, optimization algorithms are implemented to quickly optimize the remaining feature space. Although this approach can achieve satisfactory outcomes in several instances, it disregards the interactions between features, impeding the subsets from attaining the global optimum.

Chen [11] proposed a new PSO algorithm that utilizes correlation. By utilizing the correlation between features and labels to guide particles towards better exploration directions, this method effectively incorporates the features information to produce efficient results. In comparison to other algorithms, this approach achieves superior results in 25 classification problems. Although it considers interactions between features, this approach overlooks the additional information generated through feature combinations. Moreover, calculating correlation information between features and labels consumes a significant amount of time.

2.4 Reinforcement Learning Based Feature Selection Algorithm

EC is widely employed in feature selection due to its potent search capabilities. However, a limitation lies in its tendency to prioritize local information at the current search point, neglecting global information. This constraint hampers decision-making, especially for intricate problems involving high-dimensional data. In contrast, reinforcement learning, a robust machine learning algorithm, excels in decision-making by extracting patterns and regularities from historical experiences to guide decision optimization. Recognizing this advantage, researchers have explored combining reinforcement learning with evolutionary computation to enhance decision-making capabilities.

Xu and Pi [17] proposed a PSO algorithm that incorporates reinforcement learning for dynamic topology communication. This approach can modify the communication structure among particles and outperform static topology in various benchmark functions. However, the efficiency of this algorithm depends heavily on the specific characteristics of the problem at hand. If the problem characteristics are unclear or rapidly changing, the algorithm may struggle to adapt and optimize effectively. Moreover, the use of this strategy may lead to unsatisfactory results, because different problems may require different optimal topology structures.

Emary [22] proposed the Enhanced Grey Wolf Optimization (EGWO), which combines reinforcement learning with the Grey Wolf Optimization (GWO) algorithm. This variant of GWO outperforms the original GWO and other algorithms, such as Genetic Algorithms (GA) and PSO, on multiple data sets. However, it is important to note that this reinforcement learning strategy is specifically designed to optimize the GWO algorithm and may not be applicable to other algorithms with different parameter shapes. Therefore, it cannot be considered a universally applicable approach.

In summary, while EC-based feature selection algorithms have demonstrated promising outcomes, there are still limitations in effectively mining data information through features and leveraging population experience. To address these constraints, numerous studies have commenced the integration of reinforcement learning into evolutionary computation algorithms, utilizing reinforcement learning to extract and apply historical information from the population for optimizing decision-making at the feature level. However, a universally applicable reinforcement learning strategy framework for the majority of evolutionary computation algorithms is currently lacking. Hence, the primary objective of this research is to develop a universal reinforcement learning framework, efficiently exploring relationships between feature combinations and aiding evolutionary computation algorithms in optimizing decision-making.

3 The Propose Method

We first describe the feature optimization framework based on double-layer reinforcement learning as a whole. We then provide a detailed description of the lower-layer feature optimization framework and the upper-layer length control strategy based on the construction of state, action, reward, and transition equations.

3.1 Double-Layer Reinforcement Learning Based Feature Optimization Framework

In this subsection, we present a framework for feature optimization based on double-layer reinforcement learning. Our proposed approach leverages the ability of reinforcement learning to extract insights from previous experiences and inform decision-making. The goal is to harness reinforcement learning to enable a comprehensive exploration of the experience gained from evolutionary computation in feature selection, and create a roadmap for populations to pursue more promising solutions.

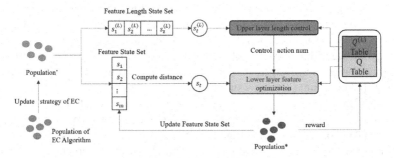

Fig. 1. Sketch of Double-layer Reinforcement Learning based Feature Optimization Framework

Our proposed framework is illustrated in Fig. 1, where we integrate the individual's position in the EC into the reinforcement learning framework using the standard update method of the EC algorithms. We then produce a modified individual through reinforcement learning. In the reinforcement learning framework, we employ a double-layer Q-Learning algorithm. The upper layer acts as the feature length control layer, determining the number of selected features for the current individual feature subset and the optimal feature subset length for the next state based on the current state. This information is transmitted to the lower layer. The feature optimization layer, situated below, utilizes the optimal length information and the feature data stored in the Q-Table to choose or eliminate specific features from the current subset, aiding in optimizing the subset for enhanced performance. The optimal individual obtained through evolutionary computation serves as the lower-level state representation set for reinforcement learning, facilitating improved learning of dominant individuals' information. Simultaneously, the Q-Table in reinforcement learning extracts feature information through feature search, comprehensively exploring feature relationships, identifying advantageous features, and guiding optimization of evolutionary populations.

3.2 Lower-Layer Feature Optimization Algorithm Based on Q-Learning

In this subsection, we present feature selection as a reinforcement learning task and introduce a lower-level feature optimization algorithm based on Q-Learning (QLFS) to address this task. Reinforcement learning tasks are commonly modeled as Markov Decision Problems (MDP), in which the state, action, reward, and policy functions are the fundamental components. The model for selecting features in MDP includes the quadruple $<S, A, r, \pi>$, with the following specific definition.

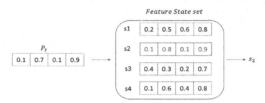

Fig. 2. Feature state instance diagram

State S: Take the best individuals in evolutionary computation as a representation of the state, designated as $S = (s_1, s_2, \ldots, s_m)$. The set is made up of the location data of m individuals with the most successful population history, called a feature subset of states. The current state of the feature subset is determined by calculating its Euclidean distance from all individuals in the feature state subset. The state corresponding to the closest individual is selected as the current feature subset state, as illustrated in Fig. 2. The current input EC individual position is P_t. The shortest distance exists between P_t and the subset stored in state 2, so the corresponding state of this individual is s_2.

Action A: There are 2n actions in total, with the initial n actions representing the non-selection of corresponding features, and the final n actions representing the selection of corresponding features, denoted as $A = \{a_1, a_2 \ldots a_n \ldots a_{2n}\}$. The algorithm assesses actions based on two dimensions: selection and removal of features, ultimately determining the feature subset through their interaction.

Policy function π: $\pi(S, A)$ represents the transfer function from state S to action A. In this study, once the agent identifies the current state, it will conduct Q-Value sorting aligned with the current feature subset in the initial h actions. Simultaneously, for the currently selected feature, the corresponding action for selection, as well as the non-selection action for the unselected feature, should not be executed. h is obtained by multiplying the length of the current feature subset by a scaling factor β.

Reward r: The reward attained after performing h actions, denoted as r, is determined by evaluating the accuracy and length of the feature subset in the preceding and subsequent iterations, as depicted in Eq. (5):

$$r = \alpha(acc_t - acc_{t-1}) + (1 - \alpha)\frac{(L_{t-1} - L_t)}{n} \tag{5}$$

where $\alpha(\alpha \in (0, 1))$ represents the importance constant of rewards. acc_t and acc_{t-1} denote the classification accuracy of the current and previous iterative feature subset. L_t And L_{t-1} denote the length of the current and previous iterative feature subset.

After obtaining the immediate reward r, the agent will update the corresponding Q-values of all state-action pairs executed in this iteration using Eq. (3).

Assuming the input position of the framework is $P = \{p_1, p_2, \ldots, p_{popSize}\}$. In the algorithm 1's main loop, the agent calculates the Euclidean distance of all feature state subsets P and S. The state corresponding to the minimum value is then considered as the agent's current state s_t. The Q-Table is queried to obtain the Q-Value of the corresponding action in the current state. The Q-Values are sorted in descending order to obtain an action sequence F_Q based on the Q-Value. Assuming that there are 4 actions to be executed based on the policy function, select 4 actions from the top ranked actions of F_Q that do not conflict with the feature subset. Then obtain the set of actions to be executed $\{a_{n+1}, a_5, a_{n+6}, a_3\}$. Since actions with subscripts of n or less represent the deletion of corresponding features in the current subset, while actions with subscripts greater than n represent the selection of corresponding features, the current agent must delete features 5 and 3, and add features 1 and 6. At this time, the positions will be updated by $1 - p[j]$, for all j in $\{1, 3, 5, 6\}$, and the resulting position will be used as input for the next iteration of evolutionary computation. Simultaneously, use Eq. (2) to convert it into a new feature subset vector, and input it into the classifier to calculate accuracy. Finally, calculate a reward and update the Q-Table using Eq. (3). Please refer to Algorithm 1 for specific algorithmic details.

Algorithm1: Lower-level feature optimization algorithm based on Q-Learning

Input: The EC Algorithm, $ECAL$; The population size, $popSize$; The state size, m; The maximum number of iterations, $iterMax$; Threshold θ; Learning rate lr; The probability β.

Output: Selected feature.

1. Randomly initialize the position $P_{posSize}$ and compute the fitness values by equation (3).
2. Choose the best m individual and assign them to the state set S based on the fitness values.
3. Set $t \leftarrow 0, Q(S, A) \leftarrow 0$.
4. **while** $t < iterMax$ **do**
5.   Update position $P_{posSize}$ by standard $ECAL$ update strategy.
6.   **for** $i = 1$ to $popSize$ **do**
7.   Compute the distance between p_i and all the Feature Subset of S.
8.   Select the state set with the shortest distance to p_i as the state s_t of the i individual.
9.   Obtain set F_Q of $Q(s_t, A)$ sorted in descending order by Q-value.
10.   Set $F_e \leftarrow$ the exist feature and $F_a \leftarrow$ the absent feature of the i individual.
11.   Calculate the action number $h = \beta L_i$. (L_i is the feature number of the i individual)
12.   Set $j \leftarrow 0, w \leftarrow 0$.
13.   **while** w < m and $j < 2n$ **do**
14.   **if** $F_Q[j] \leq n$ and $F_Q[j] \in F_e$
15.   Delete feature $F_Q[j]$ then set $p_i\left[F_Q[j]\right] \leftarrow 1 - p_i[F_Q[j]]$.
16.   **else if** $F_Q[j] > n$ and $F_Q[j] \in F_d$
17.   Select feature $(F_Q[j] \bmod n)$ then set $p_i[F_Q[j] \bmod n] \leftarrow 1 - p_i[F_Q[j] \bmod n]$.
18.   **end**
19.   Set $j = j + 1$ and $w = w + 1$.
20.   **end**
21.   Update the state position of s_t to p_i when the fitness of the p_i is less.
22.   Calculate reward by equation (5) and renew Q Value of the actions by equation (4).
23.   **end**
24.   Set $t \leftarrow t + 1$
25. **end**
26. **return** the index of the best position in history that have values larger than θ.

3.3 Upper-Layer Length Control Strategic Based on Q-Learning

The length control strategic is also designed based on the Q Learning framework. After adding this mechanism, our reinforcement learning feature selection algorithm is renamed QLLCFS. The feature subset is divided into distinct length ranges using a predefined step size, and these ranges define the states according to the subset length. Next, we utilize the Q-Learning algorithm to determine the optimal length of the feature subset at each step. This length control strategic will then guide the algorithm in Subsect. 3.2, where it will either add or delete features. Below, we briefly introduce the length control strategy for the quadruple $<S^{(L)}, A^{(L)}, r^{(L)}, \pi^{(L)}>$.

Fig. 3. Schematic diagram of length state based on feature subset

State $S^{(L)}$: Starting from 0, divide the feature dimension n into z subsets according to a certain step size l, and select different subset length ranges as different states $S^{(L)}$ to represent. The representation diagram based on subset length is shown in Fig. 3.

Action A^L: There are z actions in the action set, represented by $A^{(L)} = \{a_1^{(L)}, a_2^{(L)} \ldots a_z^{(L)}\}$. Each action corresponds to a feature subset range, which represents a state. In each iteration, an action is selected to determine the length range of the next subset of state features.

Policy function $\pi^{(L)}$: In the length control strategic, the agent executes the length action with the maximum Q-Value corresponding to Q-Table in the current state. After selecting the action, it randomly selects a length L_{basic} within the corresponding range serves as a length benchmark to guide the length of the next feature subset.

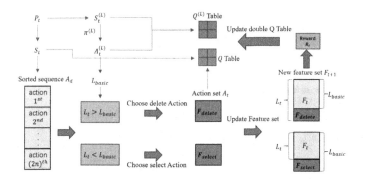

Fig. 4. Schematic diagram of a framework based on length control strategy

The Q-Learning algorithm utilizing the length control strategy is integrated into the algorithm selection action steps outlined in Subsect. 3.2, as illustrated in Fig. 4. Initially, in line with the preceding steps of Algorithm 2, acquire the sorted action sequence F_Q that corresponds to the present state s_t. Following this, the agent determines its length state $s_t^{(L)}$ by assessing the length of the current feature subset. Later, the highest corresponding Q-Value action in the $Q^{(L)}$-Table will be selected based on $\pi^{(L)}$. The length benchmark, L_{basic}, for the new feature subset will be randomly selected within the corresponding range. Technical term abbreviations will be explained upon first use. If the current state's feature subset length is less than the length benchmark, the agent will choose features from front to back in the F_Q sequence. If the opposite is true, the agent will select the action of deleting features from front to back in the F_Q sequence. After executing the action, a new subset of features will be obtained, and corresponding rewards will be obtained through the reward calculation formula. Then, the Q and $Q^{(L)}$ tables will be updated according to the Q-Value update formula. Algorithm 2 shows the specific implementation process of the Q-Learning feature selection algorithm with upper-layer length control strategic based on Q-Learning.

Algorithm2: Upper-layer length control strategic based on Q-Learning.

Input: $ECAL$; $popSize$; m; $iterMax$; θ; lr; The number of $A^{(L)}$, z.

Output: Selected feature.

1. Randomly initialize the position $P_{posSize}$ and compute the fitness values by equation (3).
2. Choose the best m individual and assign them to the state set S based on the fitness values.
3. Set $t \leftarrow 0$, $Q(S, A) \leftarrow 0$, $Q^{(L)}(S^{(L)}, A^{(L)}) \leftarrow 0$.
4. **while** $t < iterMax$ **do**
5.   Update position $P_{posSize}$ by standard $ECAL$ update strategy.
6.   **for** $i = 1$ to $popSize$ **do**
7.   Compute the distance between p_i state set S and choose the minimun one as state s_t.
8.   Obtain set F_Q of $Q(s_t, A)$ sorted in descending order by Q-value.
9.   Set $F_e \leftarrow$ the exist feature and $F_a \leftarrow$ the absent feature of the i individual.
10.   Current feature length L_t and calculate the length state $s_t^{(L)}$.
11.   Choose the action $A_t^{(L)}$ based on $\pi^{(L)}$ and calculate the L_{basic}.
12.   Set $j \leftarrow 0$.
13.   **while** $L_t \mathrel{!}= L_{basic}$
14.   **if** $F_Q[j] \leq n$ and $F_Q[j] \in F_e$ and $L_t > L_{basic}$
15.   Delete feature $F_Q[j]$ then set $p_i[F_Q[j]] \leftarrow 1 - p_i[F_Q[j]]$.
16.   **else if** $F_Q[j] > n$ and $F_Q[j] \in F_d$ and $L_t < L_{basic}$
17.   Select feature $(F_Q[j] \bmod n)$ then set $p_i[F_Q[j] \bmod n] \leftarrow 1 - p_i[F_Q[j] \bmod n]$.
18.   end
19.   Set $j \leftarrow j + 1$.
20.   end
21.   Update the state position of s_t to p_i when the fitness of the p_i is less.
22.   Calculate the reward of action by equation (5).
23.   Renew the all the two Q-Table of the action in state S_t and $s_t^{(L)}$ by equation (4).
24.   end
25.   Set $t \leftarrow t + 1$.
26. end
27. **return** the index of the best position in history that have values larger than θ

4 Experiment and Result

4.1 Dataset Description and Experiment Settings

In order to test the performance of the proposed framework for optimizing features, based on double-layer reinforcement learning, and the effectiveness of the proposed length control strategy, experiments were conducted on six datasets from UCI. To ensure the experiment's persuasiveness, it was necessary to have considerable diversity in the number of features, instances and classifications while selecting the dataset. Table 1 shows the specific information for the dataset.

Table 1. Dataset for feature selection

Dataset	Feature	Instance	Class
BCW	30	569	2
Sonar	60	208	2
LSVT	310	120	2
Colon	2000	62	2
DLBCL	5470	77	2
Brain Tumor1 (BT1)	5920	90	5
PT	10509	102	2
Lung Cancer1 (LC1)	12600	72	3

We conducted three sets of experiments in the framework validation experiment. First, to verify our framework's effectiveness, we will use PSO as an example and incorporate our two-layer reinforcement learning framework embedded with length control strategy, naming it QPSOLC. We will compare this algorithm with PSO [9], the currently advanced algorithm CUSSPSO [11], and the unprocessed feature selection process. CUSSPSO uses information from features and labels to guide the feature selection process and has demonstrated superior performance compared to most PSO-based algorithms. Our framework mines historical feature selection experiences to extract information on feature subsets. We will compare our proposed algorithm with this approach to demonstrate its superiority. Secondly, we tested the generalization ability of our framework by integrating common algorithms PSO, GA [7], and BFO [20] into our double-layer reinforcement learning framework with embedded length control strategies to generate QLLC-PSO, QLLC-GA, and QLLC-BFO. Following comparison with the base algorithms, we conducted experiments to develop a framework suited for general swarm intelligence optimization algorithms. Thirdly, to confirm the efficacy of the length control strategic in this article's framework, we will compare QLLC-PSO, QLLC-GA, and QLLC-BFO algorithms with only PSO, GA, and BFO against QLPSO, QLGA, and QLBFO obtained from the lower-level reinforcement learning feature optimization framework, which is lack of length control strategy.

In this experiment, we divided the data evenly, selecting 70% of the samples randomly for the training set and the remaining 30% for the test set. For classification prediction, KNN was used as the learning algorithm, with k set to 5. Due to its simplicity and convenience, KNN helped achieve experimental results quickly. In order to demonstrate the effectiveness of the proposed feature selection framework, this study uses accuracy and feature subset length as evaluation criteria for effectiveness.

4.2 Parameter Settings

Table 2 displays the parameters utilized in the six feature selection methods employed in the experiment. Notably, CUSSPO, PSO, GA, and BFO's parameter settings align with previous literature. The EC algorithms used in this study operate on a population of 50, as indicated by $popSize = 50$. The number of iterations is set to 100. We have established a threshold θ of 0.5 for selecting features.

Table 2. Parameter of FS Algorithms

Algorithms	Parameter values
CUSSPSO	$c_1 = c_2 = 1.49445, \omega = 0.9 - 0.5 * \frac{iter}{iterMax}, n_c = 2, A = 0.15, B = 0.05$
PSO	$c_1 = c_2 = 1.49618, \omega = 0.7298$
GA	$Sr = 0.5 * popSize$, mutation probability $P_m = 0.005$, crossover number $C_n = 0.5 * popSize$
BFO	$N_C = 100, N_s = 4, F_{re}=4, F_{ed} = 3, P_{ed} = 0.15$
QLLC	State size $m = popSize$, Length step $l = \frac{n}{20}, \alpha = 0.9, lr = 0.5, \gamma = 0.5$
QL	State size $m = popSize, \alpha = 0.9, lr = 0.5, \gamma = 0.5, \beta=0.1$

In the feature optimization frameworks QLLC and QL, the learning rate is set to $lr = 0.5$, while the discount factor is set to $\gamma = 0.5$. These values are chosen to ensure that the RL algorithms assign equal weight to historical experience, immediate rewards, and future rewards. After multiple debugging attempts, we have determined that setting the state size m to $popSize$ yields the best results. We have also found that setting the feature length step l in QLLC to 20 equal parts of the feature dimension and the proportion β of the action to be executed to 0.1 produces suitable outcomes.

4.3 Experiment Result

Table 3 presents the comparison results of the PSO feature selection algorithm. The table shows that our proposed double-layer reinforcement learning framework has enhanced the performance of PSO. QLLC-PSO attained the highest accuracy in seven datasets and featured the lowest number of features in eight datasets. From the comparison of results from datasets such as Colon, DLBCL, BrainTumor1, et cetera, it is evident that our framework exhibits greater improvement in handling datasets with dimensions exceeding a thousand, and is capable of addressing challenges posed by the extensive search space resulting from ultra-high dimensional data.

Table 3. The result of the PSO based FS algorithms

Dataset	Algorithms									
	All	PSO			CUSSPSO			QLLC-PSO		
	Acc	Acc	NF	Time	Acc	NF	Time	Acc	NF	Time
BCW	96.49	**98.36**	9.1	**20.1**	97.48	6.3	29.7	98.07	**5.5**	31.6
Sonar	53.23	73.71	20.4	**14.8**	72.41	11.6	28.5	**84.68**	**10.2**	30.7
LSVT	94.74	97.37	91.8	**6.97**	95.52	39.9	21.3	**99.95**	**16.7**	27.3
Colon	68.42	80.00	636	**7.98**	84.21	71.7	98.6	**91.05**	**74.2**	140.1
DLBCL	86.96	94.78	1710.9	**73.2**	93.91	816.4	614.2	**99.13**	**394.6**	744.0
BT1	66.67	71.85	1740.5	**36.1**	72.22	533.1	473.0	**86.67**	**117.7**	549.9
PT	80.65	92.25	3271.8	**31.9**	94.51	368.8	784.01	**97.42**	**245.3**	650.7
LC1	85.25	88.19	3791.8	**44.2**	88.85	832.4	1386.2	**93.11**	**299.8**	834.2

* Acc means accuracy; NF means number of features; the unit of Time is second; All means all Feature.

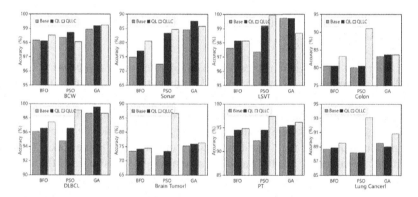

Fig. 5. Accuracy comparison of the six FS algorithms on the 8 datasets

Figure 5 and Fig. 6 presents the results of the last two experiment groups discussed in Subsect. 3.2. According to Fig. 5, it can be observed that the accuracy of PSO and BFO in seven datasets and GA in six datasets has improved after integration with QLLC. What's more, in Fig. 6, the EC algorithm has obtained a smaller subset of features than the basic algorithm in almost all experimental examples of integration into the QLLC framework. This experiment reveals that our double layer reinforcement framework possesses universality in guiding EC algorithm optimization and can be applied to many EC algorithms. In Fig. 5, a comparison is presented between RL frameworks that employ length control strategies (QLLC) and those that do not (QL). Generally, the QL framework enhances the accuracy of the basic EC algorithm, surpassing the QLLC framework on certain datasets. However, the QLLC framework improves accuracy to a greater extent in the majority of cases, albeit not all. At the same time, the QL framework typically does not permit the EC algorithm to yield a reduced set of features. This affirms the efficacy of length control tactics in RL frameworks.

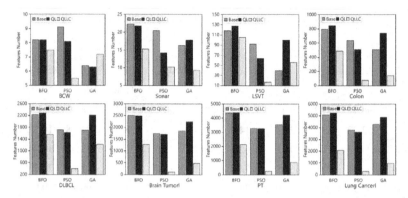

Fig. 6. Number of selected features comparison of the six FS algorithms on the 8 datasets

In the experiments, we demonstrate that our proposed double-layer reinforcement framework enhances the performance of EC algorithms in most cases. Additionally, the length control strategy is an essential part of the RL framework. The strategy facilitates the RL framework's ability to quickly find the best range of feature numbers.

5   Conclusion

In this article, a double-layer reinforcement learning framework is proposed to aid the EC algorithm in selecting feature subsets. The algorithm utilizes Q-Learning to extract the combination information of features during the iteration process of the EC algorithm, guiding optimization. The proposed length control strategy assists in determining an appropriate subset range for the population and supplying specific values for the number of actions carried out by the lower-level feature optimization framework. During the experiment, we compared the PSO algorithm combined with our QLLC framework to both the CUSSPSO algorithm and PSO alone. Additionally, we tested the effectiveness and robustness of our double-layer reinforcement learning framework by combining PSO, BFO, and GA with both the QLLC and QL frameworks. The experimental results show that QLLC enhances the effectiveness of the PSO algorithm across 7 out of 8 datasets. Moreover, the framework improves the performance of GA and BFO in most cases, while confirming the need for our upper-level length control strategy in reinforcement learning frameworks. This strategy can flexibly determine the optimal range of feature numbers and efficiently eliminate redundant information.

For future research, we aim to identify appropriate techniques to enhance the efficiency of our framework, including proxy models algorithms, to expedite optimization.

Acknowledgments. This work is supported by the National Natural Science Foundation of China (Grants Nos. 71901152), Guangdong Basic and Applied Basic Research Foundation (2023A1515010919), Guangdong Innovation Team Project of Intelligent Management and Cross Innovation (2021WCXTD002), Shenzhen Stable Support Grant (Grant Nos. 20220810100952001), and Shenzhen University-Lingnan University Joint Research Programme.

References

1. Chen, K., Xue, B., Zhang, M., et al.: An evolutionary multitasking-based feature selection method for high-dimensional classification. IEEE Trans. Cybern. **52**(7), 7172–7186 (2020)
2. Liu, K., Fu, Y., Wang, P., et al.: Automating feature subspace exploration via multi-agent reinforcement learning. In: Proceedings of the 25th ACM SIGKDD International Conference on Knowledge Discovery & Data Mining, pp. 207–215 (2019)
3. Nadimi-Shahraki, M.H., Zamani, H., Mirjalili, S.: Enhanced whale optimization algorithm for medical feature selection: a COVID-19 case study. Comput. Biol. Med. **148**, 105858 (2022)
4. Tan, M., Yuan, S., Li, S., et al.: Ultra-short-term industrial power demand forecasting using LSTM based hybrid ensemble learning. IEEE Trans. Power Syst. **35**(4), 2937–2948 (2019)
5. Paiva, F.D., Cardoso, R.T.N., Hanaoka, G.P., et al.: Decision-making for financial trading: a fusion approach of machine learning and portfolio selection. Expert Syst. Appl. **115**, 635–655 (2019)
6. Chandrashekar, G., Sahin, F.: A survey on feature selection methods. Comput. Electr. Eng. **40**(1), 16–28 (2014)
7. Zhou, Y., Zhang, W., Kang, J., et al.: A problem-specific non-dominated sorting genetic algorithm for supervised feature selection. Inf. Sci. **547**, 841–859 (2021)
8. Zhang, Y., Gong, D., Gao, X., et al.: Binary differential evolution with self-learning for multi-objective feature selection. Inf. Sci. **507**, 67–85 (2020)
9. Li, A.D., Xue, B., Zhang, M.: Improved binary particle swarm optimization for feature selection with new initialization and search space reduction strategies. Appl. Soft Comput. **106**, 107302 (2021)
10. Abdel-Basset, M., El-Shahat, D., El-Henawy, I., et al.: A new fusion of grey wolf optimizer algorithm with a two-phase mutation for feature selection. Expert Syst. Appl. **139**, 112824 (2020)
11. Chen, K., Xue, B., Zhang, M., et al.: Correlation-guided updating strategy for feature selection in classification with surrogate-assisted particle swarm optimization. IEEE Trans. Evol. Comput. **26**(5), 1015–1029 (2021)
12. Paniri, M., Dowlatshahi, M.B., Nezamabadi-Pour, H.: MLACO: a multi-label feature selection algorithm based on ant colony optimization. Knowl.-Based Syst. **192**, 105285 (2020)
13. Xu, Q., Su, Z., Lu, R.: Game theory and reinforcement learning based secure edge caching in mobile social networks. IEEE Trans. Inf. Forensics Secur. **15**, 3415–3429 (2020)
14. Mazyavkina, N., Sviridov, S., Ivanov, S., et al.: Reinforcement learning for combinatorial optimization: a survey. Comput. Oper. Res. **134**, 105400 (2021)
15. Paniri, M., Dowlatshahi, M.B., Nezamabadi-pour, H.: Ant-TD: Ant colony optimization plus temporal difference reinforcement learning for multi-label feature selection. Swarm Evol. Comput. **64**, 100892 (2021)
16. Liu, K., Fu, Y., Wu, L., et al.: Automated feature selection: a reinforcement learning perspective. IEEE Trans. Knowl. Data Eng. **35**(3), 2272–2284 (2023)
17. Xu, Y., Pi, D.: A reinforcement learning-based communication topology in particle swarm optimization. Neural Comput. Appl. **32**, 10007–10032 (2020). https://doi.org/10.1007/s00521-019-04527-9
18. Huynh, T.N., Do, D.T.T., Lee, J.: Q-Learning-based parameter control in differential evolution for structural optimization. Appl. Soft Comput. **107**, 107464 (2021)
19. Yin, S., Jin, M., Lu, H., et al.: Reinforcement-learning-based parameter adaptation method for particle swarm optimization. Complex Intell. Syst. **9**, 5585–5609 (2023)
20. Wang, H., Jing, X., Niu, B.: A discrete bacterial algorithm for feature selection in classification of microarray gene expression cancer data. Knowl.-Based Syst. **126**, 8–19 (2017)

21. Ma, W., Zhou, X., Zhu, H., et al.: A two-stage hybrid ant colony optimization for high-dimensional feature selection. Pattern Recogn. **116**, 107933 (2021)
22. Emary, E., Zawbaa, H.M., Grosan, C.: Experienced gray wolf optimization through reinforcement learning and neural networks. IEEE Trans. Neural Netw. Learn. Syst. **29**(3), 681–694 (2017)

Combinatorial Optimization Approaches

Ant-Antlion Optimizer with Similarity Information for Multidimensional Knapsack Problem

Yi Liu, Guoli Yang, Qibin Zheng$^{(\boxtimes)}$, Xiang Li, Kun Liu, Qiang Wang, and Wei Qin

Advanced Institute of Big Data, Beijing 100195, China
zhengqb@aibd.ac.cn

Abstract. The Multidimensional Knapsack Problem (MKP) is one kind of classical mathematical model that has been extensively studied by researchers. Due to its NP-hard nature, finding an exact solution for MKP in polynomial time is not feasible, and the methods based on evolutionary algorithms have been widely explored and proven successful in solving the MKP. To effectively tackle MKP, we propose a novel method called the ant-antlion optimizer with similarity information. It incorporates the similarity concept throughout the evolution process. A new evaluation measure that combines individual's fitness and the similarity degree between the elite individual and other solutions is developed. This measure is utilized to enhance its searching capability. In addition, it employs both fitness values and similarity information of the population to implement a self-adaptive mutation strategy to improve its diversity performance. To evaluate our method, a comprehensive experiment consisting of forty-eight testing instances and six well-known algorithms is carried out. The results demonstrate that our proposed approach effectively solves MKP, and the inclusion of similarity information significantly enhances its performance.

Keywords: Antlion Optimizer · Ant Colony Optimization · Similarity Information · Multidimensional Knapsack Problem · Self-adaption Mutation

1 Introduction

The knapsack problem is a challenging combinatorial problem that falls under the category of NP-hard problems and cannot be solved in polynomial time. It has significant implications in various real-world applications, including but not limited to feature selection, data imputation, scheduling, and resource allocation [1, 2]. There exist several variants of the knapsack problem, including the multiple knapsack problem, Multidimensional Knapsack Problem (MKP), and quadratic knapsack problem, among others [1]. Among these variants, MKP has drawn considerable attention from researchers and has found applications in diverse situations.

The goal of MKP is to find a subset of items filling in a multidimensional capacity-limited knapsack that maximizes the total benefit while taking into account the profit of each chosen item. Mathematically, the MKP can be represented as follows:

$$\max f(x) = \sum_{j=1}^{n} p_j x_j$$
$$s.t. \ \sum_{j=1}^{n} c_{ij} x_j \leq w_i, i = 1, \ldots, m \tag{1}$$
$$x_j \in \{0, 1\}, j = 1, \ldots, n$$

where n is the number of items and m is the number of knapsack constraints with capacity w_i ($i = 1, \ldots, m$). Decision variable $x_j = 1$ means the jth item is chosen or otherwise. An item j needs c_{ij} units of capacity and could bring p_j units of profit.

The MKP is extensively utilized for evaluating optimization methods in the fields of operational research and machine learning, and it has numerous practical application scenarios. Since the MKP is also categorized as an NP-hard problem, no deterministic approach can solve it in polynomial time.

Over the past several decades, Evolutionary Algorithms (EAs) have been extensively studied for solving different types of optimization problems, resulting in the proposal of numerous effective algorithms, including baby search algorithm, brain storm optimization, Ant-Lion Optimizer (ALO), bat algorithm, whale optimization algorithm [3, 4]. Traditional EAs are originally designed to handle continuous optimization problems and are not suitable for addressing combinatorial optimization issues due to difficulties in generating feasible solutions, leading to premature convergence issues.

In our previous research, we developed a discrete variant of ALO called Ant-Antlion Optimizer (AAO) [5]. It leverages the powerful searching ability of ants in Ant Colony Optimization (ACO) and the predation behavior of antlions in ALO. Exhaustive experiments have demonstrated its effectiveness in solving feature selection problems. However, the considered problem is a knapsack-related topic, which is comparatively easier than the MKP due to fewer constraints, and MKP remains challenging for most EAs to generate new feasible solutions. To efficiently handle the MKP, we modify AAO and propose a novel algorithm called Ant-antlion Optimizer with Similarity Information (AOSI). AOSI employs similarity information between the best solution and others, and it combines individual's fitness with its similarity values as the new fitness to evaluate the individual and guide the evolution process. Moreover, AOSI takes advantage of fitness and similarity values within populations to use self-adaption mutation procedure thereby promoting its searching performance. Forty-eight classical multidimensional knapsack testing instances and six excellent methods are taken to make a comprehensive experiment, and results demonstrated that AOSI outperforms the compared algorithms in resolving the MKP.

2 Related Works

To efficiently address the MKP, researchers primarily investigated EAs from two aspects: transforming inadequate methods into suitable alternatives, and developing robust strategies to enhance existing approaches.

Luo and Zhao [6] adopted V-shaped and S-shaped transform functions to obtain binary solution representation of grey wolf optimizer, and proposed quick repair operator to get new individuals within the limits of constraints. Besides, they employed a differentiated position updating strategy to balance between intensification and diversification. Similarly, Amirmohammad and Madjid [7] developed a binary variant of butterfly optimization algorithm by introducing three S-shaped and three V-shaped functions to binarize original algorithm. Moreover, they used an elite initial population and repair operator to further promote its ability to find feasible solutions. Feng and Wang [8] made use of two S-shaped, one V-shaped, and three other-shaped transfer functions to binarize solutions. A quick repair operator based on pseudo-utility ratio is brought to transform infeasible solution into feasible one. In addition, a self-learning flight straightly operator is proposed to improve the population diversity. He et al. [9] introduced a hybrid encoding meta-heuristic algorithm based on differential evolution. They presented a new greedy repair operator that considers the degree of violating constraint in DROP and ADD phases, respectively, to improve the quality of solutions. Furthermore, they adopted a hybrid encoding differential evolution that utilized adjuvant search space concept to resolve MKP efficiently.

Mansour et al. [10] proposed a gradual weight-based ant colony optimization method for tackling the multi-objective MKP. Its main idea is to generate a set of sophisticated weights that enable ants to reach different Pareto-optimal points in the objective space. García and Maureira [11] assessed a novel algorithm that combines the quantum cuckoo search algorithm with the k-nearest neighbor technique for handling MKP. The main idea of this algorithm is to utilize the concept of k-nearest neighbor to find better solutions around an existing solution by normalized vector operation in cuckoo search algorithm. Li et al. [12] proposed a variant of memetic algorithm that incorporates problem-dependent heuristics and a new framework. This approach used two logarithmic utility functions to measure the degree of balance between the objective and the capacity constraint. Besides, it employs a probability learning rules inspired by competitive learning and the binary Markov chain to enhance its searching ability. Gupta et al. [13] leveraged the sine-cosine algorithm and differential evolution algorithm to construct an enhanced hybrid method. The exploitation procedure of this method involves utilizing the sine-cosine algorithm's search mechanism around the best candidate individual found so far, while the exploration process utilizes the search actions of the differential evolution algorithm. Additionally, they proposed a switch parameter to control whether a candidate individual performs the exploration or exploitation process to achieve a fine tradeoff. Lai et al. [14] proposed a novel quantum particle swarm optimizer, which uses a diversity-preserving population updating strategy to maintain a healthy diversity of particles and a variable neighborhood descend procedure is applied in a probabilistic manner to reinforce search intensification.

The results of the studies demonstrate the effectiveness of the aforementioned strategies. In this research, we incorporate the ideas of two existing methods into ALO, a recently proposed EA which has a wonderful optimization ability, to develop a method called AOSI for resolving MKP. We use the behavior of ants in ACO to adapt it for discrete optimization problems, and introduce a similar measurement strategy in evaluation and mutation steps to strengthen its optimization performance.

3   Ant-Antlion Optimizer with Similarity Information

3.1   Novel Fitness with Similarity Information

AOSI uses a novel fitness indicator with similarity information instead of original fitness, which could evaluate the quality of solutions for MKP. We now illustrate it in further detail. First, we give the Jaccard similarity indicator which is shown in Eq. (2) that is employed to gain similarity information,

$$J(A, B) = \frac{|A \cap B|}{|A \cup B|} \tag{2}$$

where A and B are two sets, $|A \cap B|$ denotes the number of intersections of the elements, and $|A \cup B|$ represents the number of unions of the elements. Suppose we have obtained an elite and other solutions at Tth iteration, we adopt the Jaccard similarity indicator to determine the similarity degrees between ordinary solutions and the elite one, as illustrated in Fig. 1. In Fig. 1, The Jaccard similarity value between solution i and the elite one is 0.25, and that of solution j is 0.67. For that, AOSI assigns a higher weight to solution j for its involvement in the evolution process.

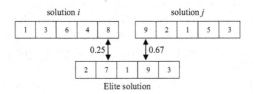

Fig. 1. The illustration of similarity information.

The decision to incorporate similarity information in our approach stems from a heuristic idea. When a solution demonstrates both fine fitness and similarity values, there is a higher likelihood for AOSI to discover superior results compared to other solutions. The novel fitness calculation between elite e and solution i is given in Eq. (3).

$$NF(i) = \alpha \times CF(i) + \beta \times J(i, e) \tag{3}$$

where CF is the evaluation value of solution i by testing instance function, α and β are two factors controlling the weights of CF and J. We improve AOSI's ability of finding excellent solutions by incorporating NF indicator.

3.2   Self-adaption Mutation

Previous studies have shown that the diversity of EAs can be enhanced by incorporating mutation operations, which have proven to be effective in various algorithms [15]. In this paper, we propose a self-adaption mutation method based on other developed similarity information. The pseudo-code for this method is provided in Algorithm 1.

Algorithm 1: Pseudo-code of self-adaption mutation
Input: All solutions P, all novel fitness values F
Output: New solutions NP
1. **FOR** each coding position
2. Find solution sets C and D in P that the solutions in the two sets have contrary values of current coding position
3. Find the maximum novel fitness value and corresponding solution in C and D, respectively
4. Obtain the distances by Jaccard similarity indicator between two corresponding solutions
5. Get the possible rate R by self-adaption probability formula
6. If random number is not larger than R, convert the state of current position
7. If new solution violates constraints, adjust it to a feasible solution and evaluate it
8. **END FOR**

The main idea behind the proposed strategy is that as the distance between two corresponding solutions increases, the probability of applying greater variation in position mutation also increases. The possible rate R in step 5 is computed by self-adaption probability formula which is shown in Eq. (4).

$$R = \gamma \times NF\_C + \lambda \times J\_C \tag{4}$$

where NF_C is the difference between the two maximum novel fitness values, J_C is the Jaccard distances between two corresponding solutions. γ and λ are constants to control the relative importance of NF_C versus J_C. Especially, if the new solution violates the constraints, we adjust it to a feasible one as follows: the selected items are successively dropped in ascending order of the pseudo utility until a feasible solution is achieved.

3.3 Procedure of Proposed Method

The procedure of the proposed AOSI is depicted in Fig. 2.

AOSI initializes the population and selects the elite antlion to begin the evolution process. It then chooses antlions based on pheromone matrices, following a similar approach as described in [5]. AOSI generates new ants by chosen antlions and the elite one, and evaluates them by novel fitness indicator outlined in Sect. 3.1. Furthermore, it implements self-adaption mutation strategy, as depicted in Sect. 3.2, and updates the elite solution and pheromone matrixes for next evolution.

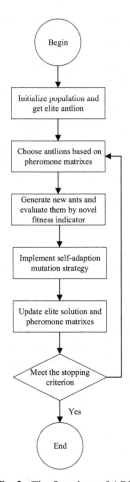

Fig. 2. The flowchart of AOSI.

4   Experiments and Results

4.1   Testing Problems and Comparison Methods

We use forty-eight typical benchmark instances of MKP from OR-library to evaluate
AOSI [16]. These instances consist of eight HP and PB problems, two SENTO problems,
thirty WEISH instances, and eight WEING benchmark instances. By using different
knapsacks and items, these instances could test our method comprehensively.

In addition, we choose six classical EAs to implement experiments, including original
AAO, Firefly Algorithm (FA) [17], Shuffled Complex Evolution Algorithm (SCEA) [18],
Genetic Algorithm (GA) [19], Particle Swarm Optimization (PSO) [20], and ACO [21].

The parameters of AOSI are initialized as follows, number of individuals is 30,
number of iterations is 2000, $\alpha = 0.7$, $\beta = 0.3$, $\gamma = 0.6$ and $\lambda = 0.4$. These parameters
are tuned through several tests to obtain a good performance of AOSI. The parameters

for other comparison algorithms are set as specified in their respective original literature, except for the number of individuals and iterations, which are set to match AOSI.

We adopt the Windows 11 operating system, Matlab 2020b, Intel i5-1135G7, and 16GB RAM as the test platform. The experiment was executed independently 20 times, and the average fitness values were taken as final results.

4.2   Simulation and Evaluation

This subsection analyses the performance of AOSI on MKP instances using the setup provided earlier. Figure 3 displays the fitness value trajectory of the proposed AOSI algorithm on the WEISH01 instance over 2000 iterations. Figures 4, 5, and 6 illustrate the fitness value trajectories on the WEISH30, SENTO2, and WEING7 instances respectively. The overall results of seven algorithms on forty-eight instances are given in Table 1. In particular, the second column titled "B/K/I" signifies the best-known value, the number of knapsacks, and the number of items for each respective MKP instance that was tested.

The result presented in Fig. 3 shows that the proposed AOSI achieved convergence in fewer than 100 iterations on WEISH01. Combined with the comparison result in Table 1 that AOSI and AAO produced the optimal fitness value on WEISH01, it can be inferred that AOSI maintained a superior searching performance on WEISH01.

Although AOSI did not yield the best-known fitness values on WEISH30 and SENTO2, its fitness values were still very close to the optimal values and higher than those of other comparison algorithms. As displayed in Figs. 4 and 5, AOSI required nearly 600 iterations to achieve convergence, which is justifiable considering that WEISH30 involves a relatively larger number of items and SENTO2 consists of a substantial amount of knapsacks and items.

Upon examining the results of the WEING7 instance presented in Fig. 6 and Table 1, it becomes evident that AOSI swiftly explored and found promising solutions within a few iterations. Subsequently, AOSI continued to iterate until convergence was achieved.

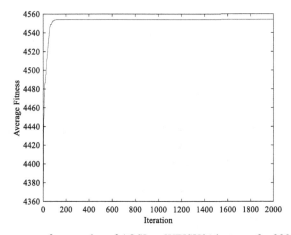

Fig. 3. The average fitness value of AOSI on WEISH01 instance for 2000 iterations.

The ultimate fitness achieved by AOSI closely approximated the optimal fitness and outperformed other algorithms.

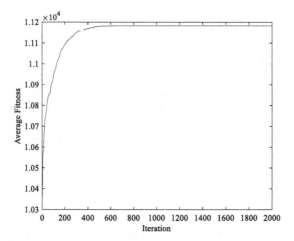

Fig. 4. The average fitness value of AOSI on WEISH30 instance for 2000 iterations.

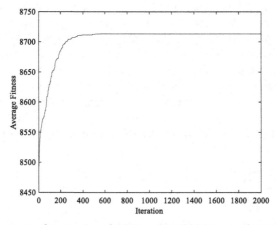

Fig. 5. The average fitness value of AOSI on SENTO2 instance for 2000 iterations.

If we tend to look at the figures again, it can be inferred that AOSI exhibits notable convergence ability, thus indicating its proficient search performance.

Table 1 shows that AOSI successfully generated optimal values for the HP and PB instances, apart from PB2, PB4, and PB5. The results obtained from the SENTO and WEING instances indicate AOSI's superior performance when compared to other algorithms, except for the instance WEING6 where AAO outperformed AOSI. For all 30 instances of WEISH, the proposed AOSI method achieved optimal fitness, except for the WEISH29 instance. Nevertheless, the fitness of AOSI closely approximated that of AAO in the particular instances which AAO yielded the best performance.

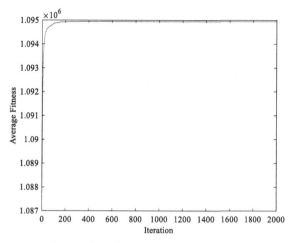

Fig. 6. The average fitness value of AOSI on WEING7 instance for 2000 iterations.

Upon further analysis of the overall results presented in Table 1 and in comparison to other algorithms, AOSI emerged as the winner in 27 out of the 48 instances, tied in 16 instances, and only lost in 5 instances. In the cases of tied instances, AOSI consistently achieved the best-known fitness values. With regard to the instances where AOSI did not win, it still produced fitness values that were very close to those of the top-performing algorithms, except for PB4. Additionally, when considering the best-known fitness values of the instances, AOSI achieved a total of 18 instances. Turning to the six comparison algorithms, only AAO won AOSI in 5 instances, other algorithms could not achieve the best-known fitness values except for ACO on WEISH04 and WEISH05. In summary, AOSI demonstrated superior performance compared to other algorithms in the majority of the tested MKP instances, providing strong validation of its exceptional capability for solving MKP problems.

Furthermore, to statistically confirm the superiority of AOSI, the Mann-Whitney U test is conducted for verification. The significance level is set to 0.05, and as the fitness values on different instances vary in a large range, we used the normalized mean fitness values, which are ranged in [0, 1] and calculated as Eq. (5).

$$Norm = (f_a - \min(f)) / (\max(f) - \min(f)) \tag{5}$$

where f_a represents the mean fitness value of the algorithm on the test instance, and $\max(f)$ and $\min(f)$ represent the maximum and the minimum mean fitness values between seven algorithms on the test instance. The Mann-Whitney U test results are given in Table 2. The findings suggest that every other algorithm rejects the null hypothesis, proving that AOSI is significantly superior to other algorithms.

As we analyzed, the proposed AOSI method has a superior performance on the test instances when compared with other six algorithms. Among the comparison algorithms, only AAO won AOSI and achieved best-known fitness values on several instances, and the fitness values of other algorithms even had a great gap from best-known fitness values. It is due to that our proposed method inherits AAO's characteristic of effectively

Table 1. Results of seven algorithms on forty-eight instances.

Instance	B/K/I	AOSI	AAO	FA	SCEA	GA	PSO	ACO
HP1	3418/30/40	**3404.6**	3404.5	3384.15	3385.8	3355	3322.75	3386.2
HP2	3186/30/37	**3176.05**	3164.5	3146.75	3120.65	3103.85	3066.1	3118.1
PB1	3090/4/28	**3079.3**	3076.55	3056.25	3059.2	3017.35	3025.8	3060.65
PB2	3186/4/35	3176.25	**3178.25**	3148.35	3150.05	3098.75	3067.95	3121.85
PB4	95168/4/27	93228.2	**94139**	93913.7	92534.8	91784.3	88293.3	90527.6
PB5	2139/4/34	2131.35	**2133.9**	2098.9	2114.8	2075.25	2076.85	2132.6
PB6	776/2/29	**769.7**	766.9	739.3	725	692.65	639.1	752.05
PB7	1035/10/20	**1029.9**	1027.55	1014.35	997.85	1003.9	928.7	975.05
SENTO1	7772/30/60	**7758.8**	7748.4	7716.1	7369.5	7490.1	6616.2	7446.2
SENTO2	8722/30/60	**8713.55**	8711.4	8662.4	8517.15	8573.15	8074.15	8273.3
WEISH01	4554/5/30	**4554**	**4554**	4526.7	4515.75	4510.95	4302.85	4504.15
WEISH02	4536/5/30	**4536**	4535.5	4512.65	4504.35	4488.45	4263.7	4499.9
WEISH03	4115/5/30	**4115**	**4115**	4087.6	4077.45	4040.9	3797.1	4103.7
WEISH04	4561/5/30	**4561**	**4561**	4555	4511.8	4476.5	4021.8	**4561**
WEISH05	4514/5/30	**4514**	**4514**	4510.55	4452.2	4412.4	3973.1	**4514**
WEISH06	5557/5/40	**5549.65**	5547.8	5503.05	5479.3	5453.05	5274.45	5369.05
WEISH07	5567/5/40	**5567**	**5567**	5537.8	5430.45	5445	5208.9	5389.6
WEISH08	5605/5/40	**5604.6**	5603.75	5582.75	5531.8	5519.35	5192.3	5430.1
WEISH09	5246/5/40	**5246**	**5246**	5220.2	5184.1	5134.9	4433.75	5146.05
WEISH10	6339/5/50	**6339**	6336.65	6294	6138.95	6183.1	5590.75	6087.75
WEISH11	5643/5/50	**5642.05**	5641.1	5576.8	5458.65	5359.55	4587.2	5470.85
WEISH12	6339/5/50	**6339**	**6339**	6291.8	6105.05	6163.8	5419.05	6089.7
WEISH13	6159/5/50	**6159**	**6159**	6097.8	5980.15	5977.45	5393.85	5936.1
WEISH14	6954/5/60	**6948.75**	6945.65	6882.85	6599.4	6736.35	5921.9	6442.5
WEISH15	7486/5/60	**7486**	**7486**	7430.4	7096.75	7158.3	6112.65	7084.1
WEISH16	7289/5/60	**7287.45**	7283.95	7234.1	6975.5	7155.65	6384.85	6826.75
WEISH17	8633/5/60	**8632.45**	8631.1	8617.05	8521.65	8541.8	8145.9	8042.6
WEISH18	9580/5/70	**9573.35**	9569.95	9493.3	9215.05	9401.2	8559.5	8559.45
WEISH19	7698/5/70	**7696.5**	7695	7582.95	7256.85	7348.3	6364.5	6962.2
WEISH20	9450/5/70	**9450**	**9450**	9365.2	9015.6	9214.3	8178.6	8492.6
WEISH21	9074/5/70	**9074**	**9074**	9003.65	8603.2	8821.1	7627.2	8236.3
WEISH22	8947/5/80	**8928.75**	8915.35	8856.25	8343.95	8627.05	7619.45	7706.85
WEISH23	8344/5/80	**8341**	8339.05	8235.8	7732.15	7915.6	6974.4	7353
WEISH24	10220/5/80	**10208.8**	10204.3	10133.9	9696.4	10009.2	9027.65	8969.9
WEISH25	9939/5/80	**9933.35**	9924.85	9848.4	9423.25	9733.3	8641.45	8850.05
WEISH26	9584/5/90	**9574.55**	9572.05	9427	8587.1	9171.75	7741.7	8187.6
WEISH27	9819/5/90	**9818.6**	9817.25	9617.95	9034	9408.45	7876.2	8244.15
WEISH28	9492/5/90	**9490.85**	9485.85	9308.25	8657.25	9061	7431.75	8080.35
WEISH29	9410/5/90	9399.35	**9401.2**	9227.2	8538.85	9028.3	7585.5	8072.9

(*continued*)

Table 1. (*continued*)

Instance	B/K/I	AOSI	AAO	FA	SCEA	GA	PSO	ACO
WEISH30	11191/5/90	**11186.3**	11184.9	11084.4	10443.7	10955.5	9928	9617.5
WEING1	141278/2/28	**141278**	**141278**	140904	140932	140136	137734	140333
WEING2	130883/2/28	**130883**	**130883**	130731	130168	130260	126344	129592
WEING3	95677/2/28	**95677**	**95677**	95404.1	95003.5	89762.1	90338.7	94496.5
WEING4	119337/2/28	**119337**	**119337**	118412	118163	112994	113254	118856
WEING5	98976/2/28	**98796**	**98796**	98548.8	97800.6	96315.7	93979.4	95850.6
WEING6	130623/2/28	130565	**130584**	130264	130175	129389	124264	129572
WEING7	1095445/2/105	**1094942.9**	1094813.85	1090167.1	1085875.15	1088104.9	1077326.3	1072965.55
WEING8	624319/2/105	**621848.35**	621504.95	607817.2	553628.6	571459.65	477602.95	544195.9

combing the powerful searching ability of ants in ACO and the predation behavior of antlions in ALO, and meanwhile, we develop and incorporate a novel fitness indicator with similarity information and a self-adaption mutation strategy to further improve the performance of the method.

Table 2. Mann-Whitney U test p value results.

Indicator	AAO	FA	SCEA	GA	PSO	ACO
Normalized mean fitness value	**1.07e-05**	**2.67e−17**	**1.71e−18**	**1.38e−18**	**3.96e−20**	**3.24e−17**

5   Conclusions

MKP is an NP-hard problem got widely studied by many researchers, and a plenty of methods based on EAs are developed to handle it. Traditional approaches either update inappropriate components or adopt some strategies to enhance their performance. In this paper, we propose a novel algorithm named AOSI, which combines ALO with similarity information, building upon conventional ideas. AOSI introduces a novel evaluation measure based on Jaccard similarity indicator, effectively leveraging similarity information between elite individual and other solutions to improve its ability. Besides, AOSI employs a self-adaptive mutation strategy that explores the fitness values and similarity information of populations, further enhancing its capabilities. To evaluate our method, we conduct experiments using forty-eight typical MKP instances and compare against six prominent algorithms. The experiment results demonstrate that AOSI exhibits excellent coverage ability and surpasses other approaches in terms of searching capability, thereby affirming the effectiveness of our proposed idea. In the future, we intend to apply AOSI to real-world optimization problems to validate its practical usability.

Acknowledgements. This work was partially supported by National Science Foundation for Young Scientists of China (72201275), Young Elite Scientists Sponsorship Program by CAST (2022QNRC001).

References

1. Cacchiani, V., Iori, M., Locatelli, A., Martello, S.: Knapsack problems — an overview of recent advances. Part I: single knapsack problems. Comput. Oper. Res. **143**, 105692 (2022)
2. Liu, Y., Zheng, Q., Li, G., Zhang, J., Ren, X., Qin, W.: Discrete baby search algorithm for combinatorial optimization problems. In: 2022 3rd International Conference on Big Data, Artificial Intelligence and Internet of Things Engineering (ICBAIE), pp. 595–599. IEEE (2022)
3. Liu, Y., Li, M., Zheng, Q., Qin, W., Wang, J.: Baby search algorithm. In: 2021 4th International Conference on Advanced Electronic Materials, Computers and Software Engineering (AEMCSE), pp. 502–508. IEEE (2021)
4. Mirjalili, S.: The ant lion optimizer. Adv. Eng. Softw. **83**, 80–98 (2015)
5. Li, M., Ren, X., Wang, Y., Qin, W., Liu, Y.: Advanced antlion optimizer with discrete ant behavior for feature selection. IEICE Trans. Inf. Syst. **E103-D**, 2717–2720 (2020)
6. Luo, K., Zhao, Q.: A binary grey wolf optimizer for the multidimensional knapsack problem. Appl. Soft Comput. **83**, 105645 (2019)
7. Shahbandegan, A., Naderi, M.: A binary butterfly optimization algorithm for the multidimensional knapsack problem. In: 2020 6th Iranian Conference on Signal Processing and Intelligent Systems (ICSPIS), pp. 1–5. IEEE (2020)
8. Feng, Y., Wang, G.: A binary moth search algorithm based on self-learning for multidimensional knapsack problems. Future Gener. Comput. Syst. **126**, 48–64 (2022)
9. He, Y., Zhang, X., Li, W., Wang, J., Li, N.: An efficient binary differential evolution algorithm for the multidimensional knapsack problem. Eng. Comput. **37**, 745–761 (2021). https://doi.org/10.1007/s00366-019-00853-7
10. Ben Mansour, I., Alaya, I., Tagina, M.: A gradual weight-based ant colony approach for solving the multiobjective multidimensional knapsack problem. Evol. Intell. **12**, 253–272 (2019). https://doi.org/10.1007/s12065-019-00222-9
11. García, J., Maureira, C.: A KNN quantum cuckoo search algorithm applied to the multidimensional knapsack problem. Appl. Soft Comput. **102**, 107077 (2021)
12. Li, Z., Tang, L., Liu, J.: A memetic algorithm based on probability learning for solving the multidimensional knapsack problem. IEEE Trans. Cybern. **52**(4), 2284–2299 (2020)
13. Gupta, S., Su, R., Singh, S.: Diversified sine-cosine algorithm based on differential evolution for multidimensional knapsack problem. Appl. Soft Comput. **130**, 109682 (2022)
14. Lai, X., Hao, J., Fu, Z., Yue, D.: Diversity-preserving quantum particle swarm optimization for the multidimensional knapsack problem. Expert Syst. Appl. **149**, 113310 (2020)
15. Liu, Y., Qin, W., Zheng, Q., Li, G., Li, M.: An interpretable feature selection based on particle swarm optimization. IEICE Trans. Inf. Syst. **E105-D**(8), 1495–1500 (2022)
16. Beasley, J.E.: Orlib operations research library, (2005). http://people.brunel.ac.uk/~mastjjb/jeb/orlib/mknapinfo.html
17. Nand, R., Sharma, P.: Iteration split with firefly algorithm and genetic algorithm to solve multidimensional knapsack problems. In: 2019 IEEE Asia-Pacific Conference on Computer Science and Data Engineering (CSDE), pp. 1–7. IEEE (2019)
18. Baroni, M.D.V., Varejão, F.M.: A shuffled complex evolution algorithm for the multidimensional knapsack problem using core concept. In: 2016 IEEE Congress on Evolutionary Computation (CEC), pp. 2718–2723. IEEE (2016)

19. Berberler, M.E., Guler, A., Nuriyev, U.G.: A genetic algorithm to solve the multidimensional knapsack problem. Math. Comput. Appl. **18**(3), 486–494 (2013)
20. Bansal, J.C., Deep, K.: A modified binary particle swarm optimization for knapsack problems. Appl. Math. Comput. **218**, 11042–11061 (2012)
21. Fidanova, S., Atanassov, K.T.: ACO with intuitionistic fuzzy pheromone updating applied on multiple-constraint knapsack problem. Mathematics **9**(14), 1456 (2021)

Efficient Graph Sequence Reinforcement Learning for Traveling Salesman Problem

Yiyang Liu[✉] and Lin Li

Northwestern Polytechnical University, Chang'an District, Xi'an, Shaanxi, China
549778180@qq.com, linli@nwpu.edu.cn

Abstract. The Traveling Salesman Problem is formulated as a sequence to sequence problem, and then policy gradient, graph convolutional networks, and multi-head attention techniques are applied to generate the according sequence model. The model is trained and tested by reinforcement learning on small-scale graphs. In addition, we use the 2-optimization algorithm to improve the model's generation performance during the testing process. The results demonstrate that the proposed method, which is called Graph Sequence Reinforcement Learning Model, can be trained on small-scale graphs effectively without supervision and can be applied to solve TSP with large-scale graphs directly. Moreover, the performance of the proposed surpasses some of the state-of-the-art heuristic algorithms with high performance, and the ablation experiment shows that each part of the model is helpful for improving performance.

Keywords: Policy Gradient · Graph Convolutional Networks · Multi-Head Attention · 2-Optimization

1 Introduction

The Travelling Salesman Problem (TSP) is an NP-hard problem [1]. Given a set of city coordinates, a salesman needs to find which is the shortest path that allows him to visit each city exactly once and return to the starting point. Variants of TSP exist in many practical applications, such as vehicle routing [2], warehouse management [3]. TSP is often solved by two classes of traditional algorithms: exact algorithms and approximate algorithms [4]. Exact algorithms aim to find the best possible solution, but it is difficult to solve the problem as the size of the problem increases. In contrast, approximate algorithms prioritize computational speed over obtaining the optimal solution, often resulting in an upper bound on worst-case performance [5].

In this paper, the main objective is to explore the deep learning techniques for solving TSP, one of the most famous combinatorial optimization problems. Deep learning models have demonstrated remarkable advancements in computer vision [6] and natural language processing [7], functioning as potent feature extractors that learn directly from data. Researchers are curious whether deep learning can replace heuristics methods by learning from observed data when dealing with combinatorial problems like TSP. The paper focuses on the following key points.

Y. Tan and Y. Shi (Eds.): DMBD 2023, CCIS 2017, pp. 256–267, 2024.
https://doi.org/10.1007/978-981-97-0837-6_18

- Deep learning operates in a continuous space, which allows the utilization of gradient-based methods. However, TSP typically involve discrete solutions, posing a challenge for traditional deep learning approaches [8].
- When solving large-scale TSPs, deep learning often requires lots of memory and computation, and complex graph networks often lead to insufficient memory [9].
- Accurate solvers are difficult to solve on large-scale data, the lack of labeled data leads to limiting the usability of the supervised learning.

In the past, deep learning methods for solving the TSP included sequence to sequence methods represented by pointer networks [10] and adjacency matrix solving methods represented by graph convolution [11]. Training methods include supervised learning methods [12] and reinforcement learning methods [13]. In contrast, our main contributes are as follows.

- The policy gradient with baseline method is used in reinforcement learning for training to avoid the requirement for labeled data set and ensures the stability of training.
- Recurrent neural network and graph convolutional network are used to encode the city features, which can embed features from both graphs and nodes, and reduce the memory required for training.
- A weighted multi-head attention mechanism is used as the decoder to generate the probability distribution of the cities to be selected, and the accuracy is guaranteed without adding too much memory and calculation.

2 Related Work

Recently, deep learning models in combinatorial optimization, especially models for solving TSP, have made great progress [14]. This can be divided into two main approaches: autoregressive methods and non-autoregressive methods.

2.1 Autoregressive Methods

One of the earliest reinforcement learning methods for TSP originates from [10], which uses the pointer network of [15] as a model to output a policy that instructs the agent on the sequence of cities to visit. The policy is trained via policy gradient, and visits are constructed by greedy decoding, sampling, or using active search.

The attention and transformers are introduced in [16]. The model is trained on randomly generated TSP instances, using the same policy gradient scheme as in [10], with a greedy algorithm as the baseline. On TSP50, the optimal gaps for greedy search and beam search are 1.76% and 0.52%, respectively. Recently, some researchers define TSP as a translation problem [14], and utilize the transformer architecture in the encoder and decoder to construct an effective solution. Similarly, they train the model using a policy gradient method on TSP50, and achieved optimal gaps of 0.31% with greedy search and $4e-3$% with beam search.

The next city selected by these methods is predicted based on the embedding vector of the current part of the route. In [14, 17], the transformer decoder is continuously queried to build the embedding vector of this partial path and to find the next city. In contrast, the loop mechanism of pointer network naturally realizes this sequence generation process [10].

2.2 Non-autoregressive Methods

Another approach is to predict the entire adjacency matrix of the TSP, and treat the adjacency matrix as a probability heatmap. Each edge represents its probability in a path, and the solved path is obtained from the adjacency matrix heatmap. One of the earliest attempts [12], uses a supervised learning approach. First each data sample is passed through an exact solver to generate a solution path as a label. Then they used a graph convolutional neural network to encode cities. The authors reduce memory usage by only considering each city's k-nearest neighbors to form a graph. They obtain optimal gaps of 3.10% and 0.26% using greedy search and beam search, respectively.

Following this work, some researchers propose a method to combine the small-scale solutions generated by the model in [12] into a larger solution. Their work uses the model in [12] to generate heatmaps for a 20-node TSP, then utilizes these heatmaps and combines them through a heuristic to construct a heatmap for a 50-node TSP. This final heatmap is then subjected to a Monte Carlo tree search to generate a large set of possible solutions, from which the best solution.

set is then obtained. Recently, others introduce a heuristic algorithm named Deep Policy Dynamic Programming [18] to explore the space of possible solutions given the model in [12]. Essentially, their algorithm provides a way of beam search to produce high-quality solutions. Combined with multiple efficient implementations, these efforts yield a set of highly competitive results. Neither of these jobs involve training a model, but instead use heuristics to search.

Whether using autoregressive or non-autoregressive methods, both involve searching or sampling to overcome local optimum or poor solution quality. Currently, autoregressive methods are often trained by reinforcement learning, constructing solutions step by step using the embedded feature, which can be slower, while non-autoregressive methods typically use graph neural networks for feature embedding, which can generate edge probabilities and infer faster to find efficient paths directly, but often resulting in lower-quality solutions.

This paper proposes a hybrid encoder-decoder-search structure to approximately solve large-scale TSP, which is trained on small-scale TSP. The following describes how to effectively combine recurrent neural networks with graph neural networks as an encoder structure, utilize a weighted multi-head attention as the decoder and use 2-opt to improve greedy sampling.

3 Graph Sequence Reinforcement Learning Model

Since feature embedding considers the representation of city nodes in graphs and sequences, and the policy gradient training method belongs to reinforcement learning, the model proposed in this paper is called the Graph Sequence Reinforcement Learning Model (GSM), as shown in Fig. 1.

In GSM, the node coordinates of the traveling salesman are used as input, the input is expanded and processed through the graph convolutional network, and the historical node information is retained by the Long Short Term Memory (LSTM). After obtaining the embedding feature, the probability of the cities to be selected is calculated by the weighted multi-head attention mechanism.

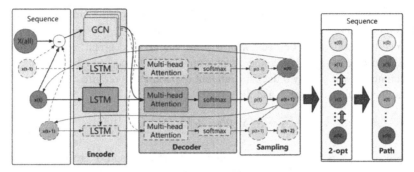

Fig. 1. It depicts the overall structure of our method, which consists of three main modules: a hybrid encoder to learn latent representations from both current city's relationships and last city's information, a weighted multi-head attention decoder to generate efficient city probabilities and generate paths, and the 2-opt algorithm to improve the generated paths.

Due to the lack of a large amount of training data, we train the model via policy gradient in deep reinforcement learning to minimize the solution sequence path by maximizing the reward. Since the cities are generated sequentially as output, the characteristics of each node will pass through the graph convolutional network and the LSTM separately. This allows for the effective representation of the attributes associated with an uncertain number of nodes. Therefore, the model trained on the small-scale TSP can be directly applied to the large-scale TSP and predict the permutation distribution of the output cities.

According to our research, GSM can fully demonstrate the ability of graph neural network and deep reinforcement learning to learn to solve the TSP under unsupervised conditions. Moreover, the comparison experiments with other heuristic methods and deep learning methods prove that our proposed framework exhibits good node prediction performance and expansion performance.

3.1 Hybrid Encoder

Hybrid encoder for GSM consists of two parts, one part is responsible for the embedding of the graph information, and the other part is responsible for the encoding of historical information. Each city node will be embedded as a high-dimensional feature through a linear layer:

$$\tilde{x}_i = wx_i. \tag{1}$$

where $\tilde{x}_i \in \mathbb{R}^d$, $w \in \mathbb{R}^{d \times 2}$, d is the dimension of the hidden layer, and all nodes share parameters.

After that, we pass the high-dimension features of the current city node $\tilde{x}_i$ to LSTM for encoding to obtain hidden variables h_i. Hidden variables h_i are passed to the decoder and kept for the latter city's LSTM. After the city coordinates are input into the network, for all city nodes $X_{all} = \left[\tilde{x}_1^T, \tilde{x}_2^T, \cdots \tilde{x}_N^T\right]^T$, we use the coordinates of all city nodes $X_i = \left[\tilde{x}_i^T, \tilde{x}_i^T, \cdots \tilde{x}_N^T\right]^T$ to make a vector subtraction to the coordinates of the current city node to obtain a vector pointing to other cities from the current city $X = X_{all} - X_i$, and then input the graph convolution for node embedding.

Since the problem to be dealt with is a fully-connected graph, and the adjacency matrix is a matrix of all 1s, using graph convolution to perform feature embedding between nodes will greatly reduce the amount of parameters required. The definition of the graph convolution layer is as follows:

$$X^{l+1} = \gamma\sigma\left(X^l W_1^l + b\right) + (1 - \gamma)X^l W_2^l. \tag{2}$$

where $W_1^l, W_2^l \in \mathbb{R}^{d_l \times d_{l+1}}$, γ, b are trainable parameters and σ are ReLU activation functions, it contain both linear and non-linear parts.

The city node coordinates will obtain the features of LSTM encoding and the features of graph convolution embedding after hybrid encoder.

3.2 Weighted Multi-head Attention Decoder

The decoder is based on the weighted multi-head attention mechanism, the feature representation of the GSM hybrid encoder is used as input, and the pointer vector u_i is output, and then the pointer vector u_i is passed to the softmax layer to calculate the distribution of the next candidate cities, similar to pointer network [10, 13]. The weighted multi-head attention mechanism and pointer vector u_i are defined as:

$$u_i^{(j)} = \begin{cases} \sum_{m=1}^{M} \lambda_m v^\top \cdot \tanh\left(W_k^m k_j + W_q^m q\right) & \text{if } j \neq \sigma(n), \forall n < j \\ -\infty & \text{otherwies} \end{cases}. \tag{3}$$

where W_k and W_q are trainable matrices, λ is the trainable weight and multi-head attention vectors are summed to obtain a pointer vector u_i. $u_i^{(j)}$ indicates that for the current node i, the multi-head attention vector of the jth city node is selected. If the jth city node has not been selected, its multi-head attention pointer vector is calculated, otherwise it is set to be infinitesimal. GSM uses the hidden variable h_i from the LSTM encoding as the query vector q, and the j-th row k_j from the deep features X^L of the graph embedding as the key vector, i.e. $q = h_i$, $k_j = X_j^L$.

The output obtained from the decoder is a set of pointer vectors, each corresponding to a candidate city, and the number of these vectors matches the number of input cities. The probability distribution of the candidate cities is obtained by solving the value of the pointer vector through softmax:

$$\pi_\theta(a_i|s_i) = p_i = softmax(u_i) \tag{4}$$

According to the strategy $\pi_\theta(a_i|s_i)$, we can predict the next city to visit as our action in a sampling or greedy way $a_i = x_{\sigma(i+1)}$.

3.3 2-Optimization Algorithm

After solving the initial traveling salesman route according to the GSM encoder-decoder-sampling structure, two adjacent cities in the current route is considered to exchange order, and then the total travel distance of the new route is calculated. If the distance of the new path is shorter than the original path, the new path is kept. Otherwise the original path stays unchanged. This process is repeated until when there is no better path generated.

The advantage of 2-optimization is that it is simple and efficient, and it can locally improve the existing path without the need for a global search. Although 2-optimization is not guaranteed to find a globally optimal solution, it usually improves the initial path significantly and runs fast.

3.4 Policy Gradient

In the process of training, 2-optimization is not used for improvement, and the complete path is obtained through the encoding-decoding-sampling structure. We update our policy through policy gradient obtained on the complete path. The following will introduce how to apply the idea of reinforcement learning to traveling salesman question. For a traveling salesman problem, it can be defined as follows.

Given N city coordinates $\{x_1, x_2, \cdots x_N\} \subset \mathbb{R}^2$, we need to find an optimal permutation of cities σ to minimize travel length:

$$L(\sigma, X) = \sum_{i=1}^{N} \left\| x_{\sigma(i)} - x_{\sigma(i+1)} \right\|_2. \tag{5}$$

where $\sigma(N + 1) = \sigma(1)$, it means that the salesman arrives at the first city he visits, $\sigma(i)$ represents the i-th city among the N cities in the arrangement, and when $i \neq j$, we have $\sigma(i) \neq \sigma(j)$, $X = \left[x_1^T, x_2^T, \ldots, x_N^T \right] \subset \mathbb{R}^{N \times 2}$ represents all city nodes in the classic traveling salesman problem.

Here the TSP is described in terms of reinforcement learning, where S denote the state space and A denotes the action space. The state $s_t \in S$ represents all the cities visited at the moment t, and the action $a_t \in A$ represents the action to be taken at the next moment, that is the city to be visited at the moment $t + 1$. For city permutations σ, $a_t = X_{\sigma(t+1)}$, due to $\sigma(N + 1) = \sigma(1)$, $a_N = X_{\sigma(N+1)} = X_{\sigma(1)}$, that is, returning to the starting city.

Given the collection of cities s_t that have been visited, there is an access strategy $\pi_\theta(a_t|s_t)$ for the city a_t to be visited that can give the probability distribution of the candidate cities. We use neural network to fit the access strategy π_θ where θ represents the weight parameters that the network can learn. For the reward function of reinforcement learning, We use the Euclidean distance of the city path taken action a_t from state s_t, and get $r(s_t, a_t) = - \left\| X_{\sigma(t)} - X_{\sigma(t+1)} \right\|_2$ as our reward, so the expected return is as follows:

$$
\begin{aligned}
&\mathbb{E}_{(s_t,a_t) \sim \pi_\theta} \left[\sum_{i=1}^{N} r(s_t, a_t) \right] \\
&= \mathbb{E}_{\sigma \sim p_\theta(\Gamma), X \sim \chi} \left[\sum_{i=1}^{N} - \left\| X_{\sigma(i)} - X_{\sigma(i+1)} \right\|_2 \right] \\
&= \mathbb{E}_{\sigma \sim p_\theta(\Gamma), X \sim \chi} [L, (\sigma, X)].
\end{aligned}
\tag{6}
$$

where χ represents the space of city set X, Γ represents the space of all possible existence paths in χ, and $p_\theta(\Gamma)$ represents the probability distribution of possible existence paths Γ predicted by the neural network. To minimize the traveling path, that is, to maximize the expected return, the objective function of TSP is $J(\theta) = -\mathbb{E}_{\sigma \sim p_\theta(\Gamma), X \sim \chi}[L(\sigma, X)]$, according to the REINFORCE with baseline method [19], the policy gradient is:

$$\nabla_\theta J(\theta) = \frac{1}{B} \sum_{i=1}^{B} \left[\left(\sum_{t=1}^{B} r(s_{i,t}, a_{i,t}) - b_i \right) \times \left(\sum_{t=1}^{N} \nabla_\theta \log \pi_\theta(a_{i,t}|s_{i,t}) \right) \right]. \quad (7)$$

where B is the size of a batch, π_θ is the policy function with parameter θ, $r(\cdot|\cdot)$ is the reward function, and b is the baseline. The specific formula is as follows:

$$b_i = \sum_{i=1}^{N} \left(r(s_{i,t}, a_{i,t}) \right) + \left[\frac{1}{B} \sum_{t=1}^{B} \sum_{i=1}^{B} \left(r(s_{i,t}, a_{i,t}) - r(\tilde{s}_{i,t}, \tilde{a}_{i,t}) \right) \right]. \quad (8)$$

where the action $\tilde{a}_{i,t} \sim \pi_\theta^{Greedy}$ is obtained by greedy sampling, and $\tilde{a}_{i,t}$ is the corresponding state. The second item is the difference between the summed rewards obtained by the probability sampling and greedy sampling methods [13]. The difference between the reward function and the baseline function is obtained by the advantage function, and then multiply the advantage function with the logarithm of the gradient of the model parameters at each step yields the policy gradient of the policy function.

After sampling a batch, the parameters can be updated using gradient ascent:

$$\theta \leftarrow \theta + \alpha \nabla_\theta J(\theta). \quad (9)$$

where θ is the parameter of the policy function π_θ, α is the learning rate, and $\nabla_\theta J(\theta)$ is the policy gradient obtained by the REINFORCE with baseline method.

4 Experiment

In our experiment, GSM model's graph convolutional layers are set to be 3, and each layer has a dimension of 128. Our training data is generated on a $[0, 1]^2$ uniform distribution randomly, and real world instances are proportional scaled in $[0, 1]^2$. We choose Adam as our optimizer, the batch size is 32 and the learning rate is set to 1e−3, with a decay rate of 0.96 after each 2400 instances. The main performance for TSP is the inferring time and the solution length, and we design the ablation experiment and the comparison experiment below.

4.1 Ablation Experiment

To make sure each part of our GSM model can make a better improvement. In our ablation experiment, different GSM models are separately trained on 20, 50, 80, 100, and 120 nodes' TSP instances, which are generated randomly on a particular set of seeds and has 24000 instances on each size, and the models are tested on 150 nodes' TSP while they are trained.

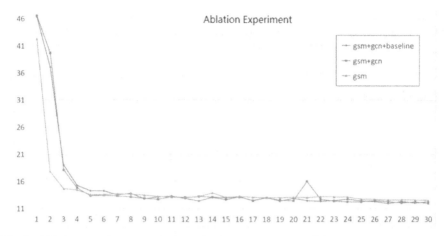

Fig. 2. Ablation experiment, the horizontal axis represents the training epoch, and the vertical axis represents the average test path length.

The models that have both graph convolutional networks and baseline improvement are considered as the whole GSM model, which is called gsm+gcn+baseline in Fig. 2, and their average performance on testing are considered the GSM performance while training on 5 different sets of nodes. At the same time, the models only have graph convolutional networks is called gsm+gcn in Fig. 2. It is trained by REINFORCE method, we are testing the improvement led by baseline through comparison between gsm+gcn and gsm+gcn+baseline. Similarly, the models without graph convolutional networks is trained by REINFORCE without baseline method and it is called gsm in Fig. 2. It can help us test the improvement led by graph convolutional networks through comparison between gsm+gcn and gsm+gcn+baseline.

Since GSM is developed from the pointer network [10, 13], which has good scalability and can be applied to the large-scale traveling salesman problem after training on a small-scale TSP, GSM also gains a good performance on scalability. The ablation experiment we designed above is models, in different settings, trained on the same batch data to predict the TSP path length of 150 nodes. The results of the ablation experiments show that:

1. The GSM model trained on the small-scale TSP can be effectively applied to the large-scale TSP problem and predicts the TSP path length of 150 nodes.
2. The REINFORCE training method that introduces the baseline improvement makes the test results more stable. Compared with the test results without baseline, the results with baseline are more reliable.
3. The training with graph convolution has better convergence effect than the test results without graph convolution. After 20 rounds of training, the test results of the model with graph convolution are significantly better than those without graph convolution.
4. As show in Fig. 2, the scalability of this encoding-decoding architecture is remarkably high, to the extent that even models without graph convolutional networks or baseline improvements are able to achieve notable performance on testing TSP-150.

4.2 Comparison Experiment

Along with ablation experiment, we also design a performance comparison, which is on the same seeds, among GSM, some heuristic methods, the existing pointer networks and attention models. We test some open-source heuristic methods and make a comparison of the inferring time and the solution length with GSM model, pointer networks and attention models. The test results are shown in Table 1 and Table 2. Optimal gap is the gap between our solution length and optimal solution path generated by Concorde [20].

Table 1. Average Length of Different Method

Average length	TSP 50	TSP 100	TSP 500	TSP 1000	TSP 5000	TSP 10000
Concorde	5.59	7.81	16.56	22.95	–	–
GA	5.79	8.34	18.64	–	–	–
SA	5.82	8.36	19.72	27.87	–	–
SOM	**5.68**	**8.09**	19.79	–	–	–
TS	5.79	8.22	**18.09**	–	–	–
NN	6.80	10.09	20.77	28.71	63.07	88.94
2-opt	6.02	8.48	18.80	26.15	57.98	81.61
Pointer	7.66	–	21.41	32.71	–	–
Attention	5.80	–	24.79	34.06	–	–
GSM	6.26	8.77	19.67	27.54	64.06	92.12
GSM+2opt	5.91	8.30	18.12	**25.04**	**56.96**	**80.97**
Optimal gap	3.93%	4.99%	8.81%	9.1%	–	–

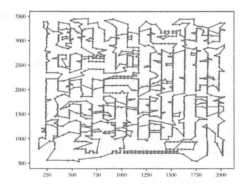

Fig. 3. GSM+2-opt test path on PCB vias of different sizes(442TSP, 1173TSP).

In addition, to make sure GSM model can work on real-life instances, we test on open-source real data [21] and plot some pictures of the testing results. The optimal solution path length is given by TSPLIB [21]. The test results are shown in Fig. 3 and Table 3. The whole comparison experiment can be concluded as Table 3.

Table 2. Average Time of Different Method

Average time	TSP 50	TSP 100	TSP 500	TSP 1000	TSP 5000	TSP 10000
concorde	0.9 s	1.4 s	57.6 s	3357.8 s	–	–
GA	3.8 s	36 s	1440 s	–	–	–
SA	2.4 s	4.2 s	19.2 s	40.8 s	–	–
SOM	7.7 s	30 s	540 s	–	–	–
TS	3.9 s	28 s	144 s	–	–	–
NN	**<0.01 s**	**<0.01 s**	**0.02 s**	**0.05 s**	**1.5 s**	**5.0 s**
2-opt	0.02 s	0.2 s	0.3 s	2.0 s	126.3 s	457.6 s
Pointer	3.5 s	–	280 s	3133 s	–	–
Attention	2 s	–	14 s	136 s	–	–
GSM	<u>0.01 s</u>	<u>0.02 s</u>	<u>0.08 s</u>	<u>0.2 s</u>	<u>8.8 s</u>	<u>33.5 s</u>
GSM+2opt	0.02 s	0.03 s	0.4 s	1.3 s	106 s	461.9 s

Table 3. GSM+2-opt Test Results on PCB Vias

PCB example	time cost	optimal solution ratio
PCB 442	1.22 s	1.06
PCB 1173	4.82 s	1.10

- The solution quality of GSM+2-opt on small-scale TSP still has a certain gap compared with the self-organizing map which has the best quality in the heuristic method, but the solution time of GSM+2-opt is shorter, which is close to 2-opt but performs better.
- For medium-scale and large-scale TSP instances, due to the seriously prolonged execution times of certain heuristic methods, their solutions were not employed. GSM+2-opt has better solution quality than the rest of the commonly used heuristics, and the running time is relatively short.
- With the increase of TSP scale, the optimal gap of GSM+2-opt is slowly increasing, but on large-scale TSP, GSM+2-opt is still the method with the best combination of running time and solution quality.

5 Conclusion

The experiments in this paper showcases the effectiveness and scalability of the proposed GSM in solving TSP. We conduct ablation experiments, which show that the GSM model trained on small-scale TSP data, can effectively handle large-scale instances and accurately predict TSP path lengths for 150 nodes. Furthermore, introducing baseline improvement in the REINFORCE training process enhances test result stability and reliability. The inclusion of graph convolution significantly improves convergence, surpassing models without it in just 20 training rounds.

Comparing GSM+2-opt with common heuristics, pointer networks, and attention models, we find that it strikes an optimal balance between running time and solution quality. Although it is slightly lower in solution quality compared to the best heuristic, its shorter solution time makes GSM+2-opt a practical choice.

For medium-scale and large-scale TSP instances, GSM+2-opt outperforms commonly used heuristics in both solution quality and running time. As the TSP scale increases, GSM+2-opt remains the preferred method, delivering the best combination of running time and solution quality. Notably, the fully-connected graph convolution reduces model parameters, allowing GSM+2-opt to efficiently handle very large-scale TSP problems with memory consumption mainly dependent on the size of the 2-opt distance matrix.

In conclusion, our findings highlight GSM+2-opt's potential as a reliable and efficient approach for solving diverse TSP instances. Combining policy gradient improvement, graph convolution, and the 2-opt optimization technique paves the way for further research and real-world application, particularly in scenarios with prevalent large-scale TSP instances.

References

1. Hartmanis, J.: Computers and intractability: a guide to the theory of np-completeness (michael r. garey and david s. johnson). Siam Rev. **24**, 90 (1982)
2. Robust, F., Daganzo, C.F., Souleyrette, R.R., II.: Implementing vehicle routing models. Transp. Res. Part B Methodol. **24**, 263–286 (1990)
3. Zunic, E., Besirevic, A., Skrobo, R., Hasic, H., Hodzic, K., Djedovic, A.: Design of optimization system for warehouse order picking in real environment. In: XXVI International Conference on Information, Communication and Automation Technologies (ICAT), pp. 1–6. IEEE (2017)
4. Anbuudayasankar, S., Ganesh, K., Mohapatra, S.: Models for Practical Routing Problems in Logistics. Springer, Cham (2016). https://doi.org/10.1007/978-3-319-05035-5
5. Goh, Y.L., Lee, W.S., Bresson, X., Laurent, T., Lim, N.: Combining reinforcement learning and optimal transport for the traveling salesman problem. arXiv preprint arXiv:2203.00903 (2022)
6. Le, N., Rathour, V.S., Yamazaki, K., Luu, K., Savvides, M.: Deep reinforcement learning in computer vision: a comprehensive survey. Artif. Intell. Rev. **55**(4), 2733–2819 (2021). https://doi.org/10.1007/s10462-021-10061-9
7. Arkhangelskaya, E.O., Nikolenko, S.I.: Deep learning for natural language processing: a survey. J. Math. Sci. **273**, 533–582 (2023). https://doi.org/10.1007/s10958-023-06519-6
8. Bengio, Y., Lodi, A., Prouvost, A.: Machine learning for combinatorial optimization: a methodological tour d'horizon. Eur. J. Oper. Res. **290**, 405–421 (2021)
9. Qiu, R., Sun, Z., Yang, Y.: DIMES: a differentiable meta solver for combinatorial optimization problems. In: Advances in Neural Information Processing Systems, vol. 35, pp. 25531–25546 (2022)
10. Bello, I., Pham, H., Le, Q.V., Norouzi, M., Bengio, S.: Neural combinatorial optimization with reinforcement learning. arXiv preprint arXiv:1611.09940 (2016)
11. Kipf, T.N., Welling, M.: Semi-supervised classification with graph convolutional networks. arXiv preprint arXiv:1609.02907 (2016)

12. Joshi, C.K., Laurent, T., Bresson, X.: An efficient graph convolutional network technique for the travelling salesman problem. arXiv preprint arXiv:1906.01227 (2019)
13. Ma, Q., Ge, S., He, D., Thaker, D., Drori, I.: Combinatorial optimization by graph pointer networks and hierarchical reinforcement learning. arXiv preprint arXiv:1911.04936 (2019)
14. Bresson, X., Laurent, T.: The transformer network for the traveling salesman problem. arXiv preprint arXiv:2103.03012 (2021)
15. Vinyals, O., Fortunato, M., Jaitly, N.: Pointer networks. In: Advances in Neural Information Processing Systems, vol. 28 (2015)
16. Vaswani, A., et al.: Attention is all you need. In: Advances in Neural Information Processing Systems, vol. 30 (2017)
17. Kool, W., Van Hoof, H., Welling, M.: Attention, learn to solve routing problems! arXiv preprint arXiv:1803.08475 (2018)
18. Kool, W., van Hoof, H., Gromicho, J., Welling, M.: Deep policy dynamic programming for vehicle routing problems. In: Schaus, P. (ed.) CPAIOR 2022, vol. 13292, pp. 190–213. Springer, Cham (2022). https://doi.org/10.1007/978-3-031-08011-1_14
19. Kielak, K.: Importance of using appropriate baselines for evaluation of data-efficiency in deep reinforcement learning for Atari. arXiv preprint arXiv:2003.10181 (2020)
20. Cook, W.J., Applegate, D.L., Bixby, R.E., Chvatal, V.: The Traveling Salesman Problem: A Computational Study. Princeton University Press (2011)
21. Reinelt, G.: TSPLIB—a traveling salesman problem library. ORSA J. Comput. **3**, 376–384 (1991)

Many-Constraint Multi-objective Optimization of Grid-Connected Hybrid Renewable Energy System

Mengjun Ming[✉], Xin Zhou, Rui Wang, and Tao Zhang

National University of Defense Technology, Changsha, China
mingmengjun11@nudt.edu.cn

Abstract. Grid-connected hybrid renewable energy system (G-HRES) is demonstrated as effective in making use of renewable energies, e.g., solar, wind. This study proposes a novel multi-objective model and algorithm for optimizing the size of a typical G-HRES that is composed of photovoltaic (PV) panels, wind turbines, battery banks and diesels. Noticeably, the proposed model considers objectives of economy and environment under the premise of satisfying many constraints, and enables a decision maker to optimize both the number and the type of PV panel, wind turbine, battery and diesel generator as well as the PV panel installation angle, the wind turbine installation height. To effectively solve the model, in particular, dealing with many linear constraints, an adaptive multi-stage evolutionary algorithm is proposed. Lastly, a case study is presented to demonstrate the effectiveness and efficiency of the proposed model and algorithm.

Keywords: Grid-connected Hybrid Renewable Energy System (G-HRES) · Constrained Multi-objective Optimization · Multi-stage Evolutionary Algorithm

1 Introduction

Due to the depletion of conventional energy sources, e.g., oil and coal, as well as the increase of green house effect, the development of renewable energy sources like solar and wind which are clean and sustainable has attracted a great deal of attentions since the last decade. Despite the advantages of solar and wind energy sources, they are often criticized by their unpredictable and intermittent nature for power generation. However, it is noticed that in many regions the two energy sources complement each other by means of daily and seasonal variations. Therefore, the combination of solar and wind energy sources has the potential to reduce the impact of uncertainties, leading to a more reliable grid-connected hybrid renewable energy system (G-HRES) [24].

On the design of a G-HRES, it is necessary to optimize the size of the considered G-HRES components. The problem itself is multi-objective in nature,

Y. Tan and Y. Shi (Eds.): DMBD 2023, CCIS 2017, pp. 268–282, 2024.
https://doi.org/10.1007/978-981-97-0837-6_19

that is, multiple objectives like the system life time cost, system reliability and greenhouse gases emissions are to be optimized. Typically, a constrained multi-objective optimization problem (CMOP) can be written as follows (for minimization) [5]:

$$\min \mathbf{F}(\mathbf{x}) = (f_1(\mathbf{x}), \ldots, f_m(\mathbf{x})), \mathbf{x} \in \Omega,$$

$$\text{s.t.} \begin{cases} g_j(\mathbf{x}) \leq 0, & j = 1, \ldots, q, \\ h_j(\mathbf{x}) = 0, & j = q+1, \ldots, p, \end{cases} \tag{1}$$

where $\mathbf{x}$ is a decision variable vector in the decision space Ω, and $\mathbf{F}(\mathbf{x})$ is an objective vector with m real-valued function values. $g_j(\mathbf{x})$ and $h_j(\mathbf{x})$ are the jth inequality and equality constraints, respectively, whose numbers are q and $p - q$, respectively. The constraint violation of $\mathbf{x}$ against the jth constraint is usually calculated as [23].

$$CV_j(\mathbf{x}) = \begin{cases} \max\{0, g_j(\mathbf{x})\}, & j = 1, \ldots, q, \\ \max\{0, |h_j(\mathbf{x})|\}, & j = q+1, \ldots, p. \end{cases} \tag{2}$$

And the overall constraint violation $\phi(\mathbf{x})$ is defined as:

$$\phi(\mathbf{x}) = \sum_{j=1}^{p} CV_j(\mathbf{x}). \tag{3}$$

Given a decision variable vector (i.e. a solution), it is feasible only if the overall constraint violation is zero. For two feasible solutions, $\mathbf{x}_1$ and $\mathbf{x}_2$, $\mathbf{x}_1$ is said to dominate $\mathbf{x}_2$ if $f_h(\mathbf{x}_1) \leq f_h(\mathbf{x}_2)$ for $\forall h \in \{1, \ldots, m\}$ and $f_g(\mathbf{x}_1) < f_g(\mathbf{x}_2)$ for $\exists g \in \{1, \ldots, m\}$. A solution is called Pareto-optimal when no other feasible solution dominates it. All Pareto-optimal solutions in the decision space constitute the Pareto-optimal set. The image of all Pareto-optimal solutions in the objective space is the Pareto front (PF). When solving a CMOP, the goal is to approximate the PF with a set of well-converged and well-distributed feasible solutions [21].

There has been a number of studies regarding the optimal design of G-HRES via multi-objective optimization. Evolutionary algorithms are often adopted to handle such problems since they have demonstrated their niche in solving unconstrained multi-objective optimization problems (MOPs) [4]. Readers are referred to [10] for a comprehensive survey.

CMOPs are usually much more challenging than unconstrained MOPs. For example, the constraints can make a significantly large proportion of the search space infeasible, divide the feasible space into narrow disconnected regions, and/or make the PF of unconstrained MOP partially or completely infeasible [16]. Consequently, the PF may be disconnected and/or the Pareto-optimal solutions may lie on the boundary of the feasible region, causing it hard for algorithms to obtain the desired solution set.

However, the existing methods share a common ground, i.e., dealing with all constraints simultaneously as a whole. They may be less effective on many-constraint optimization problems (MCOPs), for the reasons that—i) searching a feasible solution in an MCOP is more difficult than in a general MOP. This is because the feasible search space becomes even more complex; and ii) the *handling-difficulty* of different constraints is not considered. That is, a solution that violates an easy constraint or a hard constraint is treated equally. Additionally, when the number of constraints is large, decision-makers may have their priorities, i.e., some of constraints should be satisfied first. The above institutive observation motivates us to re-investigate constrained optimization problems, especially when the number of constraints is large.

This study therefore presents an adaptive multi-stage evolutionary algorithm to deal with G-HRES. In order to effectively handle it, the "divide-and-conquer" concept is proposed. It first divides all constraints into different levels according to their *handling-difficulty*. Then the constraints are sequentially added into the evolutionary search. In this study "the most interesting first" principle is followed which aims to maximize the degree of constraint satisfaction of decision-makers. It is worth noting that when decision-makers have no priority on constraints "the most interesting one" is interpreted as "the most difficult one" so as to distribute as much search effort as possible to handle those challenging constraints. A simple yet effective framework, namely, an adaptive cascaded constraint-handling (ACCH) is proposed. The initial results show that the ACCH framework can significantly improve the effectiveness of algorithms on MCOPs.

The rest of this paper is organized as follows. Section 2 formulates the mathematical models. Section 3 elaborates the proposed ACCH framework, following the introduction of ACCH-PPS. In Sect. 4, the performance of the ACCH-PPS is examined by comparing with five state-of-the-art CMOEAs on a set of benchmarks and the G-HRES application. Section 5 concludes the paper and identifies future studies.

2   Mathematical Model of G-HRES

The considered G-HRES consists of PV panels, wind turbines, diesel generators and batteries. Based on the load demand, the best configuration of G-HRES can be designed. The mathematical models of the G-HRES components considered in this study are described below.

First, assuming that the PV array is grouped by N_S in series and N_P in parallel of PV panels, the maximum output power is computed as (4) where β is the filling factor and I_{PV} denotes the current [13].

$$P_{\text{pv}} = \beta \cdot N_S \cdot N_P \cdot I_{PV} \tag{4}$$

Second, the output power from a wind turbine is obtained with the wind speed v in (5) [25].

$$P_{\text{wg}} = \begin{cases} 0 & v < V_c \\ \frac{1}{2}C_p\rho A_{wg}v^3 & V_c \leqslant v < V_r \\ P_{wgr} & V_r \leqslant v < V_f \\ 0 & v \geqslant V_f \end{cases} \tag{5}$$

with

$$v = v_r \left(\frac{H_{wg}}{H_r} \right)^{\frac{1}{7}} \tag{6}$$

where C_p is a coefficient defined as the ratio of the actual power output divided by the maximum wind power, ρ is the air density, A_{wg} is the cross section of the rotor, and P_{wgr} is the wind turbine rated power. Besides, the cut-in wind speed V_c, the rated wind speed V_r and the cut-off wind speed V_f are set as 4 m/s, 14 m/s and 20 m/s, respectively. The wind speed v at the height of H_{wg} is transferred by the measurable wind speed v_r at the reference height H_r.

Third, to ensure safety, most of the battery models confine the battery state of charge (SOC) with maximum and minimum constraints. The change in SOC is based on the renewable energy production and the load. We use (7) to calculate the SOC of the battery at each simulation step.

$$SOC(t_s + 1) = SOC(t_s) + \frac{(P_{bat}(t)/V) \cdot \Delta t_s \cdot \eta_{bat}}{C_n \cdot N_{bat}} \tag{7}$$

where $P_{bat}(t_s)$ is the battery input/output power (positive for charging models and negative for discharging models), V is the DC voltage and Δt_s is the simulation time, and is set to 1 h. η_{bat} is the round-trip efficiency, and is set to 80% during charging and 100% during discharging, respectively. The C_n denotes the nominal capacity of the battery. The N_{bat} denotes the total number of the battery.

Ultimately, if a diesel generator is used, its fuel consumption F_{cons} is assumed to be a linear function of the power output [9] as (8).

$$F_{cons} = \gamma_1 P_{dgr} + \gamma_2 P_{dg} \tag{8}$$

where P_{dgr} is the rated power of diesel generator, P_{dg} is the actual output power, and γ_1, γ_2 denote the coefficients of fuel consumption.

The operating mechanism of G-HRES is as follows: First the power produced by PV panels and wind turbines directly supplies the load demand. The surplus power will be saved into the battery storage till it is fully charged. On the contrary, when the load goes beyond the produced power, the battery will supply power to the load. If the battery cannot meet the demand, diesel generators will be used as emergency power-supply. In case that the diesel generators still cannot cover the supply-load gap, the unmet load will be cut.

The variable symbols mentioned above continue to be used here, but 4 different models of photovoltaic panels and wind turbines are considered. Here, P_{pv1}, P_{pv2}, P_{pv3} and P_{pv4} are used respectively to represent the power of four different types of photovoltaic panels, while P_{PV} represents their total power, that is:

$$P_{PV} = P_{pv1} + P_{pv2} + P_{pv3} + P_{pv4}. \tag{9}$$

Similarly, P_{wg1}, P_{wg2}, P_{wg3}, and P_{wg4} represent the power of the four different types of wind turbines, respectively, and their total power P_{WG} is:

$$P_{WG} = P_{wg1} + P_{wg2} + P_{wg3} + P_{wg4}. \tag{10}$$

The optimization of G-HRES will select types of photovoltaic panels and wind turbines, and quantify the selected equipment. Here, the variables s_{pv1}, s_{pv2}, s_{pv3} and s_{pv4} are used to indicate whether four different types of photovoltaic panels are selected. Use N_{pv1}, N_{pv2}, N_{pv3} and N_{pv4} to indicate the number of photovoltaic panels configured for the corresponding model. Because choosing too many types of photovoltaic panels is not conducive to maintenance and management, the selected photovoltaic panels should not exceed three types, subjecting to the following constraints:

$$
\begin{aligned}
&s_{pv1} + s_{pv2} + s_{pv3} + s_{pv4} \leq 3, \\
&s_{pv1} = \text{Logical}(N_{pv1}), s_{pv2} = \text{Logical}(N_{pv2}), \\
&s_{pv3} = \text{Logical}(N_{pv3}), s_{pv4} = \text{Logical}(N_{pv4}),
\end{aligned}
\tag{11}
$$

where $\text{Logical}(\cdot)$ is used to take logical values, for example, when $N_{pv1} \geq 1$, $\text{Logical}(N_{pv1})$ is 1.

Similarly, the variables s_{wg1}, s_{wg2}, s_{wg3} and s_{wg4} are used to indicate whether four different types of wind turbines are selected, respectively. N_{wg1}, N_{wg2}, N_{wg3} and N_{wg4} indicate the corresponding number of different wind turbines. The selection of wind turbines shall not exceed three types, which will result in the following constraints:

$$
\begin{aligned}
&s_{wg1} + s_{wg2} + s_{wg3} + s_{wg4} \leq 3, \\
&s_{wg1} = \text{Logical}(N_{wg1}), s_{wg2} = \text{Logical}(N_{wg2}), \\
&s_{wg3} = \text{Logical}(N_{wg3}), s_{wg4} = \text{Logical}(N_{wg4}).
\end{aligned}
\tag{12}
$$

In addition to the 16 variables mentioned above, the decision variables in this problem also include the number of batteries N_{bat}, the number of diesel generators N_{dg}, the height of the wind tower H_{wg} and the installation angle of the photovoltaic panel α.

It is worth noting that the constraints additionally include the height range of the wind tower, the installation angle range of the photovoltaic panel, and the relevant constraints on the power reliability in a specific time period.

The optimization objective of this problem mainly considers the minimization of the system annualized cost target (f_{ASC}) and the minimization of the proportion of electricity supplied by non-renewable energy sources (f_{NRE}), as follows:

$$
\min \mathbf{F}(\mathbf{x}) = (f_{ASC}(\mathbf{x}), f_{NRE}(\mathbf{x})),
$$

$$
f_{ASC}(\mathbf{x}) = C_{initial} + C_{rep} + 2 \sum_{t_s=1}^{T_s} F_{cons}(t_s) \cdot e_f,
\tag{13}
$$

$$
f_{NRE}(\mathbf{x}) = 1 - \frac{\sum_{t_s=1}^{T_s} (P_{PV}(t_s) + P_{WG}(t_s)) \, \Delta t_s}{\sum_{t_s=1}^{T_s} P_{load}(t)}.
$$

The annualized cost f_{ASC} mainly includes the initial investment of devices ($C_{initial}$) and the expenditure in repair and maintenance (C_{rep}) and the cost of fuel consumption. T_s is the biggest simulation of the system time, Δt_s is the simulation step size, $P_{\text{load}}(t_s)$ is load demand of the simulation time t_s.

Overall, the optimization of G-HRES is a minimization optimization problem with two objectives and many constraints. Note that the parameter values can be referred to [17].

3 Adaptive Multi-stage Evolutionary Algorithm: ACCH-PPS

3.1 ACCH Algorithm Framework

Algorithm 1 provides pseudo-code for the ACCH algorithm framework. As shown in lines 1–6, initialization is performed first.

The main loop of ACCH is shown in lines 7–17. In the process of evolution, it is necessary to first determine whether the conditions for starting to consider constraints are met. Once the conditions are met, the remaining constraints need to be sorted, and the constraints with higher priority should be selected to enter the next stage and the evolution time should be allocated for this stage. In subsequent stages, if the evolutionary generation satisfies the time requirement, it proceeds to the next stage. Accordingly, new constraints need to be added based on the priority of constraint processing. If any of the conversion conditions are not met, the evolution continues at the current stage. The reproduction process of each generation is shown in lines 14–15, where N offspring are generated by crossing and compiling operations after selecting parent individuals. The N solutions that survive the environmental selection not only circulate as the new population into the next generation, but also update the external population, as shown in line 17. The main loop is executed until the maximum evolutionary generation is reached, eventually returning the population as the final result, as shown in line 18.

ACCH provides a basic framework for processing many constraints in multiple stages, and it needs to be combined with constrained multi-objective evolutionary algorithms to play an effective role. In principle, most algorithms such as NSGA-II [8], SPEA2 [26], PPS-MOEA/D [11] can be integrated into the ACCH framework.

3.2 Constraint Cascading Handling Strategy

In order to "divide and conquer" many complex constraints, this section proposes a new strategy for cascading constraints. The newly proposed strategy is based on the constraint cascaded handling (CCH) strategy we proposed in 2019 [18], with further improvements to be suitable for dealing with MCOPs. Here, the newly proposed strategy is named ACCH.

The main idea of ACCH is to adaptively divide the evolutionary process into different stages, and add constraints step by step, so that different constraints can be graded. For an optimization problem with m objective functions and

---

Algorithm 1: ACCH algorithm framework

Input: population size: N; maximum generation gap: $T_{\max}$.
Output: final population (or population archive).
1 Initialize the generation counter: $t \leftarrow 1$;
2 Generate initial population randomly: $P \leftarrow \{\mathbf{x}_1, \mathbf{x}_2, \ldots, \mathbf{x}_N\}$;
3 Compute the objective vector $\mathbf{F}(\mathbf{x}_i) = (f_1(\mathbf{x}_i), \ldots, f_m(\mathbf{x}_i))$ for $i = 1, \ldots, N$;
4 Initialize population archive: $A \leftarrow P$;
5 Mark the current stage: $Stage \leftarrow 1$;
6 Make the currently considered constraint set empty: $\mathcal{C} \leftarrow \emptyset$;
7 **while** $t \leq T_{\max}$ **do**
8 | **if** *satisfy the condition to start adding constraints* **then**
9 | | $Stage \leftarrow Stage + 1$;
10 | | Sort and add constraints, allocate the evolution time t_{update};
11 | **if** $Stage > 1 \wedge t = t_{update}$ **then**
12 | | $Stage \leftarrow Stage + 1$;
13 | | Sort and add constraints, allocate the evolution time t_{update};
14 | Select parent individuals and produce offspring ;
15 | Considering only the current constraints, the solutions are compared, and the better N solutions are selected to enter population P;
16 | $t \leftarrow t + 1$;
17 | Update population A using feasibility rule;
18 **Return** A.

---

p constraints, under the ACCH strategy, the original problem is transformed into an unconstrained optimization problem in the first stage. After entering the second stage, the problem under consideration is automatically transformed into: min $\mathbf{F}(\mathbf{x}) = (f_1(\mathbf{x}), \ldots, f_m(\mathbf{x}))$, s.t. $c_{j_1}(\mathbf{x}) \leq 0$. This stage is always optimized with only c_{j1} constraints considered (where c_{j1} has the highest priority among the p constraints). By analogy, each time the transformation enters a new stage, the constraint with the highest current priority is selected from the remaining constraints to be added to the problem, and the optimization of this stage needs to consider all the constraints that have been added. In the final stage, all constraints are added to the problem, that is, the problem at that stage is restored to the original problem. Note that $j_1, j_2, \ldots, j_p \in \{1, 2, \ldots, p\}$ and $j_1 \neq j_2 \neq \ldots \neq j_p$.

3.3 Prioritization of Constraints

As mentioned above, in multi-objective optimization problems with many constraints, each constraint usually has different processing difficulties, that is, some constraints are easy to find the corresponding feasible solutions, and some constraints cause great difficulties in finding feasible solutions. In addition to the difficulties posed by the constraints themselves, decision makers may also have a preference for the relative priority of constraint satisfaction. In view of the differences between constraints, it is necessary to sort constraints in the process of hierarchical processing, so as to provide a criterion for the selection of constraints and maximize the satisfaction of the final output solution set for constraints. The following mainly discusses the prioritization of constraints when the decision maker does not provide preference information.

This paper adopts the principle of "the more difficult the priority", and its difficulty is measured by the proportion of infeasible solutions, that is, the infeasible rate of the population under each constraint to be added, calculated as shown in (14). (Suppose j is the number of a constraint that is not currently added.)

$$r_j = \frac{N_j}{N},\tag{14}$$

where N_j is the number of solutions in the current population that violate the j constraint, and N is the population size. During the stage transformation, the infeasible rate of the population under each constraint to be added should be calculated, and the constraint with the highest infeasible rate should be selected to be added to the next stage. It is important to note that in addition to this simple strategy, there are other advanced indicators that can be used, which are also worth further investigation.

3.4 Conversion Conditions at Different Stages

The conversion from the current stage to the next stage needs to meet the corresponding conversion conditions; Otherwise, continue optimizing in the current stage. In the ACCH strategy, the conversion conditions are divided into two categories: the first type is used in the first stage to determine whether to start considering constraints; the second type is used in subsequent stages to determine whether to add new constraints.

Specifically, moving from the first stage to the next requires that the following conditions be met: within the l_{gap} generation, the rate of change of the population is less than a given threshold. From the second stage, while adding new constraints, evolutionary generation can be assigned to the stage to be entered according to the infeasibility rate of each constraint. To move from the current stage to the next stage, the following conditions must be met: the time in the current stage (evolutionary generation) reaches the time allocated.

3.5 Implementation of ACCH-PPS

In this section, the proposed ACCH-PPS algorithm is introduced in detail. It integrates PPS-MOEA/D [11] into the ACCH framework.

The pseudocode for the ACCH-PPS algorithm is shown as Algorithm 2. Lines 1–6 are the initialization stage of the algorithm. First, the initial algebra is 1, the initial population is generated randomly, and the objective vector of each solution in the initial population is calculated. The initial population is then copied to the population as an initialization of the population. Then, the symbol *Stage* is used to mark the Stage of the current population, and *stage* = 1 indicates that the population is currently in the first stage, and so on. In addition, make

---

Algorithm 2: ACCH-PPS

    Input: population size: N; maximum generation: $T_{\max}$; generation gap: l_{gap};
           maximum tolerance generation for unconstrained evolution:T_c; threshold
           value:δ; weight vector set: $\Lambda \leftarrow \{\boldsymbol{\lambda}_1, \boldsymbol{\lambda}_2, \ldots, \boldsymbol{\lambda}_N\}$.

    Output: final population.

 1 Initialize the evolutionary generation counter: $t \leftarrow 1$;

 2 Generate initial population randomly: $P \leftarrow \{\mathbf{x}_1, \mathbf{x}_2, \ldots, \mathbf{x}_N\}$;

 3 Calculate the objective vector $\mathbf{F}(\mathbf{x}_i) = (f_1(\mathbf{x}_i), \ldots, f_m(\mathbf{x}_i)$ for each solution $\mathbf{x}_i$
    $(i = 1, \ldots, N)$;

 4 Initialize the population archive:$A \leftarrow P$;

 5 $Stage \leftarrow 1, \mathcal{C} \leftarrow \emptyset$;

 6 **while** $t \leq T_{\max}$ **do**

 7   **if** $t \geq l_{gap}$ **then**

 8   Calculate the rate of change r^t;

 9   **if** $t < T_c$ **then**

10   **if** $r^t \leq \delta \wedge Stage = 1$ **then**

11 $Stage \leftarrow Stage + 1$;

12   Add new constraints and allocate evolution time;

13   Calculate the degree of constraint violation for each solution under
               the current constraint: $\phi_c(\mathbf{x}_i) \leftarrow \sum_{c_j \in \mathcal{C}} CV_j(\mathbf{x}), i = 1, \ldots, N$;

14 $\varepsilon_0 \leftarrow \max_{i=1,\ldots,N} \{\phi_c(\mathbf{x}_i)\}$;

15 $\varepsilon(t) \leftarrow \varepsilon_0$;

16   **if** $Stage > 1$ **then**

17   **if** $t = t_{update}$ **then**

18 $Stage \leftarrow Stage + 1$;

19   Add new constraints and allocate evolution time;

20   Calculate the degree of constraint violation for each solution
                   under the current constraint:
                   $\phi_c(\mathbf{x}_i) \leftarrow \sum_{c_j \in \mathcal{C}} CV_j(\mathbf{x}), i = 1, \ldots, N$;

21   Calculate the proportion of feasible solutions under the current
               constraints r_f;

22   Update $\varepsilon(t)$;

23   **else**

24 $\varepsilon(t) \leftarrow 0$;

25   **for** $i \leftarrow 1$ **to** N **do**

26   Select the mating pool and produce a new solution $\mathbf{x}_{\text{new}}$;

27   Calculate the objective vector of the new solution $\mathbf{F}(\mathbf{x}_{\text{new}})$ and the
           violation degree under the current constraints $\phi_c(\mathbf{x}_{\text{new}})$.

28   Update the solution in the corresponding subregion of the mating pool;

29 $t \leftarrow t + 1$;

30   Update the population archive;

31 **Return** A.

---

the current constraint set empty (i.e. $\mathcal{C} = \emptyset$) so that no constraints need to be considered during the initial population stage.

Next, the algorithm enters the main loop, running repeatedly from line 7 to line 31 until the termination condition is met (i.e. $t \leq T_{\max}$). Finally, the population is returned as the output of the ACCH-PPS (as shown on line 32).

4 Experimental Study

4.1 Experimental Setup

This section uses C-NSGA-II [8], ToP [15], PPS-MOEA/D [11], and CMOEA-MS [22] and C-TAEA [14] are used as competitors to compare with ACCH-PPS. In these algorithms, C-NSGA-II, CMOEA-MS, and C-TAEA use the simulated binary crossover operator [6] and the polynomial mutation operator [7] to generate descendant solutions. ToP, PPS-MOEA/D, and ACCH-PPS use differential evolution (DE) [19] to generate new solutions.

IGD [3] is used to quantitatively evaluate the performance of each algorithm when the results obtained from independent experiments are compared. And based on the IGD results are under the 0.05 significance level of nonparametric Wilcoxon rank-sum test [12]. "+","−" or "≈" means that the competitor is superior to, inferior to or approximately equal to ACCH-PPS. The best average value obtained on each test problem is highlighted in gray.

DASCMOP Test Suite. As can be seen from Table 1, among the 9 DASC-MOP problems with variable dimension 10, ACCH-PPS obtained the best IGD average value in 7 of them, while PPS-MOEA/D obtained the best IGD average value in DASCMOP3 problem although it did not obtain the best value. However, the statistical results were not significantly different from those of PPS-MOEA/D. On DASCMOP5, CMOEA-MS performed best, and ACCH-PPS ranked second. As can be seen from Table 2, among the 9 DASCMOP problems with variable dimension of 30, ACCH-PPS obtained the best IGD average on 6 of them. The performance of DASCMOP3 and DASCMOP5 is inferior to that of PPS-MOEA/D and CMOEA-MS respectively, thus ranking second in these two problems, and there is no significant difference between DASCMOP5 and the algorithm that gets the best IGD (that is, CMOEA-MS).

The comparison results of these algorithms are explained in detail next. DASCMOP1-DASCMOP6 in DASCMOP test suite is a 2-objective optimization problem, each problem has 11 constraints. DASCMOP7–DASCMOP9 is a 3-objective optimization problem, each with 7 constraints. The constraint forms in these problems are divided into three types: 1) Obstacle to algorithm convergence is formed by multiple separated infeasible domains; 2) Discontinuous feasible domains and discontinuous PF challenge the ability of algorithms to maintain diversity; 3) The small area of feasible region makes it difficult for the algorithm to find feasible solution. According to Table 1 and Table 2, ACCH-PPS obtains the best average IGD for most DASCMOP problems. This is because

Table 1. IGD results of ACCH-PPS and competitors on the DASCMOP test suite ($n = 10$).

	C-NSGA-II	ToP	PPS-MOEA/D	CMOEA-MS	C-TAEA	ACCH-PPS
DASCMOP1	6.95e-2 (1.44e-1) −	2.09e-2 (1.05e-1) −	1.95e-3 (5.71e-4) −	8.67e-2 (1.31e-1) −	1.11e-2 (1.89e-3) −	1.44e-3 (1.21e-4)
DASCMOP2	3.28e-2 (2.70e-2) −	3.78e-3 (1.17e-4) −	3.87e-3 (1.01e-4) −	1.61e-2 (1.52e-2) −	7.41e-3 (4.61e-4) −	2.82e-3 (4.53e-5)
DASCMOP3	1.83e-1 (5.98e-2) −	9.95e-2 (9.60e-2) −	1.91e-2 (1.24e-3) ≈	1.22e-1 (5.88e-2) −	3.00e-2 (8.28e-3) −	1.92e-2 (1.23e-3)
DASCMOP4	4.60e-2 (1.27e-1) −	4.92e-1 (1.80e-1) −	1.65e-3 (6.13e-5) −	9.85e-3 (4.85e-2) −	1.12e-2 (2.50e-3) −	1.16e-3 (1.42e-5)
DASCMOP5	3.55e-3 (1.34e-4) −	3.41e-1 (2.77e-1) −	4.04e-3 (1.41e-4) −	2.65e-3 (4.60e-5) +	7.09e-3 (4.30e-4) −	2.78e-3 (9.59e-5)
DASCMOP6	1.88e-2 (9.60e-3) ≈	5.72e-1 (2.32e-1) −	1.98e-2 (5.30e-3) ≈	2.51e-2 (2.13e-2) ≈	2.41e-2 (3.26e-3) −	1.74e-2 (3.31e-3)
DASCMOP7	4.77e-2 (2.84e-3) −	3.08e-1 (1.89e-1) −	5.78e-2 (4.58e-3) −	3.06e-2 (6.27e-4) ≈	5.14e-2 (6.17e-3) −	3.05e-2 (7.34e-4)
DASCMOP8	5.81e-2 (2.77e-3) −	3.71e-1 (2.31e-1) −	8.33e-2 (1.01e-2) −	3.89e-2 (8.71e-4) −	8.13e-2 (7.90e-3) −	3.83e-2 (9.02e-4)
DASCMOP9	6.48e-2 (3.44e-3) −	6.06e-2 (3.39e-3) −	6.06e-2 (3.17e-3) −	4.03e-2 (1.01e-3) −	8.96e-2 (5.86e-3) −	3.86e-2 (1.10e-3)
+/ − / ≈	0/8/1	0/9/0	0/7/2	1/6/2	0/9/0	

Table 2. IGD results of ACCH-PPS and competitors on the DASCMOP test suite ($n = 30$).

	C-NSGA-II	ToP	PPS-MOEA/D	CMOEA-MS	C-TAEA	ACCH-PPS
DASCMOP1	7.18e-1 (3.23e-2) −	7.59e-1 (2.91e-2) −	3.62e-3 (1.29e-3) −	6.89e-1 (3.85e-2) −	2.53e-1 (4.53e-2) −	1.81e-3 (2.30e-4)
DASCMOP2	2.83e-1 (3.47e-2) −	6.75e-1 (1.94e-1) −	3.88e-3 (1.26e-4) −	2.42e-1 (3.90e-2) −	1.06e-1 (2.12e-2) −	2.87e-3 (5.71e-5)
DASCMOP3	3.58e-1 (4.20e-2) −	6.71e-1 (1.55e-1) −	1.84e-2 (2.34e-3) +	3.40e-1 (4.69e-2) −	1.32e-1 (2.30e-2) −	1.92e-2 (1.27e-3)
DASCMOP4	1.89e-2 (6.73e-2) −	NaN (NaN)	1.25e-1 (9.99e-2) −	1.14e-1 (1.35e-1) ≈	1.07e-2 (2.15e-3) −	1.17e-3 (2.56e-5)
DASCMOP5	3.56e-3 (1.55e-4) −	9.49e-1 (0.00e+0) ≈	4.14e-3 (3.97e-4) −	2.63e-3 (2.39e-5) +	7.08e-3 (6.00e-4) −	2.85e-3 (9.75e-5)
DASCMOP6	2.65e-1 (1.68e-1) −	NaN (NaN)	6.54e-2 (5.04e-2) −	4.85e-2 (7.88e-2) ≈	2.32e-2 (3.15e-3) −	1.87e-2 (5.13e-3)
DASCMOP7	4.74e-2 (2.11e-3) −	NaN (NaN)	6.53e-2 (2.80e-2) −	3.05e-2 (5.53e-4) ≈	3.65e-2 (6.21e-3) −	3.08e-2 (7.42e-4)
DASCMOP8	5.94e-2 (3.75e-3) −	NaN (NaN)	7.78e-2 (1.31e-2) −	3.91e-2 (8.08e-4) ≈	5.93e-2 (1.83e-2) −	3.86e-2 (1.48e-3)
DASCMOP9	3.46e-1 (6.66e-2) −	6.16e-1 (2.17e-1) −	8.53e-2 (5.25e-2) −	3.21e-1 (6.62e-2) −	1.61e-1 (3.33e-2) −	5.80e-2 (5.72e-2)
+/ − / ≈	0/9/0	0/4/1	1/8/0	1/4/4	0/9/0	

when ACCH-PPS deals with DASCMOP problems, in the process of adding constraints step by step, it can adaptively deal with constraints that affect the convergence process at a later stage, which is conducive to ACCH-PPS fast forward search. However, most of these constraints do not affect the shape of PF, that is, PF is not at the boundary of the feasible domain formed by these constraints. In addition, the solution obtained by ACCH-PPS in the early search may be conducive to the later search. For example, for the problem of PF discontinuity, if ACCH-PPS can temporarily ignore the constraint on PF in the early stage and search the entire PF, it will help to avoid the local optimal in the later search for discontinuous PF. Here, DASCMOP1 and DASCMOP9 are taken as examples to show the objective vector distribution of the solution set obtained by ACCH-PPS and the competitors (see Fig. 1).

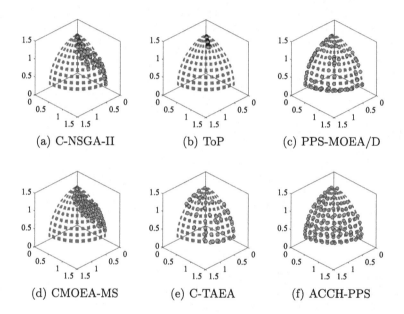

(a) C-NSGA-II   (b) ToP   (c) PPS-MOEA/D

(d) CMOEA-MS   (e) C-TAEA   (f) ACCH-PPS

Fig. 1. Objective vector distribution of the solution set obtained by ACCH-PPS and competitors on DASCMOP9 ($n = 30$).

By comparing IGD results of various algorithms on DASCMOP test suite with different variable dimensions, it can be found that for the same problem, even if the dimensions of decision variables change, the relative advantages and disadvantages of different algorithms will not change greatly. Specifically, in For DASCMOP1 problem, ACCH-PPS performs best regardless of variable dimension 10 or 30, PPS-MOEA/D ranks second and C-TAEA ranks third. For DASC-MOP5 problem, regardless of its variable dimension, CMOEA-MS ranks first and ACCH-PPS ranks second. However, when the variable dimension is larger, the relative difference between algorithms is greater. When the variable dimension is 10, although there is a significant difference between the performance of the algorithms, there is little difference in the distribution of the objective vector in some problems. When the variable dimension is 30, not only the IGD means of the algorithm have significant differences, but also the distribution differences of its objective vectors are obvious, as shown in Fig. 1. It can be seen that when the dimension of the variable increases, the solution difficulties existing in the test problem will become more prominent. However, ACCH-PPS can perform better in DASCMOP test suite with variable dimensions of 10 or 30, significantly better than other algorithms, which reflects the effectiveness and robustness of ACCH-PPS.

Optimization of G-HRES. ACCH-PPS and the competitors are used to solve the optimization problem of G-HRES. Since the true PF of this problem is unknown, the non-dominated solution of the combinatorial solution set (that is, the solution set obtained by all the algorithms involved in the comparison and then extracted) is chosen as the reference point set for IGD calculation. The average IGD value and standard deviation obtained from 31 independent runs of each algorithm are shown as Table 3. As can be seen from Table 3, ACCH-PPS achieves the best results in solving this problem.

Table 3. IGD comparison results of ACCH-PPS and its competitors on G-HRES.

	C-NSGA-II	ToP	PPS-MOEA/D	CMOEA-MS	C-TAEA	ACCH-PPS
G-HRES	1.25e+1 (9.06e-3) −	6.29e-1 (9.07e-2) ≈	6.301e-1 (9.06e-2) ≈	6.28e-1 (8.07e-2) ≈	6.31e-1 (1.42e-1) −	6.27e-2 (9.07e-2)

According to the optimal solution set provided by ACCH-PPS algorithm and preference information, decision makers can choose the solution that best meets the needs. For example, if decision-makers want to limit the proportion of electricity supplied from non-renewable sources to 60% (i.e. $f_{\mathrm{NRE}} \leq 60\%$). You can then select the solution with the lowest system annualized cost of $f_{\mathrm{NRE}} \leq 60\%$ from the solution of f_{ASC} (Table 4).

Table 4. Scheme selected from the ACCH-PPS optimal solution combined with preference information.

s_{pv1}	s_{pv2}	s_{pv3}	s_{pv4}	N_{pv1}	N_{pv2}	N_{pv3}	N_{pv4}	s_{wg1}	s_{wg2}	s_{wg3}
1	1	0	0	29	15	0	0	1	0	0

s_{wg4}	N_{wg1}	N_{wg2}	N_{wg3}	N_{wg4}	N_{bat}	N_{dg}	H_{wg}	α	f_{ASC}	f_{NRE}
0	3	0	0	0	0	0	28.83	70	674	59%

In general, ACCH-PPS algorithm shows the best performance in the test problem, and solves the fixed capacity optimization problem of grid-connected hybrid renewable energy system well.

5   Conclusion

In this paper, we proposed an adaptive multi-stage evolutionary algorithm, called ACCH-PPS, for constrained multi-objective optimization problems (CMOPs). We compared c-DPEA with five state-of-the-art CMOEAs on DASC-MOP test suite, as well as grid-connected hybrid renewable energy system (G-HRES). The experimental results exhaustively demonstrated that ACCH-PPS is either significantly superior or comparable to the five compared CMOEAs on most test problems and the real-world application.

References

1. Abedi, S., Alimardani, A., Gharehpetian, G.B., Riahy, G.H., Hosseinian, S.H.: A comprehensive method for optimal power management and design of hybrid RES-based autonomous energy systems. Renew. Sustain. Energy Rev. **16**(3), 1577–1587 (2012)
2. Auger, A., Bader, J., Brockhoff, D., Zitzler, E.: Theory of the hypervolume indicator: optimal μ-distributions and the choice of the reference point. In: The Tenth ACM SIGEVO Workshop on Foundations of Genetic Algorithms (2009)
3. Bosman, P.A., Thierens, D.: The balance between proximity and diversity in multiobjective evolutionary algorithms. IEEE Trans. Evol. Comput. **7**(2), 174–188 (2003)
4. Coello, C.A.C.: Theoretical and numerical constraint-handling techniques used with evolutionary algorithms: a survey of the state of the art. Comput. Methods Appl. Mech. Eng. **191**(11), 1245–1287 (2002)
5. Deb, K.: Multi-Objective Optimization Using Evolutionary Algorithms. Wiley, Chichester (2001)
6. Deb, K., Agrawal, R.B., et al.: Simulated binary crossover for continuous search space. Complex Syst. **9**(2), 115–148 (1995)
7. Deb, K., Goyal, M.: A combined genetic adaptive search (GeneAS) for engineering design. Comput. Sci. Inform. **26**, 30–45 (1996)
8. Deb, K., Pratap, A., Agarwal, S., Meyarivan, T.: A fast and elitist multiobjective genetic algorithm: NSGA-II. IEEE Trans. Evol. Comput. **6**(2), 182–197 (2002)
9. Dufo-López, R., Bernal-Agustín, J.L.: Multi-objective design of PV-wind-diesel-hydrogen-battery systems. Renew. Energy **33**(12), 2559–2572 (2008)
10. Dufo-López, R., Contreras, J.: Optimization of control strategies for stand-alone renewable energy systems with hydrogen storage. Renew. Energy **32**(7), 1102–126 (2007)
11. Fan, Z., et al.: Push and pull search for solving constrained multi-objective optimization problems. Swarm Evol. Comput. **44**, 665–679 (2019)
12. Hollander, M., Wolfe, D.A., Chicken, E.: Nonparametric Statistical Methods, vol. 751. Wiley, Hoboken (2013)

13. Koutroulis, E., Kolokotsa, D., Potirakis, A., Kalaitzakis, K.: Methodology for optimal sizing of stand-alone photovoltaic/wind-generator systems using genetic algorithms. Sol. Energy **80**(9), 1072–1088 (2006)
14. Li, K., Chen, R., Fu, G., Yao, X.: Two-archive evolutionary algorithm for constrained multiobjective optimization. IEEE Trans. Evol. Comput. **23**(2), 303–315 (2019)
15. Liu, Z., Wang, Y.: Handling constrained multiobjective optimization problems with constraints in both the decision and objective spaces. IEEE Trans. Evol. Comput. **23**(5), 870–884 (2019)
16. Ma, Z., Wang, Y.: Evolutionary constrained multiobjective optimization: test suite construction and performance comparisons. IEEE Trans. Evol. Comput. **23**(6), 972–986 (2019)
17. Ming, M., Wang, R., Zha, Y., Zhang, T.: Multi-objective optimization of hybrid renewable energy system using an enhanced multi-objective evolutionary algorithm. Energies **10**(5), 674 (2017)
18. Ming, M., Wang, R., Zhang, T.: Evolutionary many-constraint optimization: an exploratory analysis. In: Deb, K., et al. (eds.) EMO 2019. LNCS, vol. 11411, pp. 165–176. Springer, Cham (2019). https://doi.org/10.1007/978-3-030-12598-1_14
19. Price, K., Storn, R.M., Lampinen, J.A.: Differential Evolution: A Practical Approach to Global Optimization. Springer, Heidelberg (2006). https://doi.org/10.1007/3-540-31306-0
20. Shi, Z., Wang, R., Zhang, T.: Multi-objective optimal design of hybrid renewable energy systems using preference-inspired coevolutionary approach. Sol. Energy **118**, 96–106 (2015)
21. Tanabe, R., Oyama, A.: A note on constrained multi-objective optimization benchmark problems. In: Proceedings of the IEEE Congress on Evolutionary Computation (CEC), pp. 1127–1134 (2017)
22. Tian, Y., Zhang, Y., Su, Y., Zhang, X., Tan, K.C., Jin, Y.: Balancing objective optimization and constraint satisfaction in constrained evolutionary multiobjective optimization. IEEE Trans. Cybern. **52**(9), 9559–9572 (2021)
23. Wang, J., Ren, W., Zhang, Z., Huang, H., Zhou, Y.: A hybrid multiobjective memetic algorithm for multiobjective periodic vehicle routing problem with time windows. IEEE Trans. Syst. Man Cybern. Syst. **50**(11), 4732–4745 (2018)
24. Wang, R., Li, G., Ming, M., Wu, G., Wang, L.: An efficient multi-objective model and algorithm for sizing a stand-alone hybrid renewable energy system. Energy **141**, 2288–2299 (2017)
25. Yang, H., Lu, L., Zhou, W.: A novel optimization sizing model for hybrid solar-wind power generation system. Sol. Energy **81**(1), 76–84 (2007)
26. Zitzler, E., Laumanns, M., Thiele, L.: SPEA2: improving the strength Pareto evolutionary algorithm. TIK-report 103 (2001)

Author Index

Printed in the United States
by Baker & Taylor Publisher Services